CHINA'S MEDIA GO GLOBAL

As part of China's 'going out' strategy, China is using its media to promote its views and vision to the wider world and to counter negative images in the US-dominated international media. *China's Media Go Global*, the first edited collection on this subject, evaluates how the unprecedented expansion of Chinese media and communications is changing the global media landscape and the role of China within it.

Each chapter examines a different dimension of Chinese media's globalization, from newspapers, radio, film and television, to social media and journalism cultures and practices. Topics include the rise of Chinese news networks, *China Daily* as an instrument of China's public diplomacy and the discussion around the growth of China's state media in Africa. Other chapters discuss entertainment television, financial media and the advertising market in China.

Together, this collection of essays offers a comprehensive evaluation of complex debates concerning the impact of China on the international media sphere, and makes a distinctive addition to Chinese media studies, as well as to broader global media discourses. Beyond its primary readership among academics and students, *China's Media Go Global* is aimed at the growing constituency of general readers, for whom the role of the media in globalization is of wider interest.

Daya Kishan Thussu is Professor of International Communication at the University of Westminster, UK.

Hugo de Burgh is Professor and Director of the China Media Centre, University of Westminster, UK.

Anbin Shi is Professor and Director of the Israel Epstein Center for Global Media and Communication at Tsinghua University, Beijing, China.

Internationalizing Media Studies

Series Editor: Daya Kishan Thussu
University of Westminster

CHINA'S MEDIA
GO GLOBAL

Edited by Daya Kishan Thussu,
Hugo de Burgh and Anbin Shi

Routledge
Taylor & Francis Group

LONDON AND NEW YORK

First published 2018
by Routledge
2 Park Square, Milton Park, Abingdon, Oxon OX14 4RN

and by Routledge
711 Third Avenue, New York, NY 10017

Routledge is an imprint of the Taylor & Francis Group, an informa business

© 2018 selection and editorial matter, Daya Kishan Thussu, Hugo de Burgh and Anbin Shi; individual chapters, the contributors

The right of Daya Kishan Thussu, Hugo de Burgh and Anbin Shi to be identified as the authors of the editorial material, and of the authors for their individual chapters, has been asserted in accordance with sections 77 and 78 of the Copyright, Designs and Patents Act 1988.

British Library Cataloguing-in-Publication Data
A catalogue record for this book is available from the British Library

Library of Congress Cataloging-in-Publication Data
A catalog record for this book has been requested

ISBN: 978-1-138-66584-2 (hbk)
ISBN: 978-1-138-66585-9 (pbk)
ISBN: 978-1-315-61966-8 (ebk)

Typeset in Bembo
by Sunrise Setting Ltd, Brixham, UK
Printed and bound by CPI Group (UK) Ltd, Croydon, CR0 4YY

Every effort has been made to contact copyright-holders. Please advise the publisher of any errors or omissions, and these will be corrected in subsequent editions.

CONTENTS

FIGURES

TABLES

CONTRIBUTORS

Anbin Shi is Ministry of Education Changjiang Endowment Professor of Global Communication, Associate Dean of International Development with the School of Journalism and Communication, and Director of the Israel Epstein Center for Global Media and Communication, Tsinghua University, in Beijing. His research interests include intercultural communication, global communication, public communication, press and politics. He has published *Crisis Communication and Media Relations in the Era of Omni-Media* (in Chinese, 2014); *A Comparative Approach to Redefining Chinese-ness in the Era of Globalization* (2003); edited the anthology *Mapping Out the Future for Global Communication and Journalism Education* (in Chinese, 2014) and co-authored *Negotiating Asymmetry: China's Place in Asia* (University of Hawaii Press, 2009).

Hong Cheng is the Director and a Professor of the Richard Robertson School of Media and Culture at Virginia Commonwealth University in the United States. His research interests centre on international communication, cross-cultural advertising, and social marketing. He co-authored (with Guofang Wan) *Becoming a Media Savvy Student* (2004) and co-edited (with Kara Chan) *Advertising and Chinese Society: Issues and Impacts* (2009) and (with Philip Kotler and Nancy Lee) *Social Marketing for Public Health: Global Trends and Success Stories* (2011). His latest edited book is *Handbook of International Advertising Research*, published in 2014.

Hugo de Burgh is Professor of Journalism at the University of Westminster and SAFEA (State Administration of Foreign Expert Affairs) Foundation Professor at Tsinghua University. Formerly a British television journalist and producer, his book *Investigative Journalism*, the first edition of which was published in 2000, has been followed by many books and articles on China and Chinese journalists. His seven-part series 'The West You Really Don't Know' was transmitted in the Spring Golden Period on China Central Television in 2014, when the companion book was also published.

David Feng has a PhD in Communication from the Communication University of China, Beijing, where he is a lecturer. Among his research interests are social media in China and the comparative analysis of social media perceptions. He also has extensive experience of working for various radio stations as a multilingual live presenter, including for the English-language channel Radio Beijing, China National Radio and China Radio International. Among his key publications in Chinese are Trends and Development of China's Social Media, part of *New Media Industries Frontiers* (2013), edited by Hu Zhengrong *et al.*

Yukun Gong is a doctoral student at the Institute of Communication Studies at Communication University of China. Her research interests include corporate communication and international communication.

Zhenzhi Guo is a Professor at the School of Journalism and Communication, Tsinghua University in Beijing. Apart from the main area of media history, Dr Guo's academic interests also include journalism and communication theories, and media studies. She is the author/editor of several Chinese books, including *A History of Chinese Television* (1991), *On North American Media and Communication* (1997) and *Korean Culture and Communication* (2004). Her recent research is focused on law and regulations, including new media governance, and international communication of Chinese media.

Falk Hartig holds an MA (Sinology and Journalism) from the University of Leipzig and a PhD in International Communication from the Queensland University of Technology in Brisbane. He is currently a post-doctoral researcher at the Inter-Centre Programme on new African–Asian Interactions (AFRASO: Africa's Asian Options) at Goethe University in Frankfurt and a Contributing Scholar with the USC Center on Public Diplomacy, University of Southern California, Los Angeles. His research focuses on China's public diplomacy, China's global image and the internationalization of Chinese media. He is the author of a book about the Chinese Communist Party and a book entitled *Chinese Public Diplomacy: The Rise of Confucius Institutes.*

Zhengrong Hu is President and Professor of Communication at Communication University of China (CUC), and Director of the National Centre for Communication Innovation Studies. His research areas include media policy and institutional transition, international communication, new media, and political economy of communication. Professor Hu is the author or editor of more than 30 books, including the *Annual Report of China's International Communication Development* (2014–2016), *Annual Report of Global Media Industries* (2011–2016), *Thirty Years of Chinese Media: 1978–2008* (2008), and a number of refereed journal articles. He was the chair of China Communication Association from 2006 to 2011.

Kuo Huang is a Professor in the English Service of China Radio International in Beijing. Before joining CRI, she worked as Associate Professor at the Center for

International Communication Studies, China International Publishing Group in Beijing, and Associate Professor at Heilongjiang University in China. She has a PhD from Macquarie University, Australia. Her research interests include international communications, audience studies and new media. She is the author of *Chinese Boxes: Reality TV and Audience Participation* (2014) and *Multimedia Technology: How It Changes Classroom and Communication* (2008).

Deqiang Ji, PhD, is Associate Professor of Communication at the National Centre for Communication Innovation Studies at CUC. He is the Vice-Chair of the International Communication Section of International Association of Media and Communication Research. His research interests include political economy of communication, anti-corruption communication and international communication. He is leading several research projects on both anti-corruption communication and international communication.

Jingwei Piao teaches at Xiamen University of Technology in China. She has a PhD in financial media, globalization and China's economic integration, from the University of Westminster. She is currently working towards publishing her pioneering work in book form.

Hong Li is a PhD candidate at the China Media Centre, University of Westminster. She is working on international circulation of television formats. She was a television format researcher and developer for the 2013 television programme *The Gadget Show China*.

Shanshan Lou is Assistant Professor in the Department of Communication at Appalachian State University in the United States. She has a PhD from the University of Ohio in the United States and her research mainly focuses on the effects of new media technologies on audiences' attitudes and behaviours and intercultural advertising. She has been actively involved in creative fields as well, including advertising, film and television. She was one of the 25 professors across the country to be awarded NATPE's (the National Association of Television Program Executives) prestigious faculty fellowship for 2014. She was also selected to attend the 2013 Time Warner College Professors Thought Leadership Seminar at Time Warner Medialab in New York City.

Vivien Marsh is completing her PhD at the University of Westminster in London, comparing the English-language news of Chinese state television (CCTV) with that of BBC World News TV. Previously an experienced London-based BBC global news editor, reporter and trainer, she has latterly specialized in Asia-Pacific (particularly Chinese) news.

Miao Mi has a PhD in comparative journalism. Her research fields include media convergence, comparative journalism, and newspapers in China and the UK. She works as the London representative of Houghton Street Media, TV Production Company, Beijing as well as production/format coordinator for North One Television (UK)/Houghton Street Media. She has also worked for the Shenzhen Broadcasting Group.

Wanning Sun is Professor of Media and Cultural Studies in the China Research Centre at the University of Technology in Sydney. From 2000 to 2008 she was with the School of Media, Communication and Creative Arts at Curtin University, Western Australia. She is the author of *Leaving China: Media, Migration, and Transnational Imagination* (2002), *Maid in China: Media, Morality and the Cultural Politics of Boundaries* (2009) and *Subaltern China: Rural Migrants, Media, and Cultural Practices* (2014).

Daya Kishan Thussu is Professor of International Communication and Co-Director of the India Media Centre at the University of Westminster in London. Among his main publications are: *Electronic Empires* (1998); *International Communication – Continuity and Change*, third edition (forthcoming); *War and the Media: Reporting Conflict 24/7* (2003); *Media on the Move – Global Flow and Contra-flow* (2007); *News as Entertainment* (2007); *Internationalizing Media Studies* (2009); *Media and Terrorism: Global Perspectives* (2012), *Communicating India's Soft Power: Buddha to Bollywood* (Palgrave, 2013) and *Mapping BRICS Media* (Routledge, 2015).

Jing Wu is Professor and Deputy Dean at the School of Journalism and Communication at Peking University. She received her PhD in Communication from the Department of Communication Studies, University of Iowa in 2002. Her research areas include media and cultural studies, social theories of mass communication, media and the public sphere, identity and ideology, media and modernity. She has published articles in both Chinese and English on topics concerning various aspects of media, culture and society. Her most recent book is entitled *Visual Expressions of Cultural Modernity: Ways of Seeing and Communication*.

Mei Wu is Associate Professor at the Faculty of Social Sciences, University of Macau. She was a Visiting Fellow at the Oxford Internet Institute, Oxford University in 2011. She has written extensively on media in China and among her recent publications are: *Social Media, Digital Network and Globalization* (2013); and Symbolic Reality: Symbolic Convergence Theory and China's International Communication, in China Foreign Languages Bureau (eds.) *New World Order and China's International Communication: Problems and Strategies*.

Yanni Wu is a PhD candidate at the School of Public Administration at Tsinghua University in Beijing.

Yu Xiang is completing her PhD at the University of Westminster, where she also did an MA in Global Media. Her topic is how foreigners view China. She has translated books from English into Chinese and had extensive experience of the media industry in both China and the UK. Her current work with Xiaoxing Zhang is an article on *Revisiting Cultural Imperialism At the Inter-Section of Class and Nation: A Case Study of Sino-African Media Flows* forthcoming in the *Chinese Journal of Communication*.

Suzanne Xiao Yang is a lecturer in Chinese Public Governance and International Relations at the Lau China Institute at King's College, London, where she leads the Chinese Governance Innovation Centre of the China Institute. Prior to joining King's, Dr Yang was Deputy Director of Leadership Programmes for China at the University of Oxford. From 1996 to 2001 she was a Research Fellow at the Institute for European Studies at the Chinese Academy of Social Sciences, Beijing. Currently she is a Senior Research Fellow at the Centre for International and Strategic Studies, Peking University.

Jiao Yang is Associate Professor in the Department of Literature and Journalism at Dianchi College of Yunnan University in China. Her research interests include minority media and alternative journalism in China.

Guoqiang Yun is an Associate Professor at the School of Journalism and Communication of Beijing Language and Culture University. He has a PhD in Communication from the School of Journalism and Communication at Peking University. His research interests include philosophy of communication and history of communication theories, cultural studies of film and television, media studies, new media and social movement.

Rong Zeng obtained her PhD at the University of Westminster in 2008, where she remains a Research Fellow. She was a Wolfson Fellow at Cambridge University. Zeng is founder and Managing Director of Houghton Street Media (HSM/恆頓傳媒), the Sino-British television production company which develops and produces programmes for China Central Television, Shanghai Media Group and Jiangsu Television as well as new media platforms iqiyi, Youku and Sohu. Her publications include *Television News and the Limits of Globalization: BBC World and Phoenix Television Today* (2012) and *China's Environment and China's Environment Journalists* (2012).

Xiaoling Zhang is a lecturer in the School of Politics and International Relations at Nottingham University in the UK. Her research interests span the transformation of media, culture and society in China and she has published widely on the shifting cultural and media landscapes in China, especially the new media technologies. More recent work has focused on exploring how China promotes its soft power through the expansion of its media and communication channels around the world, with a special project on Sino-African dynamics through cultural exchange and translation. Among her publications is a co-edited volume, *China's Media and Soft Power in Africa: Promotion and Perceptions* (2016).

Qing'an Zhou is Associate Professor and Associate Dean of School for Journalism and Communications at Tsinghua University in Beijing.

INTRODUCTION

Daya Kishan Thussu, Hugo de Burgh and Anbin Shi

In May 2017, representatives of 68 countries from across the globe, including 28 heads of government, gathered in Beijing to witness China's President Xi Jinping formally launch the 'Belt and Road Initiative' (BRI – formerly known as 'One Belt, One Road'). It will become the world's largest infrastructural intervention, encompassing 900 projects (valued at about $1.3 trillion) and involving 65 countries, 4.4 billion people and 29 per cent of global Gross Domestic Product (GDP). The 'Belt' in BRI refers to the land route being built to link China to Central Asia and Europe, while the 'maritime silk road' will create a sea route from China to the Indian Ocean and the Mediterranean. Creating information and communication networks is part of the BRI projects, backed by a new $40 billion Silk Road Infrastructure Fund, capitalized mainly by China's foreign exchange reserves, estimated in 2017 to be more than $3 trillion. The China-initiated Asian Infrastructure Investment Bank – set up in 2016 – together with the Shanghai-based New Development Bank, established in 2014 by the five BRICS (Brazil, Russia, India, China and South Africa) nations, are also involved in financing these projects.

The Western version of neoliberal globalization, spearheaded by the United States government and the Bretton Woods institutions (the World Bank, the International Monetary Fund and the World Trade Organization), is being challenged. China is increasingly becoming the champion of a different kind of globalization, at a time when the role of the US and Western Europe as the main engines of global growth appears to be diminishing. The US withdrawal from the Trans-Pacific Partnership (TPP) trading agreement, as well as the uncertain future of the Transatlantic Trade and Investment Partnership, which linked the European Union with the US, are two other recent developments that indicate the relative retreat of the West. (Despite its Asia-Pacific focus, China was excluded from the TPP.) US President Donald Trump's announcement that the US would leave the 2016 Paris Climate Accord is another indication that a space has been created, within which China could articulate a different worldview for environmental protection, given that the world's most populated country accounts for nearly 30 per cent of global CO_2 emissions.

China appears to be ready to take up such a leadership role. Speaking as a keynote at the World Economic Forum in Davos – whose theme for 2017 was 'Responsive and Responsible Leadership' – President Xi reportedly told the packed gathering of the world's financial and political elite that 'pursuing protectionism is like locking oneself in a dark room. While wind and rain may be kept outside, that dark room will also block light and air.' In a cover story, the British news magazine *The Economist* hailed China as 'the global grown-up'. Relishing the irony, the magazine, an ardent advocate of free-market capitalism, noted: 'at a time of global uncertainty and anxiety for capitalists, the world's most powerful communist is presenting himself as a champion of globalisation and open markets' (*Economist*, 2017).

While the West is looking inwards, other countries are globalizing, China in particular. On the basis of purchasing power parity (PPP), China's GDP surpassed that of the US in 2014, making it the world's largest economy, according to the International Monetary Fund. It noted that China's share of global GDP in PPP terms had grown from just over 4 per cent in 1990, to nearly 18 per cent in 2016. In the same period, the IMF reports, the share of global GDP of the G7 countries (US, Japan, Germany, Britain, France, Canada and Italy) shrank from 51 to about 31 per cent (IMF, 2017). Buoyed by the inclusion of the Renminbi in the IMF's Special Drawing Rights, making it one of the world's reserve currencies, Chinese companies – both state-sponsored and privately owned – are becoming increasingly competitive in global markets, making sizeable investments and acquisitions (Khanna, 2016). In cultural products and services, specifically, the volume of China's international trade in 2016 reached $88.52 billion, recording a surplus of $68.8 billion, while exports in entertainment and advertising services were $5.43 billion, according to China's Ministry of Commerce (*China Daily*, 2017).

As with other aspects of contemporary China – the world's most populated country and one of its fastest-growing economies – Chinese media are also going global. More than a decade and a half has passed since the launch of CCTV-9, China's first English-language news network in 2000 as part of China's 'going out' strategy, which entails, in essence, promoting China's views and vision to the wider world and countering negative portrayals of the country in the US-dominated international media. An estimated $7 billion were earmarked for external communication, including the expansion of Chinese broadcasting networks such as CCTV News (renamed in 2016 as China Global Television Network – CGTN) and Xinhua's English-language TV, CNC World.

In 2017, more than half of China's 1.3 billion people were online, making it home to the world's largest number of internet users. By 2017, CGTN news could claim 200 million viewers outside China, broadcasting in six languages, including Arabic as well as over 50 million Facebook followers – one of the largest such number for a news network. In 2012, CCTV launched an Africa-specific channel, based in Nairobi, broadcasting such programmes as *Africa Live* (a one-hour daily news programme, anchored by African journalists) and *Talk Africa* (a 30-minute weekly talk show discussing current affairs). Such media interactions are taking place within the context of growing economic ties: since 2000, the volume of trade between China and Africa grew 20-fold – from $10 billion in 2000 to $280 billion in 2015. China is now the largest donor from the developing world: in 2013 China contributed four per cent to total global development assistance, nearly half of it directed to countries in Africa and a sizeable part of it aimed at creating infrastructure, including communications. A permanent veto-wielding member of the United Nations Security Council, China is also a driving force behind many multilateral geopolitical and economic formulations, notably BRICS, which together account for 20 per cent of the world's GDP, as well as the Shanghai Cooperation Organization, which links China to Russia and countries in central Asia and India.

Despite the emergence of media from China, it is still the case that the US continues to dominate and define the global media scene, being the largest exporter of media content distributed across the increasingly interconnected and digitized globe. The US media's imprint on the global communication space is profound: US-based companies continue to own the infrastructure of global communication from satellites to telecommunication hubs and cyberspace, as well as multiple networks and production facilities. In media software, too, the US presence is formidable: from news (CNN, CNBC, *New York Times*) to documentary (Discovery); from sport (ESPN) and film, popular music, gaming and entertainment (Hollywood) to online communication (Google, Facebook, Twitter) (Thussu, forthcoming). Sales of US copyright materials – recorded music, motion pictures, television and video, software publishing and other publications including newspapers, books and periodicals – were approximately $177 billion in 2015 (Siwek, 2016: 13).

Other major non-Western powers, notably China, have emerged onto the global scene in the last decade to complement if not challenge the US hegemony in this field (Jacques, 2009). The unprecedented global expansion of Chinese media and communication networks over the past decade raises important questions about the changing global media landscape and the role of China within it. In 2016, four of the top ten internet companies in the world ranked by market capitalization were Chinese, including e-commerce giant Alibaba, search engine Baidu and social media company Tencent.

In a complex, globalized world, international media is in the process of transformation, partly as a result of an increasingly mobile and globally networked and digitized communication infrastructure, which, together with the digitization of content, are enabling global and instantaneous circulation of media content across continents. While the imbalance in the flow of images and ideas – from the media-rich North (and within it a US–UK core) to the South – continues to define global media, the traditional domination of Western, or specifically American, media is diminishing, and, arguably more importantly, being challenged by the availability of media from major non-Western nations – television news in English from such diverse countries as Russia, China, Iran, Japan and Qatar – as well as entertainment from India, Turkey, South Korea, Nigeria and Brazil, among others (Punathambekar, 2013; Christensen, 2013; Kim, 2013; Figenschou, 2014; Miller, 2016; Davis *et al.*, 2016, among others).

Media from such major non-Western nations is aiming to reach a global audience, a process facilitated by growing digital connectivity, with the convergence of mobile communications technologies and content via a multilingual internet. As more people connect, content from non-traditional actors such as China is likely to become more pronounced on the media globe. As such media globalize, the question arises whether they will develop an alternative narrative on neo-liberalism. There is little doubt that the availability of media material emanating from a major non-Western centre of global media production complicates the discourse about international media. While recognizing the limitations of a media system which operates within a one-party state, with its attendant regulatory and control mechanisms, there is ample scope to evaluate how the 'peaceful rise of China' impacts on global media policies, principles and practices. Does the impressive growth of media in China and its greater visibility across the globe indicate the end of globalization as Westernization?

This new phenomenon of Chinese media globalization has so far largely escaped academic scrutiny in a comparative and transnational perspective, partly because the focus of much international (read Western) scholarship has been on the issue of censorship and media regulation in China at the expense of engaging with the emerging contours of what is sometimes described by the official Chinese media as 'Globalization 2.0' – a Sino-globalization (Meyers, 2017). Essays in this pioneering study aim to fill this gap in scholarship. They assess the impact of exponential media growth in one of the world's fastest-growing large economies on the geopolitical environment and pose questions about the effects on global communication. Have Chinese media contributed to enriching the political discourse globally, providing an alternative to US-dominated media frames? Are the Chinese media merely instruments for Chinese soft power? Will the growing globalization of China's media contribute to further internationalization of media and communication studies?

This edited collection brings together distinguished scholars from China and those with an interest in and knowledge of the country, representing a range of experienced and fresh academic voices, to examine and discuss how the emergence of Chinese media impacts on global media and communication. The chapters contextualize the role of the Chinese media in a globalized world, evaluating the media landscape and focusing on media practices, drawing on empirical material. By interrogating the relationship between Chinese and Western media practices and perceptions, this volume provides an accessible and comprehensive guide to the complex debates about the impact of China on the media globe. Finally, the book offers a range of perspectives on emerging trends in relation to the globalization of Chinese media, a key theme within the internationalization of Media Studies.

There has been a spate of publications on media in China in recent years, as indicated by such comprehensive compilations as *Chinese Media* (Keane and Sun, 2014). On specific media and communication themes, many publications are available to the scholar, for example, on political economy of communication (Zhao, 2008); Chinese film and television (Curtin, 2007; Berry *et al.* 2010; Kokas, 2017); soft power (Kurlantzick, 2007; Wang, 2011; Lai and Lu, 2012; Zhang *et al.*, 2016); propaganda and censorship (Brady, 2012; Young, 2013; Ng, 2013; Edney, 2014); news agencies (Xin, 2012); television news (Zhu, 2012); internet (Yang, 2009; Hong, 2017); creative industries (Keane, 2013); advertising and marketing culture (Stockman, 2013); war reporting (Zhang, 2016); and diaspora (Sun, 2009). Though extremely valuable, these books focus on particular aspects of China's media and do not have the same scope as this collection, which is explicitly concerned with the globalization of China's media and seeks, at its core, to interrogate how the rise of media in China will impact on global communication, drawing on perspectives from a variety of disciplines (including sociology, journalism studies, media studies and international relations) and through a number of interrelated frames and topics.

This collection is designed with a view to being of use in courses on international media and communication, which are increasingly focusing on the media in the non-Western world and in which China, given its size and scale, is inevitably the most significant area of academic inquiry. In addition, the book should interest students, teachers and researchers in journalism, media, politics, sociology, international relations, area studies and cultural studies programmes. By examining different dimensions of Chinese media's globalization – from newspapers, radio and television, to film and documentary, to social media, advertising, and journalism cultures and practices – we hope this collection will make a distinctive addition to the literature on Chinese media studies, as well as broader global media discourses.

Beyond its primary readership among academics, *China's Media Go Global* is also aimed at the growing constituency of non-academic readers, for whom the role of the media in processes associated with globalization is a central matter of public debate. We believe that this book will be of interest to readers outside the academy: politicians and analysts seeking to understand the global impact of the 'the rise' of China, researchers motivated by a desire to develop an alternative to mainstream Western media coverage of global issues, and general readers who are curious about how the globalization of the Chinese media may contribute to changes in global communication.

The book in outline

This study of the different aspects of Chinese media's globalization is divided into four parts. The first part sets the context for the globalization of China's media and the chapters survey the main theoretical and contextual debates about Chinese media's global expansion. Chapters include discussion of the national and global context of Chinese external communication, as well as theoretical issues surrounding soft power and internationalizing practices of media institutions and professionals.

In his chapter on the global context of China's media going global, Daya Kishan Thussu suggests that Sino-globalization is central to understanding the changing power equations in contemporary world politics. His chapter examines the strengths of China's economic globalization and the communication infrastructure that is already in place for globalization of China's media. He also discusses the limitations of China's going global strategy. Thussu suggests that what he calls 'cyber-capitalism with Chinese characteristics' is likely to provide greater opportunities for Chinese content to travel across the global digital superhighways.

One of China's best-known communication scholars, Anbin Shi examines the globalization of China's media within the discourse of the 'Community of Common Destiny' (CCD), locating it within a reimagined NWICO (New World Information and Communication Order) and the WSIS (World Summit on Information Society) in their historical context and in relation to the China-initiated project of 'United Nations of Media' (UNM). Both NWICO and WSIS were consequent upon neo-liberalism and capitalist globalization, focusing on technological determinism and digitalized informatization at the expense of the moral/ethical turn and democratization, while NWICO and WSIS turned against media/cultural imperialism but ended up in reinventing an updated version of 'media/cultural imperialism 2.0'. However, the UNM, argues Shi, could take up the mantle of the unfulfilled promises of NWICO and WSIS and provide a supranational and transcultural initiative to ensure the adequate representation of 'the Rest' in the global media sphere. The project of constructing UNM as CCD registers the intellectual and philosophical integration of the West and the East, of the developed and developing world, and of the tradition and (post)modernity, thereby gaining relevance to remapping the topography of global communication.

The domestic context of the globalization of China's media is the focus of the chapter by Hugo de Burgh, Director of the China Media Centre of the University of Westminster and a long-time observer of the Chinese media scene. The desire to have China's voice heard and to weaken the hold of US–UK media – in particular, to mitigate their perceived negative framing of China – is undoubtedly important. A belief that the non-Western world will welcome an alternative take on the world from that which suits US interests and ideology is another. Political leaders recognize that media must follow investment and international activity of all kinds if these are to be represented and reported appropriately so as to enhance rather than detract from China's prestige abroad. In the information age, media are an industry and a market in which China must compete if it is not to surrender earning power, jobs and culture to competitors. Restricted from untrammelled expansion at home, wealthy and dynamic media companies want to conquer new markets abroad with their products, but, De Burgh argues, producing for abroad requires changes at home which may have implications beyond any of those imagined by the 'going out' strategists.

In their chapter on Chinese international television network CCTV's going global strategy, Zhengrong Hu, Deqiang Ji and Yukun Gong examine the dynamics of the encounter between CCTV and the global media environment in the era of media convergence. Their chapter reviews CCTV's 'going out' strategies and the challenges it faces as an 'outsider' within a Western-dominated global media market. The political or ideological relationship with the Chinese party-state is another challenge it faces. However, the declining West and the rising Rest are formulating a new world media map, perhaps implying a global power shift. Against this background, is there a historic opportunity for CCTV to become a member of the dominant players like BBC or CNN in the global market, or to develop geopoliti-cally as successfully as RT or Al Jazeera, or otherwise to break a new path of devel-opment representing the global South? They attempt to answer these questions by examining the complex media powers, domestic and international, with a broader focus on the political-economic and cultural transformation across the globe.

In her contribution, Suzanne Xiao Yang examines the strategic context of China's 'media going global' project, analysing the rationale, the methods and the beliefs underlying the policy and its implementation. Her chapter reveals how the notion of soft power is interpreted in Chinese official and intellectual discourse on China's global reach, and in what ways some of these interpretations, still contested or contrasted, play out in state initiatives to strengthen external communication in pursuing transcultural understanding, an ongoing process in which various actors are involved and their actions coordinated. Promoting China's influence within its positioning as an alternative power in the world, in contrast to what many observers believe, is as much focused on short-term economic concerns as on long-term political and cultural benefits for China. The intention to project China as it is onto the world stage, however, her chapter observes, does not seem to be well matched with the limited capability and experience of Chinese media operating effectively in a global context, acknowledged among officials, media analysts and professionals. Yang suggests that intellectual and policy engagement with the national strategy to globalize Chinese media still needs to address issues concerning cross-cultural differences in terms of perceptions, expectations, discourse rivalry and cultural frames of reference.

After setting out the contextual part of the book, Part II focuses on the pro-cesses of Chinese media's going abroad by looking at the globalizing strategies of the key media players. The Chinese government is dramatically increasing its global media presence and investing heavily in the so called 'big six' traditional media outlets: *People's Daily*, Xinhua news agency, China Central Television (CGTN since 2016), China Radio International and *China Daily* as well as the lesser known Chinese News Service, a Mandarin news agency targeting the Chinese diaspora – the world's largest - in order to increase its global media presence. Since 2017, the sphere of implementing the investment policy has been expanded into a new mode of '1+6+N', which includes the flagship CGTN, the big six, the numerous minis-tries like the International Department of the Central Committee of Chinese Communist Party中联部, media outlets like Chinese International Publishing Corporations, and non-governmental organizations like All-China Federation of Returned Overseas Chinese中国侨联. In addition, this part looks at the challenges faced by commercial print media and creative media who are also aiming to com-pete in a global market.

Vivien Marsh, a former BBC news editor and now a media researcher, reports on the ambiguities and complexities involved in CCTV's English-language news aimed at the African market. She asks whether CCTV, widely seen as a potential emissary of 'soft power' spreading the notion of a reimagined world order with a resurgent China at its centre, is adopting a different way of reporting Africa from its international rivals, and, if so, whether it is a credible alternative. Her chapter sets CCTV Africa in a global broadcasting context and investigates its news reports through content analysis, backed up by interviews with journalists and managers. CCTV Africa throws out mixed signals, Marsh concludes, simultaneously pursuing the soft power role and pushing at the boundaries of what the Chinese state broadcaster might be expected to air.

Falk Hartig's chapter discusses how the English-language *China Daily* is embracing the concept of public diplomacy – the engagement and communication with foreign publics – with an enthusiasm rarely seen in other parts of the world. China is heavily investing in instruments which are aimed at improving its global image and communicating certain narratives about China's position on the global stage. With its five international editions produced around the world, *China Daily* can be understood as a prime example of China's increasing media reach. Hartig's chapter introduces *China Daily* as an important instrument of China's public diplomacy and situates it in China's broader global communication efforts.

Kuo Huang, who has worked for China Radio International (CRI), discusses the strategies adopted by this key component of China's global communication. Huang notes that 75 years after its founding, CRI has evolved into a multimedia entity using 65 languages in its overseas broadcasting – the largest such broadcaster in the world. CRI is working towards the goal of becoming a modern, comprehensive and innovative international media group; she explains how it started the process of moving from a single-platform to an integrated media organization, from a China-based institution into an international media group.

The focus of the chapter by Guoqiang Yun and Jing Wu is on the growing internationalization of the Chinese documentary. They locate the discussion about China's new documentary, which emerged during the 1990s, in its social and political context. Their chapter explores the degree of intercultural interaction between China and Western modernism in these documentary products, and analyses its influence in China's cultural transformation. The chapter suggests that the rise of China's new documentary is a key moment in the internationalization and pluralization of traditional socialism. On the one hand, consumer culture has shaped the realist aesthetics of China's new documentary through the communicative channels of globalization and its market mechanism; on the other as a creative actor, China's new documentary has participated in the shaping of China's cultural modernity, developing mechanisms for cultural exchanges and debates between China and the West.

The globalization of Chinese magazines and newspapers is dealt with by Miao Mi in her chapter. Chinese newspapers have been widely perceived by Western media as the government's propaganda instrument, tightly controlled by the party and lacking independence. Mi's chapter argues that, although many Chinese newspapers and magazines claim to be international titles with multi-language editions, bureaux, print plants or joint ventures aboard, given current scepticism it has been extremely difficult for the Chinese media outlets to increase their brand value and credibility aboard and effectively enhance China's global image. For Chinese newspapers and magazines to function better as a platform to export China's soft power, she suggests that the practices of some Western newspapers in producing content online could be considered as a model to attract a broader readership globally.

Although China has become a formidable economic power, its cultural presence globally remains rather weak, despite government 'going out' initiatives. However, Chinese media companies have adapted to global trends, especially in economic terms. Part III of the book – discourses of Sino-globalization – includes analyses of these processes of adaptation, drawing on examples from public diplomacy, from financial journalism and television news, as well as how overseas journalistic practices influence Chinese communication strategies.

In their contribution Xiaoling Zhang and Zhenzhi Guo emphasize the importance of influence through cultural exchanges, as China has embraced the idea of soft power as a national policy. As part of this cultural 'going out' strategy, since 2004, 500 Confucius Institutes (CIs) and 1,000 Confucius Classrooms (CCs) have been opened on campuses around the world. This has also generated controversy both among the academic world and the media, questioning CIs' intent, objectives and practices. Some worry about 'the political influence of the Chinese government, as guided by the propaganda apparatus of the party-state'. What has attracted far less attention but plays the same role, Zhang and Guo argue, is the China Cultural Centre (CCC) under the Chinese Ministry of Culture. In contrast to the rapid speed and the accompanying debates around CIs and CCs, CCCs have demonstrated a different trajectory in their speed, operation, modes of collaboration and choice of host countries in spreading knowledge of Chinese language and culture. Since it attracts less criticism, the chapter asks, is the CCC more effective than the CI in promoting Chinese language and culture? Tracing the history of the CCCs and their activities, Zhang and Guo conclude that CCCs have been more successful, thanks to their gradualist and much less intrusive approach, as well as the less visible role of the Chinese government in its activities.

Public diplomacy is also the focus of the chapter by Wanning Sun, who examines it from the perspective of foreign correspondents in China and how they report and represent China to the wider world. Much work has been done to analyse the scope and efforts on the part of the Chinese government in its engagement in soft power exercises. However, Sun argues, how foreign media shape the success or failure of China's soft power initiatives is less clear. Yet knowing the answer to this question is crucial if we are to understand the depth and breadth of the challenges facing China's public diplomacy goals. Combining institutional with historical analyses, her chapter examines empirical and conceptual issues arising from the role of the foreign correspondent in China's soft power agenda. Her chapter discusses key aspects of China's public diplomacy efforts in the context of the government's management of foreign correspondents in China. She also considers the historical and geopolitical contexts which continue to shape today's foreign correspondents' work practices. Drawing on interviews, Sun analyses the institutional, professional and individual factors in the often tense relationship between the Chinese government and foreign correspondents.

Yu Xiang's chapter examines the Chinese media's presence in Africa and locates it within structural theories of centre–periphery relationships. Most Sino-African media studies concentrate on the diplomatic function of China's media in Africa to promote the soft power of China. Xiang argues that few are paying enough attention to the importance of Chinese media's reception in Africa by African audiences, which is essential to reveal the actual role of international news in mediating the autonomy of individuals and the mechanism of structure. In order to understand the ideological role of China's media in Africa, it is important to analyse the structural basis of Sino-African relations. At the same time, reception analysis of the African audiences of China's media in Africa helps to understand the dynamic process of Sino-African media flow. Her chapter provides a structural analysis of the media dynamic between China and Africa from a critical, political-economic perspective, using the case study of CCTV in Africa and empirical data from audience interviews.

Jingwei Piao's chapter looks at the role of the Chinese financial media in promoting a Chinese version of economic globalization. She discusses the evolution of China's financial media, emphasizing its important but neglected role in promoting and legitimizing China's economic globalization. Her chapter explores the inter-relationship of the Chinese economy and the role of the financial media in establishing a new economic discourse. After providing an account of the evolution of Chinese financial media, Piao argues that in the early stage of market reform, China's financial media played a successful educational role in formulating a new economic language and business culture. However, as the economic agenda has changed in the twenty-first century, the economic discourse used by the media does not seem to have developed fast enough to remain synchronous with the global norms of the neoliberal business mentality.

How have these changes influenced the discourse about international communication in China? Quing'an Zhou and Yanni Wu, in their chapter, enumerate the challenges and opportunities which Sino-globalization offers. One aspect they focus on is the Chinese media's role in nation-branding initiatives and international communication activities with increasingly diversified approaches and significant achievements, particularly since the branding of the 2008 Beijing Olympic Games. Their chapter examines the international communication patterns of Chinese media by studying six media organizations: Xinhua news agency, *People's Daily*, CCTV, CRI, *China Daily* and Chinese News Service. Research on Chinese mainstream media has shown that the way in which they participate in international communication differs from one another. The roles that traditional media and new media respectively play in international communication are also different. For Chinese mainstream media, they argue, the strengthening of international communication capacity also reflects an increasing professionalism.

The final part of the book – media with Chinese characteristics – tackles the interface between the domestic and the global in Chinese media. Chapters in this part include analysis of advertising, social media, television formats as well as flows of Chinese media to Southeast Asia, drawing on rich empirical data collected specifically for this volume.

The chapter by Shanshan Lou and Hong Cheng is about advertising in China, suggesting that, over the past four decades, the emerging global economy and booming marketplace in China are reflected in a fast-growing advertising industry. Restarting from scratch in 1979, China's advertising now ranks second in the world after the US in terms of annual advertising spend, estimated as more than $73 billion in 2015. This huge advertising industry has exerted direct and enormous impact on the economic development and sociocultural changes in China. Numerous studies have been done to examine such impact domestically but little is known about the implications and impact of China's advertising on the global scene. What does this huge advertising market mean to the global advertising and global media industries, they ask? With an increasing number of Chinese companies going global, what role does the Chinese advertising industry – especially Chinese mobile advertising – have in the international market?

Social media play an integral part in how Chinese messages are being communicated. David Feng's chapter focuses on social media in China and how it may be contributing to a global conversation. It has been nearly three decades since China 'went online' and, in those 30 years, its internet landscape has changed from one of students and technically savvy consumers using elementary systems, to a vibrant online community. From setting up accounts to Weibo and WeChat, to Twitter adopting a new-style retweet first seen on Weibo, the world's largest nation is increasingly influencing the way conversations are carried out online. Feng explores what effects Chinese ways of communication are having on the internet on a wider scale, by looking both at general trends in a scholarly context, and how the Chinese-style discourse on the internet is being exported overseas by Chinese citizens themselves.

Hong Li and Rong Zeng in their chapter focus on television entertainment and the importance of international collaborations to develop new genres. The popularity of formats in China suggests Chinese entertainment television's increasing interconnectivity with global television networks, they argue, as well as the standardization of content and technology. The chapter reviews the context of entertainment television and its development and looks at the television format business, the relationship between China and the outside world, and how changes in entertainment television are coming about through foreign involvement. It also examines how the entertainment industry is orienting itself towards export as part of the 'going out' strategy.

The final chapter in the book looks at the regional dimension of China's going global strategy. Jiao Yang and Mei Wu discuss the significance and function of local media in the regional information flow in the context of globalization. Their chapter focuses on how Yunnan media construct the rhetorical vision of the national policy which positions Yunnan as a 'gateway' to Southeast Asia. Specifically, Yang and Wu examine how *Yunnan Daily*, as a representative of Yunnan's official media, has interpreted this national strategic policy and projected Yunnan's role in regional development.

To do a semblance of justice to so vast a topic as the globalization of such a large country and civilizational power as China requires a concerted and collective effort.

We are very grateful to our contributors for being part of this book. Their valuable insights into various aspects of the globalization of China's media will, we hope, help broaden and deepen our understanding of what is arguably the most significant shift in global power relations in a generation. How Chinese media mediate Sino-globalization is going to be a very interesting and intellectually challenging project for Chinese media personnel, as well as for the community of scholars concerned with globalization with an Asian accent. We hope our volume is a modest contribution to this important debate.

Contrary to popular belief, edited volumes require much more work than most scholars give them credit for. We have been fortunate to have in Natalie Foster an excellent editor, who was involved in this project from its very inception and demonstrated admirable professionalism and a good-natured patience while we worked on putting the chapters together. We thank her and her team at Routledge, as well as Alja Kranjec of the China Media Centre, University of Westminster for her help in liaising with the authors to coordinate the material for this book.

References

Berry, Chris; Xinyu, Lu and Rofel, Lisa (2010) *The New Chinese Documentary Film Movement: For the Public Record*. Hong Kong: Hong Kong University Press.

Brady, Anne-Marie (2012) *China's Thought Management*. London: Routledge.

China Daily (2017) Chinese Overseas Investments in Sports & Entertainment Surge 188% in 2016. *The China Daily*, (European edition) 10 March.

Christensen, Miyase (2013) TransNational media flows: Some key questions and debates, *International Journal of Communication*, 7: 2400–2418.

Curtin, Michael (2007) *Playing to the World's Biggest Audience: The Globalization of Chinese Film and TV*. Los Angeles: University of California Press.

Davis, Stuart; Straubhaar, Joseph and Cunha, Isabel (2016) The construction of a transnational Lusophone media space: A historiographic analysis, *Popular Communication*, 14(4): 212–223.

Economist (2017) The New Davos Man. *The Economist*, January 21.

Edney, Kingsley (2014) *The Globalization of Chinese Propaganda: International Power and Domestic Political Cohesion*. London: Palgrave.

Figenschou, Tine Ustad (2014) *Al Jazeera and the Global Media Landscape: The South is Talking Back*. New York: Routledge.

Hong, Yu (2017) *Networking China: The Digital Transformation of the Chinese Economy*. Chicago: University of Illinois Press.

IMF (2017) *World Economic Outlook: Gaining Momentum?* Washington: International Monetary Fund, April.

Jacques, Martin (2009) *When China Rules the World: The End of the Western World and the Birth of a New Global Order*. London: Allen Lane.

Keane, Michael (2013) *Creative Industries in China: Art, Design and Media*. Cambridge: Polity.

Keane, Michael and Wanning, Sun (eds.) (2014) *Chinese Media*. London: Routledge.

Khanna, Parag (2016) *Connectography: Mapping the Future of Global Civilization*. New York: Random House.

Kim, Youna (ed.) (2013) *The Korean Wave: Korean Media Go Global*. London: Routledge.

Kokas, Aynne (2017) *Hollywood Made in China*. Los Angeles: University of California Press.

Kurlantzick, Joshua (2007) *Charm Offensive: How China's Soft Power Is Transforming the World*. New Haven: Yale University Press.

Lai, Hongyi and Lu, Yiyi (eds.) (2012) *China's Soft Power and International Relations*. New York: Routledge.

Meyers, Jessica (2017) Globalization 2.0: How China's Two-Day Summit Aims to Shape a New World Order. *The Los Angeles Times*, 12 May.

Miller, Jade (2016) *Nollywood Central*. London: BFI/Palgrave.

Ng, Jason (2013) *Blocked on Weibo: What Gets Suppressed on China's Version of Twitter (and Why)*. New York: The New Press.

Punathambekar, Aswin (2013) *From Bombay to Bollywood: The Making of a Global Media Industry*. New York: New York University Press.

Siwek, Stephen (2016) *Copyright Industries in the U.S. Economy: The 2016 Report*, Incorporated, prepared for the International Intellectual Property Alliance, November. Available at: www.iipa.com.

Stockman, Daniela (2013) *Media Commercialization and Authoritarian Rule in China*. Cambridge: Cambridge University Press.

Sun, Wanning (ed.) (2009) *Media and the Chinese Diaspora: Community, Communications and Commerce*. New York: Routledge.

Thussu, Daya Kishan (forthcoming) *International Communication – Continuity and Change*, third edition. New York: Bloomsbury Academic.

Wang, Jian (ed.) (2011) *Soft Power in China: Public Diplomacy through Communication*. New York: Palgrave Macmillan.

Xin, Xin (2012) *How the Market is Changing China's News: The Case of Xinhua News Agency*. Lanham (MD): Lexington Books.

Yang, Guobin (2009) *The Power of the Internet in China: Citizen Activism Online*. New York: Columbia University Press.

Young, Doug (2013) *The Party Line: How the Media Dictates Public Opinion in Modern China*. Cambridge: Wiley.

Zhang, Shixin (2016) *Chinese War Correspondents: Covering Wars and Conflicts in the Twenty-First Century*. London: Palgrave/Macmillan.

Zhao, Yuezhi (2008) *Communication in China: Political Economy, Power, and Conflict*. Oxford: Rowman and Littlefield.

Zhu, Ying (2012) *Two Billion Eyes: The Story of China Central Television*. New York: The New Press.

PART I

Conceptualizing the rise of China's media

1

GLOBALIZATION OF CHINESE MEDIA: THE GLOBAL CONTEXT

Daya Kishan Thussu

The accelerated globalization of China's media is coinciding with shifts in international geopolitical and economic power relations, in what has been termed variously as a 'post-American' and a 'post-Western' world (Zakaria, 2008; Jacques, 2009; Acharya, 2014; Stuenkel, 2016). It has been suggested that the 'assertive China discourse' emanating from the 'Middle Kingdom' has become a narrative widely recognized by the West and its allies. There is also a parallel narrative in China – increasingly being circulated around the world – replacing the 'keeping a low profile' approach with 'striving for achievements' (Johnston, 2013).

As the 'Washington Consensus' – based on globalization of economic liberalization, deregulation and privatization, spearheaded by the US government and the Bretton Woods institutions – faces a rupture, a 'Beijing consensus' (Halper, 2010) appears to have strengthened. Indeed, China has emerged as the most vocal champion of neo-liberal globalization. One key difference, though, is that in the Chinese version of globalization, the state continues to play a pivotal role. State intervention is seen as crucial for developmental economics, for boosting growth and maintaining social harmony, and for creating and controlling a national ideological narrative (Brady, 2012). This chapter sets out to contextualize the globalization of the Chinese media, examining it from a geopolitical perspective.

The geopolitical context of China's media rise

China's media going global has been necessitated by the extraordinary expansion of the Chinese economy in the last two decades and its rapid globalization. Since 2006, China has been the largest holder of foreign-currency reserves. In 2014, China became the world's largest economy, overtaking the United States in GDP based on purchasing power parity (PPP), according to the International Monetary Fund. By 2016, China had become the largest importer for more than

70 countries and accounted for about ten per cent of all imports globally. Chinese companies are becoming increasingly competitive in global markets, making sizeable investments and acquisitions all around the world. This is assisted by the inclusion of the renminbi in the IMF's Special Drawing Rights, making it one of the world's reserve currencies. According to the IMF, China's share of global GDP in PPP terms has grown from just over 4 per cent in 1990 to nearly 18 per cent in 2016, while that of the G7 countries – the US, Japan, Germany, Britain, France, Canada and Italy – shrank from nearly 51 per cent in 1990 to about 31 per cent in 2016. Since it joined the World Trade Organization, China's imports have surged from $243.55 billion to $1.68 trillion in 15 years, an average annual growth of more than 10 per cent. As the world's second biggest investor, China's outbound direct investment rose for a 13th straight year in 2015, reaching $145.67 billion (IMF, 2017). Such an unprecedented rise of a non-Western nation evokes concern in Western capitals (Roach, 2014; Le Corre and Pollack, 2016; Alden, 2016; RAND Corporation, 2016). Writing in the journal *Foreign Policy*, Robert Kagan of the Brookings Institute warned that the US must check assertive rising powers, such as China, arguing that accepting their spheres of influence is a recipe for disaster (Kagan, 2017).

Why China's media needs to go global

To combat such negative discourses in the mainstream international media and to provide their own version of the China story, the Chinese media have been going global for over a decade (Wang and Wang, 2014; Wang, 2014; Sun, 2015). In 2014, addressing the Central Conference on Work Relating to Foreign Affairs, President Xi Jinping announced that China should 'give a good Chinese narrative, and better communicate China's messages to the world' (quoted in Xinhua, 2014). As part of disseminating this message to the world, the state-funded 'central media' – Xinhua news agency, China Central Television (CCTV, which in 2016 changed its name to China Global Television Network – CGTN), China Radio International, *People's Daily* and the English-language *China Daily* – were generously funded for global expansion (Shambaugh, 2013). This funding came as part of a broader government effort to create internationally competitive media conglomerates in China that would make 'China's voice heard internationally' (Nelson, 2013).

Founded in 1981 and with 600,000 copies distributed overseas, via 34 print sites, *China Daily*, 'a voice of China on the global stage', claims to have 45 million readers worldwide for its print and digital versions. Apart from having various international editions – including in the US and in Europe, *China Daily* is circulated with the *Washington Post* and *Wall Street Journal* in the US and several other newspapers around the world. In addition to English, the *China Daily* monthly supplement, *China Watch*, also publishes supplements in French, German and Spanish. Since 2016, London's *Daily Telegraph* has had a sponsorship deal with *China Watch*, while a Russian edition has also been launched in partnership with leading Russian newspaper *Rossiyskaya Gazeta*. Since 1997, the online version of *The People's Daily*, People.cn – one of the top ten newspapers in the world – has been available in nine international languages. In 2017, China Radio International was broadcasting in 61 languages via its six overseas regional hubs and 32 correspondents. It had affiliations with 70 overseas radio stations and 18 global internet radio services. Apart from English, CGTN news (launched with the aim to 're-brand our product to the world, to cope with the global trend in media convergence') is available in French, Spanish, Russian and Arabic. Xinhua too has expanded its international operations – being particularly strong in the developing world and claiming to articulate a Southern news agenda. CGTN – the main instrument of Chinese global communication – is emphatic about its mission: 'we cover the whole globe, reporting news from a Chinese perspective. Our mission is to create a better understanding of international events across the world, bridging continents and bringing a more balanced view to global news reporting' (CGTN website). However, massive expansion and technological prowess have not translated into professional output: none of the Chinese international media has ever broken a major global story. As one study noted, despite its globalization and marketization, 'the lack of credibility remains Xinhua's Achilles' heel' (Xin, 2012: 129), while Chinese television news has yet to acquire global credibility as 'the perception of being propaganda vehicles for the Chinese government is hard to shake off' (Zhu, 2012: 194).

More successful have been privately funded Chinese media conglomerates, which, although following state strictures, have a greater degree of manoeuvrability to work around China's highly regulated media system (Stockman, 2013). The e-commerce giant Alibaba, labelled as the 'largest virtual shopping mall in the world' (Clark, 2016: 5), is the most prominent example: its 2014 IPO in the New York Stock Exchange raised $25 billion, the largest stock market flotation in history (Erisman, 2015; Lashinsky, 2017). What is described as the 'iron triangle' – e-commerce, logistics and finance – has made Alibaba, within a very short time, China's best-known global corporate brand (Clark, 2016: 16). Jack Ma, its founder and executive chairman, is dubbed China's Rupert Murdoch by some. Since 2013, he has acquired the Hong-Kong-based *South China Morning Post*, China's largest video-sharing site, Youku Tudou, social media outlet Sina Weibo and Alibaba Pictures. Beyond China, Ma has also invested, among others, in popular social apps Snapchat and PayTM, India's largest e-commerce venture (Ni, 2016).

Creating a communication infrastructure for going global

Such expansion has been made possible by the information and communication infrastructure that has been put in place in the past decade by Chinese government-supported infrastructural projects. One key component of this is the strengthening of China's foreign aid programme. China's foreign aid has expanded greatly since its 'going global' strategy was launched in 2005. In 2013 China contributed nearly four per cent of total global development assistance, nearly half of it directed to countries in Africa, particularly since the establishment of the Forum on China-Africa Cooperation (FOCAC) in 2000 (see essays in Zhou and Xiong, 2017). This aid is aimed at creating infrastructure, including that for communication, thus facilitating growing trade relations. China's trade with the continent has increased exponentially – from $10 billion in 2000 to $280 billion in 2015. At the second FOCAC summit in Johannesburg in December 2016, President Xi announced a tripling of aid to the continent to $60 billion (Moody, 2016).

It is no wonder that Chinese media have expanded in the continent. For example, *StarTimes*, one of China's largest pay TV companies, has been operating in Africa since 2002, reaching, in 2016, seven million subscribers in ten countries, including Nigeria, Tanzania, Uganda, Rwanda and Kenya. The firm is diversifying in mobile TV services and internet business platforms, crucial as more Africans join the digital media world. Nairobi has emerged as a hub for Chinese media's presence on the continent, with the setting up of the CCTV Africa service in 2012.

Creating information and communication networks is part of China's major infra-structure initiatives, notably the highly ambitious Belt and Road Initiative (BRI), formerly know as the One Belt, One Road (OBOR) project, outlined in 2015 by China's National Development and Reform Committee (European Council on Foreign Relations, 2015). When completed, it will have 900 infrastructure projects, valued at about $1.3 trillion and will form an economic 'belt' across the Eurasian con-tinent and a maritime 'silk road' through Southeast and South Asia to the Middle East 'to deepen economic integration and connectivity'. The 'Belt and Road' projects are backed by a new $40 billion Silk Road Infrastructure Fund, capitalized mainly by China's foreign exchange reserves. In addition, the Asian Infrastructure Investment Bank (AIIB) – established in 2016 with a membership of 70 nations, including Germany, India, Britain, Canada and Australia – together with the Shanghai-based New Development Bank, established in 2014 by the five BRICS (Brazil, Russia, India, China and South Africa) nations, are involved in financing these projects, as are leading banks such as the Industrial and Commercial Bank of China (Ti, 2016).

Given the scale and scope of change that the 'Belt and Road' projects encompass, the Chinese media and government have been putting a favourable gloss on what is essentially an economic programme with significant geopolitical connotations. 'We should enhance international exchanges and cooperation on culture and media', says a government document, 'and leverage the positive role of the internet and new media tools to foster harmonious and friendly cultural environment and public opinion' (Government of China, 2015). Many Chinese commentators echo the official line, reiterating President Xi's 'Three Nos': 'no interference in the internal affairs of other nations; no to increasing "sphere of influence" and no to striving for hegemony or dominance' (quoted in Zi, 2014).

To emphasize the cultural dimension of this expansion, the government is funding translations of Chinese literature, aiming to reach readers in countries along the routes of the 'modern Silk Road', with such Chinese publishers as China Intercontinental Press and Beijing Normal University Press being encouraged to undertake what one senior official described as 'localization operations', seen as 'an important and effective way of "going out"' (Jia, 2017). An annual 'Silk Road International Arts Festival' is regularly held in the historic city of Xi'an, the Chinese starting point of the ancient Silk Road.

At the third World Internet Conference in 2016, China suggested that the 'Belt and Road' initiative offered opportunities for the countries involved to improve their telecommunication infrastructure using Chinese investment. *China Daily* quoted a senior official as saying that 'network construction, services and applications and digital economy' were crucial for deepening exchanges and cooperation. Yang Xiaowei, General Manager of China Telecommunications, said that the mission of the Chinese telecom operators was to bridge the gap and make people all over the world part of the 'information civilization'. A forum at the conference – 'Network Connection Promotes Heart Connection' – discussed cooperation in building a better communication infrastructure to expand trade and deepen cultural ties (Liqiang, 2016).

However, the official-speak – part of China's soft power narrative – does not necessarily match the realities on the ground. Commentators note that the Chinese government is 'building networks carefully and deliberately to connect to minerals, energy sources and access to cities, harbours and oceans' (Frankopan, 2015: 516). The Chinese media need to take on board the concerns of the countries directly affected by these new routes. Moscow's traditional domination of its 'near abroad' is being increasingly eroded by Chinese investment and growing presence in central Asia, while the China-Pakistan Economic Corridor project – an integral part of OBOR – irks New Delhi as it passes through territories claimed by both India and Pakistan. Europeans too are concerned. An article in the respected German news-weekly *Der Spiegel* wondered whether the real goal of OBOR was: 'to break the West's political dominance – a plan, in a sense, to conquer the world'? (Follath, 2016).

The focus on trade and investment has eclipsed the cultural and communication aspects of this expansion. Given the name *Seidenstrassen*, the Silk Roads, in 1877 by German geographer Ferdinand von Richthofen, the communication arteries facilitated interactions among religious practices of Christianity, Buddhism, Hinduism and Islam (Frankopan, 2015). However, the Chinese media's reluctance to address religious issues, particularly pertaining to Islam, can be a limitation in a region steeped in a culture defined by religious beliefs. In China, home to more than 20 million Muslims, Islam is a religious as well as an ethnic and racial category but its coverage in any Chinese media is almost negligible. Djoomart Otorbaev, the former Prime Minister of Kyrgyzstan, told *Der Spiegel* that the Chinese 'don't understand that if you want to succeed in the long term, you need to win over people's hearts' (quoted in Follath, 2016). Winning hearts and minds of foreign populations forms a key component of China's soft power discourses (Lai and Lu, 2012; Zhao, 2013; Zhang *et al.*, 2016; Sinha-Palit, 2017). The Chinese authorities have recognized that the officially sponsored news media are less effective in achieving this and therefore the strategy seems now to be to focus on entertainment media, in collaboration with private domestic and transnational content providers.

Learning from global media leaders

One of the most significant shifts in the global entertainment arena is the acquiring of entertainment properties – both hardware and software – by major Chinese companies.

The globalization of Chinese media has been influenced by and in turn has influenced global (Western) media. One compelling example is Disney, which the Chinese government is using to globalize its own media and entertainment companies, as well as to improve the country's image abroad. During a 2010 meeting with China's propaganda minister, Disney's chief executive, Robert Iger, agreed to use the company's global platform to 'introduce more about China to the world'. Disney is collaborating with China's Ministry of Culture to help develop the country's animation industry, and with Shanghai Media Group – one of China's largest media corporations – to make films for global audiences (Barboza and Barnes, 2016). Shanghai Media Group has also formed alliances or invested in other major companies, such as Sony, Warner Bros. and DreamWorks.

Despite the strict regulation of imports of foreign films and entertainment programming, the global media giants are extremely keen to consolidate their operations within what is one of the world's largest – and fastest growing – media markets (PwC, 2016; Kantar, 2016). Co-production – in state jargon 'officially assisted production' – between Hollywood studios and Chinese companies – has become increasingly common: 42 films were co-produced between 2002 and 2013. This co-production process often requires the scripts to be vetted and edited so as not to offend the sensibilities of an overly sensitive government (Kokas, 2017). Hollywood producers have altered their films to make them China-friendly to gain market access there. For example, the 2014 film *Transformers: Age of Extinction*, made by Paramount with help from Jiaflix Enterprises and CCTV's China Movie Channel, was toned down to respect Chinese censors, while Sony deleted scenes of aliens blasting a hole in the Great Wall of China from its 2015 movie *Pixels* (Cohen, 2014; Swanson, 2015).

For their part, the Chinese producers are making films with greater technical finesse to reach a wider audience by acquiring Western special effects companies: for example, in 2016 the Shanghai-based Cultural Investment Holdings bought British visual effects company Framestore, involved in the *Harry Potter* franchise. They are also adopting or adapting Western programming for the Chinese market. There appears to be a distinct fascination with traditional British culture and a huge audience for TV shows such as *Downton Abbey* and *Sherlock*. The Chinese version of the singing competition show *The Voice*, produced by a Dutch group, was very successful, viewed by more than 120 million on TV (and 400 million-plus online), while Fremantle Media's deal with Youku to stream popular shows such as *America's Got Talent* were extremely popular. In 2011, a Mandarin version of *Mamma Mia!* was performed in China, while in 2014, a Mandarin version of *Into the Woods* had a 100-performance run in Beijing, and *The Lion King* musical in Mandarin was performed at Shanghai Disneyland, the world's largest theme park, which opened in 2016.

Part of the reason for such borrowing is the lack of exportable entertainment within China. Unlike other Asian media producers – notably Japan (animation and television entertainment), South Korea (television dramas and popular music) and India (Bollywood), China has a limited tradition of exporting entertainment for a wider global audience, though the Hong Kong-made 'action films' have had international circulation since the 1970s (Thussu, forthcoming). More recently, the global success of such films as *Crouching Tiger, Hidden Dragon* (2000), *Hero* (2002) and *House of Flying Daggers* (2004) contributed to the opening of a Chinese version of entertainment to a global audience, helped in no small way by marketing, advertising and co-production with major Hollywood studios. One way of dealing with any deficiencies is to invest in the world's most profitable and successful entertainment industry: Hollywood. One of the most significant shifts in the global entertainment arena is the acquiring of entertainment properties – both hardware and software – by major Chinese companies. For the last five years, the Dalian Wanda Group, owned by China's richest man, Wang Jianlin, has been investing heavily in entertainment companies: it owns movie theatre chains in the US, Europe (including London-based Odeon & UCI Cinemas Group, Europe's largest cinema operator) and Australia, as well as production companies such as Legendary Entertainment. It plans to build a $1.2 billion headquarters in Beverly Hills, says Wang, 'to aid in China's entry into Hollywood's film industry and generally promote Chinese culture abroad' (Barnes, 2016).

In 2016, the Dalian Wanda Group and Sony Pictures entered into a strategic alliance to co-finance Sony Pictures' releases in China. It is also building the world's largest film-making facility for $8.2 billion at Wanda Studios in Qingdao, in China. The group has developed a successful entertainment chain, comprising movie houses and studios, encompassing production, distribution, digital marketing and merchandizing. 'Optimistically, it will be at least 10 years before we can make films in English that are global', Wang told *Hollywood Reporter* in 2016. 'It's going to take us a long time to catch up with Hollywood. And this catching up will probably require a much bigger effort compared to the economic catch-up' (cited in Brzeski, 2016).

Wanda Group, together with other Chinese companies are also investing in sports media – one of the most profitable and global genres – buying stakes in top football clubs in Spain, Italy and Britain, while Alibaba joined McDonald's, Coca-Cola and Visa to be a leading sponsor of the summer and winter Olympics until 2028, as well as becoming the International Olympic Committee's official cloud services and e-commerce platform services partner. It will also become a partner in the Olympic Channel, a digital TV service (Ingle, 2017). The online platform QQ Sports of the Chinese tech giant Tencent has an agreement with Disney-owned ESPN (Entertainment and Sports Network) to provide live coverage of the National Basketball Association. In gaming too, the Chinese global presence is growing: in 2015, the Chinese mobile games market became the largest in the world, generating $7.1 billion, according to industry reports (McNeice, 2017). These developments are also reflected in financial media, a sector largely dominated by the US and UK, though the Chinese are making inroads here too. In 2017, for example, a Chinese consortium acquired the US-based International Data Group, a leading global media, market research and venture company with operations in 97 countries.

At least in the short term, the audience for Chinese content is likely to be the Chinese diaspora (the world's largest), Chinese employees working abroad, Chinese students (Chinese constitute the largest percentage of international students) and Chinese tourists: since 2013, China has been the source of the largest number of tourists, with nearly 100 million overseas trips annually. As these tourists and students start travelling to countries beyond Europe and the US, Chinese culture and media will also be globalized and become more present, especially since many leading international hotel chains are now owned by Chinese companies keen to provide Chinese information and entertainment to their guests. This will also enable accessibility of Chinese media to a wider global audience. In 2016 China's HNA Group bought a stake in Hilton Worldwide Holdings, as well as Carlson Hotels, which owns Radisson and several other brands, while another Chinese company, Anbang Insurance Group, purchased such famous hotels as JW Marriott, Essex House and Waldorf Astoria in New York, the InterContinental in Chicago and Four Seasons in Washington.

In order to supply content to this growing market, Chinese media companies are developing Chinese content, ranging from historical dramas, feature films, game and chat shows, to news and current affairs, potentially to a global audience (Keane, 2013; Bai and Song, 2015). Chinese creative industries have come of age in the last two decades, facilitated by activist state intervention, and in more recent years the goal has been to move 'beyond manufacturing to develop a "knowledge economy" or "creative economy" in which value is produced through innovation, both techno-scientific and aesthetic' (Chumley, 2016: 2).

Limitations of China's media going global

Chinese media are going global at a time when the media sphere – including the digital space – is crowded and dominated largely by US and UK media outlets. Studies have shown that mainstream anglophone media 'still play an influential role in the construction of China's national image. The mainstream media not only set the agenda for international social media in reporting China, but also influence its frame' (Xiang, 2013: 268). Chinese media have had limited success in redressing this, partly because of excessive bureaucratization and overt and covert censorship – often self-censorship – which limits the journalistic impact, as a 'Chinese angle' on world news to foreign audiences remains 'elusive' (Nyíri, 2017). In response, the Chinese authorities have been acquiring radio stations abroad and investing in other news start-ups. A Reuters investigation in 2015 showed that the 'going-out' strategy had a covert dimension: though nominally independent, many international radio stations were operating as mouthpieces for Chinese government (Qing and Shiffman, 2015), while CNN reported that China Radio International had been buying radio stations internationally to promote Chinese viewpoints – at least 33 radio stations in 14 countries (Griffiths, 2016).

The Chinese elite and the elite media appear to be more interested in the West – and within it the US – than the rest of the world, a reflection perhaps of China's traditional respect for power and hierarchy. As one commentator noted: 'Despite its claim of being a multi-ethnic nation, China has historically been a homogenous "civilization-state" and its view of the world is structured and hierarchical' (Wang, 2013: 170). However, in Africa, for instance, where the Chinese media presence is strongest, it has been suggested that the Chinese media aim to counter the negative portrayal of the continent by the mainstream Western media. 'The positive reporting of China's media', it has been argued, 'will tap into the "rising Africa" narrative, thus helping to frame China's media as allies of Africa' (Zhang and Mwangi, 2016: 78).

Monitoring the messengers

As the world's largest economy in purchasing power terms, a strong military power and a civilizational state, China attracts journalists from all over the world – in 2016, it had as many as 700 accredited foreign journalists from more than 50 different countries. However, a PEN America report noted, 'as China has modernized its economy and opened-up to the world, the government's commitment to strict domestic censorship – both online and off, has remained steadfast and its methods of control both powerful and innovative' (PEN America, 2016: 4). A 2015 survey conducted by the Beijing-based Foreign Correspondents' Club of China, with representations from more than 40 countries, found that 96 per cent of its members said conditions for foreign journalists working in China 'almost never meet international press freedom standards' (Foreign Correspondents' Club of China, 2015). Such a situation inhibits coverage of China and can contribute to the distortions of reporting about the country to a global audience, as the PEN America report points out: 'Given the strict controls on government information, domestic journalism and academic scholarship, the world has limited alternative sources that can compensate for gaps and blind spots in international news coverage of China' (PEN America, 2016: 5). Such an attitude sits oddly with frequent official exhortations about the need to 'improve international society's understanding of China' (Shambaugh, 2013: 222).

Censoring cyber-communication

China has the world's largest internet population: by 2016, the number had passed 720 million. The 'Great Firewall', the term coined in 1997 by *Wired* magazine, blocks access to foreign websites – including Google, Facebook, YouTube, Twitter and Instagram – while millions of human censors, employed by the government and the party, as well as private corporations, constantly and rigorously monitor online communication (Brady, 2012; Ng, 2013; Yang, 2015). A 2014 Harvard University study showed how the Chinese authorities allowed a certain amount of individual freedom but retained collective censorship (King et al., 2014), while a 2017 analysis by the same team estimated that the government employed up to two million part-time bloggers and social media users to fabricate and post about 448 million comments a year. This army, the study suggested, was 'devoted primarily to cheerleading for the state, symbols of the regime, or the revolutionary history of the Communist Party'. The study interpreted these activities as 'the regime's effort at strategic distraction from collective action, grievances, or general negativity, etc.' (King et al., 2017: 497). Others speak of a 'networked authoritarianism', arguing that the Chinese government has adapted to the internet, even using networked tech-nologies to legitimize party-state monopoly on discourse and narrative (MacKinnon, 2011). However, such standard criticisms of the Chinese internet mask a more complex picture. Many tech-savvy Chinese with international exposure via study, travel or work know their way around censorship regimes, using software such as virtual private networks.

Cyber-capitalism with Chinese characteristics

While the Western world, and by extension the wider international community, has been legitimately focusing on censorship issues pertaining to the media in China and particularly on China's internet, Lu Wei, China's internet chief, has argued for a balance between 'freedom and order' and between 'openness and autonomy'. China is, he told the *Washington Post*, on a path of 'cyber-governance with Chinese characteristics' (cited in Denyer, 2016).

Looking beyond the standard Western discourses about party-state control, cen-sorship and surveillance and the ideological narratives that such a system promotes, one could make an argument on very different lines. It could be argued that Chinese interactions with Western ideas have always been more complex than with other non-Western regions (Yaqin, 2014). The Chinese version of communism was in many ways starkly different from the Soviet model that inspired it (it may be useful to recall that the Sino-Soviet schism took place in the late 1950s, merely a decade after the founding of the People's Republic). As China embraced modern capitalism in the late 1970s, it followed a different, some would say a distinctive model, where the state, not the market, took the main lead in modernizing and globalizing the economy. With digital capitalism too, China has amply shown that it has its own version of what I call 'cyber-capitalism with Chinese characteristics'. These can be defined as giving high priority to cyber-sovereignty, creating and sustaining the world's largest online market for a global Sino-sphere; establishing domestic cyber properties and protecting them from competition from global digital giants by introducing and implementing strict regulatory regimes; and globalization of Chinese digital corporations. China is the only country with its own version of Google, Facebook, Amazon, Twitter, WhatsApp and many other essentially US-based digital properties.

While the international debates about the Chinese internet have focused on censorship-related issues, the Chinese government and its increasingly globalizing cyber corporations have been strengthening their digital imprints across the world. One outcome of such policies is the extraordinary growth of China's cyber-capitalism in the last decade. According to *Forbes* magazine, six of China's ten wealthiest indi-viduals are founders or top executives of internet-related companies. Baidu, Huawei, Tencent and Alibaba were listed among the world's 50 'smartest' companies in 2016 by *MIT Technology Review* – enterprises which combine innovative technology with effective business models to create new opportunities. These and other such compan-ies are now increasingly going global. Some have collaborated with major Western companies to assist their globalization process: Chinese telecommunications giant Huawei – a privately owned company – collaborated with British Telecom to create a global presence and influence (Tao *et al.*, 2016). Xiaomi has invested in more than 50 start-ups globally, including video content providers and mobile gaming apps. In 2016, Xiaomi led a $25 million investment in Hungama Digital, its first in India, as part of a strategy to introduce localized internet services and content on its smartphones in the country, the world's second-largest smartphone market. By 2016, Chinese corporations such as Vivo, Lenovo, Xiaomi and Oppo accounted for 46 per cent of the smartphones in India, helped by celebrity endorsements from Bollywood actors along with huge sponsorship campaigns by brands such as Oppo and Gionee of the popular Indian Premier League cricket franchise. Such a strategy has helped improve perception and popularity of Chinese brands (Phartiyal, 2017). As one observer noted, Chinese media have been 'actively brand-building China for securing the state's economic goals of business' (Lashinsky, 2017: 17).

Chinese companies are now also aggressively entering into future-oriented cyber-capitalism, including such areas as semiconductors and Artificial Intelligence (AI) (WIPO, 2016). Alibaba Cloud, for example, has 14 data centres, many outside China, including in the US, Japan, Australia, Germany and Dubai. It was ranked fifth in the world in an arena dominated by Microsoft and Amazon. In 2016, Tencent, which developed the mobile app WeChat, created an AI research laboratory, while China's leading search engine, Baidu, also has one (Knight, 2016). In 2016, China bought the world's fastest supercomputer, the SunwayTaihuLight, thought to be part of a broader 'Chinese push to begin driving innovation, a shift from its role as a manufacturing hub for components and devices designed in the US and elsewhere' (Barrett, 2016). As Hong has argued, this cyber-capitalism is aimed at reducing China's industrial and technological dependence upon foreign corporations while transforming itself into a global ICT leader (Hong, 2017).

De-globalization or Sino-globalization

As the US takes pride in an 'America First' attitude, cuts its international aid budget and international broadcasting – broadly following an agenda of 'de-globalization' – China may find more space to promote its version of globalization. What role will Chinese media play in this transformation? In an op-ed in the *New York Times*, Yan Xuetong, a leading Chinese analyst of international relations, suggested that the 'Trump era will offer plenty of opportunities for Beijing. China has a chance to become a full-fledged superpower if it responds to the Trump presidency by opening up more to the world economically and politically' (Xuetong, 2017: A25). Another commentator, Nathan Gardels, Executive Advisor to the Berggruen Institute's 21st Century Council, resorted to hyperbole, writing in *China Daily* that 'President Xi has become the general secretary of globalization' (Gardels, 2017).

The ascendency of China, and of Asia more generally, coincides with the relative decline of the West. Dominique Moïsi of the French Institute of International Affairs argued in his 2009 book that, although the cultural influence of the US is still pervasive, economically the West is being overtaken by Asia. While the West, he argued, was dealing with a fear of the 'other', confusion about national identity and an anxiety to maintain global relevance, and the Islamic world was preoccupied with extremism and political instability, Asia demonstrated a culture of hope (Moïsi, 2009). In 2016, the word *déclinisme* entered France's Larousse dictionary, while one of the country's best-selling philosophers, Michel Onfray, lamented the decline in his book *Decadence: The Life and Death of the Judeo-Christian Tradition* (Donadio, 2017).

Chinese media will have to take greater interest in international and intercultural issues to keep pace with the steadily expanding and enhancing global presence of China. Notes one commentator: 'The transnational exchange of information and ideas is one of the most important aspects of China's engagement with the outside world and is a crucial challenge for the Party-State's efforts to manage the forces of globalization' (Edney, 2014: 2). As a permanent and powerful member of the UN Security Council, China has contributed 33,000 military, police and civilian personnel to UN peacekeeping missions – the largest contingent among the five permanent members. In 2016, there were 2,600 Chinese peacekeeping personnel involved in ten UN peacekeeping operations. As China's geopolitical and economic interests deepen around the world, Chinese journalism too will emerge as an interpreter of international conflicts. According to a new study, 'Chinese journalists are an emerging force in contemporary war zones. They are no longer simply relaying and repackaging wired news from Western news agencies' (Zhang, 2016: 2).

In the global South, Chinese success has many admirers as well as critics. Will Sino-globalization provide new models for development in a digital age? China is stepping up and improving government services via the Internet Plus – a programme aimed at digital communication and commerce – and intends to set up a nationwide internet-based government service system by 2020, according to a State Council guideline (Xinhua, 2015). Many developing countries that have become used to operating within an international system defined by a globalization under US hegemony, will now have to negotiate in a multipolar order, in which China is already a key player (Thussu, 2015; Stuenkel, 2016).

In 2016, China's State Council Information Office issued a White Paper on the right to development, detailing the country's philosophy, practice and contribution, noting that 'through more than 30 years of reform and opening-up, China has lifted 700 million people out of poverty, accounting for more than 70 per cent of the global reduction in poverty'. Its preamble reads:

> The right to development is an inalienable human right, symbolizing dignity and honour. Only through development can we address global challenges; only through development can we protect basic civil rights of the people; only through development can we promote the progress of human society.
> *(cited in Xinhua, 2016)*

Such formulations redefine the meaning of 'human rights' and evoke concerns among Western governments (US Government, 2017). The economic success of China, achieved at considerable cost to the country's environment (Kahn and Zheng, 2016) and exploitation of its digital labour (Qiu, 2016) within an authoritarian, state-capitalist system, could increase the appeal of the model as an alternative to free market capitalism, further undermining liberal democracy (Kurlantzick, 2016). Daniel Bell, of Beijing's Tsinghua University, speaks of 'The China Model' – a political, not an economic one. The authoritarianism intrinsic to China's success, Bell argues, could be a viable model of governance, manifested in recent decades through 'benign authoritarianism' and built on what he calls 'political meritocracy' (Bell, 2015).

The success of state-led capitalism is underlined by other accounts too. Sarah Eaton, for example, has convincingly mapped the journey from private-led growth to state-led growth. 'The advance of the state, more than being a point of inception', she writes, 'is a moment of culmination—a product of 20 years of sustained effort to mould state-owned national champions in key industries' (Eaton, 2016: 4). Lin Chun advocates a New Left alternative for China where the country should lead the way in resisting the dominant capitalistic discourse, saying that this would encourage similar resistance movements across developing countries. She sums up the history of China as 'blending paradigms of revolution, modernisation and globalisation' (Chun, 2013: 212). A French account notes China's 'dual strategy', where the party–state

> has one foot in the international system and one foot outside. It is combining the military tools of strategic realism with commercial diplomacy. It is combining a command economy with market competition. It controls society while allowing the individual to flourish.
>
> *(Godement, 2016: 212)*

The role of media is central to this; their narratives have contributed to making an average Chinese person optimistic about her future, despite regular and routinely negative reporting in mainstream Western media about human rights violations and suppression of free expression. A 2016 Pew survey reported that 75 per cent of the Chinese people believe that their country plays a more important role in the world than a decade ago. In contrast, only 21 per cent of Americans and 23 per cent of Europeans believe their nation is more powerful (Pew Research Center, 2016).

The rise of China represents what has been termed 'Easternization', manifest in 'the long-term shift in global economic power – which has made it harder for the US and Europe to generate the military, political and ideological resources needed to impose order in the world' (Rachman, 2016: 6). Media are important ideological resources and a more subtle and sophisticated globalization of Chinese media would go a long way in managing 'the process of Easternization' (Rachman, 2016: 255). There might be clues as to how to achieve this in a compilation of President Xi's speeches and writings, *The Governance of China*, published in 2015, which has so far sold more than three million copies and been translated into five languages, including Russian, Portuguese and Arabic. *The Guardian*'s correspondent in Beijing wondered 'how long it will be before the Chinese president starts work on his next bestseller, 'The Governance of the World' (Phillips, 2017).

References

Acharya, Amitav (2014) *The End of American World Order*. Cambridge: Polity.

Alden, Edward (2016) *Failure to Adjust: How Americans Got Left Behind in the Global Economy*. Lanham (MD): Rowman & Littlefield.

Bai, Ruoyun and Song, Geng (eds.) (2015) *Chinese Television in the Twenty-First Century: Entertaining the Nation*. London: Routledge.

Barboza, David and Barnes, Brooks (2016) Seeing Its Tomorrowland, Disney Courted China. *New York Times*, 15 June, A1.

Barnes, Brooks (2016) A Chinese Carrot for Hollywood. *New York Times*, 18 October, B1.

Barrett, Brian (2016) China's New Supercomputer Puts the US Even Further Behind. *Wired*, 21 June.

Bell, Daniel (2015) *The China Model: Political Meritocracy and the Limits of Democracy*. Princeton: Princeton University Press.

Brady, Anne-Marie (2012) *China's Thought Management*. New York: Routledge.

Brzeski, Patrick (2016) Wanda Chairman Reveals Ambitious Plan to Invest Billions in 'All Six' Hollywood Studios. *Hollywood Reporter*, 11 November.

CGTN (2017) Official website of China Global Television Network. Available at: www.cgtn.com/home/info/about_us.do [Accessed 12 May 2017].

Chumley, Lily (2016) *Creativity Class: Art School and Culture Work in Post-Socialist China*. Princeton: Princeton University Press.

Chun, Lin (2013) *China and Global Capitalism*. New York: Palgrave/Macmillan.

Clark, Duncan (2016) *Alibaba, the House That Jack Ma Built*. New York: Harper Collins.

Cohen, David (2014) 'Transformers': A Splendidly Patriotic Film, if You Happen to be Chinese. *Variety*, 3 July.

Denyer, Simon (2016) China's Scary Lesson to the World: Censoring the Internet Works. *Washington Post*, 23 May.

Donadio, Rachel (2017) In France, a Boom of Gloom. *New York Times*, 4 February, C1.

Eaton, Sarah (2016) *The Advance of the State in Contemporary China: State–Market Relations in the Reform Era*. Cambridge: Cambridge University Press.

Edney, Kingsley (2014) *The Globalization of Chinese Propaganda: International Power and Domestic Political Cohesion*. London: Palgrave.

Erisman, Porter (2015) *Alibaba's World: How a Remarkable Chinese Company is Changing the Face of Global Business*. New York: Palgrave Macmillan Trade.

European Council on Foreign Relations (2015) 'One Belt, One Road': China's Great Leap Outward. *China Analysis*, European Council on Foreign Relations.

Follath, Erich (2016) China Heads West: Beijing's New Silk Road to Europe. *Der Spiegel*.

Foreign Correspondents' Club of China (2015) *FCCC Annual Working Conditions Report 2015*. 27 May. Beijing: Foreign Correspondents' Club of China. Available at: www.fccchina.org/2015/05/27/fccc-annual-working-conditions-report-2015/.

Frankopan, Peter (2015) *The Silk Roads: A New History of the World*. London: Bloomsbury.

Gardels, Nathan (2017) China Emerges as the Leader of an Open Global Economy. *China Daily*, 13 January.

Godement, Francois (2016) *Contemporary China: Between Mao and Market*. Lanham (MD): Rowman & Littlefield. Originally published in French as *Que veut la Chine? De Mao au capitalisme*.

Government of China (2015) *Vision and Actions on Jointly Building Silk Road Economic Belt and 21st-Century Maritime Silk Road*. Issued by the National Development and Reform Commission, Ministry of Foreign Affairs, and Ministry of Commerce of the People's Republic of China, with State Council authorization, 28 March. Available at: http://en.ndrc.gov.cn/newsrelease/201503/t20150330_669367.html.

Griffiths, James (2016) *From Xi to Shining Xi: China's Propaganda Machine Goes into Overdrive.* CNN, 23 February.

Halper, Stefan (2010) *The Beijing Consensus: How China's Authoritarian Model Will Dominate the Twenty-First Century.* New York: Basic Books.

Hong, Yu (2017) *Networking China: The Digital Transformation of the Chinese Economy.* Chicago: University of Illinois Press.

IMF (2017) *World Economic Outlook: Gaining Momentum?* Washington: International Monetary Fund.

Ingle, Sean (2017) Chinese Company Alibaba Signs Deal to be Major Sponsor of Olympic Games. *The Guardian,* 19 January.

Jacques, Martin (2009) *When China Rules the World: The End of the Western World and the Birth of a New Global Order.* London: Allen Lane.

Jia, Mei (2017) Belt and Road Opens New Chapter for Authors. *China Daily,* 10 March.

Johnston, Alastair (2013) How new and assertive is China's new assertiveness? *International Security,* 37(4): 7–48.

Kagan, Robert (2017) Backing into World War III. *Foreign Policy,* February.

Kahn, Matthew and Zheng, Siqi (2016) *Blue Skies over Beijing: Economic Growth and the Environment in China.* Princeton: Princeton University Press.

Kantar (2016) *China Social Media Impact 2016.* London: Kantar.

Keane, Michael (2013) *Creative Industries in China: Art, Design and Media.* Cambridge: Polity.

King, Gary; Pan, Jennifer and Roberts, Margaret (2014) How censorship in China allows government criticism but silences collective expression, *American Political Science Review,* 2(107): 1–18.

King, Gary; Pan, Jennifer and Roberts, Margaret (2017) How the Chinese Government fabricates social media posts for strategic distraction, not engaged argument, *American Political Science Review,* 111 (3): 484–501.

Knight, Will (2016) A Chinese Internet Giant Enters the AI Race. *MIT Technology Review,* 8 December.

Kokas, Aynne (2017) *Hollywood Made in China.* Los Angeles: University of California Press.

Kurlantzick, Joshua (2016) *State Capitalism: How the Return of Statism is Transforming the World.* New York: Oxford University Press.

Lai, Hongyi and Lu, Yiyi (eds.) (2012) *China's Soft Power and International Relations.* London: Routledge.

Lashinsky, Adam (2017) How Alibaba's Jack Ma is Building a Truly Global Retail Empire. *Fortune,* 24 March.

Le Corre, Philippe and Pollack, Jonathan (2016) *China's Global Rise: Can the EU and U.S. Pursue a Coordinated Strategy?* Washington: The Brookings Institution, Geo-economics and Global Issues, Paper 1.

Liqiang, Hou (2016) Companies to Champion Telecom Infra Creation. *China Daily,* 19 November.

MacKinnon, Rebecca (2011) China's 'networked authoritarianism', *Journal of Democracy,* 22(2): 32–46.

McNeice, Angus (2017) Chinese Gaming Giant Enters Europe. *China Daily,* 15 February.

Moïsi, Dominique (2009) *The Geopolitics of Emotion: How Cultures of Fear, Humiliation, and Hope are Reshaping the World.* New York: Doubleday.

Moody, Andrew (2016) Bright Future for Africa. *China Daily,* 28 October.

Nelson, Ann (2013) *CCTV's International Expansion: China's Grand Strategy for Media?* Washington: Report to the Center for International Media Assistance. 22 October.

Ng, Jason (2013) *Blocked on Weibo: What Gets Suppressed on China's Version of Twitter (and Why).* New York: The New Press.

Ni,Vincent (2016) Is China's Media Tycoon Jack Ma the New Rupert Murdoch? *BBC News*, 5 May.

Nyíri, Pál (2017) *Reporting for China: How Chinese Correspondents Work with the World*. Seattle: University of Washington Press.

PEN America (2016) *Darkened Screen: Constraints on Foreign Journalists in China*. New York: PEN America.

Pew Research Center (2016) *Chinese Public Sees More Powerful Role in World, Names U.S. as Top Threat*. Washington: Pew Research Center.

Phartiyal, Sankalp (2017) *China Nibbles at Samsung Share to Take 50 Per cent of India's Smartphone Market*. Mumbai: Reuters, 6 January.

Phillips, Tom (2017) How Xi Jinping's Global Ambitions Could Thrive as Trump Turns Inward. *The Guardian*, 11 February.

PwC (2016) *PwC Annual Global Entertainment and Media Outlook*. London: PriceWaterhouse Cooper.

Qing, Koh Gui and Shiffman, John (2015) *Beijing's Covert Radio Network Airs China-Friendly News Across Washington, and the World*. Beijing/Washington: Reuters, 2 November.

Qiu, Linchuan Jack (2016) *Goodbye iSlave: A Manifesto for Digital Abolition*. Chicago: University of Illinois Press.

Rachman, Gideon (2016) *Easternization: War, Peace and the Asian Century*. London: Vintage.

RAND Corporation (2016) *War with China: Thinking the Unthinkable*. Santa Monica, CA: RAND Corporation.

Roach, Stephen (2014) *Unbalanced: The Co-dependency of America and China*. London: Yale University Press.

Shambaugh, David (2013) *China Goes Global: The Partial Power*. New York: Oxford University Press.

Sinha-Palit, Parama (2017) *Analysing China's Soft Power Strategy and Comparative Indian Initiatives*. New Delhi: Sage.

Stockman, Daniela (2013) *Media Commercialization and Authoritarian Rule in China*. New York: Cambridge University Press.

Stuenkel, Oliver (2016) *Post-Western World: How Emerging Powers Are Remaking Global Order*. Cambridge: Polity.

Sun, Wanning (2015) Slow boat from China: Public discourses behind the 'going global' media policy, *International Journal of Cultural Policy*, 21(4): 400–418.

Swanson, Ana (2015) Stephen Colbert's 'Pander Express' is a Brilliant Takedown of How Hollywood Sucks Up to China. *Washington Post*, 10 October.

Tao, Tian; Cremer, David and Chunbo, Wu (2016) *Huawei: Leadership, Culture and Connectivity*. New Delhi: SAGE.

Thussu, Daya Kishan (2015) Digital BRICS: Building a NWICO 2.0?, in Nordenstreng, K. and Thussu, D. K. (eds.) *Mapping BRICS Media*. London: Routledge: 242–263.

Thussu, Daya Kishan (forthcoming) *International Communication: Continuity and Change*, third edition. New York: Bloomsbury Academic.

Ti, Zhuan (2016) Boosting the Belt and Road Initiative. *China Daily*, 27 October.

US Government (2017) *Global Trends: The Paradox of Progress*. Washington: National Intelligence Council.

Wang, Jian (2013) *Shaping China's Global Imagination*. New York: Palgrave Macmillan.

Wang, Jianwei and Wang, Xiaojie (2014) Media and Chinese foreign policy, *Journal of Contemporary China*, 23(86): 216–235.

Wang, Zheng (2014) The Chinese dream: Concept and context, *Journal of Chinese Political Science*, 19(1): 1–13.

WIPO (2016) *World Intellectual Property Indicators 2016*. Geneva: World Intellectual Property Organization.

Xiang, Debao (2013) China's image on international English language social media, *Journal of International Communication*, 19(2): 252–271.

Xin, Xin (2012) *How the Market is Changing China's News: The Case of Xinhua News Agency*. Lanham: Lexington Books.

Xinhua (2014) Xi Eyes More Enabling International Environment for China's Peaceful Development, Xinhua, 30 November.

Xinhua (2015) China Unveils 'Internet Plus' Action Plan to Fuel Growth. Xinhua, 4 July.

Xinhua (2016) The Right to Development: China's Philosophy, Practice and Contribution Source. Xinhua, 1 December.

Xuetong, Yan (2017) China Can Thrive in the Trump Era. *The New York Times*, 25 January, A25.

Yang, Guobin (ed.) (2015) *China's Contested Internet*. Copenhagen: Nordic Institute of Asian Studies.

Yaqin, Qin (2014) Continuity through change: Background knowledge and China's international strategy, *Chinese Journal of International Politics*, 7(3): 285–314.

Zakaria, Fareed (2008) *The Post-American World*. London: Allen Lane.

Zhang, Shixin (2016) *Chinese War Correspondents: Covering Wars and Conflicts in the Twenty-First Century*. London: Palgrave/Macmillan.

Zhang, Xiaoling; Wasserman, Herman and Mano, Winston (eds.) (2016) *China's Media and Soft Power in Africa: Promotion and Perceptions*. London: Palgrave.

Zhang, Yanqiu and Mwangi, Jane (2016) A perception study on China's media engagement in Kenya: From media presence to power influence, *Chinese Journal of Communication*, 9(1): 71–80.

Zhao, Yuezhi (2013) China's quest for 'soft power': Imperatives, impediments and irreconcilable tensions?, *Javnost*, 20(4): 17–30.

Zhou, Hong and Xiong, Hou (eds.) (2017) *China's Foreign Aid: 60 Years in Retrospect*. Singapore: Springer.

Zhu, Ying (2012) *Two Billion Eyes: The Story of China Central Television*. New York: The New Press.

Zi, Shi (2014) One Road & One Belt: New thinking with regard to concepts and practice. Lecture delivered at the 30th anniversary of Conference of the Schiller Institute, Germany, 14 October. Available at: http://newparadigm.schillerinstitute.com/media/one-road-and-one-belt-and-new-thinking-with-regard-to-concepts-and-practice/

2

CHINA'S ROLE IN REMAPPING GLOBAL COMMUNICATION

Anbin Shi

Echoing Chinese President Xi Jinping's recent and frequent calls to build a 'community of common destiny' (CCD) on various diplomatic occasions, this chapter elaborates upon the urgency and necessity of rethinking the legacies of the New World Information and Communication Order (NWICO) and the World Summit on Information Society (WSIS) in a historical context, and of implementing the China-initiated project of constructing a 'United Nations of Media' (UNM) as part of CCD. In general, both NWICO and WSIS were concerned with neoliberalism and capitalist globalization, focusing on either technological determinism or digitized informatization. Theoretically, both NWICO and WSIS aimed to oppose media/cultural imperialism, but in practice, both ended up reinventing an updated version: 'media/cultural imperialism 2.0'.

The China-initiated project of constructing the United Nations of Media as a community of common destiny, by contrast, is not necessarily an anti-US or anti-Western alternative, but rather inherits the unfulfilled promises of the New World Information and Communication Order and World Summit on Information Society. More importantly, without being solely dependent upon either nationalism, neoliberalism or market-driven logic, the UNM as CCD is a truly supranational and transcultural initiative to ensure the adequate representation of 'the Rest' (as opposed to the West) in the global media sphere (Hall, 1992). In terms of theoretical foundations, UNM as CCD intertwines the classical Chinese philosophy of *tianxia* (i.e. under the heaven 天下) with the Euro-American concept of cosmopolitanism. In many ways, the project of constructing UNM as CCD aims for the intellectual and philosophical integration of the West and the East, the developed and developing world, and tradition and (post)modernity, thereby gaining its potency and relevance to remapping the topography of global communication.

To further evince the potency and relevance of this, the chapter offers two case studies of the World Media Summit (WMS) sponsored 'Global Journalism Award'

and 'the World Internet Conference Wuzhen Summit' to elaborate upon the historical/
geopolitical continuities and disjunctures of global communication as manifested in
the project of constructing UNM as CCD. Finally, this chapter will uncover the
potential challenges for UNM as CCD as well as opportunities for further development through possible collaboration of emergent power blocs such as BRICS
(Brazil, Russia, India, China and South Africa), among others (Nordenstreng and
Thussu, 2015).

Historically, the endeavours of reshaping global communication are characterized by the following landmark events: the United Nations Educational, Scientific
and Cultural Organization (UNESCO) debate, spanning the 1970s and early 1980s,
known as the New World Information and Communication Order, and the more
recent International Telecommunications Union (ITU)-sponsored negotiations at
the WSIS, Phase I of which was held in Geneva, 2003 and Phase II in Tunis, 2005.
These two well-intentioned and ambitious agendas, however, achieved little and
were hardly implemented. Their relevance needs to be reassessed in a constantly
changing landscape of global geopolitics and economy since 2008, with the rise of
China and the diminishing of US hegemony.

As globalization and mediatization constitute the keynotes of the new millen-
nium, China's recent efforts to launch the project of UNM as CCD do not merely
reflect the remapping of global communication in this reoriented historical and
geopolitical landscape, but also crystallize the disjuncture from the historical legacies of NWICO and WSIS. Consequently, Sino-globalization, in contrast with
Anglobalization and Americanization, looms larger as the main way to bridge the
communication gap between the global North and South, thereby fulfilling the
promises of NWICO and WSIS.

Theoretical foundations: Integrating cosmopolitanism with *Tianxia*

Both the New World Information and Communication Order and the World
Summit on Information Society were based upon the concept of 'international
communication', which foregrounded the trans-border flow of news and data, with
the modernist imaginary of the nation state as its conceptual groundwork. A case in
point is international broadcasting, typified by such media outlets as the BBC World
Service, Voice of America, Voice of Russia (a.k.a. Radio Moscow) and China Radio
International (a.k.a. Radio Beijing).

By contrast, global communication can be aptly defined as a real-time, diachronic
and synchronic flow of news, data, images and opinions, which are shared and circulated across divergent cultural, linguistic, geographic and ideological communities,
let alone nation states. There is no more telling manifestation of this than the ubiq-
uitous and omnipotent World Wide Web and, more recently, transnational Internet
companies like Google and Facebook. Interestingly, the 2.2 billion global Facebook
users would constitute the largest country in the world, surpassing the populous China (1.4 billion) and India (1.2 billion). Thus, such modernist discourses as

nationalism, statism or ethnocentrism cannot account for the complexities and intricacies of present-day global communication.

If international communication rests upon the modernist notion of the nation state, global communication would naturally refer to the Hellenic vision of cosmopolitanism as its theoretical foundation. Etymologically, the term 'cosmopolis' is a dialectical hybrid of the words for universe or world (cosmos) with that for community of people or cities (polis), registering a postmodern condition that can be adequately experienced in such globally 'nodal cities' as New York, London and Beijing. Ideologically, cosmopolitanism embodies the Utopian vision of the Kantian commonwealth, wherein all human beings belong to a single community, and would therefore be able to sustain a 'perpetual peace'. As Miriam Sobré-Denton succinctly put it, cosmopolitanism 'encapsulates the notion of belonging to a larger world than our localities, and simultaneously remaining locally rooted while growing global consciousness' (Sobré-Denton, 2015: 4).

Interestingly, it is no mere coincidence that the ancient Chinese conceptualization of *tianxia,* which literally means 'under the heaven', is commensurate with the ancient Hellenic imaginary of 'cosmos'. In this light, the concept of *tianxia* could safely be recontextualized to inform the changing relationship between China and the world, the East and the West, the global North and South, etc. As Zhao Tingyang accurately generalized from over 100 related proverbs and passages in such ancient Chinese classics as *Shang Shu* (尚书 *The Book of History*) and *Li Ji* (礼记 *The Book of Rites*), the multi-layered concept '*tianxia*' can be further subdivided into the following three spaces: (1) geographical or outer space, which refers to the physical world inhabited by human beings; (2) psychological or inner space, which refers to the universal values or common ethics shared by mankind, bearing semblance to the Kantian *ius cosmopolicum* (i.e. cosmopolitan law or right); (3) political or public space, which means a multifarious, well-governed world (i.e. cosmos) with negotiations and compromises between diverse groups or communities(i.e. polises) (Zhao, 2005).

In the contemporary world, with its central tenets of globalization and mediatization, and supranational and transcultural communication by way of various channels, using such new media platforms as the Internet and mobile social media have become a day-to-day routine for every cosmopolitan (i.e. citizen of the world), or in Chinese, *tianxia baixing* (all existing family names/clans under the universe). As Glynda Hull and Amy Stornaiuolo have aptly delineated in relation to a cosmopolitan mediascape or a digitalized *tianxia* in the age of new media:

> especially important for negotiating a complex and dynamic world are capacities for creatively and adaptively making and sharing meanings across nodes and media … for imagining others and imagining others imagining us … for seeing ourselves as social actors with obligations toward … and for negotiating meaning and interpretations across divergent cultural, linguistic, geographic, and ideological landscapes both on- and off-line.
>
> *(Hull and Stornaiuolo, 2010: 86)*

It is precisely based on the centrality of media communication that a new concept of 'virtual cosmopolitanism' has developed in recent years to catch up with the constantly changing mediascape of global communication. If cosmopolitanism is defined as 'an ethical and philosophical framework through which we may envision human and mediated intercultural communication in a more humane world' (Sobré-Denton and Bardhan, 2013: 174), virtual cosmopolitanism can be viewed as an updated version of 'cosmopolitanism 2.0', wherein 'cultural and social capital may be transmitted through social media networks, allowing for a greater transnational spread of ideas' (McEwan and Sobré-Denton, 2011: 252–53), in contrast to corporeal cosmopolitanism (cosmopolitanism 1.0).

In every respect, the China-initiated project of constructing a United Nations of Media as a community of common destiny is fully committed to integrating the Hellenic notion of 'cosmopolitanism' with the traditional Chinese heritage of 'tianxia' philosophy. Following the logic of the United Nations, the new order of global communication is shaped in accordance with the common destiny shared by all people, rather than with national sovereignty in the case of NWICO, and market-driven logic in the case of WSIS. The blueprint of 'UNM as CCD' pays adequate tribute to political, economic, social and cultural differences and disparities in the West and the Rest, or in the developed and developing nations, thereby differentiating itself from the US–UK duopoly that dominated in the sphere of international communication in past decades. It is precisely on this ground that the emergent Sino-globalization diverges from the media/cultural imperialist model of Anglobalization and the subsequent hegemonic model of Americanization in the past two centuries.

Moreover, the prospect of CCD, alluding to the Utopian vision of *tianxia*, addresses the three spaces that constitute the Confucian 'world of great unity' (*datong shijie*大同世界) or Kantian 'commonwealth'. Here, the notion of 'common destiny' can properly be translated into 'global issues' or 'humanist concerns' more familiar to the Westerner's ears: such as climate change, energy-saving and emission-reduction, terrorism, nuclear safety and financial security, to name but a few. The geographical, psychological (personal) and political (public) spaces cannot achieve a Kantian 'eternal peace' and a Confucian 'harmony' (*hexie*和谐) until common grounds are found and universal consensuses are reached through frequent and effective communication between diverse communities and civilizations. To summarize, both *tianxia* and cosmopolitanism constitute the conceptual and theoretical foundations for reshaping the order of global communication, while China's agenda of constructing UNM as CCD offers a feasible mission and foreseeable vision in this regard.

The New World Information and Communication Order and the World Summit on Information Society: Historical continuities and unfulfilled promises of global communication

As Daya Thussu has powerfully articulated, one recurring theme in the study of international communication has been

> the continued domination of the global information and entertainment
> industries . . . by a few, mainly Western nations and the transnational corpora-
> tions based in these countries. From Marconi to Microsoft, a continuity can
> be detected . . . whether it was cabling the world, broadcasting to an interna-
> tional audience or creating a virtual globe through the Internet.
>
> *(Thussu, 2000: 259)*

It is in this context that both NWICO and WSIS aimed to disrupt such historical
continuity of Euro-American hegemony, and to reinvent a new geopolitical
continuity of communication equity between the global North and South.
As Victor Pickard succinctly put it, both NWICO and WSIS, in spite of belonging
to different periods, 'bookend a 30-year ascendance of neoliberal logic of global
communication' (Pickard, 2007: 120).

The twentieth-century Non-Alignment Movement (NAM), initiated by India,
constituted itself as a conscious counter-hegemonic bloc of the least developing
countries (LDCs). India and other NAM countries further demanded a New
International Economic Order and a concomitant NWICO. However, due to the
economic and geopolitical imbalance between the global North and South, India
and other NAM countries failed to challenge effectively the dominant US-led
order of global communication, which led the NWICO debates to piles of paper-
work rather than a foreseeable reality. Not surprisingly, such efforts did not achieve
any substantial challenge against the US–UK duopoly of global communication,
but further exacerbated the dichotomy between the West and the Rest, ending in
the US and UK's temporary withdrawal from the UNESCO in the 1980s.

The ITU-sponsored WSIS campaign, by contrast, inherited from what Daya
Thussu termed the 'continuity' of global communication (Thussu, 2000), not merely
the continuous dominance of the West (read the US and UK), but also continuous
efforts to alleviate 'forced dependencies' (Preston *et al.*, 1989) upon the West and to
guarantee communication rights for the LDCs. On the other hand, WSIS also
emerged as a disjuncture from NWICO in shifting the core of global communication
from national sovereignty to corporate control and technocracy. In other words,
such non-governmental, non-profit, private corporations as ICANN (Internet
Corporation for Assigned Names and Numbers) would replace the state as the
locomotive for reshaping the order of global communication. Not surprisingly,
what ICANN and the like represented was the interest of technocratic elites, who
were endowed with indirect ties to such government agencies as the US Department
of Commerce (Muller, 2002). One case in point is the unbalanced distribution of
Internet resources: some elite US universities like Harvard and Yale were given
more Internet protocol numbers than populous countries like China and India.

In many ways, if the NWICO debate in the 1970s and early 1980s challenged
media/cultural imperialism 1.0, which was mainly related to broadcast media and
global news flow, then Internet-oriented WSIS helped to invent media/cultural
imperialism version 2.0, which various scholars have termed 'digital capitalism'
(Schiller, 1999), 'informationalized capitalism' (Schiller, 2007), and 'communicative

capitalism' (Dean, 2009) in different socio-political contexts. In general, both NWICO and WSIS failed to gain sufficient support around the globe and faced harsh criticism from both academia and industry. NWICO's overemphasis upon national sovereignty enabled the liberal intellectuals to claim it was curtailing the free flow of information and freedom of speech, which culminated in the US and UK's concerted retaliation against UNESCO in the late 1970s and their leaving the organization. In the same vein, WSIS's overt reliance on neoliberalism was attacked by the left as a conspiracy of corporate control, which was furthermore evinced by the 2008 financial meltdown and the 2013 PRISM-gate scandal leaked by Edward Snowden, the former employee of the US National Security Agency (NSA). As Dan Schiller succinctly put it, 'US backing for speech rights itself has been incomplete and contingent' (Schiller, 2014: 357) and the American cyber-hegemony based on the government rhetoric of 'Internet freedom' has therefore lost any moral appeal and ethical legitimacy for global netizens. Not surprisingly, the US authorities, including the Department of Commerce, decided to withdraw the contract of the Internet Assigned Names and Numbers Authority from the ICANN in March 2015.[1]

China's duality and Sino-globalization: Laying groundwork for remapping global communication

As one of five permanent members of the UN Security Council, China was conspicuously absent from both NWICO and WSIS debates due to domestic and international constraints over the past three decades. Since 2008, China's emergence as a global power and its duality as a 'developing developed nation' have further complicated the reorganization of the geopolitical and economic order, thereby consolidating her unique role in bridging the economic and communication gap between global North and South, and in remapping the topography of global communication.

According to an IMF (International Monetary Fund) report, China surpassed the US as the world's largest economy in terms of purchasing power parity by the end of 2014,[2] the most significant shift in the power balance since the US overtook the UK as the No. 1 economic powerhouse in the 1870s. By November 2014, China replaced Japan as the second largest stock market in the world.[3] Moreover, on 30 November 2015, the IMF agreed to include the Chinese currency, *yuan* or RMB, into the benchmark SDR (Special Drawing Rights) currency basket,[4] both of which further consolidated China's indispensable role as a major player and decision maker in the global economy and financial system.

Despite the 'economic miracle' of China's rise into the league of developed nations, the Chinese government still insisted upon its status as a 'Less Developed Country' in terms of socio-economic development on a per capita basis. In October 2015, over 71 million people, most of whom live in interior and rural China, were still living in poverty, with an annual income estimated at 2,300 *yuan* (approx. $360) per person. It is also noteworthy that if the World Bank benchmark ($1.25 per capita per day) is applied to China, the population in poverty would be double at over 200 million. Such benchmark discrepancy between the Chinese government and World Bank itself powerfully points to China's duality and uniqueness as a 'developing developed nation'. In other words, no single label or categorization can fully encapsulate the intricacy and complexity of socio-economic development in present-day China.

In terms of media development, China can claim to be a promised land for the media industry. As the world's number one market, all types of the media and all sectors of the industry are blossoming in China, in stark contrast to the dramatically declining circulation and revenue of the press and publication in Euro-America, and to the burgeoning market for the new media in most of the LDCs. In June 2015, there were over 2,000 nationwide and local newspapers, around 10,000 magazines and periodicals, 300 radio stations, over 3,000 TV channels and three million websites in China. TV viewers were estimated to be over 1.35 billion, which means that every Chinese citizen has access to television. Internet users have reached 668 million, which implies that nearly half of the Chinese population have become 'netizens'. It is also worth mentioning that over 600 million social media users are active on the platform of Weibo (China's equivalent of Twitter) and WeChat (China's equivalent of WhatsApp).

Of the sectors of the media industry, it is film and the Internet that are growing exponentially as the major challengers of long-standing US hegemony. In 2015, China became the second largest film market after the US with annual box-office revenues of 440 million RMB (approx. US$ 68 million). In February 2015 when the Chinese celebrated their lunar new year, and in October, when they enjoyed 'golden week' holidays for the National Day, monthly box-office figures surpassed those in the US as the world's number one, anticipating the prediction that China will overtake the US as the largest film market by 2018.

Among the top ten global Internet giants, four Chinese companies, nicknamed BATJ (Baidu, Alibaba, Tencent and JD360), are vying with six US moguls; this constitutes two distinct camps demarcated by the notorious 'great firewall of China'. The competition between the GAFA (Google, Amazon, Facebook and Apple) camp and the BATJ camp provides a groundwork for the shared governance of cyberspace by the US and China.

As with its duality in terms of socio-economic development, China can also claim to be a 'developing developed media market'. Despite the above-mentioned achievements in the media industry sectors of film and the Internet, Chinese media organizations are mostly unknown to a global audience. Although it has headquarters in Beijing, Washington and Nairobi and over 60 overseas branch offices, CCTV is still unable to compete with the Qatar-based Al Jazeera and RT (formerly known as Russia Today), let alone BBC or CNN, in terms of global influence in opinion making and brand loyalty among the world's audience. By the same token, Chinese feature films are still rarely seen in the mainstream cinemas in Euro-America, even if Wang Jianlin, China's richest tycoon, has purchased the ownership of major theatres in North America, Australia and UK.

These facts and figures evidence the argument that the world is experiencing a dual-aspect Sino-globalization in the wake of the Anglobalization of the nineteenth and twentieth centuries, and the subsequent Americanization after the Second World War. The agenda of Sino-globalization is further reflected in the 'One Belt and One Road' (OBOR) Initiative, which was proposed by President Xi in September 2013, reviving the historical legacies of the land and maritime silk routes in ancient China. If Anglobalization was characterized by military conquest and politico-economic colonization and the subsequent Americanization was characterized by economic and cultural hegemony, the agenda of Sino-globalization, as outlined in the OBOR initiative, is based on trade exchange and intercultural communication, thereby emphasizing the centrality of soft power and co-cultural harmony in the course of reorganizing the world order.

In its ambitious blueprint, OBOR covers more than 100 countries in Asia, Europe, Africa, North America and Oceania, estimated to include 64 per cent of the world's population and 30 per cent of global GDP. If the India-initiated NWICO and the US-led WSIS did not transcend the age-old binary dichotomy of the West vs. the Rest, of global North and South, and of nationalism vs. neoliberalism, China's duality as a 'developing developed nation' and the agenda of Sino-globalization outlined in OBOR could map out an alternative route to reshaping the order of global communication, without resorting to economic, cultural or ideological warfare.

Constructing a United Nations of Media as a community of common destiny: Mapping the alternative to NWICO and WSIS

Constructing a UNM as a CCD is China's latest endeavour to remap global communication. In one of the earliest versions of this, Li Congjun, the former president of the Xinhua news agency, proposed the concept of UNM in an article published on 1 June 2011 in the *Wall Street Journal*. What remains the core of UNM is the FAIR doctrine, which consists of four basic principles (namely, fairness, all-win, inclusiveness and responsibility) and embodies multilateralism and co-culturalism, rejecting the binary dichotomies that characterized the NWICO and WSIS debates.

The 'fairness' principle inherits the key aim of both NWICO and WSIS: to achieve full representation of LDCs in the global media sphere. The 'all-win' principle, though, reflects the historical and geopolitical departure from the binary dichotomy between the West and the Rest, that was central to the NWICO and WSIS debates. In the same vein, the 'inclusiveness' principle aims to go beyond the age-old conflict between nationalism and neoliberalism deeply rooted in the NWICO and WSIS debates. Last but not least, the revived discourse of social responsibility in the age of social media challenges the overemphasis on sovereignty-based *realpolitik* deep-seated in the NWICO debate and on market-driven technocracy central to the WSIS debate.

The mapping of an alternative route was also elaborated by China's 'online watchdog chief', Lu Wei, Minister of the State Internet and Information Office (SIIO).

Proposed in the 7th US–China Internet Industry Forum, held in Washington on 2 December 2014, Lu's 'five mutual' principles, namely, mutual appreciation, mutual respect, mutual governance, mutual stake-holding, and mutual cooperation in cyberspace, echoed Li Congjun's earlier conceptualization of UNM. Furthermore, Lu introduced the concept of 'cyber-sovereignty' to replace the ill-defined and unfulfilled concept of 'Internet freedom', a.k.a. 'Clinton Cyberspace Doctrine', which was officially advocated by Hillary Clinton's landmark speech in January 2010, against the backdrop of the heated controversy between Google and China's SIIO.

Notably, cyber-sovereignty arose from the historical legacies of the NWICO debates, while differing from the latter's overemphasis on national sovereignty. To be more specific, cyber-sovereignty should be understood along with 'co-governance of cyberspace', which is obviously indebted to the WSIS debates, while rejecting the latter's over-reliance upon corporate control. In every respect, the 'Sino-America' co-governance of cyberspace is more relevant to the reality than the debates on 'Internet freedom'.

Finally, the China-initiated agenda of promoting nationalism-based cyber-sovereignty and co-governance has been upgraded into a cosmopolitan-oriented vision of CCD in cyberspace in President Xi's keynote speech in the 2nd World Internet Conference, Wuzhen Summit on 16 December 2015. In his definition, the Charter of the United Nations, with its core concept of national sovereignty, can be conveniently applied to the virtual world, thereby legitimatizing China's promotion of cyber-sovereignty. In this light, each nation is endowed with the absolute right to choose its own model of Internet development and governance, obviously lending a tactful excuse to China's notorious 'firewall' which blocks nearly all Western hi-tech corporations, including Google, Facebook, Twitter and YouTube from Chinese netizens. To enhance the moral appeal and ethical legitimacy of China's 'Internet philosophy', Xi focused on the centrality of cyber-security, which would be more acceptable to Western liberals' ears in the aftermath of the Islamic graphic atrocities circulated via social media by the so-called Islamic State, and the terrorist attacks in European cities.

It is also noteworthy that Xi's Internet philosophy remains integral to the aforementioned agenda of UNM, as he adopts the UN Charter as the legal basis for China's agenda of bolstering cyber-sovereignty in contrast to the US's 'Internet freedom'; the latter has been reduced to an abortive doublespeak in the wake of Edward Snowdon's exposé of NSA's secretive 'PRISM' project. Ironically, when dealing with the 'Snowden leak', the US government adeptly avoided the US rhetoric of 'Internet freedom', and deployed the discourse of national security and public safety to defend the urgency and necessity of implementing PRISM. Despite such sophisticated crisis management, the world has come to realize that the US, not China or Russia, is endowed with greater technological potential and the political ambition to act as an Orwellian 'Big Brother', with its potential for comprehensive surveillance of every global netizen.

In many ways, the UNM agenda is not a reiteration of NWICO's sole dependence on national sovereignty. Aside from the concept 'cyber-sovereignty', which is an obvious reinvention of NWICO's vision in the Internet era, Xi's call to build a CCD in cyberspace did not attract adequate attention from Western media, and therefore deserves more lengthy elaboration. Since taking over China's supreme leadership in November 2012, Xi had used the term CCD 75 times on various occasions by the end of 2015. Foregrounding China's co-development and co-prosperity with the rest of the world, CCD is derived from the Hellenic concept of 'cosmopolitanism' and more importantly, it re-contextualizes the traditional Chinese ideal of *tianxia* in the course of rebuilding the post-hegemonic world order.

It is precisely Xi's foregrounding of CCD that distinguishes the agenda of UNM from NWICO and WSIS. If NWICO highlighted national sovereignty and WSIS was built upon neoliberalism, the agenda of UNM as CCD aims to transcend the age-old dichotomy between state and market, between the West and the Rest (the LDCs in particular). To a large extent, CCD in cyberspace is not a dream, but integral to the 'One Belt One Road' initiative partly funded by the Beijing-based Asian Infrastructure Investment Bank (AIIB). This bank bridges the long-standing gap between the West and the Rest by including participants from 57 countries from Asia, Europe, Africa, South America and Oceania. Notably, the UK became the first Western power to join the AIIB, followed by France and Germany.

To be more specific, Xi envisions the CCD in cyberspace project as including the following five actions: First, following the logic of the OBOR and AIIB initiatives, China would take a lead in establishing its own Internet infrastructure and meanwhile invest in LDCs to 'network' with the world, thereby eliminating the digital gap or bridging what Xi termed as 'the last mile of the information highway' that cannot fully be achieved by the market-driven logic of WSIS.

Secondly, China would set an example in employing the Internet as a powerful platform to promote intercultural communication and dialogue between various ethnic, religious, social and ideological groups, thereby mitigating the ever-increasing risk of clashes between different civilizations as predicted by the late Harvard Professor Samuel Huntington in 1993 (Huntington, 1996).

Thirdly, by integrating China's ongoing national strategy of 'Internet Plus' into the CCD context, China would spearhead a truly global system of e-commerce and Internet marketplace based on the OBOR initiative and its AIIB-backed infrastructure. Compared to the elitist model of the US-dominated GAFA camp, the more affordable, grassroots-friendly model of the BATJ (Baidu, Alibaba, Tencent and JD360) camp has galvanized engagement and involvement among a massive number of the incumbent netizens from the developing countries in Asia, Africa and Latin America.

The fourth strand of consolidating cyber-security and the fifth of advocating global governance to replace US hegemony constitute a basis for constructing CCD in cyberspace. By contrast, NWICO's sole dependency upon national governments and WSIS' overemphasis upon corporate power did not take account of the intricacies and complexities of cyberspace. Thus, Xi calls for a co-governance of cyberspace on the basis of negotiation, and collaboration between national governments, international and inter-governmental organizations, high-tech companies, geek communities, NGOs and individual citizens.

All in all, the agenda of constructing UNM as CCD inherits from the legacies of NWICO and WSIS and furthermore registers a cosmopolitan turn of reshaping global communication. Diverging from the Utopian vision of NWICO, which lacked solid infrastructural foundation, UNM would be materialized as part and parcel of the OBOR initiative under the aegis of the AIIB. Moreover, UNM's disjuncture from WSIS is embodied in the former's recognition of national government as a key player in maintaining cyber-sovereignty as the vital and viable factor in the course of institutionalizing global governance. Despite being a tentative blueprint which needs arduous implementation and further revision, the China-initiated agenda of constructing UNM as CCD remains the central to Sino-globalization, which does not mean to replace the US with an emergent hegemon but to provide an exigent alternative to the transnational capitalist world order in the post-American century. The following two case studies will set out to explore the historical continuities and disjuncture, as well as the hopes and fears for this burgeoning agenda of constructing UNM as CCD.

Implementing a United Nations of Media as a community of common destiny – I: World Media Summit Global Journalism Awards

If NWICO relied upon national governments and WSIS upon business corporations, UNM, as its name suggests, foregrounds the central role of the media industry and organizations. Spearheading the implementation of UNM, Xinhua news agency, China's flagship media outlet, initiated a project of 'WMS Global Awards for Excellence'. The World Media Summit is an industry organization comprised of over 50 media outlets from both developed and developing countries, which might be seen as the alternative to the state-driven NWICO and the corporate-driven WSIS. The WMS award also aims to provide an alternative to those well-established yet highly parochial trophies for professionals, such as the Pulitzer Award in journalism confined to US media organizations and citizens. The first WMS award has witnessed a truly 'global' journalism award with the co-existence of the established and emergent media outlets like *USA Today* and *Chicago Tribune* on the one hand, Al Jazeera and RT on the other. The winners and honorary mentions span 13 countries, with over 60 per cent from the LDCs. Notably, India is equal with the US as the country with the greatest number of winners and honorary mentions (see Appendix).

The judges of the WMS awards were comprised of veteran journalists, editors, managers and scholars from eight countries. During the selection of the winners, the aforementioned FAIR doctrine (i.e. fairness, all-win, inclusiveness, responsibility) was further concretized into the universal benchmark of professional excellence and media innovation, eclipsing the nationalist and neoliberalist conflicts embedded in the earlier NWICO and WSIS debates. Thus, three categories of awards were inaugurated in October 2014, namely, public welfare (for news team and individual professionals separately), media innovation and new media reporting. What remains the core of the WMS Awards is the theme of 'public welfare' as the common ground of media professionals from diverse political and cultural systems, which is purported to resuscitate the 'responsibility doctrine' advocated by the Hutchins Commission (a.k.a. the Commission on the Freedom of the Press) in the 1940s, and enhances its moral appeal and ethical legitimacy in the age of social media.

As for the theme of CCD, the list of winners and honorary mentions reflects a 'cosmopolitan' turn, thereby touching upon such global issues and humanitarian concerns as climate change, terrorist threat, disease control, nuclear safety and poverty alleviation.

Aside from WMS, it is also worth mentioning that Xinhua sponsored the first BRICS Media Summit on 30 November–1 December 2015 in Beijing, consolidating the concept of BRICS as a new constellation of international relations. Following the WMS model with the nexus of media industry and organizations rather than state and corporate agencies, the BRICS Media Summit was jointly launched by five mainstream media outlets from these five emergent nations (namely, China's Xinhua news agency, Russia Today International Information Agency, Brazil Communication Company, The Hindu Group and South Africa's Independent Media) and has recruited 25 member organizations, with five from each country to maintain a balanced power bloc.

In the same vein, the *People's Daily* launched the 'Silk Road Media Forum' in 2014 to realize the OBOR initiative. Renamed the OBOR Media Cooperation Forum in 2015, it has extended its membership to 136 media organizations from over 60 countries involved in the One Belt One Road initiative. It is likely that both the BRICS Media Summit and the Silk Road Media Forum, like the aforementioned WMS, will play a more significant part in the future in implementing the agenda of UNM as CCD. In essence, all these new constellations of reshaping global communication, mainly spearheaded by China, hope to transcend the historical legacies of NWICO and WSIS, thereby opening new avenues for remapping the topography of global news flow and opinion making.

Implementing the United Nations of Media as a community of common destiny – II: The World Internet Conference

As the global sphere of traditional media is still dominated by the US–UK duopoly, China could gain more advantage and effectiveness in the realm of new media. In fact, the timeliness of US–China co-governance is becoming more relevant with the diminishing US dominance over ICANN and WSIS on the one hand, and on the other, by increasing tensions between the two Internet moguls, US-based GAFA and China-based BATJ. It is in this light that China launched the World Internet Conference Wuzhen Summit to gain an upper hand in preempting the emerging 'digital cold war' and in dictating new rules of the game for cyberspace. It is noteworthy that Wuzhen in East China's Zhejiang Province, an ancient river town, rather than metropolitan Beijing or Shanghai, was chosen as the permanent venue for the World Internet Conference. Wuzhen is close to Jack Ma's Alibaba headquarters; it was thought that by taking place in the first wi-fi village in China, the conference would galvanize more attention from developing countries in relation to closing the digital gap and embarking upon the information highway, in comparison with the more elitist and expensive model of 'Silicon Valley'.

The inaugural conference was held in November 2014 under the banner of 'an interconnected world shared and governed by all', with over 1,000 delegates from more than 100 countries. ICANN sent its president and CEO to speak at this event, along with Chinese Internet chiefs. Google, Facebook, and other global Internet moguls, censored by the 'great firewall of China' held discussions with their potential local competitors: among others, the aforementioned BATJ.

The Wenzhen Summit, however, did not become truly 'global' until the second conference in December 2015, attended by state leaders, which attracted over 2,000 delegates from around 120 countries and 20 international organizations. As mentioned in the previous section, President Xi delivered a keynote speech along with leaders from seven countries (Russia, Pakistan, Uzbekistan, Kazakhstan, Kyrgyzstan, Tajikistan and Tonga) and secretary-generals from the United Nations, ITU and World Economic Forum. Aside from the official motto of 'an interconnected world shared and governed by all', Xi's call for 'constructing a cyber community of common destiny', an updated version of constructing UNM, added a new dimension and loomed larger as a central tenet for reshaping global communication with a more realistic mission and vision.

The evolving conceptualization of UNM as CCD is aptly embodied in the 'Wuzhen Declaration 2014' for the first conference, and the 'Wuzhen Initiative 2015' for the second conference. Both documents address the common concerns of current cyberspace development: the digital divide, e-commerce, cyber-security, cyber terrorism, cutting-edge high technology like cloud-computing and big data, and most importantly, cyber-sovereignty as promoted by the official Chinese discourse. However, the overt emphasis on cyber-sovereignty and implicit anti-US undertone in the 'Wuzhen Declaration 2014' is reminiscent of NWICO's canon 'One World, Many Voices' (the MacBride Report), and more ironically, reads like the new-leftist 'Internet Communist Manifesto'. It is no surprise that the 'Wuzhen Declaration 2014' was boycotted by a great number of delegates, mostly Western technical tycoons and liberal intellectuals, and was therefore not officially endorsed, but instead merely given in a news release at the closing ceremony.

By contrast, the 'Wuzhen Initiative 2015', with CCD at its core, adopts a more cosmopolitan vision to soften the nationalistic tone of China's advocacy on cyber-sovereignty. The latter concept is adroitly deployed to defend cyber-security and intellectual property; instead, global co-governance on the basis of CCD is highlighted as the central tenet of the World Internet Conference. In line with Xi's cosmopolitan vision of building CCD for mankind and his ambitious OBOR initiative, the concept of UNM as CCD aims to break new grounds for eclipsing the digital Cold War and reinventing a truly Kantian commonwealth or ancient Chinese notion of *tianxia* (universe) in cyberspace.

Conclusion

Both the New World Information and Communication Order and the World Summit on Information Society, as well as 'United Nations of Media as a community of common destiny', reflect a historical and geopolitical continuity by sharing a common mission: alleviating or even eliminating the LDC's 'forced dependencies' (Preston *et al.*, 1989) upon Western (read US) media outlets, content and technology. However, the three projects' disjuncture lies in their different geopolitical contexts: NWICO in the Cold War era, WSIS in the US-dominated unipolar world, and 'UNM as CCD' in the coming of the 'Chinese century', or more precisely, the making of a multipolar world.

China's duality as a 'developing, developed nation' opens up new avenues for reshaping the order of global communication, as manifested by the new agenda of 'UNM as CCD', which is deeply embedded in multilateralism and co-culturalism. Despite controversies and conflicts, the recent efforts in implementing UNM, the WMS Global Journalism Award and the World Internet Conference, demonstrate the shift from a Euro-centric binary dichotomy of state vs. market, nationalism vs. neoliberalism, freedom vs. censorship, democratization vs. informatization, etc., which entrenched the NWICO and WSIS debates. Rethinking the historical and geopolitical continuities and disjuncture, or the (dis)continuities, of NWICO, WSIS and the emergent 'UNM as CCD' becomes urgent and relevant to any serious endeavour of mapping out a new information structure.

Admittedly, there still exist tremendous theoretical challenges and practical uncertainties with regard to the efficacy and viability of implementing such an ambitious project as constructing UNM as CCD. Thus far, both the Hellenic conceptualization of cosmopolitanism and the classic Chinese heritage of *tianxia*, which lay the groundwork for UNM as CCD, are still at early stages of theorization for the constantly changing mediascape of global communication (Shi, 2005; Nordenstreng and Thussu, 2015; Hamelink, 2015; Hepp, 2015). Compared to the modernist discourse of nationalism and neoliberalism that inherited the philosophical legacies of the Enlightenment and embodied the universal values of freedom, democracy and equality, both cosmopolitanism and *tianxia* would still need deeper exploration into their intellectual heritage and more detailed elaboration upon their conceptual universality. Simply put, would UNM as CCD assume a 'melting pot' or 'salad bar' model? Obviously, the latter model is more welcome to this age of cynicism and consumerism. What the case study of WMS Global Journalism Awards reflects is the trend away from politics and ideology, to an overemphasis upon the technical and technological aspects of journalism as well as the 'professional excellence' of the journalistic genres. By the same token, the World Internet Conference Wuzhen Summit did not manage to get beyond the binary dichotomy of 'Internet freedom' vs. 'cyber-sovereignty', but reduced both its 2014 Declaration and 2015 Initiative to technological determinism and mercantilism, which entrenched the earlier WSIS debate.

On the praxis level, the aforementioned industry-based institutions have been established to materialize the project of UNM as CCD, namely the World Media Summit and BRICS Media Summit sponsored by Xinhua news agency, the Silk

Road Media Forum (later renamed as OBOR Media Cooperation Forum) sponsored by *People's Daily*, and the World Internet Conference Wuzhen Summit sponsored by the Internet Society of China under the aegis of the SIIO and Zhengjiang Provincial Government.

Despite different missions, visions and participants, these institutions lack a coherent systematic mode of operation, therefore more often than not overlapping with each other and diminishing their efficiency and efficacy. Moreover, since the sponsors such as Xinhua and *People's Daily* are official media organizations, their affinity with government and the consequent over-politicized nature of these institutions cast doubt upon their independence and autonomy. For example, the BRICS Media Summit, copying the logic of the BRICS Summit, galvanized media organizations from the five nations on the basis of geopolitical economy with little regard to their own media logic and cultural nuances.

For that matter, the Wuzhen Summit attracted even more doubts and accusations, particularly from the mainstream Western media, for its heavy-handed governmental invention and excessively politicized agenda. The participating leaders from China, Russia, Pakistan, Uzbekistan, Kazakhstan, Kyrgyzstan and Tajikistan were coincidentally those from the Shanghai Cooperation Organization, thereby reducing a world league to a regional coalition. If the UNM as CCD registers the future prospect for global communication, what we have witnessed so far is no more than a parochial and loose network characterized by turn-taking monologues rather than insightful and foresighted dialogue with a common ground and shared beliefs. Thus, the 'salad bar' metaphor still seems more applicable to the UNM; whereas the CCD, to which the 'melting pot' metaphor should bear more potency and relevance, is still more a myth than a reality.

While there is still a lot to watch at the level of theory and praxis, the China-initiated project of constructing UNM as CCD both inherits the historical legacies and registers a disjuncture from NWICO and WSIS, thereby contributing to reinventing a more diverse and multi-perspectival media globe. Despite its challenge and uncertainties, the inevitable coming of the Chinese century and the consequent Sino–globalization will surely lead to remapping the topography of global communication, which would bookend the two centuries' dominance of the US/UK duopoly, and unless otherwise warped or corrupted, create 'one world with many voices' as envisioned in the landmark MacBride Report, or a truly 'United Nations of Media' as the 'community of common destiny' conceived by President Xi Jinping.

Appendix

Acknowledgement and Funding

The author would like to thank his doctoral research assistants, Ms. Liu Ying, Mr. Liao Dieer, and Mr. Sheng Yang for their help with needed bibliographic search and data collection.

This research receives no specific grant from any funding agency from the public, commercial or not-for-profit sectors.

List of the World Media Summit Global Awards for Excellence 2014

Public Welfare Awards: Award for exemplary news teams in developing countries

Winner: 101 East, Al Jazeera English

Honourable Mentions:

This Week in Palestine
Truth vs. Hype, New Delhi Television
Rural Damascus, Al Jazeera
Outlook India

Public Welfare Awards: Award for exemplary news professionals in developing countries

Winner: Sainath Palagummi, *The Hindu*, India

Honourable Mentions:

Meera Srinivasan, *The Hindu*, India
Surendra Paudel, Nepal Republic Media, Nepal
Tan Ee Long, Nanyang, Malaysia
Sheuli Akter, Ns NewsWire, Bangladesh
Adow Jubat, The Standard Group, Kenya

Award for media innovation

Winner: Behind the Bloodshed, *USA Today*

Honourable Mentions:

Sea Change: The Pacific's Perilous Turn, *Seattle Times*
Live Blog of Israel–Gaza Conflict, *Haaretz*, Israel
3D Animated Videographics, AFP
The Change for Health App, The Standard Group, Kenya
Putin's Q & A, as it Happened: All the Best Quotes and Realtime Reaction, RT

Award for new media reporting

Winner: Myanmar Emerges, *Global Post*, US

Honourable Mentions:

Chicago Under the Gun, *Chicago Tribune*
Meteorite hits Russian Urals, RT
Privacy and Information Security, Al Jazeera
Overdose, *ProPublica*, US
Mandela: The Father of the Rainbow Nation, Al Jazeera

Notes

1 http://yro.slashdot.org/story/12/03/10/2134253/us-government-withdraws-iana-contract-from-icann (downloaded 25 December 2015).
2 www.foxnews.com/world/2014/12/06/china-surpasses-us-to-become-largest-world-economy/ (downloaded 9 December 2015).
3 www.bloomberg.com/news/articles/2014-11-27/ china (downloaded 9 December 2015).
4 www.cnbc.com/2015/11/30/imf-agrees-to-include-chinas-rmb-in-benchmark-sdr-currency-basket.html (downloaded 9 December 2015).

Bibliography

Cui, Baoguo崔保国 (ed.) (2015) *Zhongguo meiti chanye lanpishu (The Bluebook for China's Media Industry*中国媒体产业蓝皮书*).* Beijing: Sheke wenxian chubanshe（社科文献出版社）.

Dean, Jodi (2009) Communicative capitalism: Circulation and foreclosure of politics, *Cultural Politics*, 1(1): 51–74.

Hall, Stuart (1992) The West and the Rest, in Hall, S. and Gieben, B. (eds.) *Formation of Modernity*. Milton Keynes: The Open University Press: 275–320.

Hamelink, Cees (2015) *Global Communication*. London: Sage.

Hepp, Andreas (2015) *Transcultural Communication*. Oxford: Wiley Blackwell.

Hull, Glynda and Stornaiuolo, Amy (2010) Literate art in a global world: Reframing social networking as cosmopolitan experience, *Journal of Adolescent and Adult Literacy*, 54(2): 85–97.

Huntington, Samuel (1996) *The Clash of Civilizations and the Remaking of World Order*. New York: Simon & Schuster.

Hutchins Commission (Commission of the Freedom of the Press) (1947) *A Free and Responsible Press: A General Report on Mass Communications – Newspapers, Radio, Motion Pictures, Magazines, and Books*. Chicago: University of Chicago Press.

International Commission for the Study of Communication Problems (1980) *Many Voices One World* (MacBride Report). Available at: http://unesdoc.unesco.org/images/0004/000400/040066eb.pdf [Accessed 30 December 2014].

Kant, Immanuel (1999) Toward Perpetual Peace, in Gregor, M. (ed. and transl.) *Practical Philosophy—Cambridge Edition of the Works of Immanuel Kant*.Vol. 8. Cambridge: Cambridge University Press.

McEwan, Bree and Sobré-Denton, Miriam (2011) Virtual third cultures: Social media, cultural capital and the creation of cultural spaces, *Intercultural New Media Forum: Journal of International and Intercultural Communication*, 4: 252–258.

Muller, Milton (2002) *Ruling the Root: Internet Governance and the Taming of the Cyberspace*. Cambridge, MA: MIT Press.

Nordenstreng, Kaarle and Thussu, Daya Kishan (eds.) (2015) *Mapping BRICS Media*. London: Routledge.

Pickard, Victor (2007) Neoliberal visions and revisions in global communications policy from NWICO to WSIS, *Journal of Communication Inquiry*, 31(2): 118–139.

Preston, William; Herman, Edward and Schiller, Herbert (1989) *Hope and Folly: The United States and the UNESCO, 1945–1985*. Minneapolis: University of Minnesota Press.

Schiller, Dan (1999) *Digital Capitalism: Networking the Global Market System*. Cambridge, MA: MIT Press.

Schiller, Dan (2007) *How to Think About Information?* Urbana-Champaign: University of Illinois Press.

Schiller, Dan (2014) Rosa Luxemburg's internet? For a political economy of state mobilization and the movement of accumulation in cyberspace, *International Journal of Communication*, 8: 355–375.

Shi, Anbin (2005) The taming of the shrew: Chinese media in global perspective, *Global Media and Communication*, 1(1): 33–35.

Shi, Anbin (2012) Imagining/mapping/implementing Chinese communication, *Chinese Journal of Communication*, 5(4): 72–75.

Shi, Anbin (2015) Re-orienting 'charm offensive' to 'charm defensive': A critical review of China's media development in Africa, *African Journalism Studies*, 36(1): 135–140.

Sobré-Denton, Miriam (2015) Virtual intercultural bridgework: Social media, virtual cosmopolitanism, and activist community-building, *New Media and Society*, 15(1): 1–17.

Sobré-Denton, Miriam and Bardhan, Nilanjana (2013) *Cultivating Cosmopolitanism for Intercultural Communication: Communicating as a Global Citizen*. London: Routledge.

Thussu, Daya Kishan (2000) *International Communication: Continuity and Change*. New York: Oxford University Press.

Thussu, Daya Kishan and Shi, Anbin (2014) Quanqiu chuanbo de Chonggou he ZhongYin yiti de jueqi (Remapping Global Communication and the Rise of ChIndia 全球传播的重构和中印一体的崛起)Xinwenjie (*Journalism and Press*《新闻界》)March: 35–50.

Xu, Jilin 许纪霖 and Qing, Liu刘擎 (eds.) (2015) *Xin tianxia zhuyi (Towards a New Philosophy of Cosmopolitanism*新天下主义*)*. Shanghai: Shiji wenji chuban jituan(世纪文景出版集团).

Zhao, Tingyang 赵汀阳 (2005) *Tianxia tixi: Shijie zhidu zhexue daolun (The Institution of the Cosmos: Introduction to the Philosophy of World System* 《天下体系：世界制度哲学导论》). Nanjing: Jiangsu Jiaoyu chubanshe (江苏人民出版社).

Zhao, Yuezhi (2015) The BRICS Formation in Reshaping Global Communication: Possibilities and Challenges, in Nordenstreng, K. and Thussu, D. K. (eds.) *Mapping BRICS Media*. London: Routledge.

3

DOMESTIC CONTEXT OF CHINESE MEDIA'S GLOBALIZATION

Hugo de Burgh

Before Xi Jinping became President, disagreements about what the media were for, and how they might operate, were often interpreted outside China as reflecting a struggle between 'Marxists' and 'Westernizers'. Disaffected journalists, sometimes working in universities or think tanks overseas, were thought of as typical of the frustrated modern media worker. This approach may have been rendered outdated. China's establishment has clarified its rejection of universalism and of the idea that the Anglophone model might be the ultimate aim. More cogently than previous leaders, President Xi has expressed pride in a Chinese civilization that has its own political tradition and moral values that are by no means inferior to any others. From his pronouncements, it would seem that how the media operate is an expression of this tradition, modernized.

In this chapter I attempt to summarize and characterize the media system and to summarize it in terms of its history and cultural context. I then give a cursory look at its advantages and disadvantages, when compared to the Anglophone paradigm, and also lay out the criticisms made of the Anglophone media in China, objections to which have been a main motivator of the 'going out' policy that is the topic of this book. Finally, I try to assess whether the Chinese media will be able to earn the loyalty and respect that are attributed to the Anglophone media and look at the parts played in determining this by the specific characteristics of the domestic media.

The Chinese media system

Communications media today comprise a plethora of forms, platforms and genres, such that it is difficult to generalize except at an almost silly level of abstraction. Nowhere is this more obvious than in China, where social media appear as unfettered as offline media are vetted, and more intensely used than in the Anglosphere;

where offline media – newspapers and television – are moving online; where supposedly regimented media are becoming ingenious in competing internationally; when interactivity is intensifying and where the sheer variety and quantity defy compartmentalization.

Nevertheless, some useful things can be said as to how China's media differ from those of the Anglosphere and why, no matter whether we are looking at national policy or personal use. The declared values of Anglophone media are well-known and have often been assumed by their promoters to be universal, while those of Chinese media have often been confused with Marxist-Leninist doctrine. Not only are the origins of modern media in both civilizations different, but the contexts in which they operate are different too.

The Anglosphere's modern media had a long gestation, starting with the English Civil War of the 1640s, when its principles were famously enunciated by John Milton and when the monarchy's monopoly of information was first seriously challenged by the Protestants and other proto-socialists and crypto-democrats. The relative freedom of the twentieth-century press from party political and commercial pressures was the fruit of many struggles and the hopes of great exemplars such as Cobbett. There came about an ideology of the media which held that they should be the adversaries of power, of cultural complacency and of social stasis as well as bearers of truth and witnesses to history.

By contrast, at the very time that Anglosphere journalists, for example during the American Civil War and the Crimean War, were establishing their professionalism and their detachment from authority, literate Chinese were beginning to seize upon newspapers and periodicals as weapons in the battle to revitalize China so that it might withstand imperialism. In the Treaty Ports, foreign businessmen and their ideological associates, the Christian missionaries, inspired or set up organs of practical information and propaganda, providing useful models. Over the hundred years to 1949, modern Chinese media (in ownership and culture, as in language) evolved, thanks both to the technical and managerial lessons learnt from the imperialists, and to the intellectually enquiring and highly literate 'gentry' (Zhang, 2007: Chapter 6). There were periodicals that sought to be detached and pragmatic (Lee, 2005: 119), though many more that were committed to a particular line, especially once foreign ideologies, such as Russian communism, spread. The common assumption, though, was that the purpose of journalism, as with the purpose of art and literature, should be the revival of China, the ejection of its enemies and the unification of all Chinese in this great task. Such media are often called 'advocacy media'.

In 1949, the Communists conquered the country and proceeded to eradicate all competing visions of how China might develop. They imposed their beliefs with a savagery and thoroughness learnt from their Russian associates; media workers conformed or died and the media were converted into publicity arms of the Party. There were from time to time periods of relative liberality until the Cultural Revolution (1965–1975) brought about a total emasculation of the official media. In reaction, something approaching a revolution took place in the 1980s, particularly in the south, with a revival of radio and newspapers; it was partially attenuated after the Tiananmen Massacre of 1989, but by the mid-1990s television journalism, in particular, was flowering.

Media workers showed that they could be innovative, investigative and irreverent despite the horrors they had suffered. Commercialized in the 1990s, the media found that they were not interfered with as long as they followed the general guidelines, avoided the few particularly sensitive areas of public policy or the national leadership and did not offend public taste. That is not to say that they are independent. The state insists that it is not for media workers to decide the tone, tenor or themes of media production; these are matters for the Party. Practitioners must use all their professional skills and executive abilities within a framework provided by the Party. Whether you are a drama producer, talk show host, reality programme director or newspaper editor, you must know your place. The audience is to be informed, uplifted, motivated and inspired. You are given prescriptions and post facto evaluation; as with the BBC or the *Wall Street Journal*, the criteria of success of the moral arbiters transcend those of the business managers, which are presumably ratings, advertising and sponsorship income.

Values of Chinese and Anglophone media contrasted

Visitors to Chinese cities today notice that walls are plastered with exhortations, often accompanied by pretty illustrations, to show solidarity with the older and younger generations, behave courteously or study hard in order better to serve the nation. These, and many other expressions of paternal solicitude or moral exhortation, should be interpreted as reflecting deeply rooted communitarianism. What I mean by communitarianism is the belief that, far from being independent individuals, we are first and foremost members of a community; to be moral is to adhere to the precepts of the community and to put conformity before individual self-realization. Moreover, this community is made up, as Burke put it, of the living, the dead and the yet unborn; those to whom we owe most are first our progenitors and second those who inherit from us, to whom we transmit the values of our own parents and grandparents. Anthropologists in recent years have clarified the gulf which separates Anglophone society with its exceptional individualism, from communitarian societies of various types (Hsu, 1981; Fei, 1992; Chiu and Hong, 2006; Bond and Cheung, 2009; MacFarlane, 2015). What are the implications of these predilections for other aspects of society?

China's economic development has been much more successful than that of many countries with greater resources, smaller populations or better infrastructure. Among the explanations given for this by economists is that, as it sloughed off its debilitating ideology, China was able to draw upon its traditional culture. Let me use the analogy of England. It used to be assumed that Britain had the Industrial Revolution and then became the world's first modern market society, whereas in fact, as the Cambridge Group for the History of Population and Social Structure found, 'the truth is exactly the other way round, we were already the world's first market society and were therefore ripe for the industrial revolution' (Willetts, 2010: 6). The reason England was the first market society is largely to do with its particular family forms, so different to those on the European continent (Willetts, 2010: 11). As if in echo, economists studying China have argued that it is Chinese culture that has underpinned Chinese development (Perkins, 2000).[1] For modern societies, culture may well be a more significant predictor of development and of ideology than are economic conditions.[2] So what are the manifestations of this 'culture'?

Fei (1992) called the social system the 'differential mode of association' 差序格局. In brief, a person is a member of a unit, the first one being the family, before he or she is an individual, and progresses through life as a member of many other units or networks, towards which he/she has prescribed responsibilities and duties which override duties to the self. People are not trapped in fixed categories. 'A person in the course of his or her life time moves from being a child obedient to parents, to being a parent expecting obedience, and so on' (Feuchtwang, 2015: 148). 'Obedience' today would probably best be replaced by 'consideration'.

The notion of equality is different from that encountered in Europe. Christian ideas of equality over a period of some centuries overturned assumptions of 'natural hierarchy' and eventually animated reforms of the legal system and revolts against unrepresentative authority. In China, there was equality of subjection to moral law, law which institutionalized difference, but difference of role rather than of class prescription, let alone caste. Li Jin writes (of today) that it is how a person fulfils the role assigned within a network or community that is more important than the expression of individual personality (Li, 2012: 37).

To make these abstractions more concrete, some instances of how culture affects attitudes and behaviour in the media as elsewhere may be helpful. Membership of, and conformity to, the work unit is a more important aspect of life than it is normally expected to be for an Anglophone, and there is considerable emotional engagement with it (Bretton and Gold, 2012: 519–520). In a newspaper or website office, social life often revolves around the work unit and there people expect to make close friends, whom they will consult on every personal concern. It is not that this membership is the only membership they have, for there seems to be no contradiction in belonging to several networks at once (Nakane, 2013: 22). Once a network is formed, constituents soon know each other very well, including their family life, their love affairs[3] and personal habits.

The implications for politics and journalism are many. Anglophones assume the autonomy of individuals, but Chinese often see themselves as members of a group first, such that the norms of the group (or indeed the views of the leaders of the group) rather than the opinions of the individual will be decisive in determining a course of action.[4] Moreover personal obligations can override professional values, explaining why a story can be spiked lest it upset a friend, or a friend of a friend.

One of the features of this kind of society is that business relationships have traditionally been based on trust and the personal friendship or at least mutual respect which is usually required to precede business (Hamilton, 2015).[5] Trust is essential to business transactions: In the Anglosphere it is guaranteed by adherence to impersonal laws and contracts observed by both sides, in China by a shared ethic as to how you behave towards those with whom you are in a relationship.

Networks, whether familial or otherwise, are not quite like Anglophone civil associations. They bring people together with a common, often emotional, bond such as shared membership of a cultural group, lineage, temple congregation or college. The relationship predominates over the purpose. Moreover 'pseudo families' are not really civil associations but more precisely characterized as mutual support groups.

Because loyalty to relatives and networks takes precedence over loyalty to abstractions, notwithstanding efforts to prise away those loyalties by both the Chinese Communist Party and the Kuomintang, it has proved difficult to establish a concept of public service, adherence to professional ethics or a universal morality as opposed to loyalty to Party or leader. Since, by tradition, there are no abstract universal principles of morality, but only ethical principles governing relationships, to be dutiful is to serve well not an ideal but those involved in the relationship.

As an instance of what exists instead of the professional ethic, we might say that a Chinese investigative journalist performs his or her role by serving those whom he as a journalist should serve, rather than because it is necessary as a journalist to behave in a certain way. She or he may interpret the object of service differently, although for many it will simply be the person who appointed them.

Despite knowledge of and interest in the Anglophone idea of journalism and its professionalism, the doyens of the 'Golden Period' generally saw themselves as activists in the patriotic endeavour, rather than as adherents to a professional creed, although the *Workers' Daily* was proud of its impartiality (Lee, 2005: 111). The journalist will be honest and trustworthy to her colleague or the subject of her report, not because some ideal told her to treat all equally, but because she has entered into a relationship of trust.

Another aspect of Chinese society which may inhibit the assertion of professional authority is the assumption of hierarchy. A professional is not necessarily offended in submitting to authority, or to authority's version of events and anyway, hierarchy is tempered by the personalizing of relationships.[6] The journalists who in 1989 joined protests demanding that they not be 'forced to lie' had been pushed too far but it is unlikely they objected to the principle of authority influencing the media; rather they disliked the usurping of that power for nefarious ends.

Television events with audience involvement, showcases of common peoples' talents such as the *China Dream Show*, online newspapers seeking collaboration from readers and of course social media have all served to widen the group of those who participate in national conversations and expect to have their voices heard, tentatively at least, on an equal footing with the leaders or the supposed experts. How has this affected traditional hierarchy?

It may be that the paternalist and communitarian assumptions are giving way to, or may turn into, something more familiar to Anglophones, not only thanks to such media but also as enterprises become more knowledge-based and participatory.[7] Yet still, even in huge organizations, when a senior decision maker moves post, because the relationships in Chinese organizations are so personal, many colleagues will move as well, according to the principle of 'new king, new ministers'

一朝天子一朝臣. Media executives may be more like disciples than colleagues, and there are obligations anticipated for both the junior and the senior, as many a foreign professor or employer has discovered. Hierarchy is clear, as are its responsibilities (Chang, 2008: 193).

Such deference contrasts with the adversarial attitude of many Anglophone journalists and with Anglophone journalists' prioritizing of getting 'the truth' and reporting 'facts'. So too does its corollary: the sense that media workers are teachers before they are reporters and must tailor their output according to its moral implications and potential effects.

We may understand this better if we agree that role recognition is a more important concept for understanding Chinese institutions than is hierarchy. At a workshop on investigative journalism for young CCTV reporters in 2010, two Anglophone editors and a Chinese editor were asked at the end to summarize the day. The Anglophones proceeded to describe the techniques that had been discussed and the criteria for effective revelation; how to get the scoop. When his turn came, Zhang Jie张杰, then Editor of *Newsprobe*, made a rousing speech, in which he related investigative journalism to enlightening and educating people to be better citizens and serve the common weal; his focus was entirely upon the higher purpose, rather than on the processes. He enjoined the 250-odd youngsters, from among whom would be selected a wave of foreign correspondents, to grasp their roles as teachers and patriots.

The critique of Anglophone media

In the British Parliament, in 2012, Zhao Qizheng, Chairman of the Foreign Relations Committee of the Consultative Conference and former head of the State Council Information Office, reiterated a point he has been making for a very long time, that the Anglophone-dominated global media, far from presenting an impartial picture of China to the world, 'demonize' China and that, because of this, China must provide 'accurate' sources of information. In the same year, President Hu Jintao opined that 'we must clearly see that international forces are intensifying the strategic plot of Westernizing and dividing China'. He considered that it was through ideology and culture that they wished to subvert his country (Rawnsley, 2015: 466). Anglophone observers tend to write this attitude off as paranoia or else blame the Chinese for deluding themselves (Callahan, 2010: 194). Yet, from a Chinese perspective, influential foreign media misrepresent China by emphasizing the negative and imposing a detrimental framing upon the reporting of it.

People in China can find it difficult to accept that the Anglophone media are reporting in good faith. Since the invasions of Iraq and Afghanistan – to say nothing of the Vietnam War a generation ago – caused terrible suffering, they see the Western media's 'obsession' with 'China's human rights violations' as hypocritical. The constant reiteration of the Tiananmen Massacre of nearly three decades ago, the Tibet issue, and the emphasizing of 'dissidents'[8] is rather as if the US were to be written off as iniquitous by those whose only reference points were the Trail of Tears, the My Lai Massacre, and Abu Ghraib.

That the US media evaluate foreign countries according to their own ideology and, as Lee puts it, while justifying US interests abroad, 'undermine the legitimacy of its rivals', is really not in question (Lee, 1991: 20). There are grounds in empirical research for Chinese beliefs that the Anglophone press is hostile to China (Sparks, 2010),[9] indeed that political discourse in the USA is being permeated by a 'China threat' (Nathan and Scobell, 2012). According to Nathan and Scobell, 'The United States constantly pressurizes China over its economic policies, and maintains a host of government and private programmes that seek to influence Chinese civil society and politics' and they go on to say that

> Chinese officials consider that the United States uses the ideas of democracy and human rights to delegitimize and destabilize régimes that espouse alternative values, such as socialism and Asian-style developmental authoritarianism. And that it is only a short step from this to attack.
>
> *(ibid.: 39)[10]*

In such an atmosphere it is not difficult to find ordinary Chinese who support restrictions on foreign propaganda, whether accusations of China's nefarious trading, or films promoting individualism and violence. For, while being conscious of the deficiencies of their own media, Chinese may still reject the Anglophone assumption that their media are free of propaganda or impartial.

Many are of the conviction that the Anglophone media treat China as an enemy and that they are disgracefully ignorant of that which they vilify. Closing a seminar on public service media in January 2013, Bai Yansong asked a prominent Anglosphere TV anchor what the Chinese media should learn from him. After a long answer, a disquisition on the wonders of a free press and, by implication, condemnation of China's, the anchor politely asked what he should learn from China. Bai Yansong replied tersely, 'Chinese'.

Assessing the 'going out' policy

Such is the climate in which the Chinese media abroad hope to be equals of the Anglophone media and to undermine the idea that somehow the Anglophone media are reliable whereas theirs are not. Can they do so? Foreign journalists employed by Chinese media companies acknowledge the challenge of attracting viewers who may be sceptical about news sources controlled by the state (Farhi, 2012). The prescribed role of the media in the 'guidance of public opinion' could impede its ability to wield soft power because people (Anglophones anyway) are sceptical of state-controlled media,[11] although where rival news organizations have commented on CCTV coverage of international events, they have accounted them balanced (Dong and Shi, 2007: 183).

China also faces problems of media management and technical virtuosity, because when other countries were developing their creative industries in the 1960s and 1970s, China's stood still. Although they are now catching up, the state-run institutions are slow movers. The education, training and recruitment of foreign correspondents are unsystematic[12] and inimical to good work.

Taking a helicopter view, Professor Deans, former Head of the Contemporary China Institute, and now Professor of International Affairs at Richmond University, puts the case that the Chinese media will provide an acceptable alternative, particularly in the developing world. The Anglophone assumption that a country with an authoritarian government cannot produce high-quality media is not necessarily true:

> CCTV does very good coverage of issues, unless they are related to China. I think people will increasingly turn, especially in the developing world, to a Chinese news channel as much as they would turn to the BBC. It'll be problematic, and it may never be the way that many people in the United Kingdom or the United States think is appropriate for journalism, but that doesn't mean it's not going to work, and that doesn't mean it won't be successful. Are the Chinese media, at their worst, any worse than the American media at their worst at times for bias on content, coverage and presentation? Probably not. It's not as sophisticated, [and] standards in terms of the quality aren't there yet, but they'll close up, they'll narrow that gap with technical standards. And it will be a heavily biased perspective, but probably no more biased a perspective than Fox News or even in its own peculiar way the BBC, which has a very strong bias in favour of liberalism and human rights and democracy.
>
> *(Deans, interviewed on 14 February 2012)*

Thinkers among the CCTV journalists want to be different. First, they claim that the impact of what they report is taken into consideration. Second, they want to judge themselves by their ability to promote peace and development rather than 'the need to bear witness and write the first draft of history from the front line' (Marsh, 2015). In reporting the multiple terrorist attacks of November 2015, bloodshed in Paris was played down by CCTV, lest it give heart to enemies and frighten citizens; in reporting the Kunming terror incidents of 2014 there were initially no mentions in the public media of the race of the perpetrators, lest this inspire racism.

CCTV editors think that Anglophone media are too adversarial, too combative; they themselves want to be positive and useful. The *Global Times* was balanced when it pointed out that, while the 2015 slaughter of *Charlie Hebdo* journalists was inexcusable, it was provoked by vicious assaults on Islam; observers of CCTV reports in Africa have noted a predilection for reports about attempts to end conflict, rather than reports from the conflict itself.[13] This differentiation has been theorized as 'constructive journalism', a way of explaining an approach which eschews the adversarial while adhering to common principles of truthful reporting (Zhang, 2014). Practitioners distinguish such journalism from both the negative approach they consider to be favoured in the Anglosphere and also its reviled antithesis, positive journalism. In so doing, CCTV Africa hopes to 'promote a view of Africans seeking their own solutions' (ibid.: 11). CCTV is saying that it wants to 'give a new kind of balance and shine a new kind of light on the continent'. In a discussion with the Deputy President of CCTV, he explained that selection and interpretation of news will differ from say BBC or CNN, 'because we are Asians', but that reporting would be sacrosanct (Sun, 2011).

However, there are limits to CCTV's ability to provide that to which they aspire, a 'new type of journalism', often termed 'constructive' (Zhang, 2014). Not only is there the oft-cited subservience to the political line, at least when covering China issues, but there is a lack of confidence in its reporters when making selections and assessments which makes them anodyne or drives them to rely heavily on Anglophone agencies or NGOs whose material reflects Anglophone agenda and values (Xie and Boyd-Barrett, 2015). As a consequence, CCTV is probably not reflecting a Chinese understanding of the world, something that has been suspected by academics such as Li (2005) and is being given empirical underpinning both by Jirik and Marsh.

Jirik (2009) finds that, far from being Party propaganda, CCTV's international news is barely distinguishable from that of its competitors. He suggests that this is in part because it sources so much of its material from international agencies. 'Management's claim that CCTV-I provided Chinese perspective on world events was not supported, unless a story involved Chinese interests.' This observation reflected Chang and Chen's (1998) finding a decade earlier that conformity to the 'Party line' in news in the PRC (People's Republic of China) was contingent on the relationship of the story to PRC interests.

The value to the rest of the world in having a Chinese media presence is that it might offer an alternative perspective to the dominant framings of international affairs. They might consciously be distinct or may fail and follow the same market-driven, infotainment-oriented model with its roots in the commercial media system of the US (Thussu, 2007).

Whether the Chinese media will enrich us, either through paying attention to what others have ignored, or by talking in new terms, becoming an antidote to CNN or the BBC, probably depends upon how China resolves its identity problem, because without doing so, the media will not confidently represent the revitalized Chinese culture which they aim to promote. Here we return to President Xi and the more confident face to the world.

The return of China

Shambaugh (2013: 263–267) has done a thorough audit of its soft power and is of the opinion that China's influence is very limited for several reasons. First, he considers that the Chinese government is itself unclear as to what it should establish as the Chinese image or brand. If he is right, this problem must derive from the inconvenient fact that while the official ideology is the discredited Marxism-Leninism, the proclaimed philosophy amounts to modern Confucianism; although President Xi appears to be attempting a fusion, the contradiction is unresolved. Secondly, Shambaugh holds that the government is inconsistent when it declares itself benign, and yet allows the persecution of various individuals and minorities.[14] Thirdly, he opines that China's reputation is unattractive to the rest of the world on account of its political system. Westad goes further:

> in cultural terms, China is singularly lacking in soft power: no young person of sound mind in Tokyo or Seoul, or even in Taipei or Singapore, is looking to the PRC for music to download, films to watch, or ideas to latch on to.
>
> *(Westad, 2012: 459)*

I suspect that these observers cannot see what they did not expect. Martial arts and exercises, massage, the art of food and medical practices are well established in many countries; exported films, though few, are popular; design, fashion, telenovelas and pop music are not far behind. Very large numbers are studying Chinese at school and will be media consumers before long. In a generation, China's equivalents of *The Economist* and *Wall Street Journal* are likely to become influential abroad, if only because Chinese business matters.

It is undeniable that China's position has improved in the eyes of many: opinion polls show a growing respect for China; the more countries have to do with China, the more they seem to be well disposed towards it (Pew Research Center, 2013). The Chinese model of development is admired (Leonard, 2008: 121) and it is very probable that in many areas of the world, when doing business and politics, it is Chinese values and norms that determine how things should be rather than Anglophone ones. The *One Belt One Road* initiative appears to be a potential common market but without the bureaucracy and controls of the EU. In 2015 China showed itself a leader in addressing climate change, an augury for a future in which policy and standards for global issues may be set in China rather than elsewhere. How much of this is attributable to the media, and how much to the multitude of other ways in which perceptions of China are being changed, is debatable. But what is surely true is that President Xi is both forming and reflecting a revitalized conception of China.

After 30 years of disasters, in which the condition of the people declined to below the standards of a century before, each leader since Mao Zedong has taken steps to extricate China from the ideological prison of Marxism-Leninism. President Xi appears to be going much further, reconstituting Chineseness in the face of Anglo-American 'hegemony'.

Xi Jinping is the first leader to give a speech in commemoration of Confucius' birth (Xi, 2014); he makes more references in his speeches to Confucian thinkers than to any other category (Sun, 2014), showing that by drawing upon tradition he is sidelining Marxism (which some now dub a 'Western religion'). He is fusing Marxist practices and Confucian precepts. Xi castigates corruption but does not view it as a concomitant of the system established by the Marxists (in which case he would tackle the Party's prerogatives). Rather he considers that the corrupted have not adequately internalized the Party's values (Brown, 2015: 195); although he calls for the Rule of Law (and is trying to reduce the pressures on judges), he extolled Bo Xilai's extra-legal methods of cleaning up Chongqing, which were reminiscent of the Maoist past and shocked many of his peers; in 2016 many claimed that the anti-corruption drive that he has instituted was in the same mould.

There are still elements of the Marxian vision that are serviceable: identification of destructive and dehumanizing aspects of capitalism, its global aggressiveness, its promotion of inequality and the commodification of every aspect of culture and relationships; these are the aspects of Marx's thought that still appear to have purchase.[15]

Traditional political philosophy gives priority to the responsibility of the rulers for the social and economic conditions of the people, rather than for promoting individual liberty or political participation (Perry, 2008, quoted in Creemers, 2015: 49); hence the resonance, to the political class in the last century, of 'socialism'. Today, socialism in China seems to mean just that, a political system that identifies the material conditions of the citizenry as the first consideration, in other words, that to which all modern governments of left and right aspire. Something similar has been the aspiration of Chinese government since long before European intellectuals theorized socialism.

In the society around Xi, ordinary people's daily practices appear to ever more be reflecting tradition.[16] What English speakers have translated as 'filial piety' but might be better rendered as 'role respect', 孝, is a code of duty which binds people together in mutual support; it is constantly referred to in novels and periodicals; the rebuilding of shrines and the purchase of ancestral tablets are outward signs of inner emotions.

Though it is different in character from that found in the Anglosphere, China has a vigorous civil society, in part reconstituted from pre-1949 days, in part responding to current issues such as the environment, urbanization, rapid economic change, consumer society and the revival of religion, although there is some conflict between traditional assumptions about extragovernmental associations and imported Anglophone 'missions'. The public sphere is largely in the media; think tanks, thought-provoking periodicals, chat shows, opinion polls and consultative conferences all play their part but the sharpest debate and the relatively uncon-strained opinion are on Weibo and Weixin; short of overt lobbying and demands for revolution, 'all human life is there'. Madsen, reviewing China's public sphere, suggests that there is much from which other countries can learn and writes of a 'common quest' to revitalize the public spheres (Madsen, 1993: 197). Over the last two years, it must be noted, evidence has emerged of curtailment and repression as Xi consolidates his hold as a presumed prelude to massive reforms of the armed forces and the state-owned enterprises.

As to the media, he not only enjoins them to recognize their role in the great work of rebuilding China, but also reaffirms the Marxist theory of the media, that they are the voices of the ruling class (Bandurski, 2016). So, in the world, China's media constitute an alternative model. As part of the state apparatus, they follow the lead of officials whose job it is to ensure that they serve the interests of the nation (defined by the Party), provide a public service and reflect Chinese culture; in general, these professionals see themselves as servants of Party and country, occasionally disagreeing as to how their responsibilities should be exercised. In a corollary of state-controlled media, the government argues for cyber sovereignty on the grounds that globalization really amounts to Anglo-capitalist domination of markets, of media and of ideas.

Conclusion

Such is the context within which media entrepreneurs, creatives and managers must operate. A different history and purpose; a cultural background radically different from the Anglophone; a nation asserting the equal value of its civilization to that of the heretofore unstoppable Anglophone capitalism.

These things influence the media's external activities so far to a limited extent only. State media reporters abroad should try to represent their country's points of view while reporting back objectively to their home audiences. Sellers of new media and entertainment services for foreign consumers are under no such constriction and can be as unfettered as their foreign counterparts were before they had to take account of Chinese restrictions if they wanted to pander to that vast market. Before long, Chinese drama, entertainment, culture and education will be competing in foreign markets, often tailored to be digestible abroad; the themes and the tone, the taste and the temper will come out of the context that I have attempted to describe.

Notes

1 See also Berger, P. L. and Hsiao, H. M. (eds.) (1988) *In Search of an East Asian Development Model*, New Brunswick: Transaction Books. Tai, H. (ed.) (1989) *Confucianism and Economic Development: An Oriental Alternative?*, Washington: Washington Institute Press. Chung-Hua Institution for Economic Research (1989) *Conference on Confucianism and Economic Development in East Asia*, Taipei: CIER Press. Vogel, E. F. (1991) *The Four Little Dragons: The Spread of Industrialization in East Asia*, Cambridge: Harvard University Press. Jochim, C. (1992) Confucius and capitalism: Views of Confucianism in works on Confucianism and economic development, *Journal of Chinese Religions*, no. 20.

2 The key texts are those of Emmanuel Todd (1985) *The Explanation of Ideology*, Oxford: Blackwell; and (1987) *The Causes of Progress*, Oxford: Blackwell. These describe the ramifications of the exogamous community family. For China in particular, see Chiu, C-Y. and Hong, Y-Y. (2006) *Social Psychology of Culture*, New York: Psychology Press.

3 For a very graphic illustration of the involvement of work colleagues in personal life, see Chi Li's novel *Coming and Going*, in which the protagonist, a successful businessman, is visited by his own former boss plus his wife's former boss and upbraided for wishing to divorce her. 池莉Chi Li (2009) 来来往往. 北京 Beijing: 十月文艺出版社 October Arts and Literature Publishing House.

4 For a thorough discussion of this, see Fei (1992).

5 Hamilton (2015: 139) describes the 'ideal' of how Taiwan business people organize their business dealings. The owner and the wife are the inner core, around which is an inner circle of confidantes and other concentric rings of contacts. In doing business with Chinese media companies I have found not only that they function in the same way but that the (British) unit adapts to the same formula if it is to accommodate Chinese clients and their requirements for trust.

6 What I mean is that in a detached relationship, hierarchy may be unpleasant and divisive, whereas it need not be so where the relationship is warmer. Hierarchy between parents

and children should be entirely positive and in no way diminish mutual respect and affection; similarly with teachers and pupils.

7 Changes are afoot, at least in big enterprises. Guthrie (2006: 294) states that, increasingly, 'in the work unit, labour relations have been formalised with formal recruitment procedures, proper contracts, organisational rules, grievance procedures and representation'. He also makes the point that 'the vast majority of labour disputes settled by arbitration on mediation are decided in favour of the workers who filed the suits'.

8 Whether China has 'dissidents' in the way that the USSR had – at least in Western media – is a moot point. Ai Weiwei, like other intellectuals who have criticized their government, also has accepted patronage from government; film directors and writers are one minute being lauded by China's critics as 'opponents of the regime' but the next are national exemplars. With the possible exception of Liu Xiaobo, people are rarely so simply classifiable.

9 See Sparks (2010). Also: Cao, Q. (1999) Signification of Hong Kong's handover: the case of the British press, *Journal of International Communication*, 6(2): 71–89; Mawdsley, E. (2008) Fu Manchu versus Dr Livingstone in the Dark Continent? Representing China, Africa and the West in British broadsheet newspapers, *Political Geography*, 27: 509–529; Yang, Y.E. and Liu, X. (2012) The China threat through the lens of US print media 1992–2006, *Journal of Contemporary China*, 21(76): 695–711; Sullivan, J. and Renz, B. (2012) Representing China in the South Pacific, *East Asia*. Available at: www.academia. edu/1628681/Representing_China_in_the_South_Pacific [Accessed 17 March 2016].

10 James Dobbin (former Assistant Secretary of State) argues that

> A climate of mutual distrust and suspicion clouds the US-China relationship, and is producing a potent security dilemma. If ignored, this dynamic could spiral out of control. Altering it will require both the United States and China to fundamentally rethink their national security goals and strategic assumptions in Asia and beyond.
>
> *(Rowthorn, 2013)*

11 'Any reports on breaking news are organized and managed by the State Council Information Office, which drafts the reportage on the incident, and after approval from the Central Government and the State Council, it will organize the reporting of it to the outside world. It is difficult for the Chinese media, with their lack of competitiveness, caused by strict government restrictions, to win large audiences abroad' (Zhang, 2009: 114).

12 I cannot evidence this; the comment is the result of many conversations with dissatisfied CCTV and CNC employees.

13 For more on CCTV's challenge of 'constructive journalism', see James Wan's chapter, Propaganda or Proper Journalism: China's Media Expansion in Africa in *Africa's Media Image in the 21st Century: From Heart of Darkness to Africa Rising*, edited by Melanie Bunce, Suzanne Franks and Chris Paterson (Routledge, 2016).

14 It could be – and is – countered that Anglo-America claims to be peaceful and a champion of human rights, while waging destructive wars and shattering the most elementary of human rights of large numbers of people in countries where it, or its proxies, intervene.

15 I am indebted to Leng Rong, 冷溶, Director, CPC Central Committee Party Literature Research Center, 中共中央文献研究室 for discussing these questions with me, Summer 2014.

16 I have rarely met a student who did not go annually to visit the graves of her forbears, among the many other instances of the continuation (or revival) of tradition.

References

Bandurski, P. (2016) How Xi Jinping Views the News. *China Media Project*. Available at: http://cmp.hku.hk/2016/03/03/39672/ [Accessed 5 April 2016].

Bond, M. H. and Cheung, F. M. (2009) *The Psychology of the Chinese People*. Hong Kong: The Chinese University Press.

Bretton, J. and Gold, J. (2012) *Human Resource Management: Theory and Practice*. Basingstoke: Palgrave MacMillan.

Brown, K. (2015) *The New Emperors: Power and the Princelings in China*. London: I. B. Tauris.

Callahan, W. (2010) *China: The Pessoptimist Nation*. Oxford: Oxford University Press.

Chang, L. T. (2008) *Factory Girls*. New York: Picador.

Chang, Tsan-Kuo and Yanru Chen (1998). Constructing International Spectacle on Television: CCTV News and China's Window on the World, 1992–1996. Paper presented at the Conference 'Association for Education in Journalism and Mass Communication (AEJMC): Radio-Television Journalism Division', Baltimore, MD, 5–8 August.

Chiu, C-Y. and Hong, Y-Y. (2006) *Social Psychology of Culture*. New York: Psychology Press.

Creemers, R. (2015) Evaluating Chinese Media Policy: Objectives and Contradictions, in Rawnsley, G. and Rawnsley, M. (eds.) *Routledge Handbook of Chinese Media*. London: Routledge: 47–63.

Deans, P. Interviewed on 14 February 2012. Professor Deans, former Head of the Contemporary China Institute, is now Professor of International Affairs at Richmond University.

Dong, S. G. and Shi, A. (2007) Chinese News in Transition, in Thussu, D. K. (ed.) *Media on the Move: Global Flow and Contra-Flow*. London: Routledge: 182–198.

Fan, Yun. Interviewed on 13 April 2016. Head of Personnel, CCTV.

Farhi, P. (2012) In DC China Builds a News Hub to Help Polish Its Global Image. *Washington Post*, 16 January.

Fei, X. (1992) *From the Soil: The Foundations of Chinese Society*. Berkeley: University California Press.

Feuchtwang, S. (2015) Social egoism and individualism, *Journal of China in Comparative Perspective*, 1(1): 143–160.

Guthrie, D. (2006) *China and Globalization*. London: Routledge.

Hamilton, G. (2015) What Western social scientists can learn from the writings of Fei Xiaotong, *Journal of China in Comparative Perspective*, 1(1): 143–160.

Hsu, F. (1981) *Americans and Chinese: Passages to Differences*. Honolulu: University of Hawaii Press.

Jirik, J. (2009) *The PRC's 'Going Out' Project: CCTV International and the Imagination of a Chinese Nation*. Lehigh, PA: Lehigh University. Available at: https://global.cas2.lehigh.edu/sites/global.cas2.lehigh.edu/files/Jirik_lecture.pdf [Accessed: 6 November 2013].

Lee, C. C. (1991) Mass Media: Of China, About China, in Lee, C. C. (ed.) *Voices of China: The Interplay of Politics and Journalism*. London: Guilford Press: 3–29.

Lee, C. C. (2005) The Conception of Chinese Journalists, in de Burgh, H. (ed.) *Making Journalists*. London: Routledge: 107–126.

Leonard, M. (2008) *What Does China Think?* London: Fourth Estate.

Li, J. (2012) *Cultural Foundations of Learning, East and West*. Cambridge: Cambridge University Press.

Li, X. (2005) Who Is Setting the Chinese Agenda? The Impact of Online Chatrooms on the Party Presses, in *China Sees the World Sees China, Media and Power in China Today*, School of Communication, Tsinghua University.

MacFarlane, A. (2015) *A Modern Education*. Cambridge: Cambridge Rivers Press.

Madsen, R. (1993) The public sphere, civil society, and moral community: A research agenda for contemporary Chinese studies, *Modern China*, 19(2): 183–198.

Marsh, V. (2015) Mixed messages, partial pictures? Discourses under construction in CCTV's Africa Live, compared with the BBC, *Chinese Journal of Communication*. Available at: http://dx.doi.org/10.1080/17544750.2015.1105269) [Accessed: 7 March 2016].

Marsh, V. Interviewed in 2015. Marsh is undertaking a PhD study of CCTV, comparing its programming with the international services of the BBC. She has already published several articles and chapters.

Nakane, C. (2013) *Japanese Society*. London: Pelican.

Nathan, A. J. and Scobell, A. (2012) *China's Search for Security*. New York: Columbia University Press.

Perkins, D. H. (2000) Law, Family Ties and the East Asian Way of Business, in Harrison, L. E and Huntington, S. P. (eds.) *Culture Matters: How Values Shape Human Progress*. New York: Basic Books: 232–243.

Pew Research Center (2013) *Attitudes toward China*. Available at: www.pewglobal. org/2013/07/18/chapter-3-attitudes-toward-china/ [Accessed 18 February 2016].

Rawnsley, G. (2015) Chinese International Broadcasting, Public Diplomacy and Soft Power, in Rawnsley, G. and Rawnsley, M. T. (eds.) *Routledge Handbook of Chinese Media*. London: Routledge: 460–475.

Rowthorn, R. and Coutts, K. (2013) *De-Industrialisation and the Balance of Payments in Advanced Economies*. Cambridge: Centre for Business Research, University of Cambridge Working Paper No. 453.

Shambaugh, D. (2013) *China Goes Global*. Oxford: Oxford University Press.

Sparks, C. (2010) Coverage of China in the UK national press, *Chinese Journal of Communication*, 3(3): 347–365.

Sun, X. (2014) *Xi Jinping's 300 References*, 30 November. Available at: http://news.sina.com. cn/c/2014-10-30/024831066011.shtml [Accessed 25 February 2016].

Sun, Yusheng. Interviewed on 12 November 2011.

Thussu, D. K. (2007) *News as Entertainment: The Rise of Global Infotainment*. London: Sage.

Westad, O. A. (2012) *Restless Empire: China and the World since 1759*. London: Bodley Head.

Willetts, D. (2010) *The Pinch*. London: Atlantic Books.

Xi, J. (2014) Xi Jinping's Speech in Commemoration of the 2,565th Anniversary of Confucius' Birth. *ChinaUSFocus*, 24 September. Available at: http://library.chinausfocus.com/article-1534.html [Accessed 25 February 2016].

Xie, S. and Boyd-Barrett, O. (2015) External-national TV news networks' way to America: Is the United States losing the global 'Information War'? *International Journal of Communication*, 9: 66–83.

Zhang, X. (2007) *The Origins of the Modern Chinese Press*. London: Routledge.

Zhang, X. (2009) From Propaganda to International Communication: China's Promotion of Soft Power in the Age of Information and Communication Technologies, in Zhang, X. and Zheng, Y. (eds.) *China's Information and Communications Technology: Social Changes and State Responses*. London: Routledge.

Zhang, Y. (2014) Understand China's Media in Africa from the perspective of Constructive Journalism. Paper presented at the international conference *China and Africa Media, Communications and Public Diplomacy* on 10 September 2014. Available at: www.cmi.no/file/2922-.pdf [Accessed 7 March 2016].

4

FROM THE OUTSIDE IN: CCTV GOING GLOBAL IN A NEW WORLD COMMUNICATION ORDER

Zhengrong Hu, Deqiang Ji and Yukun Gong

In 2009, China Central Television (CCTV) was designated as one of a handful of Chinese state-owned media to be part of the 'going-out' project with the support of state subsidy and its own strategic innovation. This chapter aims to investigate the dynamics of the encounter between CCTV and the global media environment in an era of media convergence. Firstly, CCTV's 'going-out' practices in history will be summarized on the basis of document analysis. Secondly, as an 'outsider' in a global media market dominated by its Western counterparts, CCTV not only challenges the existing global media structure through its rapid expansion and different geopolitical concerns, but also faces a number of challenges in the process of 'going-out'. These are, for instance, the political or ideological scepticism of its relationship with the Chinese state, the consolidated regional markets that exclude newcomers, such as North America and even some African countries, and also the huge gaps of professional competence between CCTV and the 'international leading media' (*guoji yiliu meiti*) as acknowledged by itself (Ren and Ren, 2014). A historical analysis regarding these challenges will be provided. Thirdly, the global media landscape is changing. The decline of the West and the rise of the Rest are creating a new world media map, which implies a global power shift in the arena of media and beyond (Zhao, 2014).

Against this background, is there a historic opportunity for CCTV to become a member of the dominant players like the BBC or CNN in the global market, or to develop geopolitically as successfully as RT (formerly known as Russia Today) or Al Jazeera, or otherwise to create a new path of development representing the Global South? This chapter attempts to answer these questions by examining the complexities of media power – domestic and international – within a broader context of political-economic and cultural transformation across the globe.

1 May 1958 is a historic day in the development of television in China, when the Beijing Television Station (the predecessor of China Central Television) was

founded as the only central (national)-level television station in China. Two decades later, the Beijing Television Station was renamed China Central Television (CCTV) on 5 May 1978. Almost one year later, another television station with the name of Beijing Television Station (BTV) was established on 16 May 1979. Unlike CCTV, BTV is a television station affiliated to the Beijing municipal government, one of 31 provincial satellite television stations in China. In other words, in Beijing there are two major television stations that have nationwide access and influence: CCTV and BTV, but at different administrative levels. It is necessary to point out the central–regional differences of Chinese media at the very beginning of this chapter, because most of the 'going-out' practices – or in a more precise sense, experiments – in recent years have been carried by central-level media. The Xinhua news agency, China Central Television and China Radio International are typical examples. This 'national team' of media organizations has expanded its global outreach with enormous financial support from the central government since 2009. However, the question remains whether the state-owned media can successfully compete with either their Western counterparts or the rising of the Rest, like RT and Al Jazeera in both the global and regional media markets, let alone in the promotion of China's national image, which in itself is a complex issue. We will return to this later in the discussion about the possible roles of China in a transitional world communication order.

As early as 2001, when China finally completed its accession into the World Trade Organization, the State Administration for Radio, Film and Television launched the 'going-out' project for China's electronic media. Central-level media soon jumped on board with this policy and became the flagship leading this transformation. China Central Television and China Radio International started to increase their global appearance and won a number of awards at global television festivals (Tan and Yu, 2009). This going global steadily progressed until a new policy was issued, which accelerated the process: The General Plan for Building Major Media's Capacity of International Communication (2009–2020) was announced in 2009. According to this plan, several internationally influential media groups from China were to be developed to reflect the rising status of China's political and economic influence in the world.

As one of the focal topics of media and communication studies, there is a growing body of literature that has attempted to explore the multilayered global and regional consequences of China's media going global. Taking CCTV as an example, some researchers argue that the media going global is part of the internationalization of the Chinese economy. 'If we put it in the broader context of China's emergence as a global actor, CCTV's expansion is a natural development of Chinese firms' internationalization strategies' (Chen, 2014). Chen believes that the key to the success of CCTV going global is incorporating a well-developed business model into its organization and operation. For instance, 'embedding digital interactivity in its business model has been necessary for CCTV's development' (ibid.). Some researchers believe that the outreach of CCTV should go beyond the goal of getting more attention and audience from the global market, to focus on building international influence.

According to Tan and Yu (2009), the going global strategy of CCTV should shift from the economy of 'attention' to the economy of 'influence'. Besides the strategic discussions on how to understand and even help CCTV going global, there are also many critics of China's ambitions of sending their media to the world. Taking China's CCTV and Russia's RT as examples, in an article entitled 'Authoritarianism Goes Global', Walker *et al.* (2016) argue that 'the authoritarians not only repress reform-minded voices at home but are seeking to reshape international values and norms in order to limit the global ambit of democracy'.

The field of international communication includes many highly contested matters. Against this background, CCTV going global is not only a challenge to the world from a rising China, but also a process with uncertainties and even oppositions. We will start our analysis by briefly summarizing the historical milestones of CCTV going global since the 1980s, followed by critical reflections on the relations between CCTV and the changing world communication order.

Milestones of CCTV going global

The promotion of Chinese television started in the 1980s, coinciding with the government's 'reform and opening-up policy', which was marked by the development of satellite TV. As China's biggest state-owned television broadcaster and the mouthpiece of the Chinese Communist Party, CCTV has expanded overseas since then. In 1984, a special department of CCTV in charge of publicity to foreign countries was established and produced its first international feature programme, 'A Glimpse of China', in Chinese. In 1985, CCTV opened its first English-language news programme, 'English News', to achieve the transition from the programme time to the segment time. In 1991, a foreign TV centre was set up formally and CCTV sent programmes from CCTV-1 via the leased AsiaSat 1, whose signal covered Southeast Asia to Hong Kong, Macao and Taiwan. This new satellite era ended the practice of mailing programmes abroad (Tang, 2003: 236). Meanwhile, an English news programme called 'China Today' was broadcast in the United States and several European countries. However, during this time Chinese television had not yet entered the world TV market (Liu and Wu, 2008).

The launch of satellite TV channels for international broadcasting marked a new phase in CCTV's efforts to reach out to foreign audiences. In 1992, CCTV-4, China's first international channel in Mandarin began a broadcasting service for overseas Chinese (Zhang, 2009). Then CCTV launched the 24-hour English-language channel CCTV-9 (also known as CCTV International, renamed as CCTV News in 2010 and became part of China Global Television Network – CGTN – in 2016) in 2000, as China's first TV channel broadcasting in English. But although the main goal at that time was to inform the world about China, China's voice was not getting through to the international community via either CCTV-4 or CCTV-9, with no views or reports from China on major international issues. However, in 2003 the international channels of CCTV emerged onto the world stage with the Iraq War. Using live broadcasts, spot connections via satellite, expert interviews,

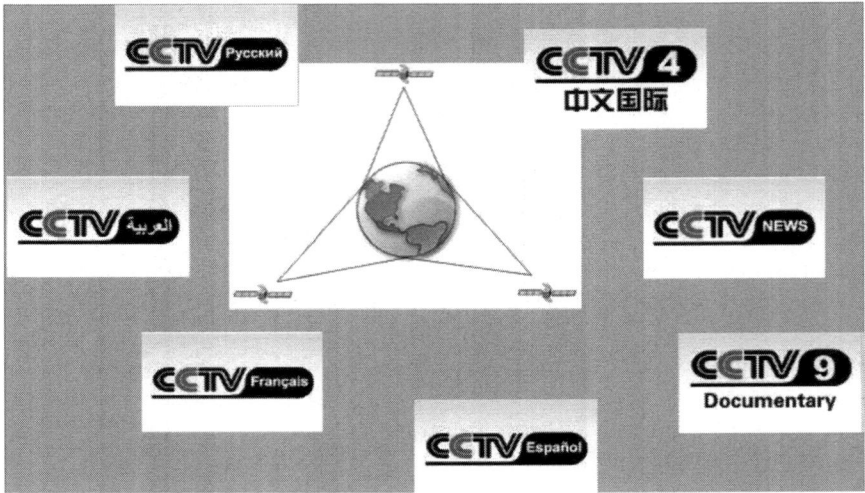

FIGURE 4.1 The global provision of CCTV International channels
Source: Si (2014).

news reviews, CCTV-4 broadcast 408 hours of war coverage, aired 2,100 pieces of war news and 15,000 television captions. CCTV-4 thus created the largest report on a single event in the history of Chinese television. CCTV-9 also provided comprehensive broadcasts and this coverage of the Iraq War resulted in a dramatic rise in the audience ratings of the two channels: CCTV-4 increased 28 times, and CCTV-9 6 times, the former becoming known as an influential Chinese media channel, while the popularity of the latter also improved (Liu and Wu, 2008).

Since 2004, driven by the government's 'going-out' policy, CCTV has accelerated the process of global expansion. Firstly, they restructured and reoriented CCTV-4 and CCTV-9 with an updated understanding of the ideas, contents and methods of international communication and increased the number of cultural and economic reports on these two channels (ibid.). CCTV-9 was renamed CCTV News in 2010, whose free-to-air satellite signals could be received by more than 85 million viewers, in over 100 countries and regions (CCTV, 2010). Then CCTV launched several international channels in different foreign languages (see Figure 4.1), including the E and F channels (Spanish and French) in 2004, which broadcast separately in 2008, and the CCTV-Arabic and CCTV-Russian channels in 2009. Finally, they opened the CCTV Documentary Channel in 2011. According to two overseas reports in 2013, the CCTV Documentary Channel reached more than 66 countries and regions, with nearly 50 million international users, which is close to the Discovery Channel, National Geographic Channel and other mainstream international documentary channels (Sohu Entertainment, 2014).

The Great Wall TV Platform, which was set up in 2004, is another example of the centrally managed and coordinated endeavour to enlarge and enhance the

Chinese media's penetration into the world media market. It is a TV package under CCTV with government-approved satellite channels mostly from China (i.e. CCTV and provincial satellite channels). It has so far launched its direct-to-home satellite service in the US, Europe, Canada, Asia, Africa and Latin America (Zhang, 2009).

In recent years, except for the construction of international channels, CCTV has gradually developed other methods to strengthen its international influence. CCTV's web-based TV, CNTV (China Network Television), which took the place of the former Chinese national broadcaster's official portal www.cctv.com, launched in 1996, started to operate in December 2009. The CNTV website claims to 'provide users with a globalized, multilingual and multi-terminal public webcast service platform. It offers interactive audiovisual services, integrating features of Internet-based operations with those of TV programming.' In addition to the website, CNTV also provides services like network TV, IPTV, mobile TV and other integrated broadcasting platforms. Through the distribution system of global online videos, CNTV reaches Internet users from more than 210 countries and regions and has launched six foreign channels in English, Spanish, French, Arabic, Russian and Korean.[1] The independent client CNTV-C Box had more than 22 million users abroad in 2013, and had become the first choice for overseas users to watch Chinese TV programmes (Ren and Ren, 2014).

On 1 January 2011, China Central Television announced the start of a new service – CCTV News Content – providing syndicated video news content to broadcasters worldwide. Produced by the CCTV's own news-gathering team, CCTV News Content comprises a combination of political, social, economic and cultural news.[2] CCTV News Content produces more than 100 pieces of news per day and foreign media institutions use this content about 1,500 times per day on average (Wang and Qin, 2014). CNN, BBC, NBC, NHK, KBS and other mainstream international media have already become subscribers to CCTV News Content.

In addition, CCTV has started to operate regional news centres around the world in an attempt to provide different perspectives on local stories and voice China's viewpoints on international affairs. In 2012, CCTV successively built two regional overseas production centres: CCTV America in Washington D.C. and CCTV Africa in Nairobi, Kenya. Both have high-technology newsrooms and employ Chinese journalists, as well as foreign correspondents and news anchors. CCTV has also focused on self-promotion on the most-used international social media platforms and since 2009 has set up several channel accounts on YouTube, Facebook, Twitter and Google+.

On 2 December 2014, CCTV launched China's first English short-news video mobile client 'CCTVNEWS APP' (IOS version and Android version). The client aims to provide English video content on China for overseas mobile users, another new venture for CCTV to expand its international influence. The CCTV News App was created by the CCTV English news channel, CCTV News, CCTV News Content and the technology department of CCTV, relying on the international news production team from the regional production centres of Beijing, North America and Africa, and provides users with 24-hour, targeted interactive services (Zou, 2014).

In recent years, in contrast to many Western television networks closing foreign bureaux, CCTV is speeding up its pace of 'going-out', actively improving its international broadcasting platforms and expanding its global news-gathering networks. In 2016, CCTV had two regional production centres in America and in Africa, five regional central bureaux, and 63 overseas correspondent stations.[3] CCTV broadcasts in six UN working languages through seven international channels, and more than 500 staff work overseas (Ren and Ren, 2014). In 2015, video materials produced by CCTV News Content were used by nearly 1,700 TV channels from 92 countries and regions. In 2016, CCTV broadcast in 171 foreign countries, had signed framework cooperation agreements with about 70 foreign media institutions and news exchange agreements with hundreds of foreign media institutions.[4]

CCTV has actively participated in important international film and TV festivals, such as the Cannes TV Festival and the 24th Sunshine Documentary Festival, and signed strategic cooperation agreements with the Austrian Broadcasting Corporation, BBC Worldwide, British Film and Television Production Association, and invested in 13 international co-produced projects, up to 33 hours in total. Through the 'multi-field, multi-mode, multi-regional' international documentary project, CCTV has played an important role in the international documentary market, not only as an investor, but also as a seller and cooperator (Ren and Ren, 2014).

Challenges of China's media

Given its history of going global since the 1980s, it is evident that CCTV as a central-level television broadcaster has tried to adapt itself to the new communication environment by applying cutting-edge information technologies and deploying new marketing and collaborating strategies. Nevertheless, this China-based, state-owned media organization not only poses challenges to the world communication order, but also faces challenges in a global media market, given the view of the rise of China as a threat due to a post-Cold War ideological mentality. The challenges from China and towards China characterize the encounters between CCTV and the global media structure.

In the closing chapter for *The Handbook of Political Economy of Communication*, Zhao (2011) concluded that the challenge of China has become more far-reaching, and China's political, economic, cultural and historical specificities within the global political economy should be carefully and critically examined. Following Zhao's theoretical claim, this chapter frames the challenge of China to the world from both the international level and the global level. At the international level, the rise of China is embodied in its increasing competency in cross-border trade and international relations. Sovereignty, economic independence and strength are always highlighted in international encounters.

At the global level, the nature of China's challenge to the existing world order and contribution to the well-being of humankind is not only to counter the scepticism as to whether China can develop well in a post-Cold War neoliberal global context given its socialist political and economic settings (for example, by greatly reducing its huge poverty levels), but also whether China can provide the world with an alternative mode of thinking for sustainable social development. The latter is perhaps best exemplified by the intellectual debates about the shift following the collapse of the Washington Consensus to the rise of the Beijing Consensus after the financial crisis in 2009 (Ramo, 2004). As a result, intentionally or not, China is now playing more of a leading role in both international relations and in the restructuring of a new world political-economic order.

Its political and economic rise drives China to pursue greater cultural influence over the world. At a symposium with Chinese intellectuals in May 2016, President Xi Jinping said: 'We have solved the problems of being beaten and starvation, now it is time to deal with the problem of being scolded in the international community.' Therefore, he suggests that a new discourse system should be developed to facilitate mutual understanding between China and the world, and finally, to promote China's soft power (Xi, 2016).

In this context, CCTV going global has a twofold meaning if the challenge of China to the established global order is to be understood. First, as with Al Jazeera and RT, CCTV's rise on the global stage represents the 'rise of the Rest' in the global media landscape and second, it also contributes to the diversity, and possibly the democratization of international communication, particularly in some specific regional markets, for example, Africa. By localizing its production, collaborating with local TV networks and internationalizing its employees, CCTV has become an emerging competitor in those markets.

Yun Fan, General Manager of CCTV News, concluded that the final goal of 'going-out' is 'from the outside in' (Fan, 2013). Borrowing the lessons from marketing, he said, in order to widen the influence and 'touch the soil' of targeted markets, CCTV has adopted a set of 'glocalization' strategies, which are proving quite successful, particularly in African countries, where the first overseas television news production centre was launched in Nairobi in 2012 (ibid.). In relation to Chinese media going into Africa, he has identified three localizing strategies, namely the localization of content (i.e. African content), production team and media channels (e.g. incorporating CCTV-developed programmes in the local TV network) (ibid.).

Similarly focusing on the localization of CCTV's ambitions in promoting its influence in Africa, Gorfinkel *et al.* (2014) conducted a small-scale pilot study from the perspective of reception/audience. They identified three challenges for CCTV Africa: attempting to simultaneously target 'African', 'Western' and Chinese audience groups, which may detract from its ability to appeal to specific international audiences; competition from other international and local broadcasters who already have a strong audience base, and a lack of accessibility, awareness and sustained interest in the channel (ibid.).

No matter how competitive those markets are, CCTV has successfully joined the battle over the global and regional television audience, but this is only one side of the story. On the other hand, the voice of China through CCTV's operation and programming is widely recognized as different from those of its Western counter-parts over global and regional affairs. Two aspects can be identified. First, the initial overseas production centre of CCTV was launched in Kenya, rather than in a Western country. As the vice director of CCTV's news department, Yi Li, said, 'The opening of CCTV's first overseas center is not only a great-leap-forward development for CCTV in Africa, but also a great leap for CCTV's international communication capacity' (Liu, 2012). This geopolitical decision shows how China's leadership and CCTV imagine the future of global communication featuring the rise of the Rest, and arguably how to rebuild the historic ties between China and Africa, and certainly other developing and underdeveloped countries, in pursuit of a just and balanced world communication order. Second, CCTV recruited a number of local employees in order not only to make the reporting familiar and close to the local audience, but also to open a space for local people to tell their own stories in their own ways. If we recognize that the essence of international communication is the internationalization of local stories, CCTV's localization strategies really capture the key to open dialogue with its audience from politically and culturally different societies. The centrality of CCTV, as implied by its name, should be reconsidered if its future is imagined and planned as an authentic global media player.

While CCTV and other Chinese media intend to play a stronger role in global communication, the challenges from the existing global media market towards China are also obvious. Changming Zhang, former vice director of CCTV, believes that there are two major challenges for CCTV's going global, or in a broader sense, for China's international communication. They are the unbalanced structure of the global media landscape in which the Western media play a dominant role, and the ideological contestation between Western media and Chinese media (Yu, 2008).

Based on a brief historical review of China's television going-out, Chang and Yu (2014) identified three challenges for strengthening the international communication capacity of China's television, including ideological differences, intercultural barriers (e.g. language and cultural tradition), and the single and monopolistic role of CCTV. They then provided a series of recommendations: first, prioritizing TV drama and documentaries that have less political colour when sustaining the mouthpiece role of news programmes; second, make the most use of new media technologies to facilitate the landing of China's television in overseas markets; and third, securing the central role of CCTV but also employing market mechanisms by including other players like regional TV stations, private TV production companies and overseas communication organizations (ibid.).

In a word, both the monopolistic market structure and post-Cold War ideological conflicts are pulling CCTV back from further global expansion and penetration. If the market structure is changing slightly because of the entrance of CCTV as a competitor from China, the ideological stereotype seems hardly to change within a short period of time. The ownership of CCTV by the Chinese state, which is led by the Chinese Communist Party, the censorship by the Party and Chinese government of international reporting and other programming, and personnel management are always the subject of intense criticism by international media. On 19 February 2016, President Xi paid a visit to three state-owned media, the *People's Daily*, the

Xinhua news agency and CCTV. At a meeting with propaganda officials and media managers after the visit, he re-emphasized the organizing principles of the state-owned media, particularly the control of the Party over those media, and pointed out innovation strategies for those media to be at the frontier of information and communication technologies, to adapt to the dynamics of the climate of opinion, and finally to secure the cultural leadership of the Party. Interestingly, if we look at the reporting of Xi's media tour by the international media, especially from the West, the focus of their narrative is overwhelmingly on Party control over media, with a simplistic understanding of the relationship between media and power in China, no matter how diversified media have developed inside and outside China.

Therefore, there is a dilemma facing CCTV's going-out practices. Though the mainstream Western media, and other regional media highly influenced by them, criticize its closeness to the Chinese state, CCTV's operation and global expansion is certainly an extension of the soft-power initiative of the Chinese state on the global stage, while the affiliation of CCTV to the Chinese state and the Party is a natural outcome drawn from its history. It seems as if no solution can be found at this moment. In the last part of this chapter, we provide a way of rethinking CCTV in a changing world communication order and a theoretical attempt to resolve the dilemma for the development of CCTV in the future.

Conclusion: CCTV and the changing world communication order

In the examination of the ambiguities of China's media going-out project, Hu and Ji (2012: 36) stated that 'the newly issued media "going-out" plan not only involves neoliberal, market-oriented ambitions, it has also inherited a historic drive for developing countries to embrace a global communications system that is so far serving Western-based transnational monopolies'. As an addition to this statement, regarding the case of CCTV, it is also important to recognize that CCTV represents a different approach of imagining and achieving a global media status. What characterizes the difference of CCTV?

First, CCTV is by definition a state-owned media organization of China, which represents the official voice of China, not a private company, and not a non-governmental entity. Thus, the operation and voice of CCTV explicitly represent the authority of the Chinese state and the national image of China. The global expansion of CCTV is accordingly the extension of China's influence in the world. Any discussion about the role of CCTV in the changing world communication order should be based on this definition.

Second, CCTV's expansion has both market and geopolitical implications. The first overseas production centre set up in Africa shows that China's official television broadcaster intended to prioritize the underdeveloped African markets and simultaneously mobilize political legacies between China and African countries from the twentieth century to enhance the competency of CCTV against Western counterparts in those markets. But the other overseas production centre of CCTV was established later on in the political centre of the US, which also means that CCTV does not want to be ignored and isolated by the most powerful country in the world. Therefore, the map of CCTV's expansion is geographically global, including both the Global South and Global North, but geopolitically incoherent. If the world is unequal and full of injustice, particularly because of the long-established centre–periphery relations between developed and developing or underdeveloped countries, how should CCTV position itself in terms of its outreach?

If CCTV simply performs like a global media company that wants to maximize audience reach and increase global and regional audience ratings in exchange for advertising income, how can it fulfil its state-owned media promise of promoting China and articulate the voice of China on a global stage? This is a potential dilemma for CCTV, namely the incompatibility between market expansion and increase of political influence. So far, the relative importance of these is ambiguous in that the political vision for a different world communication order and the role of CCTV are not clear at all.

Third, maybe because CCTV is still at the early stage of going global, the local-ization of its operation in specific markets is not well-developed. Gorfinkel *et al.*'s (2014) audience study for CCTV Africa in Kenya and South Africa revealed that demographic variables including race and education level are key to audiences accessing CCTV Africa in these two countries. In order to penetrate such societies with diverse cultural traditions and social complexities, CCTV needs to undertake more sociological analysis instead of looking only at technical and market expan-sion.

It is widely recognized in the field of media theory and practice that interna-tional communication is a largely US-originated, nationalistic-oriented, and top-down form of communication, no matter whether mediated or non-mediated (Jiang and Huang, 2009). Therefore, the space of international communication is not linear in terms of both the dissemination and reception of information, and the construction and deconstruction of meaning. Contested relations exist at both the global and regional level. Against this background, the role of CCTV in the changing world communication order is uncertain due to the interplay of outside and inside forces. There is a possibility for CCTV to become as powerful and profitable as the Western transnational media giants, but the possibility also exists for CCTV to become a globally recognized responsible media organization working for a just and democratic world communication order. The future is in our hands and the world is watching.

Notes

1 See www.cntv.cn/special/guanyunew/PAGE13818868795101875/index.shtml.
2 See http://newscontent.cctv.com/public/about_new.jsp.
3 About CCTV: www.cctv.cn/2016/02/17/ARTIoXBRYeNy9KNg3i4iTpO0160217.shtml.
4 About CCTV: www.cctv.cn/2016/02/17/ARTIoXBRYeNy9KNg3i4iTpO0160217.shtml.

References

CCTV (2010) The CCTV's International News Channel CCTV-9 is Renamed CCTV News. Available at: http://china-screen-news.com/2010/04/the-cctvs-international-news-channel-cctv-9-is-renamed-cctv-news/.

Chang, Jiang and Yu, Hongyan (2014) Problems and suggestions: Modeling the external communication for China's television, *International Communications*, 2: 30–32.

Chen, Chwen Chwen (2014) CCTV Going Global in a Digital Scenario. Available at: http://blogs.nottingham.ac.uk/chinapolicyinstitute/2014/11/17/cctv-going-global-in-a-digital-scenario-some-reflections/.

Fan, Yun (2013) From going outside to going inside: The localizing strategies of CCTV-NEWS, *TV Research*, 7: 16–18.

Gorfinkel, Lauren; Joffe, Sandy; Van Staden, Cobus and Wu, Yu-Shan (2014) CCTV's global outreach: Examining the audiences of China's 'new voice' on Africa, *Media International Australia*, 151: 81–88.

Hu, Zhengrong and Ji, Deqiang (2012). Ambiguities in communicating with the world: The 'Going-out' policy of China's media and its multilayered contexts, *Chinese Journal of Communication*, 5(1): 32–37.

Jiang, Fei and Huang, Kuo (2009) Clarifying the theoretical framework of intercultural communication, *Journalism and Communication*, 6: 53–63.

Liu, Xiaoying and Wu, Yan (2008) CCTV's international communication and influence, *Modern Communication*, 5: 42–45.

Liu, Zhen (2012) Showing a Real Africa to the World. *Guangming Daily*, 2 January.

Ramo, Joshua Cooper (2004) The Beijing Consensus. The Foreign Policy Centre. Available at: http://fpc.org.uk/fsblob/244.pdf.

Ren, Xuean and Ren, Yonglei (2014) The developing status and strategical view of CCTV's international communication. *Annual Report on the Development of China's International Communication*. Beijing: Social Science Academic Press: 98–108.

Si, Si (2014) Expansion of International Broadcasting: The Growing Global Reach of China Central Television. Available at: https://reutersinstitute.politics.ox.ac.uk/sites/default/files/Expansion%20of%20International%20Broadcasting_0.pdf.

Sohu Entertainment (2014) The Strengths of CCTV Documentary Channel. Available at: http://yule.sohu.com/20140302/n395885463.shtml.

Tan, Tian and Yu, Fanqi (2009) From going-out to going-in: On the strategic innovation of external communication for China's television, *China Television*, 9: 43–46.

Tang, Shiding (2003) *The Origin and Changes of CCTV*. Beijing: Oriental Press.

Walker, Christopher; Plattner, Marc and Diamond, Larry (2016) Authoritarianism Goes Global. Available at: www.the-american-interest.com/2016/03/28/authoritarianism-goes-global/.

Wang, Bin and Qin, Han (2014) Make concessions in order to gain advantages – an analysis of the communication concept of CCTV News Content, *International Communications*, 5: 42–44.

Xi, Jinping (2016) Building the Philosophy and Social Sciences with Chinese Characteristics. Available at: http://news.qq.com/a/20160522/035768.htm.

Yu, Miao (2008) Let CCTV's programmes touch every corner of the world: An interview with the vice director of CCTV Changming Zhang, *International Communications*, 5: 8–13.

Zhang, Xiaolin (2009) *Chinese State Media Going Global*. Available at: www.eai.nus.edu.sg/publications/files/Vol2No1_ZhangXiaoling.pdf.

Zhao, Yuezhi (2011) The Challenge of China: Contribution to a Transcultural Political Economy of Communication in the 21st Century, in Wasko, J.; Murdoch, G. and

Sousa, H. (eds.) *The Handbook of Political Economy of Communications*. Malden: Blackwell: 558–582.

Zhao, Yuezhi (2014) Communication, crisis, and global power shifts: An introduction, *International Journal of Communication*, 8: 275–300.

Zou, Linjuan (2014) New Experiment for CCTV's International Communication: Launch Ceremony of CCTV NEWS APP. Available at: www.chinadaily.com.cn/hqcj/xfly/2014-12-02/content_12823810.html.

5

SOFT POWER AND THE STRATEGIC CONTEXT FOR CHINA'S 'MEDIA GOING GLOBAL' POLICY

Suzanne Xiao Yang

This chapter examines the strategic context in which China's 'media going global' policy decisions were made, the public and intellectual discourse that has since surrounded the policy and the approaches that have so far been taken to implement the policy. It analyses the rationale, the methods and the causal beliefs underlying the policy and its implementation. In so doing, the chapter reveals how the notion of soft power is interpreted in Chinese official and intellectual discourse on China's global reach, and in what ways some of these interpretations, still contested or contrasted, play out in state initiatives to strengthen external communication in pursuing deep transcultural understanding, an ongoing process in which various actors are involved and their actions, though not always, coordinated.

It argues that the 'media going global' initiatives, as part of the national strategy promoting China's influence within its positioning as an alternative power in the world, unlike what many observers believe, are as much focused on short-term economic concerns as they are on long-term political and cultural benefits for China. The intention to project China as it is onto the world stage, however, this chapter observes, does not seem to be well matched with the limited capability and experience of Chinese media operating effectively in a global context, a painful realization acknowledged among officials, media analysts and professionals. This is captured often by the catchphrase 'discourse power deficiency' on China's part, to which the leadership want to bring changes (Li, 2008; Lu, 2010).

The policy decisions to globalize Chinese media are believed to be the key to increasing China's 'discourse power' on the world stage. Huge resources have been poured in to boost a media industry that is expected to rival BBC or CNN, with mixed and largely unsatisfactory results. Notwithstanding some degree of success in projecting an image of China as a benign rising power, mainly among developing countries, for instance, critics point to a soft-power deficit in this strategy, owing to a lack of core values that would need to appeal to the more technologically advanced and predominantly liberal societies. This chapter suggests that intellectual and policy engagement with the national strategy to globalize Chinese media still needs to address issues concerning cross-cultural differences in terms of perceptions, expectations, discourse rivalry and cultural frames of reference, as well as challenges mounted by Chinese state-run media's dual identity as both commodity and ideology.

Strategic context and intellectual and official discourse

Through the policy of economic reforms (reform and opening up 改革开放) launched in December 1978, generations of Chinese leaders since Deng Xiaoping have managed to loosen control of domestic economic liberty whilst maintaining a degree of firm control over political and social liberty (Vogel, 2011). By creating and sustaining a system of market economy with Chinese characteristics, China has thrived in the international system, despite various predictions that it would collapse (Chang, 2001; Shamburgh, 2015). Now the second largest economy in the world measured by gross domestic product (GDP) at market exchange rates, forecast to overtake the US within this decade,[1] China plays an increasingly important role in the multi-directional, transnational flow of goods, capital, information, knowledge, human resources and ideas. It is one of the main destinations for foreign direct investment as well as one of the largest outward foreign investors. A major global buyer of commodities, China's import growth remains at 6–7% in 2015–2016, as a result of a new growth model to rebalance the economy in favour of domestic consumption, still an impressive rate despite the decline from 10% a year in 2010 and 8% from 2011 to 2014 (Kireyev and Leonidov, 2016). Moreover, among the top 50 world major cities expected to be the powerhouses of global growth by 2030, China will have 17, according to a study conducted by Oxford Economics (Oxford Economics, 2015).[2] China's increasing share of world trade and GDP justifies greater use of the renminbi, which is on track to becoming a major reserve currency. Renminbi centres have been established in various major finance capitals from Frankfurt, Paris and London to New York. The Chinese renminbi has been determined to be freely useable and included as the fifth currency, along with the dollar, the euro, the pound and the yen, into the Special Drawing Rights (SDR) basket from 1 October 2016 (International Monetary Fund, 2016). Arguably, the renminbi is replacing the main part of the euro's role in the SDR. Embedding the remninbi into the international financial system helps to 'pave the way for broader use of the renminbi in trade and finance, securing China's standing as a global economic power' (Bradshernov, 2015). On a global level, China has sought to consolidate and increase its status as a major power, through what is often dubbed a 'charm offensive' (Kurlantzick, 2008), with the principle of attaching no conditionality to aid, loans and donations, extending investment and business projects to developing countries. As noted earlier, China's increasing influence in economic and financial areas is not limited to the developing world.

Perception of China as a strategic rival to the USA and as a threat to liberal values

Whilst China's economic expansion and diplomacy win cooperation and friendship across continents, particularly in parts of Africa, South America and Eastern Europe, the West casts a suspicious eye on China, uncertain whether it is using its economic influence to jeopardize or diminish the role of liberal values in international cooperation and global governance. The 'China threat theory' (Segal, 1996; Roy, 1996; Kang, 2007), widely debated since the late 1990s, with repercussions in recent years, especially in Asian countries where the South China Sea becomes a locus of contention, goes diametrically against the Chinese government's stated intention to project the image of a peace-loving and benevolent nation and benign rising power onto the world stage (Wang, H., 2003; Wang, G., 2011). China is criticized, for instance, for being at least disingenuous, at the 2014 Shangri-La Dialogue, for such claims as 'Chinese people having no tradition' or 'no gene' for invasion (Tiezzi, 2014). Analysts suggest that the dismissal of real concerns among Southeast Asian countries in relation to China's ambitions in the region creates more worries, rather than solving any problem, perceived or real (ibid.). Much as it was in the 1990s, in this view it is argued that 'American strategists are correct to label China a "threat" in the sense of a likely aspirant to regional dominance' in today's Asia-Pacific (Roy, 1996: 767). This is consistent with 'offensive realist' views about China's rise and the implications for the global order, which emphasize the so-called 'Thucydides trap' with the existing power and the emerging power colliding unavoidably. The logic for the 'China threat theory' which emerged in the 1990s primarily in Asia and has since gained influence in the US, is perhaps best captured in Roy's summary:

> If China fulfils its expected potential, it will soon be a power in the class of 19th century Britain, the Soviet Union, Nazi Germany, Pacific War Japan, and 20th century America. Each of those countries used its superior power to establish some form of hegemony to protect and promote its interests. There is no convincing reason to think China as a great power will depart from this pattern. If the opportunity arises to establish a dominant role in the region, China can be expected to seize it.
>
> *(Roy, 1996: 762)*

In responding to the question of whether China can rise peacefully, Chicago international relations scholar John Mearsheimer provides a most provocative validation, through detailed historical observation, of the offensive realism theory. For him the United States, determined to remain the world's sole regional hegemony, 'will go to great lengths' to prevent a rising China, which whilst rising rapidly, 'will seek to dominate Asia' (Mearsheimer, 2001, 2014 updated version). 'Swimming against the prevailing tide of academic opinion', Mearsheimer maintains that the tragedy of great power politics is inescapable (Roberts, 2002).

Caution against China's rise does not stop with Mearsheimer's predictions: China is viewed not only as a rival of the US in global affairs, but a danger to democracy and its associated values. Apart from the offensive realist perspective, Gary Klintworth observes other origins of such antagonist views against an emerging China: 'In our mind's eye, we have that Napoleonic image of China as an awakening Chinese dragon . . . It is non-European, non-democratic and avowedly, the last communist stronghold left in the world' (Klintworth, 1994 quoted in Roy, 1996: 765). A number of policy analysts and opinion leaders have made suggestions for major powers to contain China's rise. Ikenberry, international relations scholar at Princeton, for instance, suggests that the US alone will not be able to counterbalance China's rise and the consequence of undermining liberal values and therefore the US and Europe must unite to act in containing China to preserve and protect the liberal world. At the heart of the containment strategy is the recruitment of allies to join a coalition to balance Chinese power (Ikenberry, 2008, 2012; Krauthammer, 1995).

China's state-orchestrated, painstaking efforts so far to project itself as a peace-loving country, epitomized in the vernacular of its official statements, with state-designed memes such as 'peaceful rise' (Zheng, 2005) and 'peaceful development' (Jia, 2005; Glaser and Medeiros, 2007; People's Republic of China, Information Office of the State Council, 2011) and their lengthy elaborations and redeploy-ments, appear to have little resonance with a mainstream world media more inter-ested in its own view of an assertive China, a view that rarely shows evidence of nuanced, sophisticated analysis of China's state identity (Wang, G., 2011; Swaine, 2010; Swaine and Fravel, 2011; Johnston, 2013; Chen *et al.*, 2013–2014). Al-Rodhan (2007: 62) observes that 'journalists, strategic thinkers and pundits in the United States have sensationalized their claims by painting an all-powerful, threatening China bent on destruction of the United States'. Many media players in Europe appear to be no less inclined towards a narrow, negative depiction of China than their American counterparts. In the 2008 Olympic torch relays, mainstream Western media, BBC and CNN included, criticized China's Tibet policies and human rights issues. Protests against the Chinese government spread in all major cities through which the Olympic torch passed. For many Chinese, along with their government, this was certainly an occasion of public embarrassment. Some even took Western media's editorial choices as deliberately generated humiliation for China, which in turn provoked a strong wave of anti-West nationalism in China.

One shared sentiment was that this was yet another piece of evidence that it was difficult for China to enjoy full membership of the international system, in the sense of becoming fully accepted as 'one of us'.[3] Media analysts and practitioners regarded this as a propaganda war, a media battle between CNN, the BBC and Chinese media, which was unequal, given the disparity in terms of media communication capacity, so that China could not win despite all the statistical indicators pointing to a rising economic superpower performing remarkably well. That the editorial frame-work for decisions at various 'China critical' Western media outlets is not clear to Chinese observers (some driven by proprietors' or other stakeholder agendas, and not necessarily representational of national or regional readership's viewpoint or subscribers' view of China) serves to further widen the chasm of understanding.

Discourse power deficiency

It is widely believed in China that it has been misrepresented in Western media and that this has led to distorted views of the country in the West. Officials, media analysts and the general public in China often express frustration at the various misunderstandings of China by Western governments and media, and complain about the deep-rooted bias and prejudice against it (Barboza, 2010; Tan, 2013). For instance, despite being regarded as policy goals in Chinese public and official discourse, the peaceful rise and the harmonious world may be perceived outside China as tools Chinese politicians use to promote the position China deserves in international relations. The Chinese government's willingness to act as a responsible great power offering its services in maintaining world order and security, its participation in the global war against terrorism, and active engagement in the six-party talks concerning North Korea and in the Iranian nuclear crisis, is interpreted as serving only Sino-centric goals. At the National People's Congress in March 2010, the then Foreign Minister Yang Jiechi suggested 'people [in the West] stop looking at the country through tinted glasses, and abandon stereotyped perceptions, particularly bias'. He opined that 'China's uniqueness and national circumstances' are not appreciated in the West (Yang, 2010).

Such perception gaps exist across a number of key issue areas. Whilst the Chinese adhere to territorial integrity and sovereignty as an expression of Chinese non-aggressiveness, their claims in the South China Sea are viewed not only as assertive but as violating international norms and laws of the sea. When Chinese officials emphasize the interdependency between China's economy and the global markets, and as a result, in order to secure its economic growth and political and social stability, China does not intend to change the existing world order, Western media cite cases such as the South China Sea disputes, which are interpreted as revisionist (People's Republic of China, Information Office of the State Council, 2011, 2015; Yan, 2014; Zhang, 2015). Moreover, the historical arguments, as advanced in China's Ministry of Foreign Affairs statements, for the defensive character of Chinese foreign and security policy, tend to be dismissed.[4] The CCP's (Chinese Communist Party) Central Propaganda Department Head, Liu Qibao, argued in an article in *Guangming Daily*, 'There are always some people who wear colored glasses to see China. They view the country through the lenses of "China threat theory"' (Liu, 2014).

Perceptual gaps aside, Chinese officials and intellectuals have keenly observed a disparity between China's economic strengths and its increasing political influence in some parts of the world, and its weakness in projecting a national image that matches an emerging global power's status (Wang, H., 2003). Furthermore, they find China in an awkward position in terms of getting its messages across to their intended audiences in the world. Part of their reflection points to a self-realization about the incompetency and inadequacy of China's communication skills and media, lacking discourse power (*hua yu quan* 话语权). The lack of discourse power in part is due to the hegemony of Western media. As analysts Wang and Lv observe:

Associated Press, Agence France Press, United Press International and Reuters supply more than 80% of the news reported around the world, and about

50 top media in the West own 95% of the share of the global market, with 75% TV programmes being produced by American media; 60–80% TV programme content supply to the third world is from US media.

(Wang and Lv, 2011)

Chinese media analysts and practitioners maintain that despite the increased input in multi-media technologies and the rapidly enlarged numbers of different types of media, China is by no means a media power – as presented in the West, particularly American media – that holds discourse power. Chinese media professionals reckon that Western media power and influence cannot be easily matched (ibid.). Despite an awareness of the main role of media in the Western democracies being critical of governments and their policies, Chinese officials tend to be hypersensitive to any form of criticism, and feel unable to effectively defend their positions.

The actual or perceived deficiency of China's discourse power has been widely discussed among international relations scholars, diplomats and media policy analysts, where its features, causes and remedies are identified or suggested. For instance, in Zhang's view, the mindset of *Yu Shijie Jiegui* (与世界接轨), 'to be geared to international standard' or 'to be integrated into the global community', consistent with, and corollary of, the opening and reform policy, salient since the 1990s, means being enmeshed into the discourse of the West. According to Zhang, this contributed to the loss of China's own voice, causing its views to be aired with no input from indigenous Chinese concepts. He suggests that this approach misses the opportunity to build up China's long-term media status (Guo, 2003; Zhang, 2009).

For media analysts, the lack of input from Chinese ideas and notions or its political discourse is largely due to an inability to pass on to the world particular knowledge about Chinese culture and history. Ming Anxiang, Director of the Institute of Journalism and Communication at Chinese Academy of Social Sciences, claims that 'the *discourse power deficiency* made it hard for a nation's image not to be distorted in another nation's media', meaning first-hand information and knowledge about cultural and political differences are key to the projection of a nation's image. Ming goes on to state: 'for our genuine and authentic voice to be heard, to present an organic and truthful image of a nation, it is a must to create our own international media' (quoted from Wang and Lv 2011, author's translation and emphasis). Zhao Qizheng, Dean of the School of Journalism and Communication at Renmin University of China, put it simpler: 'If you don't tell China's stories, others will do; if you don't tell true stories (of China), false stories go far' (ibid.).

A more elaborate discussion held by media professionals about China's discourse power deficiency is seen in an article published with *Qiu Shi Magazine* (求是杂志) in its Theory Section (理论版) in 2010. This article, published in the name of Xinhua news agency Deputy Director Lu Wei, is entitled 'National Discourse Power and Information Security against the Background of Economic Globalization.[5] According to Lu, *hua yu quan* (话语权), or national discourse power, or national discourse right, can be explained by understanding the key words *hua yu*, i.e. 'discourse' and *quan*, i.e. 'power' or 'right':

> The word 'discourse' originated in cultural linguistics long ago, it refers to the exchange of meanings between a speaker and a recipient by means of language and other such symbols. Following the development of the times, the content and extent of 'discourse' have seen a profound expansion of meaning. Once 'discourse' is formed, it communicates specific value views, there are specific norms, and specific knowledge systems are built. '*Quan*' has a double meaning in law, one of 'right' and one of 'power', this means that '*hua yu quan*' not only refers to the right to speak but also to the fact that the effectiveness and power of speech must be guaranteed.
>
> *(Lu, 2010/2014)*

National discourse power, or *hua yu quan*, according to Lu,

> is the influence of a country's 'speech' in the world. It can be divided into political discourse power, economic discourse power, cultural discourse power, military discourse power, foreign affairs discourse power, public opinion discourse power, etc. Against the background of economic globalization, economic discourse power decides a country's influence, financial discourse power lies at its strength, and it includes both levels of collection power and communication power.
>
> *(Lu, 2010/2014)*

The Western developed countries, as Lu further elaborates, with strong advantages in the sectors of economy, military, science and technology, are 'the "speakers" at public occasions'; their discourse structures 'have become [the] global "prevalent discourse"'. Such discourse structures in turn contain 'latent discursive hegemony, depriving other countries of the right to speak, to say even less about their discursive power'. In contrast, and as a consequence of such hegemony, the 'current state of developing countries' discourse power can be described as a deficiency of discourse power: they are not able to communicate, what is communicated becomes distorted, they are not able to collect, and what they collect is unreliable' (ibid.).

The policy decision to globalize Chinese media

The advocates for strengthening Chinese discourse power suggest that instead of passively waiting for the Western media to alter their perspectives about China's ascendance as an economic and political power, Chinese media must take proactive steps to go global to gain discourse power. Since Western media will never 'automatically bring about positive and favourable views about China', in media analyst Sun's view, it becomes an imperative for China to act to strengthen its media communication capacity (Sun, 2010: 59). Chinese media needs to 'push Chinese perspectives and voices into the international arena in order to contest the discursive power of the West' (ibid.).

Media as a tool to consolidate and improve China's economic status

One way to do so is to start breaking the monopoly of information in the global markets of Western information organizations. Lu (2010/2014) addresses the issue of developing countries using second-hand data. In terms of how to strengthen Chinese media's communication ability, Lu suggests that it is necessary to enhance its ability to collect first-hand data. He indicates that the lack of ability to communicate in the global economic and financial markets, on the part of developing countries, China included, is due to their inability to collect information. Lu illustrates this view by describing how selective or limited stock exchange information about China is posted in Wall Street: on any particular day, information posted there tended to be disdained by the collectors' 'value system', resulting in failure to give valuable or balanced information to the global commodities market enabling objective decisions (Lu, 2010/2014). For Chinese financial information collection and communication to be meaningful it must avoid it being 'done by others according to their value system'; Lu emphasizes that China needs to have its own platform to carry out the selection and broadcasting of first-hand data, presenting China as it is (ibid.).

Recognizing this and aiming to inform their policy analysis and decision making with data collected first-hand, the Chinese CCP Central Committee together with the PRC State Council decided in 2008 to task Xinhua news agency to set up a financial information collection point in Wall Street. Dubbed 'Xinhua 08', this platform 'focuses on the renminbi market, and has become an important auxiliary project in the progress of renminbi internationalization'. Lu observes that it is so far the only such platform 'established by a developing country' (Lu, 2010/2014). As to in what ways such efforts have strengthened China's discourse power, Lu states, this 'highly efficient, reliable and safe system with indigenous intellectual property rights' has been successful in providing 'information and trading support services to financial bodies and non-financial enterprises who participate in global financial trading, filling a lacuna for developing countries' (Lu, 2010/2014). He further elaborates that Xinhua

> has successively established financial information collection points in global financial centres; it strives to expand China's market information communication power, and has established service networks in many languages and for many kinds of terminals aimed at global financial markets, it has the ability to communicate information in all kinds of weathers, and has realized three-dimensional publication for computer terminals, mobile terminals, video terminals, the Internet, the big screen, etc. Through providing renminbi asset analysis tools and pricing models, as well as renminbi asset trading support systems, it has raised pricing power over renminbi assets.
>
> *(ibid.)*

Much as the 'media going global' policy works for China on the world financial market, it should serve as a remedy for China's discourse power deficiency more broadly. China's ambition to increase Chinese media's communication capability goes beyond strengthening its ability to promote and consolidate China's economic status by way of, for example, strengthening its ability to collect and communicate first-hand information.

On a larger scale, to match the speed, extent and strength of Chinese economic and social development, Li Changchun, Minister of CCP Central Committee Propaganda Department, in a speech made in 2008 celebrating the 50th anniversary of the establishment of Central Chinese Television, stated the urgency of increasing Chinese media capacity:

> To strengthen our communication capacity is a matter of urgency. It concerns the international standing of China; it concerns the growth of China's cultural soft power; and it concerns the place and function of Chinese media in the international community of public opinion. Our first and foremost mission from now on is to strengthen our communication capacity inside and outside China. Everyone should be aware of this responsibility and mission.
>
> *(Li, 2008)*

Battle for ideas and Chinese public diplomacy

China recognizes the need for a battle for ideas to define and project its cultural, social and ideological values in the international media discourse. The Chinese government and CCP have, particularly since the Beijing Olympics in 2008, attached great importance to the role media can play in increasing China's influence over the world that is in proportion to China's economic power and its globally important rich civilization heritage and identity (Zhang, 2010a). Globalizing Chinese media and promoting Chinese public diplomacy go hand in hand as a package tool to help the outside world understand China, improving China's international image. Chinese media analysts are concerned that Western values, prevalent in international media, are often found to clash with Chinese official views or values (Zhang, 2010a). Yet Chinese media are so heavily reliant on the media monopolized by the West, in this view, that the international major news media agenda in China is actually framed by American media, illustrated by 80% CCTV world news being bought from US media organizations (Zhao, 2008). Li Xiguang, Dean of Tsinghua University School of Journalism and Communication, observes that, as a consequence of such reliance, the everyday life of Chinese people has been deeply influenced by the US in many ways, from officials, scholars and scientists, to the general public (Li, 2009).

In terms of how to break the Western media monopoly, taking into account the improvement in economic and financial information collection and communication, China must at least endeavour to change the asymmetrical and one-way flow of communication in other areas. Zhao (2008), a specialist in the study of US monopoly of world news, points out that China needs its own powerful media to project China's image by way of influencing perceptions, and the way to do it is through truthfully expressing China's viewpoints. The key for Zhao (2008) is to establish credibility and status for Chinese media over time. In doing so, China needs to promote Chinese core cultural values that are compatible with China's increasingly important economic influence, and for cultural appeal. Such values are expected to be compatible with Western views in a broader discourse.

The government has made considerable efforts to modernize its foreign propaganda apparatus, actively engaging with overseas publicity since the 1990s. The Informational Office of the State Council was set up in 1991, tasked with

> assist[ing] news media in presenting aspects of China to the world, including its domestic and foreign policies, economic and social development, and its history, science, technology, education and culture, by coordinating reports for both domestic and foreign journalists, organizing news conferences, and providing books, information, television and film products about China.[6]

In 2004, the Ministry of Foreign Affairs set up a Division of Public Diplomacy. Public diplomacy of a sort, overseas communication and overseas publicity have been a major aspect of the work of the Chinese propaganda system, initially limited to conducting communication and exchanges with developing countries in Asia, Africa and Latin America, many of whom belonged to the 'socialist camp'. For a long time, magazines and journals such as *Beijing Review*, *China Pictorial* and *China Today* played a major role in Chinese overseas publicity. Such overseas publicity was primarily concerned with political and ideological content. As Zhang has documented, until the late 1970s the main media were branches of Xinhua news agency in the developing countries, with paper media such as *People's China* and *China Construction*, and broadcaster China Radio International. The use of TV stations was limited to exchanging documentaries with communist TV stations in other countries (Zhang, 2010b: 43).

Public diplomacy activities have been centrally managed and coordinated, with CCTV taking the leading role and provincial and local TV stations mainly providing it with programmes. The State Administration of Radio, Film and Television issued a notice in 2004 stipulating that without its approval no TV station or radio station would be allowed to rent or buy airtime or establish radio and TV stations abroad. To ensure coordination and consistency in overseas publicity work, an annual conference on TV overseas publicity coordination was held with participants from both central and local TV stations (Zhang, 2010b: 47). In 2009, the decision was made to push Chinese media forward, enabling it to engage with and integrate into the world marketplace of competing ideas. Hence, Chinese media now seek to establish relationships with the foreign public as their audience, moving away from propaganda. They perform under the constraints of the party-state system, in addition to market rules. Chinese media present China's own version of events occurring inside China, Asia and the world. News reports are mainly on business, cultural activities, sports, presenting successes in Chinese economic and social sectors. It tends to 'show active defence of sensitive issues for which China is criticised, giving much prominence to China's environmental protection, political and social stability, national cohesion (especially on issues of Taiwan and Tibet), anti-corruption, human rights and reduction of poverty' (Zhang, 2010b: 47).

Culture as an industry

In tandem with the national initiatives to utilize public diplomacy to shape and enhance China's new image across the world, the 'media going global' policy aims to increase and extend China's global influence beyond the economic market to the cultural and creative industries, not only for competitiveness in the global marketplace for ideas but also for revenues (People's Republic of China, Information Office of the State Council, 2015–2016). In 2009, the Chinese State Council declared culture a strategic industry. The 17th Central Committee of the Communist Party of China approved a guideline on boosting reform of the cultural sector and cultural development at its sixth plenary session. Subsequently, huge public and private investment has flowed into the creative and cultural sector. The output of what is termed the cultural industry (文化产业) is aimed to account for 5% of China's GDP in 2016, said PRC Cultural Minister Cai Wu, adding that the culture industry should be 'a pillar of the national economy' (Cai, 2009). In 2010, governments at all levels invested more than 150 billion yuan in cultural development, doubling that of 2006.

As a result of financial and policy support, the culture industry in China has grown at a rate faster than the growth of GDP. According to the Annual Report of Chinese Cultural Innovation (2016), 'in 2002–2012, countrywide total investment into public culture increased from 30.029 billion yuan to 226.835 billion yuan', with a remarkable annual growth of 18.35% (Wang, 2016). In 2010, the total output of the culture industry in China hit 1.1 trillion yuan and, in some cities and provinces, the ratio has surpassed 5%.[7] Growing faster than GDP in 2002–2012, it has been slowing down since the 3rd Plenary Session of the 18th Central Committee of the CPC, entering into a 'new normal', in the official language, meaning it is integrating into the real economy with the prospect of becoming similar to cultural industries in developed societies. However, the Chinese cultural industry is expected to see yet another surge in the 13th Five-Year Plan period, tasked to support external cultural development for the One Belt One Road strategy. Analysts expect this will in turn help to further reform the Chinese cultural sector by establishing competent governance mechanisms, moving towards a market-oriented rather than a policy-dictated industry (Zhang *et al.*, 2015–2016).

Approaches to globalizing Chinese media

Current strategic thinking about globalizing Chinese media is still developing and is far from being static or complete. Media analysts and practitioners debate the principles of where Chinese media should go, how to get where they want to be, and indeed what Chinese media should become. They disagree with each other about the nature of Chinese media – commodity, ideology, state-owned, private sector, and so forth. Heated debates and contestations over these issues appear where social and political forces compete (Sun, 2015). The implementation of the 'media going global' policy has, to some extent, been event-driven. As the impressive host of the 2008 Beijing Olympics, China attracted unprecedented interest in Chinese culture, history and changes in society from people all over the world. Supported with the new 'media going global' policy, Chinese media conglomerates gained the momentum to globalize. The protest against China's human rights issues in the Olympic torch relay prompted Chinese media to act proactively to defuse the negative impact of Western media criticism, and to provide alternative narratives for a positive image of China. Central Chinese Television (CCTV), China Radio International, the *People's Daily*, the Shanghai Media Group and the Southern Newspaper Group made efforts to counter the rhetoric of the 'China threat' prevalent in major Western media. Chinese officials set out to broaden and change the landscape of global media with input of fresh media content and an 'image agenda' other media can follow, with the result of such initiatives being that 'in a number of developing countries, the Chinese media supply the major sources of international news' (Zhang, 2010b: 45).

On Chinese media's global expansion, officials claim that China does not want to dominate the world but only free itself from the monopoly of the US media, to project and present an image of a benign emerging China, which they insist is what it is. In other words, the 'media going global' policy is not aimed to create a new hegemony alternative to the West, but to fight for a place for China and a share of discourse power. China's activism to project its soft power onto the world, on this official view, is inherently defensive, not offensive.

The four approaches

Event-driven, problem-solving, and supported by enormous investment, the implementation of the 'media going global' policy is being undertaken methodically, with deliberations about approaches and steps, supported by expert views, media studies and communication theories.[8] Media analysts differentiate between two types of communication: direct and indirect. Direct communication refers to the use of Chinese media to report about China. In indirect communication, foreign media use materials based upon Chinese sources to report about China (Sun, 2015). It is widely acknowledged in media circles that Chinese state-owned print media tend to have low credibility on the world media stage, associated as they are with the history of communist propaganda. Media commentators suggest that it is more effective to work closely with foreign media to voice Chinese concerns and to authentically present China. This is so simply because foreign reporters and journalists, stationed in China whilst working for foreign media, are trusted by their own audiences back at home. The best approach they suggest is to establish Chinese media as the main source for international media reports. This way Chinese media will be able to set out the agenda and control the discourse for international media (Sun, 2015).

Four elements of Chinese media, or four approaches to globalizing Chinese media have been identified, either as being in use or simply suggested, and their relative advantages and weaknesses compared. The first is to globalize state-owned media, the Xinhua news agency, the *People's Daily* and CCTV included. One way for these mainstream media to go global would be to encourage them to acquire overseas media, holding shares in foreign media companies, and to merge international media enterprises. Such moves will enable Chinese media directly to produce and share media content, sources and products with their partners, a source of direct influence over organizations related to these joint ventures or shareholding companies, which in turn can become major overseas media reporting on China. As a consequence, Chinese state-owned media can become the authoritative and reliable organizations supplying news, information and thereby shape the international media discourse.

The second is participation in going global by non-state-owned Chinese media: China Net, social media, and the commercial sections of major Chinese media. As they do not take instruction from the state to conduct overseas publicity, they may enjoy more freedom on the media market. As Sun (2015) suggests, they can be complementary to the state-owned media, influencing international audiences by conducting effective publicity, targeting tourists, international students and businessmen.

The first two are forms of direct communication. The third element would be foreign journalists and reporters stationed in China. They are a direct source for the media they work for, and hence for an international audience about China. Media veterans suggest that the Chinese government, especially the propaganda or publicity departments, need to change their views about the media professionals' work – they should not be treated as enemies though they do tend selectively to report on the negative side about China (Sun, 2015). Fourth, to encourage international media that use Chinese sources, usually local media for the Chinese diasporas. One suggestion is for Chinese media to engage them as a point of contact or as agencies to broker or become partners for Chinese mainstream media. The Xinmin Evening News and Xinmin International Co, established in the US in 1994, one of the earliest efforts for Chinese media to expand beyond Asia, would have used one or more of the above approaches.[9]

The global reach of Chinese media

With political willingness and technological competency in place, commercialization and technological innovation have enabled Chinese media to go global. Even before the formal launch of the going-out policy, back in the 1990s, computers, satellite television and internet were put into use. In 1995, radio and TV stations started their own websites, as did news media and other publications. The scale of state-controlled news websites boomed in 2001 to the extent that every province had its own news website, with specifically designed websites for overseas publicity. China National Network (china.com.cn), created in 1997, was the key vehicle.

To reach overseas audiences, satellite TV channels were launched in the 1990s, broadcasting China's voice to the world. The first international channel in Mandarin was CCTV-4, launched in 1994 to target the overseas Chinese diaspora. In 2000, CCTV launched its 24-hour English-language channel, CCTV International (CCTV-9). This was followed by a Spanish-language channel in 2004 and a French-language channel in 2008, and then CCTV-Arabic and CCTV-Russian in 2009 and CCTV-Portuguese in 2010. Under CCTV, with government-approved satellite channels, i.e. CCTV satellite channel and provincial satellite channels, the Great Wall TV Platform was set up in 2004 to enhance Chinese media's penetration into the world media market (*People's Daily*, 2009). It has since launched a direct to home satellite service in Asia, Africa, Latin America, the US and Europe. China Central Television has more than 70 foreign bureaux broadcasting with UN official languages to 171 countries and regions. CCTV Africa, in Nairobi, and CCTV America, in Washington D.C., were established in 2012. Plans to launch CCTV Europe are in place.

When the 2008 financial crisis hit US and Europe severely, Western mainstream media experienced a drastic reduction in investment but the Chinese government decided to make a global media push by injecting billions of US dollars into creating media conglomerates to invigorate its global media industry. In January 2009, the *South China Morning Post* revealed that the Chinese government was prepared to invest 45 billion renminbi for the overseas expansion of state-run media, to compete with the BBC, CNN, Time Warner, News Corp, Viacom and Al Jazeera. In 2011 the Xinhua news agency launched CNC World English Channel Xinhua TV, broadcasting in English and presenting 'an international vision with a Chinese perspective' as Li Congjun, the then President noted (Xinhua, 2010).[10] The Xinhua news agency has over 180 news bureaux globally, publishing news text in eight languages and sending audio and videos, photograph programmes around the clock. The chart below, adopted from World Economic Forum, illustrates Xinhua news agency's coverage in the world.

In addition to the achievements of CCTV and Xinhua news agency, China Radio International has become one of the world's largest radio stations, second only to the BBC. It has set up 90 radio stations worldwide, broadcasting in 64 languages from 32 overseas bureaux. *China Daily* now publishes six regional editions in Hong Kong, Asia, US, Africa, Europe and Latin America. The *People's Daily* launched the *UK Weekly*, *Italy Weekly*, *Austria Weekly* and *Hungary Weekly* all in 2007, and the *Greek Weekly* in 2009.[11] In 2009, *Chinese National Geography* launched its English edition. CCP magazine *Qiu Shi* (Seeking Truth 求是杂志) has launched an English edition, with materials selected from the original Chinese edition, intended for overseas readers.

State-run media have actively engaged in English-language social media. In March 2015, Xinhua news agency launched its global social media platforms under the brand of 'New China' using Facebook, Twitter and YouTube, 'in response to a wider global trend of media transformation' as 'Xinhua must not only develop its traditional business, but also build an "online news agency" to enhance its influence through new media', to quote a high-level executive, with 7,929,769 Facebook, 4,599,580 Twitter followers respectively, for 'China insight and global view'.[12] As indicated

Regional Office

Eurasia(Moscow)

Europe(Brussels)

North America(New York)

Asia-Pacific (Hong Kong)

Latin America(Mexico City)

Middle East (Cairo)

Africa(Nairobi)

180 Foreign Bureaus, **7** Regional Offices

8 Languages in Chinese, English, French, Russian, Spanish, Arabic, Portuguese and Japanese.

600 news and **700+** photos every 24 hours

Cover **5.5** Billion Population in **200+** Countries and Regions

◆ **Numbers of news bureaus of the world's major news agencies**

AP	AFP	Reuters	TASS	Kyodo	Xinhua
280	200	200	138	95	180

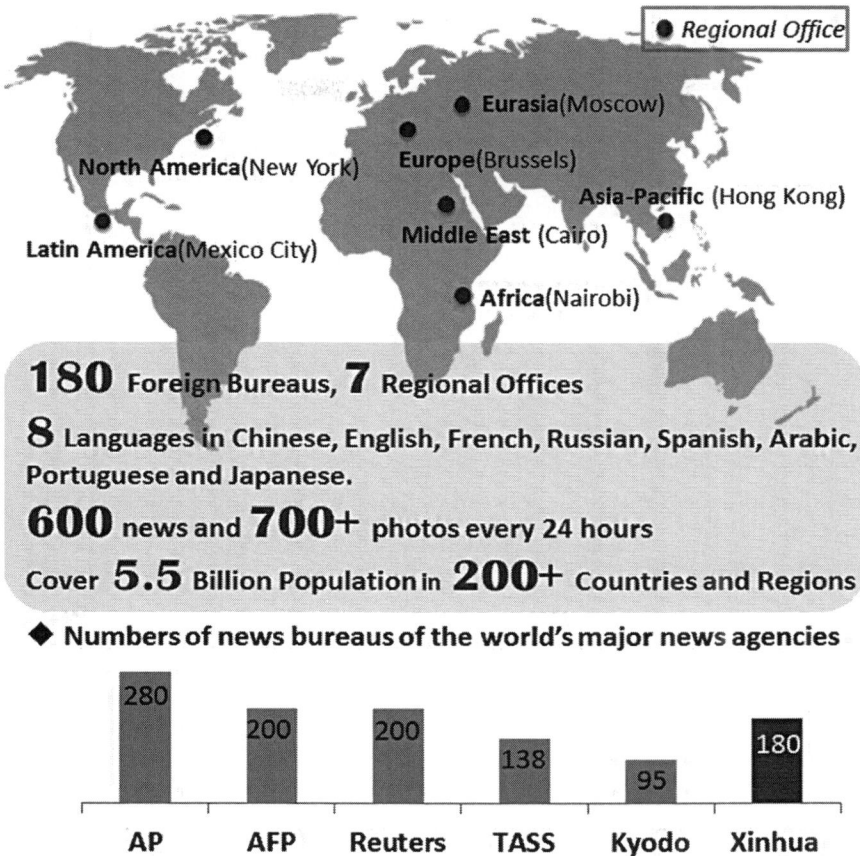

FIGURE 5.1 Xinhua news agency in numbers

Source: Vivian Yang (2015), 'How Chinese media is going global', World Economic Forum www.weforum.org/agenda/2015/08/how-chinese-media-is-going-global/.

in the chart above (see Figure 5.1), among English-language news outlets, only the BBC has more Facebook fans than CCTV and CCTV News. Fox News, *New York Times* and the rest bar CNN and BBC, have fewer Facebook fans than the *People's Daily*.

The *Global Times* (an English newspaper under the *People's Daily* Group) and the *People's Daily* are stepping up their efforts. Along with CCTV News and *China Daily*, they are active players on English social media. Their hourly updated content features not only Chinese stories, but also increasingly global news that appeals to a broader range of social media users. Figure 5.2 shows the number of people on Facebook who have 'liked' the Facebook pages of news outlets, in millions, as of 28 April 2016, as gathered from individual Facebook pages.

29 25.3 23.4 21.3 18.1 12.3 11.3 11.1 9.6 8.5 8.1 7 7.1 6.6 5.7 5.3 5.2 5.2 4.7 4.3 4 3.8 2.2

BBC NEWS | CCTV | CCTV NEWS | CNN | PEOPLE'S DAILY | FOX NEWS | CNN INTERNATIONAL | NEW YORK TIMES | TIME | TIMES OF INDIA | ABC NEWS | NBC NEWS | AL JAZEERA ENGLISH | THE ECONOMIST | THE GUARDIAN | CHINA DAILY | CHINA XINHUA NEWS | VICE | WALL STREET JOURNAL | USA TODAY | WASHINGTON POST | DAILY MAIL | GLOBAL TIMES

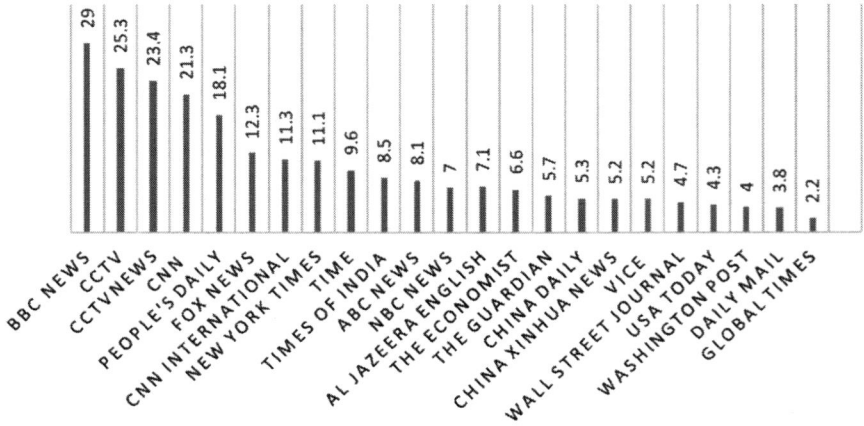

FIGURE 5.2 Facebook fans of English-language news outlets, in millions

Source: adapted with data from http://qz.com/671211/chinas-propaganda-outlets-have-leaped-the-top-of-facebook-even-though-it-banned-at-home/.

Soft power and media's policy agenda-setting role

For Chinese policy-makers, in a globalized world where China has gained increasing influence, media must be employed as the tool to increase its soft power. China's 'media going global' policy, in generating international reach and projecting positive images of China, has set out more specific goals: to promote understanding of Chinese political and economic objectives and policies, to promote Chinese culture by establishing a cultural industry with global reach and to help Chinese enterprises gain more business opportunities globally. The Chinese government is determined to fund all the efforts to enhance soft power, including promoting public diplomacy and broadening cultural reach whilst strengthening the competitiveness of Chinese culture in the marketplace of ideas. Often still viewed as a CCP mouthpiece, Chinese state-owned media, with the dual goals of commodity and ideology, are tasked both with increasing the share of Chinese media in the global market and strengthening the capacity to project Chinese soft power on the world stage (Bandurski, 2009).

Remarkable recent achievements in its media's global expansion notwithstanding, Chinese analysts acknowledge that media exposure alone does not generate credibility and international endorsement of what China does. Thus Chinese media must employ the leverage of the soft power of attraction to project the image of a benign emerging power. Analysts and officials also count on what public diplomacy can achieve in filling the apparent gaps in perception and the cultural frame of reference and in helping understand the difference in ideology, world views, history, and culture between China and the West. China's soft-power deficit seems to be closely associated with the lack of an effective public diplomacy that can operate on a par with the aspirations of the Western public, their media and intellectual circles, NGOs and cultural industries.

On closer examination, the concepts of soft power, public diplomacy and external publicity are used interchangeably in media circles in China as in the public discourse. Chinese analysts and practitioners do not tend to differentiate the notions of public diplomacy or external publicity from that of soft power. Whilst they can be closely related, for Nye (2005) soft power is the capacity to influence the behaviour of a foreign public through attraction but not coercion and to win their hearts and minds in order to achieve the desired outcomes. For Chinese officials, soft power is not so much the capacity of a society to attract people from other societies as the state's ability to project or persuade. External publicity and public diplomacy are intertwined in projecting a country's soft power. The question for China, therefore, may not lie so much in whether Chinese media are able to employ public diplomacy and external publicity effectively to project China's soft power. Rather, it may well lie in what sort of soft power to project, or even in whether soft power can indeed be projected through state-orchestrated initiatives at all.

As noted earlier, a decade or so ago Chinese officials and media practitioners felt that China's rise in soft power was constrained by the way in which Western media tended to report on China, with criticism prevailing about China's party-state system, ideology, human rights record, and domestic and international policies (Lai, 2006). Now Chinese officials and media professionals increasingly realize that what China lacks is not so much the capacity to communicate, but soft power: the capability to articulate 'values that the rest of the world can aspire to and emulate' (ibid.).

Policy advisers and decision makers on public diplomacy in Beijing hope to engage with the world through transforming Chinese traditional propaganda systems into a globally recognized and indeed friendly media industry. The Chinese government's decision to globalize Chinese media was in tandem with their strategy for global cultural reach, aiming to build China 'into a socialist cultural superpower' to match its economic superpower status (Communiqué, 2011).[13] External communication is the key to increasing the competitiveness of cultural appeal and soft power. Mainstream media are urged and tasked to develop the capability to create and present narratives of China, highlighting, for instance, its great cultural traditions and Confucianist value systems, whilst promoting a sense of its own development trajectory that is different to those of advanced Western societies (Liu, 2011).

In this view, once it possesses discourse power, media can perform the agenda-setting role providing cues and salience through drawing public attention to key public issues through, for instance, front-page headlines, thus forming public opinion and influencing national policy decisions. As a Chinese media veteran suggests, the strengthening of a developing country's national discourse power at the global level and within the global structure should go hand in hand with efforts to establish 'a new, fair and reasonable international … information communication order' (Lu, 2010/2014). This will require 'the abolition of "information discrimination" levelling the "digital divide"' (ibid.).

Soft power matters. The advocacy to establish a fair global information communication order resonates at a deep level with the tendency in communication theory to develop so-called Asian communication concepts, aimed at warding off

Euro/American-centric approaches if not replacing them, with an intended paradigm shift underpinned by the various cultural and philosophical sources salient in traditional and contemporary Asia. Intellectuals with an East Asian background or intellectual connections to Asian ideational sources have, albeit with limited success, started their work to flesh out the content and features of soft power of East Asia, exemplified by and centred on China. This is largely complementary and enriching, but not subversive of the democracy and market ideology based on universal liberal values permeated in Western societies (Chen, 1999).

Conclusion

To boost the capacity of Chinese media, the state has allocated vast resources and incentive packages to encourage media groups to transform from purely state-owned organizations to an industry actively performing in the competitive global market, particularly since 2009. With the duality of media as commodity and ideology, Chinese media are faced with more challenges than Western media, to both serve the ideological functions such as party rule, and to make profits by complying with laws prevailing where they locate, managing to suit the destination countries' legal, cultural and social environment.

Chinese officials recognize media activity as a form of cultural practice, to 'mediate in a process of convening cultural products from the producers to the consumers', reflecting the views and interests of the government and society, protecting the core cultural values, and securing professional standards of the society (Hu, 2011). Mismatches in perceptions and differences in frames of references and credibility problems create communication barriers. Sun (2010: 61) suggests that Chinese media enterprises need to cross geographical and cultural distance to 'achieve affinity with, and acquire appeal to, international (especially Western) audience' by producing media content that reflects their cultural reality and expectations and representation of shared beliefs.

From a communication point of view, information recipients tend to interpret what they see or hear based on their mindset – cultural and psychological programming – which they develop through socialization into their culture (Wang and Shoemaker, 2011). Differences in culture and national experience tend to go hand in hand with difference in patterns of mindsets and psychological realities, which could be barriers to effective communication. Perception, credibility and frame of reference ultimately determine how far intercultural communication can go. Thus it is important to assess if the image projected of China is compatible with cultural expectations of the Western public. Cultural values, beliefs, attitudes, tradition, history, personal experience and psychological factors – emotions, feelings, self-concepts, subconscious biases and prejudices affect an individual's perceptual interpretation of what they hear and they see (Neuliep, 2009; Jervis, 1976). According to Fisher, our perceptions are constantly created and recreated to form our precepts and mindsets (Fisher, 1988: 2). As Chinese values, ethics, and sensibilities are conveyed to the Western public, they must be presented as compatible with what the Western public can process in their mind. As the Chinese government loosens its tight control over the media industry, consolidating it through market orientation instead of government backing, state-owned media and private media companies now enjoy a great degree of autonomy to manage their financing and business. They have more capacity to perform professionally in the global media market attracting audience from all cultures and nationalities. Moreover, Chinese media professionals have recognized the imperative of changing their own mindsets and those of the foreign public to enable them to accommodate and eventually appreciate cultural sensitivity when projecting China's image.

Notes

1 Forbes has forecasted 2018, Bloomsburg 2026.
2 The Oxford Economics Global Cities 2030 Study predicts that '[t]he aggregate GDP of China's largest 150 cities will overtake Europe's 139 largest cities as early as 2015, and North America's largest 58 cities in 2022'.www.oxfordeconomics.com/Media/Default/landing-pages/cities/oe-cities-summary.pdf, last accessed 8 July 2016.
3 For a more recent echo to such sentiment, see Fu Ying's talk about South China Sea issues, Disorder or the Reconstruction of Order?, at the Royal Institute of International Affairs, available at *People's Daily Editorial*, 9, 8 July, www.chinadaily.com.cn/world/cn_eu/2016-07/08/content_26021696.htm, and http://mp.weixin.qq.com/s?__biz=MzA4OTIyMjUyOQ==&mid=2654619123&idx=1&sn=1f4c70135b147848ef9e0a142dc17f59&scene=5&srcid=070767kC97eHjZ6XHT4Gq3M3#rd, last accessed 10 September 2016.
4 Most frequently used examples to represent the Chinese nation as non-aggressive and purely defensive and without imperial ambition include the Great Wall and the Ming courtier Zheng He's voyages.
5 Originally from *Qiu Shi Magazine*, 18 July 2010, http://theory.people.com.cn/GB/12174522.html, last accessed 6 July 2016; English version available at https://chinacopyrightandmedia.wordpress.com/2014/12/21/national-discourse-power-and-information-security-against-the-background-of-economic-globalization/, last accessed 7 July 2016.
6 www.china.org.cn/china/2014-04/15/content_32097062.htm.
7 www.chncia.org/en/leaders.php?mid=2&id=10.
8 Chinese media analysts have gone beyond journalism moving towards Communication studies, where insights and suggestions are generated to influence public discourse and policy thinking (Chen, 1999).
9 They were followed by New Tang Dynasty Television in New York (2001), and Blue Ocean Network, the first privately owned commercial TV network providing China's focused news and features about business, technology and tourism.
10 http://news.xinhuanet.com/english2010/china/2010-07/01/c_13378575.htm.
11 http://media.people.com.cn/GB/9163080.html, accessed 30 June 2016.
12 http://news.xinhuanet.com/english/2015-03/01/c_134027886.htm, last accessed 9 July 2016.
13 Communiqué of The Sixth Plenary Session of the 17th CCP Central Committee, 18 October 2011.

References

Al-Rodhan, K. R. (2007) A critique of the China threat theory: A systematic analysis, *Asian Perspective*, 31(3): 41–66.
Bandurski, D. (2009) Hard Line Mocks Beijing's Designs on Global Influence. *The Australian*, 8 April.

Barboza, D. (2010) China Puts Best Face Forward in New English-Language Channel. *New York Times*, 1 July. Available at: www.nytimes.com/2010/07/02/world/asia/02china. html?_r=0 [Accessed 1 September 2016].

Bradshernov, K. (2015) China's Renminbi is Approved by I.M.F. as a Main World Currency. *New York Times*, 6 April.

Cai, W. (2009) Report to the 14th Plenary of the 11th Standing Committee National People's Congress about Chinese Cultural Industry. *People's Daily Overseas Edition*, 29 April. Available at: http://hxd.wenming.cn/whtz/2010-04/29/content_116369.htm [Accessed 11 September 2016].

Chang, G. (2001) *The Coming Collapse of China*. New York: Random House.

Chen, D.; Pu, X. and Johnston, A. I. (2013-2014) Debating China's assertiveness, *International Security*, 38(3): 176–183.

Chen, G. (1999) An overview of communication studies: History, theory and methodology, *The Study of Journalism*, 58: 257–268.

Communiqué (2011) *The Sixth Plenary Session of the 17th CCP Central Committee*, 18 October. Available at: http://english.cntv.cn/special/6thmeeting_17thCPC/homepage/index. shtml [Accessed 17 July 2016].

Fisher, G. (ed.) (1988) *Mindsets: The Role of Culture and Perception in International Relations*. Yarmouth, ME: Intercultural Press.

Glaser, B. S. and Medeiros, E. S. (2007) The changing ecology of foreign policy-making in China: The ascension and demise of the theory of 'peaceful rise', *The China Quarterly*, 190: 291–310.

Guo, Z. (2003) Playing the game by the rules? Television regulation around China's entry into WTO, *Javnost- The Public*, 10(4): 5–18.

Hu, J. (2011) Promote Chinese Culture and Enhance its International Influence to the World. *China News*, 1 July. Available at: http://english1.english.gov.cn/2011-07/01/content_ 1897641_13.htm [Accessed 9 July 2016].

Ikenberry, G. J. (2008) The rise of China and the future of the West: Can the liberal system survive? *Foreign Affairs*, January–February: 23–37.

Ikenberry, G. J. (2012) The Rise of China, the United States, and the Future of Liberal International Order, in Shambaugh, D. (ed.) *Tangled Titans: The United States and China*. New York: Rowman and Littlefield: 53–74.

International Monetary Fund (2016) *Special Drawing Right*, 6 April. Available at: www.imf. org/external/np/exr/facts/sdr.htm/ [Accessed 11 July 2016].

Jervis, R. (1976) *Perception and Misperception in International Politics*. Princeton: Princeton University Press.

Jia, Q. (2005) Peaceful development: China's policy of reassurance, *Australian Journal of International Affairs*, 59(4): 493–507.

Johnston, A. I. (2013) How new and assertive is China's new assertiveness?, *International Security*, 37(4): 7–48.

Kang, D. (2007) *China Rising: Peace, Power, and Order in East Asia*. New York: Columbia University Press.

Kireyev, A. and Leonidov, A. (2016) China's Imports Slowdown: Spillovers, Spillins, and Spillbacks, IMF Working Paper, WP/16/51, Available at: www.imf.org/external/pubs/ft/ wp/2016/wp1651.pdf [Accessed 18 September].

Klintworth, G. (1994) Greater China and regional security, *Australian Journal of International Affairs*, 48(2): 211–228.

Krauthammer, C. (1995) Why We Must Contain China. *Time*, 31 July.

Kurlantzick, J. (2008) *Charm Offensive: How China's Soft Power Is Transforming the World*. New Haven: Yale University Press.

Lai, H (2006) China's Cultural Diplomacy: Going for Soft Power. East Asia Institute, National University of Singapore, Background Brief 308. Available at: www.eai.nus.edu.sg/BB308.pdf.

Li, C. (2008) Speech made by Minister of CCP Central Committee Propaganda Department in 2008 Celebrating the 50th Anniversary of the Establishment of Central Chinese Television. Available at: www.gxcic.net/News/shownews_83527.html.

Li, X. (2009) Interviewed by *CCTV Nine*. Available at: http://english.cctv.com/program/e_dialogue/20090930/102151.shtml [Accessed 7 September 2016].

Liu, D. (2011) Reflection of the Global Discourse of Chinese Media, International Business. *New News*, 29 March. Available at: http://news.china.com.cn/rollnews/2011–03/29/content_7058870.htm [Accessed 3 July 2016].

刘奇葆 Liu, Qibao (2014) '大力推动中华文化走向世界' (Vigorously Advance Chinese Culture to the World, 光明日报》 *Guangming Daily*, 22 May. Available at: http://cpc.people.com.cn/n/2014/0522/c64094–25050358.html, and http://epaper.gmw.cn/gmrb/html/2014–05/22/nw.D110000gmrb_20140522_1–03.htm [Accessed 30 December 2016].

Lu, W. (2010/2014) National Discourse Power and Information Security against the Background of Economic Globalization. *Qiu Shi Magazine*, 18 July 2010, http://theory.people.com.cn/GB/12174522.html [Accessed 6 July 2016]; English version available at: https://chinacopyrightandmedia.wordpress.com/2014/12/21/national-discourse-power-and-information-security-against-the-background-of-economic-globalization/ [Accessed 7 July 2016].

Mearsheimer, J. J. (2001) *The Tragedy of Great Power Politics*. New York: W. W. Norton.

Mearsheimer, J. J. (2014) *The Tragedy of Great Power Politics*. New York: W. W. Norton, updated edition.

Neuliep, James W. (2009) Intercultural Communication: A Contextual Approach. Thousand Oaks: Sage.

Nye, Joseph (2005) *Soft Power: The Means to Success in World Politics*. New York: Public Affairs.

Oxford Economics (2015) *Global Cities 2030*. Available at: www.oxfordeconomics.com/Media/Default/landing-pages/cities/oe-cities-summary.pdf [Accessed 8 July 2016].

People's Daily (2009) '人民日报海外版希腊周刊4月20日正式创刊' (People's Daily Overseas Edition Greek Weekly Launched). 21 April. Available at: http://media.people.com.cn/GB/9163080.html [Accessed 30 June 2016].

People's Republic of China, Information Office of the State Council (2011) *Chinese Peaceful Development White Paper*. Available at: www.china.org.cn/government/whitepaper/node_7126562.htm [Accessed 15 July 2016].

People's Republic of China, Information Office of the State Council (2015) *China's Military Strategy*. Available at: www.chinadaily.com.cn/china/2015–05/26/content_20820628.htm [Accessed 15 July 2016].

People's Republic of China, Information Office of the State Council (2015–2016) *Report on Development of China's Cultural Industry*. Beijing: Social Science Academic Press.

Roberts, A. (2002) Predictions of Offensive Realism, *The Times Literary Supplement*, 24.

Roy, D. (1996) The 'China Threat' issue: Major arguments, *Asian Survey*, 36(8): 758–771.

Segal, G. (1996) East Asia and the containment of China, *International Security*, 20(4): 107–135.

Shamburgh, D. (2015) The Coming Chinese Crackup. *The Wall Street Journal*, 6 March.

Sun, W. (2010) Mission impossible? Soft power, communication capacity and the globalization of Chinese media, *International Journal of Communication*, 4: 54–72.

Sun, W. (2015) Slow boat from China: Public discourses behind the 'going global' media policy, *International Journal of Cultural Policy*, 21(4): 400–418.

Swaine, M. D. (2010) Perceptions of an assertive China, *China Leadership Monitor*, 32(2): 1–19.

Swaine, M. D. and Fravel, T. (2011) China's assertive behaviour, part two: The maritime periphery. *China Leadership Monitor*, 35: 1–29.

Tan,Y. (2013) International Competition over Discourse Power: Chinese Public Diplomacy Top-Down Design, *Teaching, Learning and Research (Jiaoxue yu Yanjiu)*, 4. Available at: www.cctb.net/llyj/lldt/qqzl/201310/t20131009_295059.htm [Accessed 10 September 2016].

Tiezzi, S. (2014) Beijing's China Threat Theory. *The Diplomat*, 3 June. Available at: http://thediplomat.com/2014/06/beijings-china-threat-theory [Accessed 20 July 2016].

Vogel, E. F. (2011) *Deng Xiaoping and the Transformation of China*. Cambridge, MA: The Belknap Press of Harvard University Press.

Wang, G. (2011) Chinese National Defense in 2010. *Xinhua news agency*, 31 March.

Wang, H. (2003) National image building and Chinese foreign policy, *China: An International Journal*, 1(1): 46–72.

Wang, J. and Lv, S. (2011) Media Going Out: Improve Chinese Media's International Communicative Capability. *Qiu Shi*, 8 March. Available at: www.qstheory.cn/dd/2011/gjcbnl/201103/t20110308_71267.htm [Accessed 9 July 2016].

Wang, X. and Shoemaker, P. J. (2011) What shapes Americans' opinion of China? Country characteristics, public relations and mass media, *Chinese Journal of Communication*, 4(1): 1–20.

Wang, Y. (2016) The Ought-to-be Growth Space of China's Public Culture Investment Measuring for Related Coordination and Balance in 2012. *Report on Development of China's Cultural Industry (2015–2016)*. Beijing: Social Science Academic Press.

Xinhua (2010) Xinhua Launches CNC World English Channel, Xinhua news agency. Available at: http://news.xinhuanet.com/english2010/china/2010–07/01/c_13378575.htm.

Yan, X. (2014) From keeping a low profile to striving for achievement, *Chinese Journal of International Politics*, 7(2): 153–184.

Yang, J (2010) Foreign Minister Yang Jiechi Answers Questions from Domestic and Overseas Journalists on China's Foreign Policy, National Peoples Congress Annual Sessions, 9 March.

Yang, V. (2015) How Chinese media is going global. *World Economic Forum*. (10 August 2015). Available at: www.weforum.org/agenda/2015/08/how-chinese-media-is-going-global/ [Accessed 16 July 2016].

Ying, F. (2016) Disorder or the Reconstruction of Order?, Royal Institute of International Affairs, available at *People's Daily Editorial*, 9, 8 July, www.chinadaily.com.cn/world/cn_eu/2016-07/08/content_26021696.htm, and http://mp.weixin.qq.com/s?__biz=MzA4OTIyMjUyOQ==&mid=2654619123&idx=1&sn=1f4c70135b147848ef9e0a142dc17f59&scene=5&srcid=070767kC97eHjZ6XHT4Gq3M3#rd [Accessed 10 September 2016].

Zhang, G. (2010a) *Annual Research Report on China's Cultural Soft Power*. Beijing: Social Science Academic Press.

Zhang, J. (2015) Interviewed by Wang Yizhi for China's Defense White Paper, *Dialogue*, CCTV News, 26 May. Available at: http://english.cntv.cn/2015/05/27/VIDE1432668717544907.shtml.

Zhang, X. (2010b) Chinese state media going global, *East Asia Policy*, 2(1): 43–50.

Zhang, X., Wang, J. and Zhang, J. (2015–2016) Face 13th Five-year Plan, Step into the New Normal. *Report on Development of China's Cultural Industry (2015–2016), General Reports*. Beijing: Social Science Academic Press.

Zhang, Z. (2009) The Dilemma for China's Discourse Power. *People.cn*, 18 August. Available at: http://theory.people.com.cn/GB/9878818.html [Accessed 3 July 2016].

Zheng, B. (2005) China's 'Peaceful Rise' to great power status, *Foreign Affairs*, 84(5): 18–24.

Zhao, W. (2008) Insights for Media Management in China from Reviewing the Relationship between the American Government and the US media. *Modern Communication*, 5: 133–139.

PART II
Chinese media abroad

6

TIANGAO OR *TIANXIA?* THE AMBIGUITIES OF CCTV'S ENGLISH-LANGUAGE NEWS FOR AFRICA

Vivien Marsh

What is the purpose of CCTV's English-language news operation in Africa? The Chinese state broadcaster's Kenyan network centre, the heart of its African programming, occupies two buildings in a quiet corner of western Nairobi some 9,200 kilometres (5,700 miles) from Beijing. The physical separation calls to mind the old Chinese saying, 天高皇帝远 *tiangao, huangdi yuan*: 'heaven is high and the emperor is far away' – suggesting that CCTV could have room in Kenya to try out new journalistic ideas. However, CCTV Africa[1] is also a product of the very core of the Chinese state – a potential emissary of 'soft power', spreading the notion of a reimagined world order with a resurgent China at its centre. Such a reshaping of international relations evokes 天下 *tianxia*, the recently resurrected Chinese theory of all-embracing governance that privileges global order and harmony over notions of individual freedom (Callahan, 2007; Wang, 2016; Zhang, 2009). The contrasting interpretations of CCTV Africa's role make its journalistic output worthy of academic scrutiny. Is CCTV adopting a different way of reporting Africa from its international rivals, and – if so – is it a credible alternative? This chapter will set CCTV Africa in a global broadcasting context and investigate its news reports through content analysis, backed up by interviews with journalists and managers.

From the very beginning of such analysis, CCTV Africa throws out mixed signals, alternating between *tiangao* and *tianxia*. Not only does it have an active YouTube channel although YouTube is inaccessible in China itself, but the programmes featured on it can surprise. In late 2015, CCTV Africa's YouTube website promoted a documentary about a Kenyan satirical puppet show in which latex effigies of Kenya's former president and prime minister were depicted as convicts bickering in jail at the International Criminal Court in The Hague (Faces of Africa, 2015). The creators and writers of the satire, XYZ, were shown speaking about pushing the boundaries of what was permitted to be broadcast in Kenya – thereby simultaneously pushing the boundaries of what the Chinese state broadcaster might be expected to air.

Yet such ideological distance between China and Africa is paired with ideological consonance. Short videos on the same CCTV Africa YouTube channel feature people from various countries describing their 'African Dream'. Typical of these is a Senegalese trader who hopes for a 'peaceful and united Africa in which we can exploit our resources' (CCTV Africa, 2015a). The video series depicts African nations following a development path analogous to that outlined in Xi Jinping's concept of 中国梦 *zhongguo meng*, the China Dream:

> China Dream is very simple. The dream is to have a better life. So African Dream is the same. Because a lot of African countries are still not very strong, they are developing. So I think the Chinese brothers want to help the African people [...]. Because now, China is stronger than before, so now is our responsibility to help the people who once helped China.
>
> *[Managing editor, CCTV Africa: personal interview, 2016[2]]*

Whether the China and African Dreams are predicated on peace and stability (FoCAC China–Africa Cooperation, 2013) or the export of elite-centred Chinese ideology into Africa (Tembe, 2015), transmission of such ideas involves Chinese soft, or soft-ish, power. Can CCTV Africa transmit these messages while remaining journalistically credible?

China in Africa: delivering the message

It was indeed the search for soft power, rather than journalistic ambition, that initially propelled CCTV-News into Kenya and precipitated the launch of its African programming in 2012. The Chinese state broadcaster's multi-million-dollar expansion on the continent was the centrepiece of a broader, primarily Anglophone, media strategy to rebut the frequently unflattering impression of China disseminated by Western news organizations and to convey Beijing's outlook on the world.

The explosion of Sino-African trade in the twenty-first century was viewed by many in the West as a wholesale extraction of resources by a rival industrial force with global political ambitions. The rhetoric increased after China became Africa's largest single trading partner in 2009. The then British Prime Minister David Cameron warned African politicians against the spread of 'authoritarian capitalism' inspired by Russia and China (UK Government, 2011), while the US Secretary of State Hillary Clinton invoked the spectre of 'a new colonialism' in Africa (US State Department, 2011). Western media echoed their remarks: the BBC charted China's economic expansion in a documentary with the alarmist title 'The Chinese Are Coming' (BBC, 2011). Such framing accorded little space to Beijing's alternative, albeit contested, formulation of its role in Africa – namely, that any expropriation demanded a return, and that the Confucian system of vertical reciprocation set China apart from Africa's erstwhile colonial and imperial occupiers (Chan, 2013: 17).

The professed anti-colonial strategy in Africa that Beijing sought to promote pre-dated China's economic rise. The 'three worlds' theory as outlined by

Deng Xiaoping in 1974 viewed Asians and Africans as allies against imperialism but also placed China at the heart of this Third World, conferring on it the status of *primus inter pares* among the ranks of the oppressed (Taylor, 2006: 43). Beijing benefited from the solidarity of African nations in securing United Nations status as sole legitimate representative of China. It has granted loans and aid to African nations, including those viewed in the West as pariah states, with no strings attached. After helping disseminate and publicize China's version of Communism in the 1960s and 1970s, Chinese media in Africa offered a 'pro-development paradigm' to compete with Western media's 'fourth estate' model once African countries had gained independence (Ran, 2016: 49–50). To this was added a rhetoric of solidarity among developing countries in the 1990s, when the president of the Xinhua news agency suggested that writers 'be cheerful for Africa's progress and [should] feel sad for their temporary sufferings' (in Xin, 2012: 122). At a time when China had few commercial interests in Africa to defend, it had little difficulty in adhering to its principle of non-interference in other countries' affairs. The twenty-first century, however, brought change.

Stark economic facts are now challenging China's long-held policies in Africa. Although China still terms itself a developing country, thus aligning itself with its African partners, the economic imbalance is huge. In 2013 China represented nearly a quarter of sub-Saharan Africa's total trade and more than 2,200 Chinese firms were operating in the region, whereas sub-Saharan Africa's share of Chinese trade was just 3 per cent (Pigato and Tang, 2015). The subsequent slowdown in China's economic growth throttled demand for Africa's raw materials: African exports to China fell by 38 per cent between 2014 and 2015 (BBC News, 2016), and Chinese direct investment in African countries fell by more than 40 per cent in the year to mid-2015. However, in December 2015 President Xi Jinping renewed China's commitment to Africa with pledges of loans and assistance worth $60 billion at the Forum on China–Africa Cooperation, and the Chinese Commerce Ministry insisted that investment would total $100 billion by 2020 (Xinhua, 2015).

CCTV Africa was launched before China's economic rise began to slow: it was at the heart of a comprehensive 'going-out' strategy for Chinese media in Africa that began under Hu Jintao's presidency. As part of this, the *China Daily* newspaper launched a weekly African edition and the state news agency Xinhua joined forces with a Kenyan company to provide a news service for mobile phones (BBC News, 2012). China also stepped up its training of African journalists and helped African broadcasters and communications firms develop their infrastructure (Wu, 2012). Proclaiming itself free of the colonial baggage of Western powers and with a history of developmental engagement in Africa, China promised news consumers a different perspective on African affairs.

Compared with Xinhua, which opened its first African bureaux in the 1950s (Xin, 2012), CCTV-News was a relative latecomer to the African media market. However, it was in the vanguard of 'glocalisation' by international broadcasters, characterized by a wave of local recruitment aimed at lending credibility, immediacy and relevance to regionally targeted output. By mid-2016, according to CCTV

Africa's managing editor, its English department contained some 90 staff, about ten of them Chinese – mostly in managerial positions – and the rest mainly African. Staffing has trebled and broadened geographically since the launch, when CCTV Africa's recruitment target was for experienced and often high-profile Kenyan journalists. All of the presenters and most of the reporters are Africans (Marsh, 2016a: 61), and Africans run the news desks. Although the programmes broadcast from Nairobi are shown worldwide on CCTV-News, their stated aim is to 'focus on African news, perspectives and personalities' and 'promote communication and cooperation between China and African countries on politics, economy, trade and culture' (CCTV, 2015). One of CCTV Africa's news editors (personal interview) put it slightly differently: 'CCTV helps introduce African countries to one another and introduces the role of China.'

CCTV Africa was launched as a network centre in January 2012. As one CCTV journalist pointed out with pride, this was five months before BBC World News began 'Focus on Africa', its own specialist daily television bulletin for the continent. In addition to twice-daily African news, CCTV Africa quickly developed separate business and sports strands, along with documentaries on inspirational Africans and a weekly current affairs talk show. CCTV also broadcast a twice-daily half-hour news bulletin in French for Africa, but this had far fewer resources and was produced in Beijing (CCTV, 2016). Chinese managers say the various nationalities at CCTV Africa took time to cohere:

> In the beginning [. . .] we knew nothing about Africa and how to communicate with the Africans. [. . .] It's a learning process – even for us.
>
> *[Managing editor, CCTV Africa]*

> Some of our colleagues, they were educated in the West. I mean, even the Kenyan education system is Western-based, so their working style was kind of similar, familiar to the Western media at the beginning. And so we encouraged them to take a more objective look in [sic] the issues, and to the leaders and the leaderships – try to do all the angles, not just to interview what the opposition say.
>
> *[Deputy managing editor, CCTV Africa]*

African staff say the station has gradually grown slicker and more creative, and that Chinese managers generally give them what they need technically for their work. Reporters revel in the ability to pitch an obscure story and have it accepted: they say that funds rarely seem to be a problem. Staff say the aim is to cover every African country – no matter how small – every year. When questioned about their long-term commitment to the channel, however, journalists voiced mixed views. Some identified strongly with CCTV Africa's aims and saw it as a vehicle for African empowerment; others worried about its Chinese state media role. This chapter will interrogate this perceived dual purpose.

'Positive' and 'constructive' reporting: the credibility challenge

Early content analysis indicated that CCTV Africa might be experimenting with an alternative journalistic approach away from the state media strictures of Beijing (Zhang, 2013). While the broadcasts presented China at all times in a positive light – a subject tackled later in this chapter – they did not shy away from addressing Africa's problems and conflicts (Marsh, 2016a; Wekesa, 2014; Zhang, 2013). However, African news and discussion was as upbeat as the subject-matter permitted. Even reporting on politics and security – the main focus of CCTV Africa's news agenda – tended to be predicated on future hopes rather than past disasters: for instance, the headlines of the conflict in South Sudan were made by mediation sessions at African Union headquarters rather than news from the battlefield (Marsh, 2016a).

An optimistic approach to reporting Africa was encouraged from the very top: according to one Chinese manager (personal interview), the media depiction of Africa was so negative before CCTV Africa's launch that his own mother was worried about him working in Nairobi. Sometimes this drive for upbeat attitudes bordered on reverse Orientalism, typified by a promotional video for the channel, *The African Smile*, that showed a succession of smiling African faces and an acacia tree silhouetted against an orange sky:

> Africans, they have been in poverty for a long time: their faces are very gloomy. People will smile when they see this. It will change their mindset. [. . .] When people [are] always in the dark, of course they are accustomed to darkness. But when they see the sunshine, that will change their dark ideas.
> *[Managing editor, CCTV Africa]*

However, the commitment to reporting African nations differently was no caricature: Chinese, African and international staff at CCTV Africa were united in the aim of presenting a rounded picture of the continent. As one of the news presenters put it (personal interview): 'Africa is not just flood-hit all the time; Africa is not hopeless all the time.' The challenge for CCTV Africa was to combine a forward-looking view of African events with credible reporting that would attract viewers – as credibility in the eyes of audiences is key to the transmission of 'soft power' (Wasserman, 2016). Quite what to call this style of reporting, however – including whether it constituted journalism – was a topic that divided media scholars from the media workers themselves.

Some China-based academics have put forward the concept of constructive journalism as a fitting way for Chinese media to report on Africa (Wekesa and Zhang, 2014; Zhang, 2014a, 2014b). Constructive journalism is an evolving field which has lacked an agreed scholarly definition (McIntyre, 2015) but which is seen as drawing on positive psychology to channel people's reactions into a search for solutions to society's problems. It is described most succinctly as 'yes-we-can reporting' (Gyldensted, in McIntyre, 2015: 7), propelled by the conviction that news should be more than just a litany of disasters and conflicts. Professor Zhang Yanqiu (personal interview, 2014) at the Communication University of China links constructive journalism with what she sees as China's constructive diplomacy and constructive international relations. For Zhang and Matingwina, constructive journalism 'combines the techniques of critical journalism with narratives that explore solutions' (Zhang and Matingwina, 2016: 24).

The proponents of constructive journalism insist that it produces 'rigorous, compelling reporting' and that it upholds journalism's core functions (Constructive Journalism Project, n.d.) while providing a more accurate, less negative reflection of the world. Some scholars are more sceptical: the South African journalism professor Anton Harber argues that news is 'only constructive if you want a sleepy, complacent society', while great journalism 'questions and probes … it is disruptive and discomfiting, particularly for the powerful' (Tullis, 2014). Frame analysis of three key news topics in 2014 (Marsh, 2016b) indicated that elements of 'constructive journalism' were certainly present in CCTV Africa's early reporting, whether intentionally or not, but that the reports were often devoid of critical focus on the causes of the issues they covered.

Journalists and managers interviewed at CCTV Africa in 2016 were all asked if they were aware of the concept of 'constructive journalism'. Hardly any of them had heard of the term, and nearly all of them described the reporting style of the Nairobi newsroom as 'positive' rather than 'constructive'. Positive reporting, long practised in China's official media for the purposes of propaganda and stability, has been widely derided in the West and has frustrated the public in China itself (Li, 2001). In Africa, however, CCTV staff saw positive reporting as helpful for developing countries. They insisted that a positive rather than critical approach – where this was possible – did not conflict with professional journalistic standards and did not stop them covering Africa's problems.

> You have to report on [the bombings and killings]. But after that, you must have your editorial policy. […] I tell our reporters, I say, next time, go to Somalia, not just focus on the bombing, the killing, but focus on the beautiful side of Somalia. […] And their economy now is also returning to normal. Some countries, especially Turkey, invest heavily in Somalia. So it's different. We should focus on another side of Somalia.
>
> *[Managing editor, CCTV Africa]*

> That is up to the electorate to decide, whether their leader has to go or not. But I want to know: what policies have you put in place that are working for your people? […] I want to know why is Rwanda for instance ranked number 3 in the ease of doing business, and yet Kenya is ranked, God knows, 101. What is it Rwanda is doing that Kenya should be doing?
>
> *[Presenter, CCTV Africa]*

However, CCTV Africa's approach is not now as alternative as it attests. Evidence of more upbeat and targeted reporting on Africa, using African reporters, has been proliferating across international news organizations for several years as their staffing begins to reflect a more globally mobile industry, although none of CCTV's competitors would claim to have espoused 'positive journalism'. BBC World News's *Focus on Africa* is CCTV's closest direct rival in spirit and format, offering a palette of news including 'Africa's rising economies, entrepreneurs, innovators' (BBC, 2012) as well as more routine topics. CNN Africa's coverage encompasses African trendsetters and socially engaged culture (CNN, 2016). Less optimism is discernible at Al Jazeera, where the series *Africa Investigates* aimed to expose corruption and abuse (Al Jazeera, 2016). What most sets CCTV Africa apart from its competitors, however, is its official status – an attribute that journalists from fellow broadcasters view with suspicion. The following sections of this chapter will investigate how CCTV Africa covers news that is primarily about China in Africa, and – firstly – news that is primarily about African countries themselves.

CCTV and Ebola

The character of CCTV Africa's reporting of major African news can be explored more specifically through a snapshot of a single issue: how the Ebola epidemic was framed by CCTV's *Africa Live* news programme in the second half of 2015. Ebola was chosen because it was a pan-African news event which could be expected to lend itself to the 'death, disease, destruction' framing for which traditional Western news reporting has been widely criticized (Bunce, 2015). Would CCTV offer an alternative view?

By late 2015, West African countries had weathered the worst of the Ebola crisis, but the battle against the virus was still being fought. All reporter-led news items on Ebola from this six-month period posted on CCTV Africa's YouTube channel – 36 videos in all – were subjected to frame analysis. The frames chosen were those used in Semetko and Valkenburg's (2000: 100) study of European political news, namely conflict, human interest, economic consequences, morality and the attribution of responsibility. The last of these categories was split to make clear the distinction between the attribution of responsibility for causing a problem – the 'blame frame' – and the attribution of responsibility for solving it. To these essentially Western frames were added harmony and stability (Marsh, 2016b), two concepts that surface frequently in Chinese state rhetoric (Delury, 2008; Qian, 2012, 2014; Trevaskes *et al.*, 2014; Zheng and Tok, 2007). The results appear in Table 6.1. Alongside the overall tally, separate columns show how frequently frames were evoked when reporters were 'in the field' or in the CCTV newsroom in Nairobi.

The attribution of responsibility for a solution was found to be the dominant frame. The governments of Sierra Leone, Liberia and Guinea were shown taking responsibility for steering their countries out of the Ebola crisis, sometimes with outside partnership. A United Nations spokesman's praise for 'the swift revival of the Ebola response mechanism led by the Liberian government' (CCTV Africa, 2015b)

TABLE 6.1 Frames detected in news coverage of Ebola on CCTV Africa's YouTube channel between 1 July and 31 December 2015. Percentages refer to the proportion of Ebola news items in which a given frame appeared

Overall frames (36)	Reporter on location (9)	Reporter in Nairobi (27)
Responsibility (solution) 83%	Human interest 100%	Responsibility (solution) 89%
Human interest 42%	Responsibility (solution) 67%	Harmony 37%
Harmony 39%	Economic consequences 56%	Economic consequences 33%
Economic consequences 39%	Harmony 44%	Human interest 22%
Responsibility (causal) 19%	Responsibility (causal) 11%	Responsibility (causal) 22%
Stability 8%	Stability 0%	Stability 11%
Conflict 8%	Conflict 0%	Conflict 11%
Morality 0%	Morality 0%	Morality 0%

was typical of the reporting, in which African authorities were frequently congratulated on their actions. There is consistency between the forward-looking emphasis on the search for a solution and the main principle of constructive journalism, whether consciously practised or not. Positive psychology, another attribute of constructive journalism, was evident in coverage of the release from hospital of Sierra Leone's last Ebola patient, described as 'a symbol of hope' (CCTV Africa, 2015c). A report on an Ebola treatment unit in Guinea spoke of 'an optimistic atmosphere buoyed by emptying wards' (CCTV Africa, 2015d). In all, solution-focused elements of constructive journalism were discernible in more than 80 per cent of the reports. The approach appeared part of a considered strategy:

> We are always looking at solutions [...]. If you concentrate all the time on, 'oh, hundreds of people have died in Guinea from Ebola and they're not doing this this this', it's depressing those people. Seriously! You're depressing the entire continent. Whereas if you say, 'actually, it is not all doom: Nigeria got it right, Senegal got it right', and then maybe the Guineans will be like, 'oh, what did they do? – let us follow, let's see what they did that we can borrow from'.
>
> *[Presenter, CCTV Africa]*

These findings position CCTV Africa alongside the *China Daily* in the use of constructive or positive reporting techniques to combat relentlessly negative framing of the Ebola crisis (Zhang and Matingwina, 2016). However, in its search for the positive during the long wait for a definitive end to the epidemic, CCTV Africa sometimes forsook journalistic accuracy. This was especially noticeable in items compiled in Nairobi rather than on location, when at times the reporter voice-over was over-optimistic and factually at variance with the soundbites. For example, an Ebola vaccine trial in Guinea that was headlined as 100 per cent successful contained clips of health officials whose optimism was much more cautious and hedged than the reporter's script (CCTV Africa, 2015e).

Incidence of the 'blame frame' – responsibility for causing a problem – was very low in the reports studied. This could be viewed as a deliberate strategy not to hold any authority accountable for the spread of the Ebola virus, in line with China's traditionally non-interventionist foreign policy. However, the use of Western news agency footage occasionally prompted sudden deviations from this stance. For example, on one weekend CCTV Africa broadcast a news report compiled by a newsroom journalist in Nairobi but based entirely on an Associated Press exclusive. This accused the World Health Organization of bungling procurement at the Kenema Ebola treatment centre in Sierra Leone (CCTV Africa, 2015f).

Accompanying the general distaste for attributing blame was a lack of human agency: the Ebola virus was said to 'make its way' into countries and to 'move undetected' (CCTV Africa, 2015g), while nominalization further depersonalized the way it spread ('Scientists say sexual transmission is the most likely explanation for the resurgence' (CCTV Africa, 2015h)). The stability and morality frames played no meaningful role, underlining the lack of finger-pointing in the Chinese approach to the epidemic.

Human interest was the second most prominent frame in the Ebola coverage, but the focus was generally on African healers and heroes, rather than on African victims. Tales of the lives and experiences of doctors and other medical staff were featured prominently, as were those of entrepreneurs and traders trying to rebuild their businesses. The physical effects of the Ebola virus were de-dramatized: there were few shots of bodies or suffering patients and the typical illustration of an Ebola clinic was a shot of gowned health workers, or of scientists conducting trials.

The harmony frame, also frequently used, alluded to the importance to China of the display of solidarity among nations in the Ebola outbreak. China was shown as the steadfast partner of the worst-affected African countries and was repeatedly congratulated by government and international officials for its help. China's response to the Ebola outbreak was contrasted with that of the rest of the world, such as when the visiting Chinese Foreign Minister Wang Yi remarked to his West African hosts, 'When Ebola came, many people left but the Chinese people chose to stay ... and fight Ebola together with the local people' (CCTV Africa, 2015i). China was portrayed in several CCTV reports as the country that lent expertise and demanded nothing, receiving the gratitude of African states.

Some 17 per cent of the reports in the study mentioned China and its role in fighting Ebola. Curiously, however, none of these reports was narrated by a correspondent on location, although CCTV's English output frequently borrows footage collected by its Mandarin counterpart. CCTV Africa can call on more than twenty reporters around Africa for its coverage, but its deployments at this stage of the Ebola outbreak appeared relatively sparse. Earlier in the crisis CCTV had used correspondents in all of the affected countries and had profiled Chinese doctors and other experts. In the second half of 2015, however, only a quarter of the reports in the study were filmed on location, and these were nearly all in Sierra Leone: the rest were put together in Nairobi, on the other side of Africa from the Ebola virus. At this stage in the crisis, China's role was portrayed at a distance and played down in the news reports. There was no inkling of what local people thought about China and its Ebola intervention.

Officials and other elite speakers dominated the coverage, with citizens and Ebola sufferers mostly marginalized. One-third of the reports in this study contained the pronouncements of government leaders or officials, mostly Africans: Chinese officials were represented in just three reports and the United States in a single video. Half of the videos in the study featured non-governmental 'elite' speakers, in other words United Nations and aid workers, along with medical staff, scientists and teachers. Fewer than 30 per cent of the reports carried the voices of the general public, and survivors of Ebola were given their say in just over 8 per cent. This dialogue of elites was reinforced through the choice of multiple soundbites with the same speaker. The report on Sierra Leone's last Ebola patient contained three soundbites from the president but not a single word from the survivor herself. The only exceptions to this pattern came when reporters were deployed on location, when non-elite speakers such as passers-by or families of Ebola sufferers were given more of a voice.

The results of the Ebola frame analysis indicate a blurred line between 'constructive journalism' and positive reporting. The Chinese broadcaster certainly accords agency to African leaders and countries in the depiction of their fight against the virus. However, concerns about the journalistic merits of either constructive or positive reporting are underlined by omissions of critical matter from the narrative.

CCTV and China–Africa

No such ambiguity surrounds CCTV Africa's promotion of China. As befits Beijing's definition of 'soft power' (Zhang, 2016: 5; Rawnsley, 2016: 20), it is China's economic might rather than its political system that is showcased, in a manner independent of the editorial considerations found in Western newsrooms. President Xi Jinping's visit to Africa in December 2015 for the FoCAC (Forum on China–Africa Cooperation) summit was, like Premier Li Keqiang's trip the previous year, a platform for CCTV Africa to laud China's aid, investment and cultural projects on the continent. For every day of his visit, Xi Jinping led the news agenda and dominated the running order. News coverage of the trip carried a strapline reading 'Hand in Hand'. The tone of the coverage was generally upbeat and concentrated overwhelmingly on officials and their pronouncements. CCTV's Zimbabwe reporter spoke enthusiastically about progress in agriculture, tourism and education (Mwakutuya, 2015), and South Africa was described as 'a work in progress, but we're getting there' (Njamela, 2015). A more astringent commentary was delivered by a reporter in Johannesburg (Nydoo, 2015a) who spoke of the need to rebalance 'skewed imports and exports' that were in favour of China, observing later that China's slowing growth had left most African countries 'in a bit of a slump'

(Nydoo, 2015b). Otherwise, in addition to lengthy excerpts from speeches by Presidents Xi and Zuma, CCTV ran copious footage of development seminars and spoke of 'deepening interactions' and 'concrete outcomes.'[3]

> It's just the way that Chinese media works, is that the mediation, the talks, which we've been taught is terribly boring television . . . . we do summits: we do a lot of summits. And it's considered really important. And I mean, yes, important things come out of it but it's not good television.
>
> *[Journalist, CCTV Africa]*

Away from the political stage, sidebar packages showcasing China in Africa were dominated by Chinese actions and pronouncements. A concert by Chinese and African jazz musicians in Cape Town was presented as a Chinese cultural event opened by a Chinese official; the Chinese piano soloist was named and interviewed but the musicians he played with were not (Del Carme, 2015).

Staff at CCTV Africa say the emphasis on Xi's visit was an attempt to rebalance the global news narrative, seeing Western media as having a fixation on everything Barack Obama did while in office. CCTV Africa had shown editorial interest in the US President's African visit in 2015, initially according its coverage a special 'Obama In Africa' introduction, but this was not consistent: his landmark address to the African Union was not headlined in the edition of *Africa Live* that followed it,[4] and coverage amounted to just two minutes.

Analysis of news coverage on *Africa Live* revealed a lack of focus on problems associated with the Chinese presence in Africa. One journalist said anything that reflected poorly on Africa–China relations 'certainly wouldn't be given prominence and might not be treated at all'. A report from the Kruger National Park (Su, 2015) trod the finest of lines: the reporter interviewed a Chinese actor about the need for conservation but avoided specific reference to widespread Chinese consumption of endangered animal parts. Although the item had been specially filmed for Xi Jinping's Africa trip, it was not headlined in the programme. For CCTV's management, non-official Chinese activity in Africa is not a priority:

> You see some Chinese buying ivory. We also criticize this and we condemn this. [. . .] But that is a minority of the people. [. . .] Of course, you see, we come here not to report on Chinese. Our aim is to report Africa.
>
> *[Managing editor, CCTV Africa]*

Management says 'very little' editorial control resides at the broadcaster's Beijing headquarters, and that everything is approved in Nairobi. Exceptions to this concerned any problems involving Chinese nationals in Africa: one producer said this meant running 'whatever CCTV Beijing is doing or whatever Xinhua is doing. So that's the official sort of state broadcaster line that we take.'

The day-to-day prominence of the 'China in Africa' narrative in CCTV Africa's news programmes, however, should not be overplayed. In a content analysis of two constructed weeks of general news on *Africa Live* between January and March 2016, China was mentioned in 21 of 197 news items, or just over 10 per cent. However, more than half of these were non-African news packages, compiled in Beijing, about China's parliamentary 'two sessions', the 两 会 *lianghui*. This relative restraint is consistent with Wekesa's content analysis (2014) of the CCTV Talk Africa show: there, too, the incidence of Chinese-themed debates was little more than 10 per cent.

'Interference', limitations and distinctiveness

The overall reporting style employed by CCTV Africa – whether 'constructive' or 'positive' – is consistent with China's long-standing policy of non-interference in other countries' affairs. Staff say there is rarely any criticism of Zimbabwe or its president, Robert Mugabe: one news editor said he found it 'very refreshing' to see the other side of 'some places [that] we have basically dismissed as basket-cases or just dictatorships'. Managers agreed that CCTV Africa was not very critical of African governments, arguing that stability was paramount:

> Because you see, if we always criticize the government and help the people to do some radical things, like overthrow the government, it's not a help to the people. Like, Libya is the example. You see, everybody now, including President Obama, regrets what he has done in Libya. Why? Because in the past it was a normal country – but now it's not a country, it's a morgue. [...] Now you can see government, even a bad government, is better than that.
> *[Managing editor, CCTV Africa]*

It appears to be in the Nairobi newsroom that the demand for a positive outlook on the news agenda is felt most. Journalists there say it means they occasionally have to be 'a little clever and a little bit creative [...], like if you want to do a story on corruption, you're going to focus on a successful anti-corruption programme'. Although staff defend most of the editorial choices on CCTV Africa, some pointed out significant omissions such as the lack of coverage of the social rights activist and retired Anglican archbishop Desmond Tutu 'because he's great friends with the Dalai Lama'. Several journalists mentioned the decision not to cover the visit by Pope Francis to three African countries in 2015: 'We understand that it means nothing to China but it means something to our African viewers. He was right here in Kenya. They didn't send anyone to it: nothing'.[5]

Journalists who worked away from the newsroom tended to feel greater professional freedom:

> I've certainly done many stories that have come out making various African governments not look great. In that sense 1 feel comfortable about it, and I think, had I felt like I had to self-censor every time I did a story, there's no way I would have stayed.
> *[Journalist, CCTV Africa]*

I'd have still been the same me, doing the same work, had I been working for CNN, Al Jazeera, BBC – the same sort of style.

[Former correspondent, CCTV Africa]

Journalists said that occasionally Chinese managers, who perform 'second approval' on news scripts after the African editors, would scrap a story from the running order at short notice, sometimes without explanation. One Chinese manager said there were 'very few' such instances, and that most interventions concerned matters of taste, such as whether or not to broadcast news footage showing cartoons of the prophet Mohammed. Despite such restrictions, staff were generally positive about the channel:

Now I see the media in a different light. It doesn't always have to be confrontational. I don't always have to go into interviews trying to belittle you, trying to criticize you.

[Presenter, CCTV Africa]

I think we do do some amazing stuff. And I'm going to choose to focus on that rather than the restrictions because I think that as time goes by, and we do great coverage on non-controversial stories, we'll be allowed to . . . there'll be a little bit more freedom.

[African journalist, CCTV Africa]

Could CCTV-News offer more to Africa than simply 'promoting the Chinese model of development and legitimizing China's global presence' (Thussu, 2015: 259)? To borrow Thussu's comparison, CCTV Africa is certainly less alternative than Al Jazeera, less argumentative than Russia's RT. It cannot be described as a news contraflow as it still favours a dialogue of elites. Journalistically, however, there is space for a non-Western news narrative in Africa. CCTV Africa's leaning towards 'positive news' taps into widespread public disaffection with an unremitting editorial diet of gloom, but its competitors question the credibility of 'positive' reporting. The challenge for CCTV Africa lies in the dual meaning of the word 'critical' – whether it can be rigorous in its reporting while setting negativity aside. Some CCTV journalists say the channel's name has given them greater recognition and access to African leaders. Others think correspondents from rival news outlets 'look down on CCTV to some degree' and that they are 'not able to push and press the way that you might if you were working for a different organization'.

Some of CCTV Africa's editorial limitations certainly arise from its position as a state broadcaster, but others are linked to its personnel. Interviews with staff revealed frustration with the channel's inability to shape the narrative. They ascribed this to the large proportion of freelance correspondents – the very thing that distances CCTV Africa from the 'bad PR' of state control. Four reporters work directly for the channel and are based in Nairobi, but some twenty other freelance journalists around Africa are employed, some of them through agencies such as Associated Press and Feature Story News.

> For most of them [the freelancers], telling the simple story is plenty, if I can just file a simple story and get paid for it, I could do one for CCTV, I could do one for France24 and stuff like that, so you really won't get much of a distinctive [package].
>
> *[News editor, CCTV Africa]*

Limitations in deployment at CCTV Africa may also be dictated by the youth of the channel and of many of its reporters. Managers encouraged 'frontline reporting' from conflicts and were aware of the competition from other broadcasters to be seen at the heart of a story, but staff said some freelance reporters were reluctant to go into war zones or even venture out of their capital cities. Another potential source of distinctive material, the re-versioning of footage collected by CCTV Mandarin correspondents, was described by one editor as 'very limited'. CCTV Africa's focus is also blurred by the lack of reliable figures for audience research (Bailard, 2016: 449). Staff in Nairobi have varying opinions on whether their target viewers are African, Chinese or global.

Upbeat reporting alone will not make CCTV Africa stand out from its rivals. The deputy managing editor observed difficulties in finding 'a good balance' in the daily news in particular as it was impossible to ignore 'disaster' stories: he indicated it was only through business, sport and documentary programmes that equilibrium on the channel could be achieved. News feature material from some of CCTV Africa's freelance reporters is consistent with neither positive nor constructive journalism, indicating that the 'half-orchestrated, half freestyle' state described by Li and Rønning (2013) is still representative of the Chinese media's reporting of African affairs. News features for CCTV from north-eastern Nigeria by a British journalist, Katerina Vittozzi, detailed the plight and privation of citizens displaced by Boko Haram insurgents without any immediate prospect of a solution (CCTV Africa, 2015j). While reporting from the Central African Republic in 2014, Jane Kiyo witnessed a lynching and immediately ditched her planned story to cover the atrocity for the Chinese broadcaster, as any other international journalist might do (CCTV Africa, 2014). These examples lend weight to the supposition that, when left to their own devices, on-the-ground reporters for CCTV Africa and their counterparts at Western broadcasters follow much the same journalistic code.

However, a news editor pointed out that negative images of Africa could be dispelled through the provision of more information, and that this could be CCTV Africa's strength:

> I think the perception problem around Africa is not because too many bad things are happening: it's that very few people have a context to those bad things happening. [...] When it's presented as a very simple story, the over-simplification of stories in Africa, I think, is what creates the negative perception of the continent.

A challenging future

CCTV Africa has big ambitions. A doubling of output to five hours a day is planned, and managers hope eventually for a 24-hour African channel. The managing editor says CCTV Africa 'will remain here permanently'. At the same time, the Chinese state and Chinese businesses are entrenching themselves ever more deeply in the continent. Security cooperation in Africa is now a central part of China's strategy (Duchâtel *et al.*, 2016), with Beijing not only providing combat troops for peacekeeping operations, but also building a naval base in Djibouti. In 2016, the first Chinese peacekeepers were killed in action in Mali and South Sudan. The deeper the Chinese involvement in Africa, the looser its non-interference policy becomes, and the greater the test of CCTV Africa's ability to scrutinize and communicate China's objectives and actions.

Tiangao or *tianxia?* – the soft power jury is out on CCTV Africa. At first glance, it is the image of Africa that may gain from CCTV's presence rather than the image and worldview of China itself.

> I hope one day people can look back and say, actually, my idea of Africa is so different now, having watched CCTV: this is not what I thought Africa was about . . . and then it becomes the norm – oh, you can go to Africa because this is what they do.
>
> *[Presenter, CCTV Africa]*

Sustained media interest in African countries, funded from deep pockets in Beijing, may well attract admirers if the coverage is positive or uncritical. The forward-looking narrative promoted by 'constructive' or 'positive' reporting may help developing nations by not crushing them under too much early scrutiny. However, lacunae in CCTV Africa's critical focus harm its overall journalistic credibility, no matter how widely its features and some of its news reporting are praised. African journalism – rooted in Western traditions – is acquiring the tools to hold its own leaders to account. CCTV Africa may disseminate Chinese soft power, but its state media position militates against the notion that it can be a source of soft power itself (Zhang, 2016: 9). Heaven may be high but, where public trust in independent news is concerned, is the emperor ever far enough away?

Notes

1 Relaunched as CGTN Africa at the end of 2016.
2 All CCTV Africa employees in this chapter were interviewed by the author in 2016.
3 *Africa Live*, 2–3 December 2015.
4 *Africa Live*, 28 July 2015.
5 Interviews with African journalists, CCTV Africa.

References

Al Jazeera (2016) Africa news. Available at: www.aljazeera.com/topics/regions/africa.html.

Bailard, Catie Snow (2016) China in Africa: An analysis of the effect of Chinese media expansion on African public opinion, *International Journal of Press/Politics*, 21(4): 446–471.

BBC (2011) The Chinese Are Coming. Broadcast 24 February, BBC2. Available at: www.bbc.co.uk/programmes/b00ykxg9.

BBC (2012) BBC announces major new focus on Africa. *BBC Media Centre*, 7 June. Available at: www.bbc.co.uk/mediacentre/worldnews/070612focusonafrica.html.

BBC News (2012) *China Daily* newspaper launches African edition. 14 December. Available at: www.bbc.co.uk/news/world-asia-china-20722952.

BBC News (2016) Africa–China exports fall by 40% after China slowdown. 13 January. Available at: www.bbc.co.uk/news/world-africa-35303981.

Bunce, Melanie (2015) International News and the Image of Africa: New Storytellers, New Narratives?, in Gallagher, J. (ed.) *Images of Africa: Creation, Negotiation and Subversion*. Manchester: Manchester University Press.

Callahan, William (2007) Tianxia, empire and the world: Soft power and China's foreign policy discourse in the 21st century. *BICC Working Paper* Series 1: 1–24. Available at: www.bicc.ac.uk/files/2012/06/01-Callahan.pdf.

CCTV (2015) About CCTV Africa. Available at: http://cctv-africa.com/about-cctv-africa/.

CCTV (2016) Afrique Infos. Available at: http://cctv.cntv.cn/lm/afriqueinfos/index.shtml.

CCTV Africa (2014) Jane Kiyo's experience in the C.A.R., 15 February. Available at: www.youtube.com/watch?v=gSaMbFpNJng.

CCTV Africa (2015a) The African Dream – Senegal, 16 June. Available at: www.youtube.com/watch?v=yS1y3fnBBfY.

CCTV Africa (2015b) Ebola setback: Liberia steps up emergency response after virus re-emergence. Report from Nairobi by Jane Kiyo, 3 July. Available at: www.youtube.com/watch?v=BaFdx5o1KpI.

CCTV Africa (2015c) Sierra Leone's last Ebola patient discharged. Report from Nairobi by Kathryn Ogunde, 25 August. Available at: www.youtube.com/watch?v=zozPe41yXN4.

CCTV Africa (2015d) Countdown towards Guinea's Ebola-free status ends in November. Report from Nairobi by Mahia Mutua, 14 October. Available at: www.youtube.com/watch?v=rdmsk-DST5k.

CCTV Africa (2015e) Ebola vaccine trial proves 100% successful in Guinea. Report from Nairobi by Susan Mwongeli, 1 August. Available at: www.youtube.com/watch?v=HHCC5khGwNc.

CCTV Africa (2015f) New investigations say WHO failed to handle Ebola crisis. Report from Nairobi by Kathryn Ogunde, 21 September. Available at: www.youtube.com/watch?v=jFe8kFGUWoM.

CCTV Africa (2015g) Polio resurfaces in Mali from Ebola-hit Guinea. Report from Nairobi by Robert Nagila, 8 September. Available at: www.youtube.com/watch?v=bPdRSd9Oz40.

CCTV Africa (2015h) WHO: Ebola will be eradicated in 2015. Report from Nairobi by Susan Mwongeli, 10 September. Available at: www.youtube.com/watch?v=ndTozq7_KeU.

CCTV Africa (2015i) China to continue assisting Ebola-affected countries. Report from Nairobi by Kofa Mrenje, 13 August. Available at: www.youtube.com/watch?v=acgj-I31uKg.

CCTV Africa (2015j) Life in the Shadow of Boko Haram. 14–15 September. Nairobi: CCTV News. Available at: www.youtube.com/playlist?list=PLKijeAOQYrq0mzHNf3Rcjed87ZQr2_gih.

Chan, Stephen (2013) The Middle Kingdom and the Dark Continent: An Essay on China, Africa and Many Fault Lines, in Chan, S. (ed.) *The Morality of China in Africa: The Middle Kingdom and the Dark Continent*. London: Zed: 3–43.

CNN (2016) Africa News. Available at: http://edition.cnn.com/africa.

Constructive Journalism Project (n.d.) About Constructive Journalism Project. Available at: http://constructivejournalism.org/about/.

Del Carme, Rene (2015) Report from South Africa. *On Africa Live*. Nairobi: CCTV-News, 1700 GMT.

Delury, John (2008) 'Harmonious' in China. *Policy Review*. [Online]. Available at www.hoover. org/research/harmonious-china [Retrieved 2 August 2017].

Duchâtel, Mathieu; Gowan, Richard and Rapnouil, Manuel Lafont (2016) Into Africa: China's Global Security Shift. *European Council on Foreign Relations*. [Online]. Available at www.ecfr.eu/publications/summary/into_africa_chinas_global_security_shift [Retrieved 2 August 2017].

Faces of Africa (2015) The Puppet Masters Part 2, 2 November. Nairobi: CCTV News. Available at: www.youtube.com/watch?v=4ksTGzPW8YI.

FoCAC (2013) Speech by Mr Lu Shaye on the seminar of Chinese dream, African dream. *China-Africa Joint Research & Exchange Programme*, 17 July. Available at: http://wcm.fmprc. gov.cn/pub/zflt/eng/xsjl/zflhyjjljh/t1059481.htm.

Li, Shubo and Rønning, Helge (2013) Half-orchestrated, half freestyle: Soft power and reporting Africa in China. *Ecquid Novi: African Journalism Studies*, 34(3): 102–124.

Li, Xiguang (2001) Creeping Freedoms in China's Press, in Brahm, L. (ed.) *China's Century: The Awakening of the Next Economic Powerhouse*. Singapore: Wiley: 386–402.

Marsh, Vivien (2016a) Mixed messages, partial pictures? Discourses under construction in CCTV's *Africa Live* compared with the BBC, *Chinese Journal of Communication*, 9(1): 56–70.

Marsh, Vivien (2016b) Africa through Chinese Eyes: New Frames or the Same Old Lens? African News in English from China Central Television, Compared with the BBC, in Bunce, Melanie; Franks, Suzanne and Paterson, Chris (eds.) *Africa's Media Image in the 21st Century: From the 'Heart of Darkness' to 'Africa Rising'*. Abingdon: Routledge: 177–189.

McIntyre, Karen (2015) *Constructive Journalism: The Effects of Positive Emotions and Solution Information in News Stories*. PhD Thesis, Chapel Hill: University of North Carolina.

Mwakutuya, Farai (2015) Report from Zimbabwe. On *Africa Live*. Nairobi: CCTV-News, 1700 GMT.

Njamela, Yolisa (2015) Report from South Africa. On *Africa Live*. Nairobi: CCTV-News, 1700 GMT.

Nydoo, Sumitra (2015a) Report from South Africa. On *Africa Live*. Nairobi: CCTV-News, 1700 GMT.

Nydoo, Sumitra (2015b) Report from South Africa. On *Africa Live*. Nairobi: CCTV-News, 1700 GMT.

Pigato, Miria and Tang, Wenxia (2015) *China and Africa: Expanding Economic Ties in an Evolving Global Context*. World Bank, Investing in Africa forum, March. Available at: www.worldbank. org/content/dam/Worldbank/Event/Africa/Investing in Africa Forum/2015/investing-in-africa-forum-china-and-africa-expanding-economic-ties-in-an-evolving-global-context.pdf.

Qian, Gang (2012) Watchwords: Reading China through its Political Vocabulary. *JMSC Working Papers*, University of Hong Kong. Available at: http://jmsc.hku.hk/2012/11/jmsc-series-unlocks-political-jargon-china/.

Qian, Gang (2014) Reading Chinese politics in 2014. *China Media Project*, 30 December. Available at: http://cmp.hku.hk/2014/12/30/37469/.

Ran, Jijun (2016) Evolving Media Interactions Between China and Africa, in Zhang, X.; Wasserman, H. and Mano, W. (eds.) *China's Media and Soft Power in Africa: Promotion and Perceptions*. London: Palgrave Macmillan: 47–61.

Rawnsley, Gary (2016) Reflections of a Soft Power Agnostic, in Zhang, X.; Wasserman, H. and Mano, W. (eds.) *China's Media and Soft Power in Africa: Promotion and Perceptions.* London: Palgrave Macmillan: 19–31.

Semetko, Holli and Valkenburg, Patti (2000) Framing European politics: A content analysis of press and television news, *Journal of Communication*, 50(2): 93–109.

Su, Yuting (2015) Report from South Africa. On *Africa Live*. Nairobi: CCTV-News, 1700 GMT.

Taylor, Ian (2006) *China and Africa: Engagement and Compromise.* Abingdon: Routledge.

Tembe, Paul (2015) The temptations and promotion of 'China Dream': Calling for Africa's home-grown rhetoric. *CCS Policy Briefing.*

Thussu, Daya Kishan (2015) Reinventing 'Many Voices': MacBride and a Digital New World Information and Communication Order. *Javnost – The Public*, 22(3): 252–263.

Trevaskes, Susan; Nesossi, Elisa; Sapio, Flora and Biddulph, Sarah (eds.) (2014) *The Politics of Law and Stability in China.* Cheltenham: Edward Elgar.

Tullis, Ashleigh (2014) Constructive Journalism: Emerging mega-trend or a recipe for complacency? in *World News Publishing Focus*, 18 November. Available at: http://blog. wan-ifra.org/2014/11/18/constructive-journalism-emerging-mega-trend-or-a-recipe-for-complacency.

UK Government (2011) Transcript of PM's speech on aid, trade and democracy, 19 July. Available at: www.gov.uk/government/speeches/pms-speech-on-aid-trade-and-democracy.

US State Department (2011) Transcript of interview on Africa 360, 11 June. Available at: www.state.gov/secretary/20092013clinton/rm/2011/06/165941.htm.

Wang, Ban (2016) Tianxia: Imperial Ambition or Cosmopolitanism? *China Policy Institute Analysis*, 5 October. Available at: https://cpianalysis.org/2016/10/05/tianxia-imperial-ambition-or-cosmopolitanism/.

Wasserman, Herman (2016) China's 'soft power' and its influence on editorial agendas in South Africa, *Chinese Journal of Communication*, 9(1): 8–20.

Wekesa, Bob (2014) An analysis of China Central Television's Talk Africa debate show. Paper presented at the international conference, *China and Africa Media, Communications and Public Diplomacy,* CMI/CASS, 10–11 September, Beijing.

Wekesa, Bob and Zhang, Yanqiu (2014) Live, Talk, Faces: An analysis of CCTV's adaption to the African media market. Discussion paper, May, Stellenbosch University.

Wu, Yu-Shan (2012) The Rise of China's State-Led Media Dynasty in Africa. *China in Africa Project, Occasional Paper No. 117.* South African Institute of International Affairs.

Xin, Xin (2012) *How the Market is Changing China's News: The Case of Xinhua News Agency.* Plymouth: Lexington Books.

Xinhua (2015) China's investment in Africa falls 40% in H1: MOC. 18 November. Available at: www.chinadaily.com.cn/business/2015-11/18/content_22480510.htm.

Zhang, Feng (2009) The tianxia system: World order in a Chinese utopia, *Global Asia*, 4(4): 108–112.

Zhang, Xiaoling (2013) How ready is China for a China-style world order? China's state media discourse under construction, *Ecquid Novi: African Journalism Studies*, 34(3): 79–101.

Zhang, Xiaoling (2016) A World of Shared Influence, in Zhang, X.; Wasserman, H. and Mano, W. (eds.) *China's Media and Soft Power in Africa: Promotion and Perceptions.* London: Palgrave Macmillan: 3–16.

Zhang, Yanqiu (2014a) Construct Relations via Constructive Journalism: A New Paradigm of Chinese Media in Africa. Paper presented at the international symposium, *China's Soft Power in Africa*, China: The University of Nottingham Ningbo.

Zhang, Yanqiu (2014b) Understand China's Media in Africa from the Perspective of Constructive Journalism. Paper for the *China and Africa Media, Communications and Public Diplomacy conference* (CMI), Beijing.

Zhang, Yanqiu and Matingwina, Simon (2016) A new representation of Africa? The use of constructive journalism in the narration of Ebola by *China Daily* and the BBC, *African Journalism Studies*, 37(3): 19–40.

Zheng, Yongnian and Tok, Sow Keat (2007) 'Harmonious Society' and 'Harmonious World': China's Policy Discourse under Hu Jintao, in *Briefing Series,* China Policy Institute, University of Nottingham. [Online]. Available at https://nottingham.ac.uk/cpi/documents/briefings/briefing-26-harmonious-society-and-harmonious-world.pdf [Retrieved 2 August 2017].

7

CHINA DAILY – BEIJING'S GLOBAL VOICE?

Falk Hartig

In his address to the Australian parliament in November 2014, Chinese President Xi Jinping likened his country to 'a big guy in the crowd' whom others might view suspiciously, but stressed that China would continue to pursue a peaceful development path (Xinhua, 2014). Xi noted that while many people applaud China's achievements, others have concerns 'and there are also people who find fault with everything China does' (Xi, 2014). Others naturally wonder how the big guy will move and act, and they may be concerned that the big guy may push them around, stand in their way or even take up their place' (ibid.). Xi dismissed those concerns, vowing that his country remains unshakeable in its resolve to pursue peaceful and common development.

While critics may discount such a statement as rhetorical window-dressing, it clearly illustrates that the Chinese leadership 'is aware that China's reputation in other countries can be a major factor in their assessments of Chinese intentions and in their corresponding responses to China's rising capabilities' (Ross and Johnston, 2006: 5). There is increasing acknowledgement that China's concern over its international image and status is 'a driving force in China's foreign relations' (Li, 2012: 33). A number of studies (Barr, 2011; Wang, 2011; Li, 2009; Ding, 2008) suggest that the PRC in 'its search for status as a global power [...] has discovered the importance of international image and soft power' (Shambaugh, 2013: 207) and 'image considerations weigh heavily on the minds of Chinese decision-makers' (Rabinovitch, 2008: 32). These considerations are reflected in the increasing awareness of public diplomacy by both Chinese academics and officials, who see it as the instrument to shape China's international image and to tell China's story to the world (Hartig, 2016). This increasing awareness, in turn, leads to increasing funding for public diplomacy. According to the latest estimates, China is annually investing about $10 billion in its conduct of public diplomacy (Shambaugh, 2015).

Essentially China uses similar public diplomacy instruments to other countries, including international media, publications, academic exchanges and seminars, international exhibitions, cultural and arts performances, and cultural institutes abroad. China also conducts 'panda diplomacy' and recently started to engage in 'First Lady diplomacy'. Panda diplomacy (*xiongmao waijiao*) refers to China's loan of giant pandas to selected countries around the world. Officially sent to promote and support animal conservation and biological research, giant pandas are a strong symbol of China's foreign policy, used by the Chinese government to win hearts, and maybe minds, abroad. Normally, a pair of pandas is on loan for ten years and hosting zoos have to pay about $1 million annually which makes them a cost-saving tool of Chinese public diplomacy (Hartig, 2013b). First Lady diplomacy (*diyi furen waijiao*) refers to the strategic utilization of the international image and activities by First Lady Peng Liyuan, who, according to Chinese reports has 'charmed the world' with 'her personal appearance to convey Chinese culture', her 'charity actions to communicate love and care', her 'music to open communication' and her 'successful marriage to the leader' (Luo, 2015).

Although there is recognizably an increasing variety of instruments, the 'Chinese government considers the media to be the major instrument of China's public diplomacy' (d'Hooghe, 2015: 164). This chapter takes d'Hooghe's finding as a starting point and introduces the English-language newspaper *China Daily* as one instrument of China's public diplomacy. It starts with a brief discussion of public diplomacy in China and of *China Daily* as one of its instruments. It then looks at the newspaper in China before it investigates the recent global ambitions of the newspaper group with a special focus on Africa and Europe.

Conceptual framework – public diplomacy in China

Broadly understood, public diplomacy is 'a country's engagement and communication with foreign publics' (Wang, 2011: 3) and its practice can be divided into six elements: 'listing, advocacy, cultural diplomacy, exchange diplomacy, international broadcasting, and psychological warfare' (Cull, 2009: 10). As China becomes increasingly engaged with the rest of the world (and vice versa), the Chinese government has realized the importance of favourable international public opinion (*lianghao guoji yulun*) to the development of the country. As a result, public diplomacy has become an important part of China's overall diplomacy (Zhao, 2012). From the Chinese point of view, there is an urgent need to communicate better with the wider world, as the scepticism towards China mostly results from an incorrectly perceived picture of the PRC. This argument holds that it is up to China to talk back and to explain its real self, or the real China (Zhao, 2007). According to Zhao Qizheng, one of the leading figures in China's public diplomacy debates, public diplomacy should be characterized by a self-confident approach, illustrated in his statement: 'China should not only listen, but talk back' (Zhao, 2007). Zhao furthermore urges China's public diplomacy to present the 'true image' of the 'real China' (Zhao, 2010).

Taken together, China's public diplomacy

> informs and is informed by a specific political agenda and a determination to project an image of strength, affluence, and political responsibility that

surmounts the popular impression of China as a state which routinely violates human rights and threatens global stability.

(Rawnsley, 2009: 282)

Therefore such diplomacy should help with 'promoting business activities both within and outside China' (Aoyama, 2007: 5). In this regard, Chinese scholars frankly state that the principal goal of public diplomacy, similar to that of traditional diplomacy, is to safeguard and promote national interests (*weihu he zengjin guojia liyi*) (Liao, 2009; Zhang, 2009).

While the non-Chinese discourse focuses on mutuality, exchange and reciprocal communication in the context of new public diplomacy (Melissen, 2005), the Chinese understanding tends to define public diplomacy more functionally, as China is more concerned to get its message out and convince the world of its benign intentions (d'Hooghe, 2015). These goals go beyond normative notions of new public diplomacy into realist calculations where world politics is driven by competitive self-interest (Hartig, 2016).

China Daily as an instrument of China's public diplomacy

In 2011, Liu Binjie, then director of the General Administration of Press and Publication (*Xinwen Chuban Zongshu*), stated that the country would increase investment in mainstream media organizations until 2020, 'especially those targeting overseas readers' to 'better present a true picture of China to the world' (quoted in Qiu, 2011). The major mainstream organization targeting overseas readers is the China Daily Group. The group, according to its mission statement, 'is an authoritative provider of information, analysis, comment and entertainment for global readers with a special focus on China' (*China Daily*, n.d.). It runs 16 print publications in China and abroad and is in charge of eight website clusters and three mobile platforms (ibid.).

China Daily in China

In China, the group runs *China Business Weekly*, the *Shanghai Star*, *Beijing Weekend*, *21st Century*, *21st Century Teens Senior Edition*, and *21st Century Teens Junior Edition* (*China Daily*, n.d.1). The flagship publication, and name giver of the whole group, however, is the newspaper *China Daily*. The newspaper was founded on 1 June 1981, and publishes 24-page editions Monday to Friday, plus 16-page editions on Saturday and Sunday in broadsheet format. The paper undertook a major relaunch in March 2010, not only to broaden 'its international appeal' but also to claw back domestic readership from the *Global Times*[1] (Shambaugh, 2013: 234). Shambaugh further notes that the relaunch 'resulted in a complete makeover for the paper, leaving it much more readable and informative' (ibid.).

According to its mission statement, *China Daily* is committed 'to helping the world know more about China and the country's integration with the international

community' (*China Daily*, n.d.1). It is regarded as one of the country's most authoritative English media outlets and an important source of information on Chinese
politics, economy, society and culture. It is often described as the 'Voice of China'
or 'Window to China' (ibid.). According to Qu Yingpu, *China Daily*'s deputy editor-
in-chief, the paper has five main priorities in reporting: 'What is happening in
China; why is it happening; what are the future trends; what is the impact on the
outside world; and how Chinese people perceive the outside world' (quoted in
Shambaugh, 2013: 235).

Readers within China are mainly foreign diplomats and the growing number of
foreign expatriates, as well as 'high-end nationals' such as Chinese diplomats and
governmental policy makers (ibid.). Additionally, as Liu (2011: 137) points out,
Chinese people who want to improve their English also read the paper. Overseas
subscribers are mostly government officials, members of parliament, staff members
of international organizations and multinational corporations, professors, researchers
and students in universities and institutes.

It remains, however, somewhat unclear how many people the paper reaches.
China Daily itself notes an average daily circulation of more than 200,000 copies,
one-third of which is abroad and these numbers appear in the few academic analyses
as well (Chen, 2012, 2013). Other, more journalistic, accounts mention roughly
500,000 copies (Meyer, 2013: 15). David Shambaugh (2013: 234), referring to an
interview with *China Daily* deputy editor-in-chief Qu Yingpu in 2010, reports a
global circulation of more than 400,000 (280,000 domestic, 50,000 in Hong Kong
and Macao, and 100,000 overseas). While concrete numbers remain vague, it is clear
that the distribution has broadened in China in recent years. Some years ago, Chen
(2004: 678) noted that the newspaper 'is not even available to buy on the street and
is instead circulated by public subscription', a situation that has changed: nowadays
one can buy copies for ¥1.50 in book stores and in newsstands in major Chinese
cities, although the paper is easier to find in places close to tourist spots, international hotels or foreign embassies.

China Daily is owned by China's principal Chinese-language newspaper and the
mouthpiece of the Chinese Communist Party (CCP), the *People's Daily* (*Renmin
Ribao*) and is therefore described as the 'English-language sister paper' (Chen, 2012:
309) and as the 'mouthpiece for the Party in its efforts to communicate with the
wider world' (Chen, 2012: 309). Due to the close connection to the *People's Daily*,
the *China Daily* not only draws on many of the same sources of information and
adopts the same line on major news items (Chen, 2004), but also party control is
exerted on the *China Daily*, as on other Chinese newspapers, through the CCP's
Publicity Department (ibid.). This leads some to describe *China Daily* as a 'propaganda effort by the central government, in the guise of news reporting, about government policy on social issues of the day' (Lanigan, 2015: 506), while others note
that the editorial policies of *China Daily* 'are considered to be slightly more liberal
than other Chinese-language newspapers' (Liu, 2011: 138) and that *China Daily*
'often covers delicate issues in China that receive little or no coverage in the
Chinese-language media' (Hays, 2008). Markus Wanzeck, a German journalist who

participated in a German–Chinese journalism exchange programme and worked for *China Daily* in 2009, describes the newspaper quite aptly as a corporate publishing project of the Chinese government: 'partially it provides professional, informative fare; partially, especially when dealing with "sensitive" topics such as Tibet or Taiwan, it functions as a display or selling window for official party politics' (Wanzeck, 2013: 184).

Foreigners, mainly English native speakers, play an important role within *China Daily* because, as outlined above, the newspaper is written in English by Chinese journalists, 'whose work is then "polished" by foreign journalists working as sub-editors' (Chen, 2004: 679). Although these polishers may participate in editorial meetings they have 'virtually no influence on, and often little knowledge of, decisions involving the most sensitive matters' (Conley and Tripoli, 1992: 27, quoted in Chen, 2004: 680). As Chinese media is expanding, the number of foreign journalists working for Chinese media is also increasing, as is the number of reports about working as 'a "polisher" in a Chinese news factory' (Swan, 1996: 33; see also Needham, 2007; Newham, 2011; Radtke, 2013). Those accounts, although at times rather sensationalist in style, present interesting insights into the work of this state-run newspaper. Needham, an Australian journalist with *The Sydney Morning Herald*, worked for three months for *China Daily* in 2004. She describes her work as 'polishing strident editorials in the daily mouthpiece' and what she calls 'the art of the foreign expert language polisher [...] to tweak propaganda enough that it read as English, without inadvertently triggering war' (Needham, 2004).

This assessment, then, raises the question how to understand the very term 'propaganda'. Propaganda is probably 'the oldest and most prominent type of information initiative that political entities use with publics' (Zaharna, 2009: 89) and originally, propaganda 'in the most neutral sense means to disseminate or promote particular ideas' (Jowett and O'Donnell, 2006: 2). Nowadays, however, there are two opposing academic understandings of propaganda, described by Brown as the 'moralist school' and the 'neutralist school' (Brown, 2006). The moralist school states that propaganda is intrinsically misleading and therefore morally reprehensible while the neutralist understanding – in the words of Brown (2006) the 'no-nonsense view' – is reflected in Lasswell's statement: 'propaganda as a mere tool is no more moral or immoral than a pump handle' (quoted in Sproule, 1997: 69).

Rawnsley (2000a: 136) also notes that propaganda 'is (wrongly) associated with manipulation, and we are naturally suspicious of any form of manipulation since it implies the secret exercise of power that is beyond our immediate control'. According to him, it is essential to understand 'that propaganda is merely the means to a predetermined end', and 'it should be without moral judgment, since history has demonstrated that propaganda can serve either constructive or destructive interests' (Rawnsley, 2000b: 3). This, however, is essentially an academic debate whereas the public understanding relates propaganda to 'lies, distortion, deceit, manipulation, mind control, psychological warfare, brainwashing, and palaver' (Jowett and O'Donnell, 2006: 2–3). Those considerations point to one of the most salient debates about whether government-sponsored activities 'are manipulative "propaganda" or valid "public diplomacy"' (Zaharna, 2004: 219). This perspective sees propaganda as something done by 'others', while 'we' do public diplomacy. Gilboa describes this as the distinction made by officials between providing 'civilized persuasion [thus public diplomacy] rather than distortions, half-truths, and innuendos [thus propaganda]' (Gilboa, 1998: 58). Looking particularly at the case of China,[2] Rawnsley notes that one may suspect

> that the Chinese do not separate clearly their understanding or their practice of propaganda and public diplomacy, and that often the activities are so blurred that the cynic might suggest that, in the Chinese world, public diplomacy is merely a euphemism for propaganda.
>
> *(Rawnsley, 2013: 148)*

While, then, it is ultimately in the eye of the beholder whether those communicative practices are propaganda or public diplomacy, it is clear that *China Daily* presents the official version of China to its readers.

Wanzeck (2010) recalls how *China Daily* adjusts international news items to official Chinese narratives. When Taiwan's former President Chen Shui-bian went on trial in March 2009 accused of a series of corruption charges, *China Daily* released a modified news item from Associated Press (AP). The modification included the cutting of the sentence 'Taiwan and China split amid civil war in 1949' that was included in the AP piece. Furthermore, while AP noted Chen had 'anti-Chinese views', *China Daily* described those as 'political views' and AP's description of Chen as the 'former president' of Taiwan was modified into 'former "president"' (Wanzeck, 2010: 44). Needham (2004) also describes the usage of inverted commas in the case of Chen Shui-bian, which was meant to 'ridicule legitimacy'. These examples illustrate how control of public language is applied in order to support state power in the PRC, a phenomenon that Schoenhals (1992) discussed in his book *Doing Things with Words in Chinese Politics*.

China Daily around the world

Li Changchun, in charge of propaganda in the Hu-Wen administration, explained in late 2008 why China was becoming more and more active in international communication. According to Li, 'communication capacity determines influence' (Li, 2008). In this day and age, Li continued, 'whose communication methods are [most] advanced and whose communication capacity is the strongest, it will be [this nation] whose culture, ideas and worldview can spread far and wide and [this nation] has the most power to influence the world' (ibid.). Therefore, Li said,

> strengthening the setup of our domestic and international communication capacity is related to the overall situation of China's reform and opening up and modernization; it is related to China's international influence and

international status; it is related to the upgrading of our nation's cultural soft power and the role of our nation's media in the international public opinion structure.

(ibid.)

In late 2014 Xi Jinping made a similar statement which illustrates the Chinese leadership's 'growing sensitiveness to how it is perceived by the international community' (Chen, 2013: 82). Xi delivered an address at the Central Conference on Work Relating to Foreign Affairs in which he noted that it is necessary to 'give a good Chinese narrative, and better communicate China's message to the world' (FMPRC, 2014).

One instrument to better communicate China's message to the world is *China Daily* which is not only distributed in China but also globally. Next to the 'mother newspaper' in mainland China, the China Daily Group also publishes the Hong Kong, US, European, African, Asian and Latin American editions of *China Daily*, with, according to its own statistics, a total circulation of 900,000 copies (*China Daily*, n.d.). While *China Daily* in mainland China is published on a daily basis, there are two different forms of appearance outside the mainland. There is a *China Daily Hong Kong* edition and a *China Daily USA* edition, both with daily frequency, and there are weekly editions for Asia, Europe, North America, Africa and Latin America. The newspaper also publishes *China Watch*, which is circulated as a monthly supplement with the *Washington Post*, *Los Angeles Times* and London's *Daily Telegraph*.

China Daily USA was launched in 2009. It publishes 16 pages from Monday to Friday and a 20-page Friday edition and it is distributed in the US and Canada. Circulation includes the headquarters of the United Nations, government agencies, think tanks, major financial institutes and leading companies. *China Daily*'s activities in the US, furthermore, include direct mail campaigns and setting up coin boxes on the streets of major cities. Overall, as Shambaugh (2013: 234) notes, '*China Daily* is aggressively marketing in the United States'. In 2012, *China Daily North America* was launched, a 20-page weekly that reaches 'mainstream political, business and academic circles in Canada' (*China Daily*, n.d.). *China Daily Asia Weekly*, launched in 2010, offers 32 pages each week, and is distributed throughout the Asia-Pacific region, in countries including Australia, Japan, Korea, Indonesia, India, Thailand, Singapore, Malaysia and the United Arab Emirates. *China Daily Asia Weekly ASEAN Edition* was launched in May 2013. The 32-page weekly is circulated around Southeast Asia (ibid.).

According to the Media Profile 2013, *China Daily Asia Weekly* has a total circulation of 273,100 copies which are regionally distributed as shown in Table 7.1.

According to *China Daily*'s own statistics, 77 per cent of the readers of *China Daily Asia Weekly* are between 25 and 44 years old, 81 per cent have a college degree or above and 58 per cent are described as being 'senior executives' (China Daily Asia Pacific Limited, n.d.: 21).

China Daily European Weekly was launched in 2010. Each edition has 32 pages and is distributed in about 30 European countries, including Britain, Germany,

TABLE 7.1 Regional distribution of *China Daily Asia Weekly* (2013)

Country/Region	Distributed via	Circulation
Hong Kong and Macau	Bundled with *China Daily Hong Kong*	20,000
Mainland China	Standalone copy	5,000
Indonesia	Bundled with *The Jakarta Post*	58,000
India	Bundled with *The Mint*	40,000
Japan	Bundled with *The Wall Street Journal*	5,100
South Korea	Standalone copy	10,000
Australia	Standalone copy	30,000
United Arab Emirates and Gulf Countries	Bundled with *Gulf News*	30,000
Singapore	Bundled with *The Straits Times*	20,000
Thailand	Bundled with *The Nation*	20,000
Malaysia	Standalone copy	30,000
Nepal	Bundled with *Nepali Times*	5,000

Source: Adapted from China Daily Asia Pacific Limited (n.d.).

Belgium and France. *China Daily Africa Weekly*, launched in 2012, offers 32 pages each week. Circulation covers countries such as Kenya, South Africa, Nigeria, Ethiopia, Tanzania and Ghana. Most recently, *China Daily Latin America Weekly* was launched in 2013, which offers 16 pages each week. Circulation currently covers places such as Brazil's Sao Paulo and Brasilia (*China Daily*, n.d.).

China Daily in Africa and Europe

A closer look at two editions of *China Daily* provides further insights into this tool of China's public diplomacy with regard to international perception and audiences. In recent years, Chinese media organizations have been expanding in Africa and the flourishing China–Africa relationship has been matched by Beijing's concerted effort to build an 'impressive' media presence in Africa (Wan, 2015). According to Mary Harper, Africa editor of the BBC World Service, who has reported on events on the continent since the early 1990s, 'Chinese media is much more visible now in Africa' (quoted in Shek, 2013). 'Even though there have been Chinese media operations in Africa ever since I started working on the continent, I've noticed a really dramatic rise in their presence,' says Harper (ibid.). African cable television audiences have access to CNC World, the English-language television channel of Xinhua news agency while China Central Television (CCTV) uses its office in Nairobi as a base to cover news on the continent, and the English-language edition of *China Daily* has extended the newspaper's reach to English-language readers in major African centres, as well as online (Wasserman, 2013: 1–2). China Radio International and Xinhua have also grown their presence on the continent. Xinhua, for example, is planning 200 overseas bureaus and 'more than 20 are in Africa' (Harber, 2013: 150).

The key Chinese media with a presence in Africa are: China Radio International (first broadcast from Kenya in 2006); Xinhua news agency (established a regional office in Kenya in 1986, re-calibrated into Africa regional headquarters in 2006); *StarTimes* (established first office in Rwanda in 2007); *China Daily Africa* edition (published since December 2012, launched January 2013 with African headquarters in Nairobi); *China Africa* magazine (set up an African office in South Africa, 2012); *People's Daily* (set up Africa base in Johannesburg in 2011); and CCTV Africa (Wekesa and Zhang, 2014: 4). The presence of CCTV in Africa has attracted the attention of scholars: Gagliardone (2013: 25), for example, argues that CCTV Africa is not directly offering an alternative narrative about China, but it is much more concerned with 'advancing new ways of looking at Africa'. Marsh also shows, comparing a CCTV Africa programme with its BBC counterpart, that the CCTV 'did indeed show signs of developing an alternative to the "Western gaze", which reduces Africa to a litany of conflicts and famines. Chinese subject matter and Chinese interests had a disproportionate effect on its editorial agenda' (Marsh, 2016: 56; Gorfinkel *et al.*, 2014). The notion of a non-Western representation of Africa is confirmed by another recent study which finds that 'CCTV Africa has, to a large extent, managed to approach African issues from a different and new perspective' (Zhang and Matingwina, 2016: 103).

While we know something of China's TV operation on the African continent, not much information so far is available concerning its print media such as *China Daily*. *China Daily Africa Weekly* was started in 2012 as a 24-page weekly introducing economic, trade cooperation, and cultural exchanges between China and different countries in Africa. It circulates among government offices, institutions, diplomatic personnel, think tanks, commercial enterprises, universities and international organizations across Africa. At the launch of the newspaper, officials from both sides highlighted the importance of the newspaper and situated the paper in the context of Sino-African friendship and South–South solidarity. Chinese State Councillor Dai Bingguo stated that *Africa Weekly* would be a channel of good communication between Chinese and African people, while Foreign Minister Yang Jiechi urged the newspaper to report the voice of China and advance Sino-African friendship, and Chinese Minister of Culture Cai Wu said the new weekly would give African people a comprehensive and reliable guide to China (*China Daily*, 2012). Abdul'ahat Abdurixit, President of the Chinese–African People's Friendship Association, said the launch of an African edition by *China Daily* 'will surely help better communication, both at the official and people-to-people level, between China and Africa', while Nkosazana Dlamini-Zuma, chairperson of the African Union Commission, noted that this 'edition by China's leading English-language newspaper is an eloquent testimony of the cordial and excellent relations between Africa and China, which have passed through several stages of evolution' (*China Daily*, 2012).

At the launch of the Africa edition, Zhu Ling, *China Daily*'s publisher and editor-in-chief, noted that the 'relationship between China and the African continent is one of the most significant relationships in the world today. It is growing and complex and not always understood – not just by those in other parts of the world but Africans and Chinese, too' (China Daily, 2012).Zhu also pointed out that *China Daily Africa* hopes 'to set that straight, and that is why China Daily [. . .] is launching an Africa edition' (ibid.). According to its mission statement, the state-run paper 'will look at the precise nature of Chinese involvement in Africa and also the prominent role many Africans play in China' (ibid.).

When reading the printed edition or browsing the newspaper's online archive, one cannot escape the impression that the nature of Chinese involvement in Africa is all about business and economic relations. A randomly picked selection of front page stories of the printed editions illustrates this: the front page of the initial issue states that 'as African economic prospects brighten, there is debate about which growth model would best suit its development'. The lead story of the second issue was quite similar, with a headline explaining: 'As China-Africa trade and investment soar, many leaders see relationship as central to continent.' The fourth issue opened with a story whose headline runs: 'Chinese companies playing major role in African infrastructure development despite tough conditions.'

More recent issues also focus on the business dimension. Vol.2, No.41 (4–10 October 2013) opens with a discussion of economic growth models and notes that 'African nations must study China's experience before pressing on', while the next edition of the newspaper explains how 'Chinese companies use sustainable development to chart a new course in Africa'. The edition published on 14 March 2014 describes how 'Private companies give a fillip to Chinese business and investment in Africa' while on 19 September 2014 *China Daily Africa* opened with a story about how 'Chinese carmakers rev up African sales'. On 24 April 2015, the cover story explained 'Why the bulls keep running' and noted that the 'Chinese stock market has been described by at least one analyst as being "on fire"'. The cover story of the first edition in 2016 was on 'Growth and reform' and noted of 2016: 'This will be a crucial year if China is to meet its target of joining the high-income club of nations.'

This focus on business undeniably reflects one important part of the reality of Sino-African relations. The 2013 White Paper on 'China–Africa Economic and Trade Cooperation', issued by the information office of China's State Council, not only points out that China has replaced the US as Africa's largest trade partner, but also that in 2012 China–Africa trade hit $198.5 billion, after annual growth of 19 per cent from 2009 and accounting for 16 per cent of the continent's trade with the rest of the world. It is also well-known that there is a growing Chinese presence in Africa's infrastructure building sector and that China invests $2 billion a year in Africa. And the debates on how this economic development may influence Africa are also well documented, mainly referring to the discussion of China as the new 'neo-colonialist', which partially explains this focus on business and the economy; nevertheless one may doubt whether this kind of reporting really portrays 'the precise nature of Chinese involvement in Africa' (Hartig, 2013a).

Another common topic is exchange, cooperation and mutual benefit. On 18 April 2014, *China Daily Africa* opened with a story entitled 'Shared dreams' which explained that the 'concept of the Chinese dream resonates in Africa more than anywhere else as the continent looks for inspiration'. 'Degree of success', published one week before, reported on how a 'new wave of Africans returning home after studying in China is bringing with them the skills and know-how to help fuel the continent's most important partnership of the modern era'. The edition from 22 January 2016 includes the cover story on the 'Road to prosperity', which explains to its readership that 'Egypt has positioned itself to benefit greatly from China's Belt and Road Initiative'. On 20 November 2015, *China Daily Africa* opened with a story entitled 'Passport to the future', a piece outlining how 'enthusiasm for learning Mandarin is taking hold in Africa as students, workers and businesspeople increasingly see the language as a ticket to academic, career and commercial success'. On 17 April 2015, the cover story was on the 'Urban role model', which discussed the idea that 'even as Africa looks to China as an exemplar while the continent's industrialization continues apace, it also hopes to avoid some of the costly mistakes China inevitably made in more than 30 years of rapid economic growth'. The last piece is of particular interest here as it illustrates that *China Daily Africa* 'does not entirely avoid critical engagement with state policy', as Green (2012) observes. Nevertheless 'it tends to report on the topic within very narrow bounds' (ibid.). According to a study by Zhang (2013), *China Daily* and Xinhuanet have a tendency towards positive news on Africa, though negative reporting outweighs positive reporting on occasion (see also Wekesa and Zhang, 2014: 16). One can argue in favour of this positive reporting because 'the current China–Africa narrative, beset by hyperbole and inaccuracy, hardly shows journalism at its best' (Green, 2012). But Green makes it also clear that the story of '*China Daily*'s launch mirrors the broader story it will report on' (Green, 2012) and that is one of prosperity and mutual benefit.

Another and related aspect is of interest here. *China Daily*, as Harber notes,

> symbolically stepped into the shoes abandoned by London's *Financial Times*. As the pink paper announced it was stopping its South African print run, the red paper hired the same people to move into the same print and distribution arrangements, almost seamlessly.
>
> *(Harber, 2013: 150)*

But it is not only Western media that are struggling against falling revenues, resulting in cuts in the number of correspondents around the world and decreasing coverage of world affairs; a number of African newspapers 'are operating on a shoestring, and many journalists in the likes of Sudan, Ethiopia, Equatorial Guinea and Eritrea face hostility from their governments' (Green, 2012). There, as Green concludes, a 'deep-pocketed new Chinese outfit, working under the umbrella of the Chinese government, will likely have an easier life' (Green, 2012) and it remains to be seen whether and how *China Daily Africa* and other media outlets in Africa can really turn into a 'testing ground for the construction of a discourse that China envisages as an alternative' and a 'Chinese-style world order' (Zhang, 2013: 79).

China Daily in Europe

China Daily European Weekly was launched in December 2010. Published in London and Brussels, it is available in most major European cities. After an initial launch in eight cities, the newspaper is now available in 27 countries on the continent, either in bookstores or newsagents in major train stations or airports or from distributors. It covers politics, business, culture and society, 'delivering in-depth analyses on news and issues that are of interest to European and Chinese readers' (*China Daily*, 2011). The 32-page weekly newspaper aspires to be 'a newspaper that provides a window for China to be understood by and understand the world' (*China Daily*, 2010). In 2014, *China Daily European Weekly* won the International Newspaper of the Year award for its 'superb design, attractive layout and exceptional print' (*China Daily* Online, 2014). Nevertheless, in early 2016 the newspaper underwent a makeover and was relaunched with a slightly different layout mainly affecting the front page. Until December 2015, the newspaper caught the attention of readers with a huge comic-like graphic display related to the cover story and a few opening paragraphs of that story. Since January 2016 there are two stories printed on the front page, both of which continue within the newspaper.

On the occasion of the launch, Lord Prescott, Britain's former Deputy Prime Minister, pointed out that

> most people need to be much better informed about the economic, political and social issues of importance to China, and the way in which these issues are being addressed. And they need to know more about China's achievements. *China Daily* therefore has a big part to play in developing an informed debate about these issues.
>
> (*quoted in* China Daily *Press Release, 2011*)

The Chinese Ambassador to Britain, Liu Xiaoming, described the overall goal as opening 'a new window on China' for European readers' (ibid.). Qu Yingpu, deputy editor-in-chief of China Daily Media Group, said:

> As China and Europe face a host of common problems – a patchy global economic recovery, sovereign debt crises, diminishing resources, environmental challenges, trade disputes – the two sides should talk more and do more. Talk to each other, not past each other. Do more together, not pull in different directions
>
> (*quoted in* China Daily, *2011*)

Qu also reassured potential audiences by saying: 'We do not shy away from contentious issues – we provide a rational perspective and try to be the voice of reason. On various issues, we provide balance with comment from Europeans and Chinese' (ibid.).

Zhi Renzhong, General Manager of *China Daily UK*, said:

> We identified a gap to provide a useful source of news and analysis to
> European businesses seeking to better understand and engage with China.
> As more partnerships develop between China and the West, it is crucial that
> there exists a regular source of insight on changing trends.
>
> *(Xinhua, 2010)*

Zhi furthermore said the *China Daily European Weekly* seeks to provide a more
in-depth review of headlines of the week and serve to help European readers better
understand the emerging opportunities existing between China and Europe
(Xinhua, 2010).

The focus on business clearly corresponds with the newspaper's audience.
In early 2013, the newspaper had its first ABC audit,[3] which revealed an average
distribution of 86,752 copies in the period July to September 2012 (Greenslade,
2013), which meant a bigger circulation than Britain's *Independent* newspaper for
the same period (Rushton, 2013). The latest available numbers for the second half
of 2014[4] provide further insights into the circulation of this newspaper. In the second
half of 2014, *China Daily European Weekly* had an average distribution of 93,579
copies. In the UK and the Republic of Ireland there were 34,790 copies while in
other European countries there were 58,789. While the ABC audit gives no further
details on other European countries, the 2012 Readership and Distribution Analysis
provides some further insights here.

The 2012 average circulation was 88,095 copies, and the majority of *China Daily
European Weekly* was distributed throughout Western Europe (65 per cent of circulation) (China Daily UK Co. Ltd, 2013: 14). In 2012, the UK accounted for *China
Daily*'s largest circulation market (39%) and altogether the top ten markets account
for 89% of total circulation (China Daily UK Co. Ltd, 2013: 15). The top ten markets in 2012 were the following: Britain (with 34,203 circulated copies), Italy
(10,517), Germany (9,220), Belgium (5,088), Spain (4,691), Poland (4,456), France
(4,185), Netherlands (3,837), Turkey (2,584), Switzerland (2,346) and the remaining 6,968 copies were distributed to 26 other countries (ibid.).

Returning to the average distribution of 93,579 copies in the second half of
2014, the decisive point, however, is the very fact that 94 per cent, or 88,208 copies,
reached their audience via monitored free distribution. Copies are delivered to
hotels, businesses, schools, airport lounges, airlines, leisure centres, medical establishments, and other travel points 'for free pick up' (ABC, 2015: 1). The vast majority,
that is 40,971 copies, goes to hotels, followed by 26,808 copies for airports and/or
airlines, 13,728 copies for offices and 5,060 copies for educational establishments
(ibid.). The newspaper is distributed weekly and 'some London based points are
being checked and re-filled every second day' (ibid.).

Another interesting item concerns retail and single copy sales. According to the
most recent ABC audit, in the second half of 2014, *China Daily European Weekly*
sold on average 660 copies in this category. It sold 309 in Britain and Ireland (for a

price of £2) and 351 in other countries (for €3). This mode of distribution apparently explains the reported readership of the newspaper. According to its Readership and Distribution Analysis 2012, the majority of *China Daily*'s readership are employed in the private sector (81 per cent) of which the majority of all readers are in senior level positions (65 per cent). The majority of *China Daily European Weekly*'s readership have had business dealings with China both at home (70 per cent) and in China itself (61 per cent) demonstrating a highly internationally professional and globally mobile readership (China Daily UK Co. Ltd, 2013: 6).

Conclusion

Taking into account the content provided by *China Daily* (as outlined with regard to the African edition) as well as the readership (as outlined with regard to the European edition), it can be summarized that *China Daily*'s global editions have a clear focus on economic and business relations. While this seems to be a justifiable focus, it nevertheless raises questions about the proclaimed aim of the newspaper – and China's public diplomacy more broadly – to 'better present a true picture of China to the world' (Qiu, 2011).

While business and economy are clearly one important aspect of contemporary China, the true or real picture would require a variety of aspects, stories and information. From an international reader's point of view, this would also include stories about issues and problems as well as challenges for China's development. This is not to say that those stories do not appear in global editions of *China Daily*, but the focus on business and positive stories nevertheless presents a rather narrow, and not really a true, picture of China. This is further reinforced when recalling the outlined working mode and the notion of *China Daily* being a corporate publishing project of the Chinese government (Wanzeck, 2013).

The fundamental question, then, is whether government-funded media outlets can provide 'true' pictures of China to the world (Mattimore, 2011). As Mattimore correctly points out: 'China's government can help the media present a "true" picture of China, but that truth will always be subjective' (ibid.). He further notes that

> the ultimate arbiter of the value of that media will be the market. That will be the truth test. If international consumers want the Chinese media products because they come to trust them or believe the media represent a valuable alternative to other perspectives, that will be a good thing for the world and for China.
>
> *(Mattimore, 2011)*

Overall, it can be argued that *China Daily* is clearly Beijing's global voice (next to other media organizations as discussed in this volume), mainly due to its potentially global reach. The crucial question, however, is whether this voice is heard globally and if so, how international audiences react to its messages. *China Daily* clearly provides the infrastructure to globally communicate with people abroad, but in the end, it is up to these people to decide whether they want to listen to Beijing's global voice or not.

When looking at the small circulation numbers presented above, one can get the impression that Beijing's global voice does not reach a significant number of readers (yet). This, in turn, raises the question why China is running several editions of *China Daily* as well as other instruments of global communication. As the practical utility is limited – and this fact cannot go unnoticed in Beijing – it seems there must be other factors driving China's global media outreach, of which *China Daily* is an important part. One reason might be related to Zhao Qizheng's dictum, according to which China should use its public diplomacy to 'talk back' (Zhao, 2007). Related here is the understanding that China, after solving the problems of being beaten (by the Western powers, *aida*) and being poor (*ai'e*), now has to deal with the problem of being insulted and verbally abused (*aima*) (Yu, 2012: 85). Public diplomacy in this regard is seen as a means for telling China's story to the world and thereby countering the negative accounts of the country in foreign, mainly Western, media. Against this background, one may argue, it is not that important whether people actually read *China Daily*, but what is much more important is the message – to the world and to domestic audiences – which is implicit in the establishment of *China Daily* and its overseas operations, namely that China does not leave the prerogative of interpretation of what China is and what it stands for to external stakeholders anymore.

Notes

1 The *Global Times* (*Huanqiu Shibao*) is a daily Chinese tabloid under the auspices of the *People's Daily* (*Renmin Ribao*), focusing on international issues. The *Global Times* differentiates itself from other Chinese newspapers in part through its more populist approach to journalism, coupled with a tendency to court controversy (for more on the *Global Times* see Carlson and Oaks (2012) and Edney (2014)).
2 With regards to China, things get even more complicated because in Chinese the term propaganda (*xuan chuan*) does not have the negative connotations as in the Western public mind (Wang, 2008: 259).
3 The Audit Bureau of Circulations or ABC was founded in 1931 by the ISBA (Society of British Advertisers) to provide an independent verification of circulation/data figures to facilitate the buying and selling of advertising space within UK national newspapers.
4 The Combined Total Distribution Certificate for July to December 2014 was issued on 12 February 2015 (ABC, 2015: 4).

References

Aoyama, Rumi (2007) *China's Public Diplomacy*. Tokyo: Waseda University.
Audit Bureau of Circulations (ABC) (2015) Consumer Magazines Combined Total Distribution Certificate July to December 2014. *China Daily European Weekly*. Berkhamsted, Hertfordshire: ABC - Audit Bureau of Circulations Ltd.
Barr, Michael (2011) *Who's Afraid of China: The Challenges of Chinese Soft Power*. London: Zed Books.
Brown, John. (2006) Two Ways of Looking at Propaganda. *The CPD Blog*, 29 June. Available at: http://uscpublicdiplomacy.org/index.php/newswire/cpdblog_detail/060629_two_ways_of_loo king_at_propaganda/.
Carlson, Allen and Oaks, Jason (2012) Is China's Global Times Misunderstood?, *The Diplomat*, 14 September. Available at: http://thediplomat.com/2012/09/is-chinas-global-times-misunderstood/1/.

Chen, Lily (2004) Evaluation in media texts: A cross-cultural linguistic investigation, *Language in Society*, 33(5): 673–702.

Chen, Lily (2012) Reporting news in China: Evaluation as an indicator of change in the *China Daily*, *China Information*, 26(3): 303–329.

Chen, Lily (2013) Could or should? The changing modality of authority in the *China Daily*, *Journal of the British Association for Chinese Studies*, 2: 51–85.

China Daily (2010) United Kingdom: *China Daily* Launches European Edition. *China Daily*, 2 December.

China Daily (2011) Window Opens with Launch of *China Daily European Weekly*. *China Daily*, 21 January.

China Daily (2012) *China Daily* Launches Africa Edition. *China Daily*, 13 December.

China Daily (n.d.) About China Daily Group. *China Daily Online*. Available at: www.chinadaily. com.cn/static_e/2011about.html.

China Daily (n.d.1) About China Daily. *China Daily Online*. Available at: www.chinadaily.com. cn/english/static/aboutchinadaily.html.

China Daily Asia Pacific Limited (n.d.) *China Daily—Your Global Newspaper. China Daily Media Kit 2013*. Hong Kong: China Daily Asia Pacific Limited.

China Daily Online (2014) *China Daily European Weekly* Wins Media Award. *China Daily Online*, 2 April.

China Daily Press Release (2011) *China Daily* Europe Edition Receives Thumbs-up. *China Daily*, 19 January. Available at: www.chinadaily.com.cn/china/2011-01/20/content_ 11885238.htm.

China Daily UK Co. Ltd (2013) *China Daily European Weekly: Readership and Distribution Analysis 2012*. London: China Daily UK Co. Ltd.

Conley, Jean & Tripoli, Stephen (1992) Changes of Line at 'China Daily': Fluctuating Party Policy or Fluctuating Control? In Porter, Robin (ed.) *Reporting the News from China*, London: Royal Institute of International Affairs: 26–39.

Cull, Nicholas (2009) *Public Diplomacy: Lessons from the Past*. Los Angeles: Figueroa Press.

d'Hooghe, Ingrid (2015) *China's Public Diplomacy*. Leiden: Brill.

Ding, Sheng (2008) *The Dragon's Hidden Wings: How China Rises with Its Soft Power*. Plymouth: Lexington Books.

Edney, Kingsley (2014) *The Globalization of Chinese Propaganda: International Power and Domestic Political Cohesion*. New York: Palgrave.

FMPRC (2014) The Central Conference on Work Relating to Foreign Affairs was Held in Beijing. *Ministry of Foreign Affairs of the People's Republic of China online*, 29 November. Available at: www.fmprc.gov.cn/mfa_eng/zxxx_662805/t1215680.shtml.

Gagliardone, Iginio (2013) China as a persuader: CCTV Africa's first steps in the African mediasphere, *Ecquid Novi: African Journalism Studies*, 34(3): 25–40.

Gilboa, Eytan (1998) Media diplomacy: Conceptual divergences and applications, *The Harvard International Journal of Press/Politics*, 3(3): 56–75.

Gorfinkel, Lauren; Joffe, Sandy; van Staden, Cobus and Wu, Yu-Shan (2014) CCTV's global outreach: Examining the audiences of China's 'new voice' on Africa, *Media International Australia*, 151(1): 81–88.

Green, Adam Robert (2012) *China Daily* Launches Africa Edition. *This is Africa Online*, 14 December. Available at: www.thisisafricaonline.com/News/China-Daily-launches- Africa-edition?ct=true.

Greenslade, Roy (2013) *China Daily*'s European Edition Gets ABC Certification. *The Guardian*, 4 February.

Harber, Anton (2013) China's soft diplomacy in Africa. *Ecquid Novi: African Journalism Studies*, 34(3): 149–151.

Hartig, Falk (2013a) China and Africa: All About the Economy?. *The AFRASO Blog*, 7 November. Available at: www.afraso.org/de/node/353.

Hartig, Falk (2013b) Panda diplomacy: The cutest part of China's public diplomacy, *The Hague Journal of Diplomacy*, 8: 49–78.

Hartig, Falk (2016) *Chinese Public Diplomacy: The Rise of the Confucius Institute*. New York: Routledge.

Hays, Jeffrey (2008) Chinese Newspapers and Magazines and Their Battle Against Corruption and Censorship. *Facts and Details*.

Jowett, Garth and O'Donnell, Victoria (2006) *Propaganda and Persuasion*. London: Sage.

Lanigan, Richard (2015) Netizen communicology: *China Daily* and the internet construction of group culture, *Semiotica*, 207: 489–528.

Li, Changchun (2008) Nuli goujian xiandai chuanbo tixi tigao guonei guoji chuanbo nengli [Vigorously Build a Modern Communication System in order to Improve Domestic and International Communication Capabilities]. *Xinhuanet.com*, 23 December 2012. Available at: http://news.xinhuanet.com/politics/2008-12/23/content_10545118.htm.

Li, Mingjiang (2009) *Soft Power: China's Emerging Strategy in International Politics*. Plymouth: Lexington Books.

Li, Mingjiang (2012) International Status: China's Pursuit of a Comprehensive Superpower Status, in Kavalski, E. (ed.) *The Ashgate Research Companion to Chinese Foreign Policy*. Farnham: Ashgate.

Liao, Hongbin (2009) Gonggong waijiao: guoji jingyan yu qishi [Public diplomacy: International experiences], *Dangdai shijie yu shehui zhuyi*, 1: 100–103.

Liu, Youling (2011) External Communication as a Vehicle for Disseminating Soft Power: A Study of China's Efforts to Strengthen its Cultural Soft Power in the Age of Globalization. PhD Thesis, University at Buffalo, State University of New York.

Luo, Wangshu (2015) First Lady Plays Key Role in Diplomacy. *China Daily*, 16 April.

Marsh, Vivien (2016) Mixed messages, partial pictures? Discourses under construction in CCTV's *Africa Live* compared with the BBC, *Chinese Journal of Communication*, 9(1): 56–70.

Mattimore, Patrick (2011) Chinese Media Step Forward. *China Daily*, 6 January.

Melissen, Jan (2005) *Wielding Soft Power: The New Public Diplomacy*. The Hague: Clingendael.

Meyer, Daniela (2013) Der Elefant mit gelbem Haar, in Radtke, O. (ed.) *China in den Augen deutscher Medienbotschafter*. Beijing: New Star Press: 1–28.

Needham, Kirsty (2004) Dear Iris, the Truth is This . . . . *The Sydney Morning Herald*, 23 August.

Needham, Kirsty (2007) *A Season in Red: My Great Leap Forward into the New China*. Crows Nest, NSW: Allen and Unwin.

Newham, Mark (2011) *Limp Pigs and the Five Ring Circus*. Brighton: Pen Press.

Qiu, Bo (2011) Investment in Media to Present True Picture of China. *China Daily*, 4 January.

Rabinovitch, Simon (2008) The rise of an image-conscious China, *China Security*, 4(3): 32–46.

Radtke, Oliver (ed.) (2013) *China in den Augen deutscher Medienbotschafter*. Beijing: New Star Press.

Rawnsley, Gary (2000a) *Taiwan's Informal Diplomacy and Propaganda*. Basingstoke: Palgrave Macmillan.

Rawnsley, Gary (2000b) Selling Taiwan: Diplomacy and propaganda, *Issues and Studies*, 36(3): 1–25.

Rawnsley, Gary (2009) China Talks Back: Public Diplomacy and Soft Power for the Chinese Century, in Snow, N. and Taylor, P. (eds.) *The Routledge Handbook on Public Diplomacy*. New York: Routledge.

Rawnsley, Gary (2013) 'Thought-Work' and Propaganda: Chinese Public Diplomacy and Public Relations After Tiananmen Square, in Auerbach, J. and Castronovo, R. (eds.) *The Oxford Handbook of Propaganda Studies*. Oxford: Oxford University Press: 147–159.

Ross, Robert and Johnston, Alastair (2006) Introduction, in Johnston, A. and Ross, R. (eds.) *New Directions in the Study of China's Foreign Policy*. Stanford: Stanford University Press.

Rushton, Katherine (2013) European Version of *China Daily* Overtakes. *The Independent, The Telegraph*, 4 February.

Schoenhals, Michael (1992) *Doing Things with Words in Chinese Politics: Five Studies*. Berkeley: University of California at Berkeley, Center for Chinese Studies.

Shambaugh, David (2013) *China Goes Global: The Partial Power*. Oxford: Oxford University Press.

Shambaugh, David (2015) China's Soft Power Push: The Search for Respect, *Foreign Affairs*, 94(4): 99–107.

Shek, Colin (2013) Chinese Media Expands Africa Presence. *Al Jazeera Online*, 24 January. Available at: www.aljazeera.com/indepth/features/2013/01/201312071929822435.html

Sproule, Michael (1997) *Propaganda and Democracy: The American Experience of Media and Mass Persuasion*. Cambridge: Cambridge University Press.

Swan, Jon (1996) I was a 'polisher' in a Chinese news factory, *Columbia Journalism Review*, 34(6): 33.

Wan, James (2015) Propaganda or Proper Journalism? China's Media Expansion in Africa. *African Arguments*, 18 August. Available at: http://africanarguments.org/2015/08/18/propaganda-or-proper-journalism-chinas-media-expansion-in-africa/.

Wang, Jian (2011) *Soft Power in China: Public Diplomacy Through Communication*. New York: Palgrave Macmillan.

Wang, Yiwei (2008) Public diplomacy and the rise of Chinese soft power, *The ANNALS of the American Academy of Political and Social Science*, 616(1): 257–273.

Wanzeck, Markus (2010) Im Land der Morgenröte, *Medium Magazin*, 1-2: 44.

Wanzeck, Markus (2013) Interkulturelle Kostbarkeiten, in Oliver, R (ed.) *China in den Augen deutscher Medienbotschafter*. Beijing: New Star Press: 179–205.

Wasserman, Herman (2013) China in Africa: The implications for journalism, *Ecquid Novi: African Journalism Studies*, 34(3): 1–5.

Wekesa, Bob and Zhang, Yanqiu (2014) *Live, Talk, Faces: An Analysis of CCTV's Adaption to the African Media Market*. The Center for Chinese Studies Working Paper, Stellenbosch University.

Xi, Jinping (2014) Full Text of Chinese President Xi Jinping's Address to Australia's Parliament, 19 November. Available at: www.straitstimes.com/news/asia/australianew-zealand/story/full-text-chinese-president-xi-jinpings-address-australias-parl.

Xinhua (2010) *China Daily to Launch European Edition in UK*. *Xinhua Net*, 2 December. Available at: http://news.xinhuanet.com/english2010/china/2010-12/02/c_13632562.htm.

Xinhua (2014) Xi Jinping zai Aodaliya lianbang yihui fabiao zhongyao yanjiang [Xi Jinping Delivered Important Speech at the Australian Federal Parliament]. *Xinhua Net*, 17 November. Available at: http://news.xinhuanet.com/world/2014-11/17/c_1113283064.htm.

Yu, Wanli (2012) Guanyu Zhongguo Guajia Xingxiang de Guoji Zhengzhi Sikao – jiyu dui liangfen guoji mindiao baogao de jiedu [Some Thoughts About China's Image from the Perspective of International Politics – Based on Two International Opinion Polls], in Fangming, H. (ed.) *Zhongguoren de guoji xin xingxiang – Chinese Image Abroad [The New International Image of the Chinese People]*. Beijing: Xinhua Chubanshe: 85–100.

Zaharna, Rhonda (2004) From Propaganda to Public Diplomacy in the Information Age, in Snow, N. and Kamalipour, Y. (eds.) *War, Media, and Propaganda: A Global Perspective*. Lanham: Rowman and Littlefield: 219–225.

Zaharna, Rhonda (2009) Mapping Out a Spectrum of Public Diplomacy Initiatives: Information and Relational Communication Frameworks, in Snow, N. and Taylor, P. (eds.) *Routledge Handbook of Public Diplomacy*. New York: Routledge: 86–100.

Zhang, Weiwei (2009) Tuozhan you zhongguo tese de gonggong waijiao [Further develop public diplomacy with Chinese characteristics], *Guoji Wenti Yanjiu*, 4: 12–16.

Zhang, Xiaoling (2013) How ready is China for a China-style world order? China's state media discourse under construction, *Ecquid Novi: African Journalism Studies*, 34(3): 79–101.

Zhang, Yanqiu and Matingwina, Simon (2016) Constructive Journalism: A New Journalistic Paradigm of Chinese Media in Africa, in Zhang et al. (eds.) *China's Media and Soft Power in Africa*. New York: Palgrave: 93–106.

Zhao, Kejin (2012) Zhongguo jueqi fanglüe zhong de gonggong waijiao [Public diplomacy within the strategy of China's peaceful rise], *Dangdai Shijie*, 5: 30–34.

Zhao, Qizheng (2007) Better Public Diplomacy to Present a Truer Picture of China. *People's Daily*, 30 March.

Zhao, Qizheng (2010) *Gonggong waijiao yu kua wenhua jiaoliu. [Public Diplomacy and Communication between Cultures]*. Beijing: China Renmin University Press.

8

THE 'GOING OUT' OF CHINA RADIO INTERNATIONAL

Kuo Huang

Radio developed in China in the 1920s and 1930s with the main purpose of communication. China Radio International (CRI) was first established under the name of Xinhua New Chinese Radio (XNCR) in December 1941, in Taihang Mountain by the Communist Party of China (CPC). It was then renamed Radio Peking when it moved to Beijing, then Radio Beijing, and finally, in 1993, China Radio International. From the very beginning CRI had the aim of outbound communication from China. Its first programme was in Japanese because it was produced during and for the purpose of China's war of resistance against Japanese aggression. The following five years saw the process of professionalization and popularization of Chinese radio. Programme formats and contents were developed and formalized and the most popular programmes were news, war bulletins, official announcements and arts and literature. In September 1947, six years after CRI's establishment, China's voice reached the English-speaking world for the first time. During the Chinese civil war, English-language programmes were broadcast to provide information about the newly liberated areas, as well as to communicate CPC's political and cultural perspectives to the world at large.

Seventy-five years after its founding, CRI is now a multimedia entity using 65 languages in its overseas broadcasting, which makes CRI the media organization with the largest number of language services of any mainstream global broadcaster. Such rapid progress is due to the 'great transformation' initiated in 2004, the attempt to develop a modern broadcasting network to improve the capacity for international communication, and 'going out' is one of the strategies to accomplish this. Working towards the goal of becoming a modern, comprehensive and innovative international media group, CRI started the process of moving from a single-platform media organization to an integrated media group incorporating all mass communication means, shifting from focusing on traditional communication to new media orientation, as well as changing from a China-based institution into an international media group.

From 'content going out' to 'overall going out'

It is debatable which year marks the start of the Chinese media 'going out' project. Some scholars consider 2009 as the launch, since three Chinese media organizations stepped up their move towards globalization in that year: China Central Television revamped the 24-hour English-language news service CCTV News, Xinhua news agency launched the 24-hour English-language television channel CNC World and *China Daily* expanded its overseas distribution and bureaus (Hu and Ji, 2012; Zhao, 2013). Some believe that the Chinese media 'going out' project started several years earlier, since such results (branches, stations and channels) take years to achieve. According to Jiang (2016: 84), the Chinese government launched the strategy of 'going out' in 2000, mainly focusing on economics, and later, in 2001, the State Administration of Radio, Film and Television of the People's Republic of China (SARFT, known as SAPPRFT from 2013) issued 'Regulations on the Implementation of Radio, Film and Television "going out"'. The Chinese media 'going out' policy was implemented with governmental support in policies and funding and in 2009 the strategy to enhance Chinese media's international communication capacity was added. CRI's example of launching its first overseas FM radio station supports Jiang's argument. It was launched in Nairobi, Kenya in February 2006 and in the same year CRI opened its 13th Confucius Classroom for Chinese-language learners, which extended CRI's Confucius Classrooms to Kenya, Japan, Russia, Mongolia, Pakistan, Bangladesh, Nepal, Sri Lanka, Italy, Tunisia, Australia and Tanzania.

There is more agreement among scholars on the purpose of Chinese media's 'going out' project than on the date of its initiation. The goals most frequently mentioned are 'building influence and spreading a positive image of China' (Li and Rønning, 2013a: 118), as well as providing information counter-flow and building a new and balanced world information order (Huang and Li, 2017), or patriotic comments, such as

> China's launch of media 'going-out' project was under the pressure of the media imperialism and the negative China threat and irresponsibility theses. With its own transnational media institutions, China not only tries to counteract the ideological attack, but also voice its benign messages as a responsible power in areas like economy.
>
> *(Zhao, 2015: 28)*

Before 2004, CRI focused on proving information for the world outside, a form of 'content going out'. In order to reach a wider international audience, CRI went online in 1997 with the test-launch of its English-language website CRIENGLISH. com. A year later, on 26 December 1998, a multi-language website CRI Online was officially launched, providing content first in Mandarin, Cantonese, English, German and Spanish, and later in 61 languages, attracting visitors from over 180 countries and regions (Wang, 2011: 220). Li Changchun, a member of the Standing

Committee of the Political Bureau of the CPC Central Committee, stated in his speech in 2004 that CRI should set up a 'modern international broadcasting system therefore CRI can play a bigger role and exploit the advantages to the full in facilitating China's international communication' (Wang, 2007: 10). Such comments guided CRI to initiate a 'great transformation' to put effort into building a modern communication system to improve its domestic and international communication capability.

In 2007, CRI launched its online television programme and mobile radio services. In 2009, CRI Online started its mobile version, becoming China's first multimedia English-language website optimized for mobile devices. Mobile phone users only need to type 'm.cri.cn' to gain access to news, business, showbiz and travel information, as well as a Chinese-language learning studio, and audio and video content. The French and Spanish versions were launched two years later. On 18 January 2011, the China International Broadcasting Network, or CIBN, was formally established. CIBN relies on the rapidly developing internet and mobile communication technology to interact with a global audience through multilingual, multi-type, multi-terminal forms of communication, and covers a wide range of online audio-visual programs, mobile radio and TV, internet TV, IPTV, CMMB and other new media forms. The establishment of CIBN marks the full entry of CRI into the new media field and started the process of media convergence. Such efforts allow international audiences to access CRI more easily and freely and, at the same time, CRI's decisive step towards establishing a modern, comprehensive and innovative international media group enables its content to circulate globally.

Alongside the media platform and technology developments, in 2003 CRI started the process of localization, which is also part of the 'going out' strategy. During the period of 'content going out', CRI cooperated with foreign media organizations to co-produce programmes, in that CRI provided China-related programme components and foreign partners did the editing and packaging to accommodate foreign audiences. Such cooperation is still carried on today and the Finland-based FutuVision Media Ltd. is one such partner. In this way, CRI introduced topics and views from China to broaden the foreign public's agenda and even to stimulate new perspectives. In addition, CRI tried to 'present' itself overseas. One way is that CRI established radio stations in Guangxi, Inner Mongolia Autonomous Region, Jilin, Heilongjiang, Hainan and Yunnan provinces, which border neighbouring countries. In doing so, CRI established a network of radio stations targeting audiences in the countries and regions that border China. The other way was to set up overseas radio channels and stations, and the preparation work started in late 2005, while the first full frequency overseas radio station was launched in Nairobi, in February 2006 (Wang, 2011: 220). By the end of 2015, CRI had about 130 overseas radio stations, and cooperation agreements with 160 radio channels globally (Wang, 2016: 5). Besides overseas radio channels and stations, CRI has established six overseas main regional bureaus and 32 overseas correspondent bureaus and 4,112 overseas audience clubs.

'Going out' for soft power and public diplomacy

The shift from 'content going out' to the policy of 'overall going out' shows that CRI embraced warmly the opportunity of and government support for China's national policy. Since 2000, the Chinese government has announced several strategies so that 'the global image and influence match the status and reputation of China'. Such strategies include 'Chinese culture going out', 'Chinese media going out', 'special university programmes for international communication', and an 'international communication plan', supported by policies and funding to facilitate international communication-related research and practice. Key phrases such as 'cultural soft power', 'modern communication systems' and 'enhancing international communication capacity' appeared in the high-level documents, including Chinese President Hu Jintao's keynote speech to the 17th National Congress of the Communist Party of China in 2007, Hu's report to the 18th National Congress of the Communist Party of China in 2012, and the current Chinese President Xi Jinping's address to the third Plenary Session of the 18th CPC Central Committee in 2013 (Jiang, 2016: 84). The Chinese government's investment in international communication has been interpreted as having two goals:

> Firstly, it is using its media resources to impress and remind the world that it cannot be taken advantage of again following the humiliations of the 19th and first half of the 20th centuries. The second is the endeavour to depict China as an attractive, internationally responsible and respected member of the global community.
>
> *(Vincent, 2016: 48)*

Both goals aim to enhance China's soft power.

CRI benefited from the government's call and support for improving soft power and has played an important role in terms of 'going out', to balance the media presence in countries and regions outside China. Being one of the 'three central broadcasting organizations in China', along with China National Radio and China Central Television (CCTV), CRI has evolved and been shaped by global events, threats and conflicts like other international broadcasting organizations, such as the British Broadcasting Corporation (BBC) and the Voice of America (VOA), which commenced transmitting in 1932 and 1942 respectively. Based on the definition of international broadcasting as

> the elegant term for a complex combination of state-sponsored news, information, and entertainment directed at a population outside the sponsoring state's boundaries. It is the use of electronic media by one society to shape the opinion of the people and leaders of another
>
> *(Vincent, 2016: 45)*

it is understandable that CRI's 'going out' is for the purpose of enhancing China's soft power and funded partly by government projects related to such goals.

CRI is clear about its role as an integral element of China's soft power project, working to 'mount a counter-offensive on the Western media's ideological assault on the rest of the world' (Vincent, 2016: 48), and to 'gain as much as possible approval by international public opinion', which is considered as being 'at the top of [the] agenda of the Chinese government in its international expansion' (Chen *et al.*, 2010: 3). Besides constructing a convergent multimedia platform for easier international access and setting up international channels, stations and bureaus, CRI also moved from propaganda to international communication by adopting public diplomacy methods, and thus achieved the 'going out of influence' which is the core of soft power.

CRI benefited from its media convergence after the establishment of CIBN when it realized that video products had more impact compared to traditional audio products. As a result, a project to translate, dub and reproduce Chinese TV series and films to be broadcast overseas was set up in 2011. A centre for translating and producing was then founded in 2012. Since 2011, several Chinese TV series, such as 'A Beautiful Daughter-in-law Era', 'Kintaro's Happy Life', 'Love Story of Beijing' and 'Du Lala Getting Promoted', were dubbed into English, French, Swahili and Hausa and screened on television channels in countries including Tanzania, Kenya, Uganda, Botswana, Senegal, Gabon, Burundi and Togo.

The most significant example is 'A Beautiful Daughter-in-law Era', which was renamed 'Doudou and Her Mothers-in-law' for African audiences. In November 2011, the Swahili version of 'Doudou and Her Mothers-in-law' was premiered on Tanzania's national television channel TBC1. It broke records by hitting a 52 per cent rating and was re-run four times due to audience demand. Being the first Chinese TV drama dubbed in native African languages, the show aroused a strong response in the Swahili community: television channels in Kenya, Uganda and Burundi also screened 'Doudou and Her Mothers-in-law', which made the TV series reach an audience of over 100 million Swahili speakers. Chinese President Xi Jinping highly commended the show during a speech delivered on his visit to Tanzania in 2013, saying that 'the Chinese dream will be more easily accepted by foreign audiences when it is manifested in small and touching stories'. In 2014, a national multi-language movie and TV translation and production base was established as part of CRI, supported by the State Administration of Press, Publication, Radio, Film and Television (SAPPRFT, formerly known as SARFT) of the People's Republic of China.

With a mission to be one of China's voices overseas, CRI needs to be recognized in overseas markets, so it makes full use of its main overseas regional and corre-spondent bureaus, global partners and audience clubs to organize international events and activities. It has developed new activities in order to expand name recognition, mainly focusing on public relations. CRI has held online dialogues in cooperation with foreign media partners, for example the Annual Online Dialogue between China and Japan, and meetings with sister cities between a foreign city and a city in China. CRI also carried on face-to-face activities, and an International University Camp and dialogue between Chinese and foreign college students entitled 'From University to the World', an international singing competition between China and Vietnam, and International Knowledge Competition for global audiences, are conducted on yearly basis.

The most important example is the joint mega events organized with a peer foreign media organization. In 2006, CRI and ITAR-TASS News Agency of Russia co-organized the 'The Trip of Sino-Russian Friendship'. Journalists from 11 organizations in China and Russia were invited to join the trip and report on stories along their journey through over 20 Russian cities. The journey started from Tiananmen Square, Beijing and covered nearly 15,000 km over 42 days, eventually winding up at Red Square, Moscow. According to the statistics, media from China and Russia released over 2,000 reports, over 800 pictures and more than 20 hours of radio and television broadcasting. A China-based trip for 'Sino-Russian Friendship' was conducted the following year, and again CRI and the ITAR-TASS News Agency jointly organized a press corps consisting of 12 Russia national media and four Chinese media to interview people in 26 Chinese cities and towns over 32 days and 9,000 km. Statistics shows that media from the two countries released over 2,000 reports and more than 3,500 pictures.

Over the past decade, under the framework of 'Year of China', 'Year of Russia', based on themes of language, tourism, or youth community exchanges between China and Russia, CRI has proactively sought cooperation with five Russian media at state level, covering news agencies, newspapers, radio stations, television channels and internet media. In such ways, a stable long-term mechanism for disseminating Chinese culture in Russia has been established. In March 2013, the Chinese Vice Premier Wang Yang and the Russian Deputy Prime Minister Golovin Gertz witnessed a cooperation agreement between CRI and Voice of Russia radio station and in October 2014, the Chinese Premier Li Keqiang and the Russian Prime Minister Dmitry Medvedev were present for the agreement between CRI and RT (Russia Today).

In May 2015, CRI Director-General Wang Gengnian and Editor-in-chief of *Rossiyskaya Gazeta* Pavel Negoica signed a further cooperation agreement and this time the Chinese President Xi Jinping and the Russian President Vladimir Putin were both present. The purpose of these cooperation agreements is to develop long-term mutually beneficial partnerships between the media sectors of the two countries, and the two media organizations will further their collaboration in a programme of exchange and promotion, staff training and communication and interaction in new media areas. This was the only media cooperation document witnessed by the two presidents during Xi's visit to Russia in 2015, and it shows how much importance China and Russia attach to media cooperation and that they consider it a valuable part of public diplomacy in enhancing soft power.

'Going out' as a process of globalization and marketization

Besides playing a key role in China's soft power project, CRI aims to develop itself into an international media organization with influence, reputation and market share. According to CRI's business philosophy, it aims to 'introduce China to the rest of the world, introduce the world to China, report global affairs to the world, and promote understanding and friendship between the Chinese and peoples from other countries'. To achieve this CRI needs not only to go out, but also to undertake a process of globalization, which started in 2003, according to CRI Director-General Wang Gengnian (Wang, 2011: 225). To be globalized, CRI also needs to follow market principles, and in December 2012 it officially launched its advertising platform on CRI Online. This marks the establishment of CRI's advertising business and the starting point of the process of marketization and commercialization.

Based on experiences of localization and cooperation with foreign media organizations, CRI founded the Global Broadcasting Media Group (GMG) to operate its market-related and global business. With the help of GMG, CRI set up five overseas companies in partnership with foreign media groups in the United States, Australia, South Africa and such European countries as Portugal by means of a joint venture or holding company. CRI Director-General Wang Gengnian said that

> company cooperative operation is the expansion model of media in developed countries and CRI is following the example. Cooperative operation can help CRI to improve efficiency so as to have a better integration into the media environment in foreign countries.
>
> *(Wang, 2012: 12)*

According to Wang Gengnian, through corporatization, CRI has achieved rapid development of overseas media in terms of scale and intensity and contributed to economic independent development, including for the overseas affiliations: 'CRI's international development model, not only draws on Western mainstream media's example, but also in line with China's national condition and the trend of media globalization' (ibid.).

CRI has adopted a 'country-specific strategy' in globalization, according to the Deputy Director of CRI, Hu Bangsheng. This includes six multi-task projects in countries such as Turkey, Thailand, South Africa and Britain. The Turkey project is a good example: CRI started broadcasting in Turkish in October 1957 using the shortwave frequency and in 2010 it began an internet service and also used local FM stations in Istanbul and Ankara to reach its audience. Now CRI has set up an integrated multimedia platform, including a website focusing on events related to the Silk Road in Chinese (www.sczlw.net/) and CRI Online in Turkish (http://turkish.cri.cn/), a video channel in Turkish, and Apps for Chinese news in Turkish. Xia Yongmin, Director of the Turkish service of CRI, said that the stronger presence of CRI would help develop bilateral relations further since 'our common values are more than the differences between the Turkish and Chinese peoples, and Turks and Chinese share similar traits such as hospitality and warmth in human relations'. The listenership of CRI's Turkish Radio service is not obtainable, but CRI Online in Turkish received about 20,000 clicks in August 2016, and its Twitter account had about 990,000 impressions and 50,000 re-tweets while its Facebook account reached about 150,000 audiences and was shared about 15,000 times in August 2016.

Marketization has been identified by CRI as a new development path for Chinese state media in foreign countries. In 2010 CRI founded a joint venture company in Thailand, and rented Channel FM103 to start 17-hour live broadcasting in the Thai language in January 2011. The channel was renamed '103 Like FM' expressing the hope that the channel would be popular among Thai audiences and also that the channel would serve as the communication platform for audiences with the same interests, providing an effective link between the broadcasting programme, the internet and offline activities. The channel positioned itself as an 'urban music channel' tailored for 'modern' audience members aged between 25 and 45; therefore 80 per cent of the programmes on Like FM were local popular music and songs with 15 per cent for local and international news and about 5 per cent for advertising.

CRI Like FM is an example of localization and marketization. Among 34 staff members only one was assigned by CRI headquarters for programme supervision; all other 33 staff members, including CEO, CCO, CFO and CMO were recruited from local experienced media practitioners. Based on their rich knowledge of Thai culture and its broadcasting industry, the Like FM team developed an app and opened accounts on social media, including Facebook, Twitter, YouTube and Instagram to interact with audiences. They invited local celebrities to participate in the programme and activities so that the brand of Like FM would benefit from their fame. The team held over 30 promotional activities each year in a variety of forms; half of them were events with hundreds of participants, including concerts with audiences of 1,500–2,500. They also held cooking competition activities with a well-known local food company in tourist attractions in Thailand, so the fans and DJs of Like FM enjoyed the food as well as music together, and in this way the brand of Like FM was recognized and liked by Thai audiences. According to the audience survey conducted by Nielsen Thailand, Like FM is among the top ten media favourites.

This market-oriented operation enabled CRI Like FM to make a profit from advertising and commercial activities, and to progress beyond the old state-dependent Chinese media 'going out' model. In 2011, it gained advertising revenue of 1.35 million RMB and in 2014 revenue increased to 13.62 million RMB. The case of CRI Like FM in Thailand demonstrates that CRI's 'going out' not only responded to the call of the state to enhance China's soft power and international communication capacity with government investment, but also followed its goal of

> building itself into an international media group supported by modern technology through comprehensive communication channels . . . backed by a solid financial footing, a large number of language services for a broad and diverse audience, and a powerful influence that extends around the globe.
>
> *(China Plus, 2017)*

The case of CRI Like FM in Thailand shows that the government's policy on and support for the 'Chinese media going-out project' has no strict requirements to promote China or improve China's overseas image, but rather the government provides support to Chinese media and opportunities to go global, leaving wide open how they can develop, with the hope of competing with their Western peers in the future.

Debates, problems and the future

National economic power and international cultural influence would be expected to increase simultaneously. Chinese media consider their 'going out' process as following the example of Western media such as BBC and VOA, since both of them get support from their government, but an investigation by journalists from Reuters shows a different perspective. The report, 'Beijing's covert radio network airs China-friendly news across Washington, and the world' was published in 2015, and claimed that 'the Chinese government controls much of the content broadcast on a station that is blanketing the US capital with pro-Beijing programming. WCRW is part of an expanding global web of 33 stations in which China's involvement is obscured' (Koh and Shiffman, 2015). They particularly pointed out that CRI's 'going out' was not the same as that of VOA or other media forms:

> In some ways, the CRI-backed radio stations fulfil a similar advocacy role to that of the US-run Voice of America. But there is a fundamental difference: VOA openly publishes the fact that it receives US government funding. CRI is using front companies that cloak its role.
>
> *(Koh and Shiffman, 2015)*

The investigators further characterized CRI's action by citing CRI Director-General Wang Gengnian's concept of 'borrowed boat' strategy – using existing media outlets in foreign nations to carry China's narrative, an action precisely intended to implement President Xi Jinping's idea to 'increase China's soft power, give a good Chinese narrative and better communicate China's message to the world' (ibid.).

The report did give a voice to the Chinese side. It quoted someone close to the CPC leadership and also familiar with the CRI network as saying: 'We are not the evil empire that some Western media portray us to be', and 'Western media reports about China are too negative. We just want to improve our international image. It's self-protection' (Koh and Shiffman, 2015). Not long after, an editorial in the popular Chinese newspaper, *Global Times* (*Huan Qiu Shi Bao*), responded that 'the local American broadcasting stations are not controlled by CRI, even according to Reuters' disclosure, they just broadcast CRI programmes' (*Global Times*, 2015).

Debates on the purpose and influences of Chinese media's 'going out' have become a hot topic in recent years and much attention has been paid to Chinese media's presence in Africa. Many believe that the expansion is a key part of China's public diplomacy in Africa, that the dominant frameworks include neo-colonialism, pragmatism and information counter-flow, and the popular discourses are soft power, public diplomacy and charm offensive. In 'The Rise of China's State-led

Media Dynasty in Africa' produced by the South African Institute of International Affairs in 2012, it is reported that CRI's newscasts over the Liberia Broadcasting System has allowed Liberians access to Chinese views, rather than receiving the news from a third media source. Similar activities and interactions, such as setting up programme exchanges with the Kenyan Broadcasting Corporation and establishing its own local radio station that broadcasts in English, Mandarin and Swahili, CRI has promoted cross-cultural understanding as Africans receive more China-related stories (Wu, 2012: 17).

At a conference held in Oxford in 2010 scholars from Africa, China and Europe explored ways to approach the study of China's emerging role in the media in Africa and some scholars identified that Chinese influence in the media sector in Africa should be researched, looking at China as a prototype, a partner and a persuader. They suggested the need for a shift in the debate that tends to be polarized by images of China as either a neo-colonialist power or as a benevolent partner. To understand whether the Chinese approach to African media could have resonance beyond China, greater attention must be paid to how the ideology and political culture characterizing individual African countries, as well as the elites who establish partnerships with Chinese political leaders and companies, resonate with the Chinese approach to governance and the media (Gagliardone *et al.*, 2012).

A research project about 'The Voice of China in Africa - Media and soft power', funded by the Research Council of Norway, finished in 2016 after three years of comprehensive study following its launch in March 2013 (www.cmi.no/projects/1686-voice-of-china). The project analysed the interaction between China and Africa in areas such as communication industries, media and culture. Its authors have published several journal articles, book chapters, reports and conference speeches and believe that:

> media seem to be the pivotal connection between the Chinese public and Africa. More than obvious governmental directives are behind the media's initial interest in African issues, while the media narratives are driven by different forces and meant to meet various needs and demands.
>
> *(Li and Rønning, 2013b: 43)*

> China has been employing domestic media to engage public support to buttress its expansion in Africa. Thus to build a positive image of Africa in China must be seen as a component of the mainly economic Chinese relations with Africa.
>
> *(Li and Rønning, 2013c: 43)*

It seems that setting up more overseas channels or stations and even bureaus will not be an easy task for CRI in the future, not only because the regulations for foreign communication businesses are getting tighter globally, but also due to the changing media environment in which social media are overtaking traditional media and further changing the media industry. CRI has noted the importance of communicating to a global audience on social media and set up huge numbers of overseas social media accounts on different platforms in different languages. By the end of August 2016, CRI's social media accounts totalled 108, comprising Facebook (76), Twitter (19) and other platforms (13). The number of fans of all the CRI overseas accounts reached 15 million. There were 33 accounts followed by over 100,000 fans respectively, using 25 languages, of which the most frequently used languages were English, Japanese, Spanish, Chinese, German, Thai, Burmese, Vietnamese, Turkish and Malay.

The practice of CRI's 'going out' can be easily identified as an attempt to balance the role of a state-owned radio station delivering positive narratives of China globally, and the role of a media organization aiming to develop itself into a global mainstream media organization, capable of 'introducing China to the rest of the world, introducing the world to China, reporting global affairs to the world, and promoting understanding and friendship between the Chinese and peoples from other countries' (Wang, 2011: 232). CRI plans that during the next five years and beyond, it will further accelerate the transformation to develop into an international media group supported by modern technology, and the true challenge for it will be how to keep a solid financial footing and a large number of language services for a broad and diverse audience if it does not rely on the traditional state-dependent model.

References

Chen, C.; Colapinto, C. and Luo, Q. (2010) China radio international in the digital age: Propagating China on the global scenario, *Global Media Journal*, 9(16): 1–15.

China Plus. Who We Are. Available at http://chinaplus.cri.cn/aboutus/aboutcri/62/20170216/393.html [Accessed 18 March 2017].

Gagliardone, I.; Stremlau, S. and Nkrumah, D. (2012) Partner, prototype, or persuader? China's renewed media engagement with Ghana, *Communication, Politics and Culture*, 45: 174–196.

Global Times. (2015) Editorial: How Come the West Takes Precautions against China's Ideological Infiltration? Available at: http://opinion.huanqiu.com/editorial/2015-11/7903659.html [Accessed 11 October 2016].

Hu, Z. and Ji, D. (2012) Ambiguities in communicating with the world: The 'Going-out' policy of China's media and its multilayered contexts, *Chinese Journal of Communication*, 5(1): 32–37.

Huang, K and Li, S. (2016) Chinese Media in Africa: From the Perspective of Discourse and Influence, in Guan, J. and Huang, K. (eds.) *Research on media's construction of foreign discourse system: From the perspective of international communication.* Beijing: China Broadcasting Press.

Jiang, F. (2016) Mapping the intercultural communication theories to facilitate updating Chinese international communication strategy, *Jinan Journal* (Philosophy and Social Science Edition), 38(1): 83–95.

Koh, G. and Shiffman, J. (2015) Beijing's Covert Radio Network Airs China-friendly News Across Washington, and the World. Available at: www.reuters.com/investigates/special-report/china-radio/ [Accessed 11 October 2016].

Li, S. and Rønning, H. (2013a) Half-orchestrated, half freestyle: Soft power and reporting Africa in China, *Ecquid Novi: African Journalism Studies*, 34(3): 102–124.

Li, S. and Rønning, H. (2013b) Reporting Africa: Soft power, media and civic engagement, *China Media Report Overseas*, 9(3): 43–55.

Li, S. and Rønning, H. (2013c) China in Africa: Soft power, media perceptions and a pan-developing identity. *CMI Report* R 2013:2. Bergen: Chr. Michelsen Institute.

Vincent, E. (2016) International broadcasting as a tool of international diplomacy, *New Media and Mass Communication*, 46: 45–52.

Wang, G. (2007) Accelerating construction of a modern international broadcasting system, *China Radio and TV Academic Journal*, 1: 10–11.

Wang, G. (2011) *Strategies for International Communication*. Beijing: Chinese Communication University Press.

Wang, G. (2012) Let China integrate into the world better, *China Radio and TV Academic Journal*, 1: 10–12.

Wang, G. (2016) CRI 2016 annual report, *Journal of World Radio Film and Television*, 1: 3–12.

Wu, Y. (2012) *The Rise of China's State-Led Media Dynasty in Africa*. South African Institute of International Affairs: China in Africa Project: 1–33.

Zhao, X. (2015) A review of China's soft power projection through its transnational media institutions: Conveying discourse of economic responsibilities in media 'going-out'. for(e)dialogue, *New Directions in Media Research*, 1(1): 27–39.

Zhao, Y. (2013) China's quest for 'soft power': Imperatives, impediments and irreconcilable tensions? *Javnost-The Public*, 20(4): 17–30.

9

INTERNATIONALIZATION OF CHINA'S NEW DOCUMENTARY

Guoqiang Yun and Jing Wu

The birth and development of the independent documentary movement in China, later becoming China's New Documentary, reflects the relationship between the transformation of China's economic system and that of cultural production. Before the dramatic commercialization of media in China towards the end of the 1990s, the independent documentary movement demonstrated the potential achievements and degree of freedom that cultural producers could gain in the international market. It created heroic stories about the individual's pursuit of independence and resistance and established a pattern of representing China that still echoes in today's mass media. This pattern is by no means completely free and independent, however, but closely related to post-Cold War narratives of communist defeat and new visions of global capitalism. It is only against the economic and cultural context of international film festivals that we are able to see the heroic 'battle' between documentary filmmakers and official media in China. Moreover, because of its international acclaim and symbolic power within China, independent documentaries constitute an important pattern of discourse in representing social developments in contemporary China, through whose lens the meaning and significance of China's social changes are articulated.

To have a deeper understanding of the historical value of the independent documentary movement, we need to view it as part of wider historical changes internationally. Since the late nineteenth century, the affairs and fate of China have always been linked to the affairs and fate of the rest of the world. When studying the practices of independent documentary and other related cultural phenomena, we need to keep the dialectical sense of history between the local and the international.

The formation of documentary aesthetics in China: a historical perspective

Film technology appeared in China at the same time that Western colonial expansion reached its acme. The photographers commissioned by the Lumière brothers, the inventors of film, projected and shot films around the globe, and they achieved tremendous success. Their film practices encompassed all the features of the culture industry, including mechanical reproduction, standardized processes and quality control, mass audiences and the adoption of formal qualities of visual realism. It is notable that the success of the Lumière brothers was by no means limited to commercialization of film and management of artistic quality. They were the first to establish a modern technology-based visual system that was going to have a profound impact. The combination of camera, projector and movie screen created a 'realistic' world, which not only affected the transformation of visual systems in the West, but also influenced the organization of cultural industries in the entire modern world. Film also revolutionized the way that people perceived and comprehended reality. Thus, visual technologies such as film, a tool in the global expansion of violence and capital, rapidly became the dominating form of reproducing reality. As Martin Heidegger points out, in modern times the world is now conceived and grasped as picture. It does not merely mean that people are increasingly surrounded by pictures; it means a complete change in the relationship between the human and the world.

Movies, which entered China simultaneously with Western powers, have always been perceived as a national trauma by Chinese intellectuals. In the preface to *The Outcry* (*Na Han*), Lu Xun referred briefly to a piece of newsreel when he explained his experience of abandoning medicine for literature. In his view, movies, as exotic 'stuff', were certainly considered as a thing that amused people. Nevertheless, the 'stuff' was exactly the stimulation that spurred him to make such an important decision. Watching the newsreel in which Chinese spectators passively accepted Japanese soldiers beheading their own people, he deplored Chinese unconsciousness, or the national character that he more thoroughly criticized later on. In the films, Japanese (and other Western) invaders used their swords as both real and symbolic violence, splitting the Chinese into two parts: onlookers indifferent to the execution and 'offenders' being executed. Both onlookers and 'offenders' were objectified via the 'gaze' of the camera documenting the scene of execution, and became objects under surveillance and control. In the meantime, these Chinese people, deprived of their subject position, strengthened the subjectivity of invaders.

The issue of 'looking' raised by Lu Xun has three dimensions. The first is the 'looking' of indifferent onlookers inside the scene captured by the newsreel. They look innocently and unenlightened. The second is the 'looking' of the Western invaders at China through the mediation of the movie camera, namely the colonial gaze. Chinese civilization has been regarded as 'the other' to the West and modernity, and thus the target of Western domination by means of gunboat and camera. The third is that Lu Xun, and in the same way, Chinese intellectuals, look at the event from the perspective of the colonial gaze, recognizing the imminent crisis of national subjugation and genocide. This way of viewing represents self-awakening and national awareness of Chinese vanguard intellectuals in the modern age.

Film has become a special intermediary between seeing and being seen. China and the world 'encounter' each other both in films and in real life, which gives birth to three paradigms of understanding China's relations with the world. The first is the paradigm of empire. Filmmakers identify with the goal and psychology of Western imperialism intentionally and unintentionally. China, as an object of observation and research, was shot in the perspective of the West as subject. This kind of documentary film can be traced back to the movies produced and projected by photographers commissioned by the Lumière brothers. China's image in the movies is imbued with exotic elements, serving as the 'other' to the West. The second is the paradigm of humanism. This category of documentary movie is practised by artists, intellectuals and journalists who were influenced by the progressive documentary film movement during the mid-twentieth century. The angle of humanism in this documentary movement emphasizes respect for people, concern over the destiny of humankind in social change, as well as the pursuit of social progress. It partly pushes practitioners to transcend ethnic and regional estrangement between onlookers and persons being looked at, or observers and object of observation. It also incorporates China's social and cultural landscape into a global vision of social change. China, as explained in the movies of this humanist paradigm, is dynamic and has subjectivity (Wu, 2006).

With the founding of New China, the third visual paradigm comes into being, which we call the 'Party's gaze'. It is associated with the Chinese Communist Party (CCP) taking state power and establishing the political order of one-party rule. The Party's gaze stems from the CCP's power operations: the Party's political project resorts to visual and graphic forms to permeate almost every social institution and community with the aid of Party organizations at all levels, which has finally become the dominant framework of interpreting reality by the Chinese people. In general, the Party's gaze is a visual mechanism similar to 'perspective', which sets an invisible viewpoint for spectators by applying realistic aesthetics and visual conventions, incorporating viewers into a sense of collectivism and socialism as 'natural reality'. This style also inherits the Griersonian heavy-handed voiceover, speaking from on high to communicate truth to the audience, which has become the main target of resistance by a new generation of documentary filmmakers (Zhang, 2006).

The three visual paradigms mentioned above have established the historical and formal context in which the spirit of China's documentary coheres and gradually changes. As an art form, documentary not only visually reproduces people and events, but also constructs ideographic systems in coordination with other art forms. These systems endow the social world with specific meanings so as to make social reality visible and meaningful. In this sense, image reproduction is only the empirical 'surface' of documentary. At a more profound level, visual paradigms organize visual materials into an ordered whole in documentary films, which serve as visual social reality. Therefore, China's documentary works should be given more methodological inquiry, so that researchers can better comprehend the deep and complex relationship between China and the world through Chinese documentaries.

The independent documentary movement and the rise of New Documentary

Looking back to the twentieth century, particularly film history after the Second World War, the change of film form manifested itself through a blend of aesthetic, economic and political appeal, and ultimately was transformed into social facts through social movements. The rise of China's so-called independent documentary movement also continued this pattern. Chris Berry argues that we need to look at China's film production during the reform era in a 'post-socialist' perspective, which in China means a kind of post-modern combination of residual socialist political façade and the loss of socialist belief at the same time. Thus the 'state' has become an empty signifier against which any innovation in language and art is directed (Berry, 2008).

Bumming in Beijing (1990) by Wu Wenguang is generally considered the beginning of China's independent documentary movement. Independent productions became a trend in the early 1990s. Documentary forms, techniques and aesthetics, developed out of this era of 'independent' documentary, are generally considered and named China's 'New Documentary' (Berry *et al.*, 2011). In the meantime, CCTV began broadcasting a new non-fiction programme, *Life Space*, in 1993, with the mission of 'telling the story of ordinary people'. This programme is considered as the second milestone in the New Documentary Movement. Like those independent documentary filmmakers walking on the margins of the governmental system, *Life Space* focused on the multitudes, trying to 'present humanitarian caring and leave the future a history composed of ordinary people, in the midst of swiftly changing times'.[1] The documentaries made by independent producers outside the official media system, together with non-conventional documentary-making by those within state television such as CCTV, gave birth to China's New Documentary Movement, the occurrence and development of which had a profound impact on China's contemporary documentary culture.

To understand the features of the New Documentary Movement and independent documentary, we need to put it in the context of the transformation of China's cultural system. The Mao era was driven by radical changes of productive relations. Along with the socialist reconstruction of the economy, culture and the media, as an integral part of the socialist cause, China adopted the structure of state monopoly, public funding and strict ideological controls over content. The implementation of this culture system in the field of documentary filmmaking is to establish in visual forms the previously mentioned 'Party' gaze, which is typically represented by the documentary style of the Party's Central Newsreel Factory. The most fundamental characteristic of this kind of documentary by official agencies is the domination of a certain value system over the content. The meaning of the documentary is determined by the producers (institutions) instead of the characters.

The New Documentary Movement and independent documentary first estab-
lished their own uniqueness by dissociating themselves from this documentary
convention of 'Party' gaze. Legends say that the name of 'independent' and
'New Documentary Movement' came from a private party at the film director
Zhang Yuan's home in 1992 (Lv, 2003). Participants included Wu Wenguang,
Shi Jian, Jiang Yue, Hao Zhiqiang, Wen Pulin, Li Xiaoshan and Duan Jinchuan, most
of whom later became the backbone of the independent documentary circle.
At that party, they discussed the initiation of a movement to fight against obsolete
documentary conventions. Among those present were staff from state film and tel-
evision institutions and also individuals engaged in film and television production.
The official/grassroot dichotomy that is so essential to the New Documentary
Movement was set up at the very beginning, even though these new documentary
filmmakers were mostly from the cultural elite and worked in elite institutions.
Zhang Yuan pointed out with a challenging attitude that China's documentary is
actually a synonym for political propaganda film. He also alleged that the lack of
real documentary history leads to the hypocrisy of Chinese film, and that true movies
should be directed to express the director's inner world, express their views on the
world, provide the audience with special perspectives on their own lives, and
prompt them to think, to reflect (Fang, 2003: 361–362). Although the participants
of that party did not explain clearly what 'independence' means, this did not hinder
it from developing into a unique film movement. The obscurity of the term 'independence' offered a wider space for interpretation and imagination, and thus helped
with a broader recognition of the movement.

By prevailing professional documentary production standards, the film *Bumming
in Beijing* is undoubtedly unprofessional, plain and even crude. This is due mostly to
its extremely low budget and no expectations of being broadcast. However, its success
created a unique and new documentary spirit and documentary researchers recognize its historic and cultural value, mostly because of its theme and context. The film
changed the relationship between the photographer and the photographed, or
'seeing' and 'being seen' (Mei and Zhu, 2004). This new idea of shooting rebelled
against the documentary convention of the 'Party's gaze' and breached a lot of
spoken and unspoken norms of official institutions. As a result, many from the circle
were banned from making movies and television programmes (Fang, 2003: 346).

Circumventing capital constraints by making lower quality, community-circulating
movies and challenging the propaganda system's hegemony constitute the initial
space where pioneers of independent documentary can imagine 'independence'.
The concept of 'independent' documentaries first means creating an alternative
and unique voice beyond documentary's highly institutionalized ideology in
China's media system. 'Independence' is usually understood as individual, folk, non-
governmental, outside institution, etc. It made an implicit commitment to provide
original reality based on independent thinking and different from the mainstream
perspective. In the series of dichotomies between individual/institutional, non-
governmental/official and popular/elite, independent documentary constructed a
specific identity in China and fought for its voice and existence. Soon, in the

context of marketization of cultural institutions, it became a historical actor playing a role in the new power structure of the market economy.

By differentiating itself from the 'Party's gaze', visual conventions of the imperial and humanistic paradigms of looking are incorporated and regenerated by the New Documentary Movement as international discursive resources. The New Documentary's emphasis on the development of the individual, folk and civil discourses owes very much to the humanistic turn in cultural productions of official media institutions during the reform era. In fact, it is important to remember that both China's socialist revolution and her reform efforts, together with the cultural arm of the two political paradigms, have international precedence and influence. In the reform efforts of official media in China, international media practices become inevitable reference points. To a great extent, the New Documentary Movement has its roots in the self-reform of institutional media.

In 1992, the Central Propaganda Department of the CCP explicitly requested that the news media should pay more attention to social issues in order to strengthen communication between cadres and ordinary people (Zhang, 2013: 3). To carry out the policy, CCTV launched a series of programme reforms. Yang Weiguang, the then director of the TV station, recruited many young people with unconventional ideas and innovative spirits as producers, thus giving rise to a number of historically significant television programmes like *Oriental Horizon*, *Topics in Focus* and *News Investigation*. Emphasis on documentary style while subduing the propagandist tone became the basic consensus at this stage of reform. It served as a source of innovation for all non-fiction productions reaching beyond CCTV. The programme *Oriental Horizon*, for example, intentionally uses long shot, eye-level camera angle and less editing, showing the influence of the New Documentary grammar at the time (Zhang, 2013: 65). Programme evaluation standards also changed partially from political correctness to popularity among audiences and 'newsworthiness' judged by professionals. This sociological turn of programme-making was in accordance with the humanist documentary spirit of caring about the life and hardships of ordinary people.

The transformation of China's non-fiction film and television production is of course not unrelated to international trends. At a time when the Chinese independent documentary grew up, the Western documentary tradition was similarly undergoing a significant transformation, which is also referred to as the 'New Documentary film'. According to Linda Williams, New Documentary filmmakers believe that the camera cannot reveal the total reality of the world and that it can only represent the thought-forms and consciousness-building of competing realities presented by people from different angles. Documentary makers are making use of various audio-visual narrative methods to present the significance of events they choose to reveal (Williams, 2001: 584). Another notable feature of the New Documentary film is that subjectivity is no longer considered problematic as in traditional documentary norms, because any language is inevitably loaded with value and position. New documentaries tend to abandon the myth of objectivity and accept that subjectivity is unavoidable, making it into a clearly stated subject position that leads the audience into the filmic space.

In his historical analysis of Chinese documentary film, Shan Wanli associates the independent documentary movement in China during the 1990s with the 'direct cinema' and 'cinema vérité' movement in the 1960s, explaining the origin and development of Chinese independent documentary from the angle of technical and aesthetic similarities between these two (Shan, 2005: 424). However, the explanation based on the similarities of technical forms actually covers up the deep differences between the 1960s' independent documentary movement in the West and China's own New Documentary scene at the end of the century. Also, he completely ignores the post-revolution 'new documentary film' trend that has more socioeconomic structural similarities with China's New Documentary Movement.

The two decades of the 1960s and 1970s were the heyday of mass media professionalism in Europe and America. Independence and objectivity were then regarded as a basic indicator of media practice. Growing out of this atmosphere, direct cinema primarily followed an aesthetic style that aimed to be independent of the market and to defend society by resisting the penetration of the market into the creative processes of media. However, with the two oil crises in the 1970s causing full-blown recessions in traditional industrial and manufacturing sectors, the economic structure of the mass media was shaken too. To deal with the social and economic crises at that time, developed countries in Europe and America turned to neo-liberalism as the regime of 'innovation'. In order to overcome the crisis and maintain profit and production levels, neo-liberal economic doctrines revoked Keynesianism, which believes in active government intervention in economic life. Instead, the new economies turned to deregulation, privatization and governmental withdrawal from many areas of public services, including the media sector. Under the neo-liberal doctrine, market domination of big conglomerates deepened and media productions were increasingly forced to be responsive to market demands. This development undermined the foundation of independence and professionalism of the media, thus affecting the transformation of the documentary tradition towards subjectivism and sensationalism – the main features of the so-called New Documentary Movement.

In the Western context, the market has affected the principles of public service and gained hegemony over cultural production, which finally led to the demise of the documentary film movement that had begun in the 1960s, while in China, the New Documentary Movement developed in parallel with the marketization process. Although some pioneers of Chinese independent documentary once explicitly interpreted 'independence' as a way of providing a different perspective from the official ideology as well as reducing dependence on capital, the fact was that the main object of resistance for China's independent documentary movement was official ideology rather than market forces. Indeed, it rapidly embraced the market and global capital, which in turn helped bring partial freedom from the traditional propaganda system.

If we simply interpreted the development of Chinese independent documentary during the 1990s by linking it with the documentary movement of the 1960s in the West, we would overstate the technical and aesthetic similarities while ignoring political and economic structures of cultural production. Besides, it would blind us from seeing the influence of neo-liberalism and globalization. From a global perspective, the rise of China's independent documentary was not only a part of China's own market transformation; the mode of production of independent documentary also fits the neo-liberal economic policy as a part of the structural adjustment of capitalism. In the Chinese context, intellectual discourses usually describe China's social transformations as 'reform' or 'post-revolution', as if they were completely internal to China's own politics. It is worth noticing that a lot of 'reform' ideologies and policies are the results of 'opening up', i.e. China learning from the internationally dominant neo-liberal regime in order to gain legitimacy for reform. To some extent, the independent documentary movement is also part of this global process of the neo-liberalization of media, in the name of China's cultural reform. In the following part, the authors will be discussing how international film festivals and the international market act as structural forces in the formation of China's independent documentary mentality.

International film festivals and the internationalization of New Documentary

The rise of the New Documentary Movement and independent documentary marks a historic change in the relationship of looking between China and the world. The New Documentary Movement and independent documentary constitute a dominant reference system to understand the modern features of contemporary Chinese society, as they are internationally recognized as the most trustworthy sources of media representation in China. With the help of international film festivals, New Documentary films are able to create and maintain a particular style of documenting and narrating China, which allows them to act as a unique mechanism of social production and reproduction (Voci, 2006). When independent documentary claims to represent the social reality and becomes more and more internationally acclaimed, it also produces a public that appreciates its style and aesthetics. Therefore, it exists not only as a form of media content, but also as a producer of new kinds of consciousness. The New Documentary thus acts as an important medium through which China and the world interact with and influence each other.

Looking back at the process of internationalization of China's New Documentary since the 1990s, there are two factors that are of particular interest: international film festivals and 'pre-sell' purchases by international media conglomerates. Both of these not only provide the space for expression and dissemination of independent documentary films out of China, but also are deeply involved in the construction of the New Documentary's discursive feature and the creation of its classical style. Looking from a historical perspective, awards from film festivals like Yamagata, Amsterdam, Leipzig, France's Reality Film Festival, as well as global media organizations, such as the BBC and NHK, always go hand in hand with the landmark productions of China's New Documentaries. This creates an important interactive space for the encounter between China and the world.

The debut of China's New Documentary on the world stage dates back to the second Yamagata Documentary Film Festival in 1993. Six Chinese documentaries exhibited in the festival and Wu Wenguang's *My Red Guard life in 1966* was awarded the 'Ogawa Shinsuke Prize'.[2] Since then, a growing number of China's independent documentaries have competed for awards in various international film festivals. Meanwhile, in areas of modern art, with the efforts of brokers for the Western art establishment, a system of exhibition, collection and trade for contemporary Chinese art had formed. Considered part of contemporary art, China's independent documentary was often grafted on the vine of this system for international art exhibitions and trading. In 2013, the New York Museum of Modern Art held a film festival named 'China's reality/sight in documentary' in order to show the changes in the practices of China's documentary works. The films on show included some of China's world-famous independent documentaries like *Bumming in Beijing*, *West Zone* and *Petition*. The curators claimed that 'the pioneer directors such as Wu Wenguang, Zhang Yuan and Duan Jinchuan dissociate themselves with the mainstream media institutions and are free from the castration of censorship'. At the same time, 'they create alternative views and imaginations of society on the basis of direct observation of reality'. In addition, the festival includes other 'underground amateur videos' and 'Internet conceptual arts'.[3] Through international film festivals and art exhibitions, China's newborn independent documentary gained channels of distribution and platforms of display. Participating in film festivals and art exhibitions has gradually become a shortcut to success for independent documentary filmmakers, as it provides replicable genre formats and economic predictability.

International film festivals help to consolidate the loose uniformity of the independent documentary circle by providing prestige, authority, capital grants, etc. The pioneers of independent documentary were thus able to break the documentary conventions of official media, create significantly different shooting and expressive forms, and produce new conventions to guide the practices of documentary production. Due to limited interventions from official institutions and therefore more freedom of action for the authors, independent documentary can capture changes in social conditions more flexibly and represent social realities from more innovative angles. In competition with and opposition to official documentary both in content and form, independent documentary has accumulated plenty of 'symbolic capital'.

International film festivals also help independent documentary makers from China to step into and learn to operate in the symbolic as well as economic order of capitalist culture. They gradually incorporate China's independent documentary in the display of genres and product chains on the landscape of international documentary, turning it into a somewhat self-conscious national subject, with a particular market appeal, sphere of representation and validity of narration. More importantly, international film festivals provide China's independent documentary with a direct service to turn symbolic capital into economic capital. This kind of economic service is not merely an extra bonus for award-winning films or sales at the events. Today's film festivals have already transcended the simple role of 'intermediary' and made themselves the core hubs of the documentary industry, which not only collect

finished products together but also distribute capital, commission and organize productions all over the world. Amsterdam International Documentary Film Festival,
for example, has just set up a special 'Doc For Sale' and 'Forum' section, providing
services independent of the event for the documentary trading market – services to
'find funding for producers',[4] to encourage directors from developing countries to
apply for production funds,[5] and to link capital sources to production initiatives
more closely. This process involves a new way of dominating and constraining people's
creative efforts, grafting the symbolic capital of the independent documentary to
the circulation logic of economic capital. In the circles of independent documentary,
because of the double constraints of China's official media and entertainment market,
it has become an esteemed 'model' for directors to apply for shooting funding from
international capital, then get awards in international film festivals, and finally return
to Chinese theatres with their symbolic capital.

By the end of the 1990s, another method of distribution besides international film
festivals had been developed by television institutions to accommodate Chinese
independent documentaries. This method, commonly known as pre-sale, involves
international programme agencies seeking documentary projects they consider appro-
priate and making recommendations to television institutions. Among the projects
proposed, programme agencies select a number of themes, give their approval and pay
the independent producer in advance for the licence to broadcast the first few rounds,
while allowing the producer to hold its copyright. Television stations, such as NHK
and the BBC, had begun collaborations with independent documentary producers in
China through this method. Many pioneers in this field such as Wu Wenguang, Duan
Jinchuan, Jiang Yue and Li Hong have achieved fame and financial independence
through these collaborations. With pre-selling, these film producers are offered a comfortable and flexible environment for production, which allows them to 'produce with
the greatest independence, and express freely via their camera lens without worrying
about financial pressure' (Mei and Zhu, 2004: 116). For once, the lifelong dream of
filmmakers to produce their own documentaries independently seemed within reach.

Taking a dialectical perspective, the influence of international film festivals and
pre-selling on the internationalization process of Chinese new documentaries and
independent documentaries is certainly complex and multi-faceted. On the one
hand, it does offer Chinese documentary producers the opportunity to learn and
gain more insight through communication and interaction with their peers in other
countries. With the relative financial security it offers, it has allowed Chinese documentary producers to study excellent works by producers around the world, as well
as the chance to take active part in the vibrant and dynamic process of exchanging
their professional ideas and experiences on an international platform, exposing
them to different documentary spirits and aesthetics which appear both novel and
enlightening to them. On the other hand, this pattern also involves them in another
hegemony that is harder to resist.

The pathfinders of Chinese independent documentary have often described
their experience at international film festivals as a rather shocking one. During
Yamagata International Documentary Film Festival in Japan, the works of Shinsuke

Ogawa as well as the producer himself were said to leave the Chinese director Wu Wenguang 'astounded' (Mei and Zhu, 2004: 69), while Jiang Yue described his feeling as 'petrified' (Mei and Zhu, 2004: 162). In Wu's mind Shinsuke Ogawa epitomized the quintessential documentary spirit. 'All over the world it's unlikely to find figures like him. . . He is a milestone type of figure' (Mei and Zhu, 2004: 69). Duan Jinchuan voiced his experience in a way quite typical among Chinese directors:

> Upon seeing all those incredible works at foreign film festivals, I suddenly realized how bigoted and limited I used to be, it was truly some kind of epiphany as if a shield has been lifted and one begins to see things in a completely different light.
>
> *(Mei and Zhu, 2004: 103–104)*

He also mentioned 'feeling very much at home' at such occasions. Kang Jianning, after going to film festivals, reflected that not only his works but all domestic documentaries are more or less 'artificial and lack scientific spirit'.

Such accounts however, while claiming liberation from the previous shackles of ignorance, pay un-reflexive homage to the new standards of 'authenticity' celebrated by the international market. Commonly recognized as the defiant, uncooperative agency outside the official media, offering more personalized scope than the overwhelming mainstream discourse, independent documentary is characterized by the double features of avant-gardism and resistance. The former mainly refers to the way it renders a more close-up representation of the world in reality, and its refusal to adopt any pre-determined theme. The latter, resistance, is most evident in two aspects: first, its reluctance to succumb to the mainstream ideology, adopting a strategic rebellious attitude towards official media as a result; and secondly, its challenge to socialist realism, refusing to provide representative accounts of social forces or pointing at directions of social development as the doctrine stipulates.

Yet in this dichotomization between Chinese and 'International' media institutions, international film festivals and media platforms have become a centre for cultural hegemony, in which Chinese independent documentary faces incorporation and discipline. The independent voice producers struggle for could in fact also mean catering to the new provider of funding and symbolic capital. The culture of going to film festivals is laden with hero worship and aspirations to fame and success, which leads to alienation of both the ideals and practice of independent documentary, cultivating an attitude of utilitarianism instead of sincerity in creative activities. When independent documentary pioneers from China face such enormous cultural and institutional gaps between China and the 'world', those who take a stance openly against the dominating national media system appear as 'tragic heroes' in the eyes of the public, but in fact are immediately backed up by a more powerful financial and aesthetic establishment. In this bowing to international standards in representing China, independent documentary has, involuntarily perhaps, reinforced the orientalist or colonial gaze that defined the looking relationship between the West and China since the late nineteenth century.

After experiencing the initial shock, however, many of the pioneers start to reflect upon these issues and develop a critical understanding of the situation. Wu Wenguang realized that international film festivals could play a highly manipulative role in documentary production, controlling every aspect from the form to content, and young producers were apparently following a set pattern in order to be successful. Even his own work, he thought, had become somewhat 'manufactured and artificial'. The entire documentary film industry is 'packed with purpose and utilitarianism' (Fang, 2003: 384–385); Jiang Yue frankly used the word 'phony' to express his negative feelings towards the documentaries tailored for film festivals, declaring that 'all these festivals are phony, pretentious, in the name of solemnity and the sublime'. Li Xiao admits during a documentary forum that there actually is not much point in attending international film festivals for documentary. Film professor Zhang Tongdao finds orientalism prevailing during a film festival in Amsterdam:

> It's surprising how little the European audience know about China. The elders may have heard of Mao Zedong, and changes taken place after he ruled over China, but as for what China is like nowadays, their knowledge seems to remain in the age of Marco Polo.
>
> *(Zhang, 2003)*

The documentaries produced to cater for such an established perspective are certainly not well prepared to provide any challenging information and viewpoints.

Conclusion

The history of China's reform and opening-up policy can be divided into two stages: the reintroduction of a market economy in rural areas and small industries during the 1980s and the full-scale marketization, internationalization and privatization of key industries, and even public services in China since the early 1990s. From a global history perspective, the drastic transformation of China's economic policies has a deeper structural and systematic link with the expansion and transformation of capitalism. Neo-liberalism has been the main actor of this structural shift. David Harvey notices the link between ideologies behind China's reform and opening-up discourses and neo-liberal thinking coming mostly out of the governments and think tanks of the USA and UK. Harvey argues that both of them not only happened simultaneously but also led to similar practices both in economy and social policies, and this could not be mere accident (Harvey, 2010: 52–73). In front of the dismantled world order following the end of the Cold War, China's marketization and reform was exposed to the drastic changes in the Eastern bloc economy and the Western-led globalization. China's response to it was to actively integrate its economy into the global capitalist system, the climax of which is China's entering the World Trade Organization in 2001. In the neo-liberal economy, the commercialization of culture is one essential element. In the early part of this chapter, we discussed the marketization of public broadcasting in the West and its impact on the form and content of documentary production, and how spectacle and entertainment have mostly replaced social criticism as the rationale underlying the market for reality visual productions. This is the larger economic context within which China's independent documentaries need to be understood.

On the one hand, as we have pointed out in the international film festival analysis, desire for international capital, hero worship and fame leads to the development of utilitarianism in the circle of China's New Documentary producers. On the other hand, with the victory of the Chinese market logic, the confrontational relationship between the 'market' and the official media has collapsed. The critical meaning of 'independence', of creating different, individualized and unconventional perspectives towards social reality, has also weakened in the pursuit of mainstream recognition. Political dissent, which used to be the key self-identity of China's New Documentary, is also in danger of being emptied out when the global integration of cultural industries gradually encompasses the Chinese market.

Notes

1 *Southern Weekly* (1999) Chen Meng of *Life space*: To be like a scholar observing life, December 15.
2 The six Chinese documentaries exhibited in the festival were: Wu Wenguang's *My Red Guard life in 1966*, Hao Zhiqiang's *The tree township*, Wang Guangli and Shi Jian's *I graduate*, Jiang Yue's *God in Tibet*, Wen Pulin's *Qing Pu – the shrine of ascetic* and Fu Hongxing's *Tibetan Opera Troupe*.
3 Information on the Internet of Museum of Modern Art, New York: www.moma.org/visit/calendar/films/1371#related_screenings.
4 News on Indiewrie: 'Toolkit | Making a Pitch at IDFA's FORUM', www.indiewire.com/article/toolkit_pitch_perfect_at_idfas_forum.
5 Information on the website of Amsterdam International Documentary Film Festival: www.idfa.nl/industry/idfa-bertha-fund.aspx.

References

Berry, Chris (2008) *Post-socialist Cinema in post-Mao China: The Cultural Revolution after the Cultural Revolution*. London: Routledge.
Berry, Chris, Lu, Xinyu and Rofel, Lisa (eds.) (2011) *The New Chinese Documentary Film Movement: For the Public Record*. Hong Kong: Hong Kong University Press.
Fang, Fang (2003) *A History of China's Documentary Development*. Beijing: China Drama Press.
Harvey, David (2010) *A Brief History of New Liberalism*, translated by Wang Qin. Shanghai: Shanghai Translation Publishing House.
Lv, Xinyu (2003) On the Ruins of Utopia – New Documentary Movement in China, in *Documenting China: Contemporary Chinese New Documentary Movement* by Lv Xinyu, Beijing: SDX Joint Publishing Company.
Mei, Bing and Zhu, Jingjingjiang (eds.) (2004) *Archive of Chinese Independent Documentary*. Xi'an: Shaanxi Normal University General Publishing House.
Shan, Wanli (2005) *History of Chinese Documentary Film*. Beijing: China Film Press.
Voci, Paola (2006) Chinese Documentary: Changing China's Cinema Culture, in Jie, P. (ed.) *A New Look at Contemporary Chinese Documentary: Commentary on Contemporary Documentary by Overseas Scholars*. Shanghai: Wenhui Press: 103–113.

Williams, Linda (2001) Mirrors Without Memories: Truth, History, and the New Documentary, translated by Shan Wanli, in Wanli, S. (ed.) *Documenting the Documentary.* Beijing: China Radio and Television Publishing House.

Wu, Jing (2006) Two paradigms of 'seeing' China and the emergence of China's modern consciousness – on early modern visions of China, *Journalistic University*, 2.

Zhang, Jie (2013) It was an Era of Innovation – An Interview with Yang Weiguang, in Liang, B. (ed.) *Light Ideal Day: I and Oriental Time Twenty Years*. Beijing: SDX Joint Publishing Company.

Zhang, Tongdao (2003) Carnival of documentary: An experience at International Documentary Film Festival of Amsterdam, *World Screen*, 2.

Zhang, Yingjin (2006) Style, Theme and Perspective: Studies of Contemporary Chinese Independent Documentary, in Jie, P. (ed.) *A New Look at Contemporary Chinese Documentary: Commentary on Contemporary Documentary by Overseas Scholars*. Shanghai: Wenhui Press: 53–68.

10

CHINA'S MEDIA GOING GLOBAL: NEWSPAPERS AND MAGAZINES

Miao Mi

Aiming to improve China's image and profile abroad and to provide an alternative voice to influence key people who control media agendas, government policy and business overseas, Chinese media have in the past ten years been dramatically increasing their presence in the world. However, their success in gaining mass audiences abroad is still in doubt. Chinese media – and newspapers in particular – have been widely perceived by Western media as the instruments of government propaganda, tightly controlled by the Party and lacking independence. This chapter argues that, although many Chinese newspapers and magazines claim to be international titles with multi-language editions, bureaus, print plants or joint ventures aboard, given current scepticism it has been extremely difficult for these Chinese media outlets to increase their brand value and credibility abroad and effectively enhance China's global image.

With the internet's potential to break geographic boundaries and provide worldwide journalism, many influential newspaper brands, in particular those published in English-speaking countries, such as *The Guardian* in the UK, have been taking advantage of the internet by extending their brand, journalistic value and good practice online to reach a broader global audience. In order for Chinese newspapers and magazines to function better as a platform to export China's soft power, this chapter suggests that the good practices of some Western newspapers in producing content online could be considered as a model for Chinese newspapers and magazines to attract broader readership globally.

Following China's formal entry into the World Trade Organization in December 2001, in the same month the State Administration of Radio, Television and Film announced national strategies to encourage broadcasters in going out. After hosting the 2008 Beijing Olympics, and its failure to control Western media's coverage of the riots in Tibet and Xinjiang, the media's role in improving China's international image became more pronounced (Sun, 2013). In 2009 the Chinese government announced an ambitious 45 billion RMB funding scheme to boost Chinese media organizations' international presence (Wu and Chen, 2009) and in the same year Liu Yunshan, who is currently one of the seven members of the Politburo Standing Committee and serves as the head of the Central Propaganda Department, wrote in an article published in the Chinese Communist Party's (CCP) ideological journal *Seeking Truth*, that the Chinese media should 'make further improvement in leading public opinion, obtain the power of agenda-setting, seize initiatives and develop multi-language, widely appealing, informative, influential world leading media outlets with a global coverage' (Liu, 2009).

Again, in early 2012, the General Administration of Press and Publication released a national government document, *Suggestions on Accelerating the Going Out of Chinese News and Publishing Sector,* to further explain government policies on China's media going out. This document considered ten supporting policies, mainly related to government grant schemes, to encourage China's media to expand their global reach and at the same time, request the chief of local administration bodies to supervise the implementation of the going-out policy. For the first time, the national administration body stated that the implementation of the going-out policy would be included as an assessment indicator for government officials' promotion (*People's Daily*, 2012).

Instead of focusing on Western media's penetration into China and how China is represented by them, the Chinese media's going-out strategies and the global implications of China's soft power have become a much-researched topic (d'Hooghe, 2007; Zhao, 2013). As a part of the whole range of China's soft power initiatives, the global strategy for media is widely regarded as China's endeavour to break the Anglo-American monopoly on the setting of media and public agendas, to offer China's view and showcase China's rise as a great power in a non-threatening and non-confrontational manner (Zhao, 2013; Zhang, 2010). A report on the world's leading media companies' strategies of international communication published by the Communication University of China indicated that the voice of the Chinese government on international affairs has been significantly underrepresented. The report revealed that 50 Western multinational media companies account for 95 per cent of the world's media market and they shape the international image of China and lead public opinion on international affairs on a daily basis (Hu and Guan, 2011).

This chapter first reviews how China's newspapers and magazines have 'marched to the world' as part of the going-out initiative, what approaches have been taken, and the problems they have been facing. It then reviews the alternative strategies that China's newspapers and magazines have taken online to reach a broader global audience at a time when the future of newspapers is threatened by changes in communication technology.

China's newspapers and magazines

By the end of 2014, there were 1,921 newspaper titles in China, with 221 national titles and 792 provincial titles; 900 of them only serve cities and counties. In terms of content diversity, 823 of them were 'comprehensive newspapers', making up 43 per cent of the total newspaper titles and 1,089 were specialist titles with a special reporting perspective on technology, agriculture, military or other (Xinhua, 2015). In terms of its social function, they are classified as state-owned CCP titles and commercially driven metropolis and evening titles which are often affiliated to CCP titles. The CCP titles are managed as a state-owned public institution and have the obligation to serve the public interest. They are in broadsheet format and practise serious journalism. Most of the commercial titles in China are owned by large news groups, such as the Southern Daily News Group, the Yangcheng Evening News Group and the Wenhui-xinmin United Press Group. There are currently 40 newspaper groups in China. Although they are government-run public institutions and still receive subsidies from the government's public spending budget, competition within the newspaper groups is extremely fierce. For example, a city with a population of 14 million, such as Guangzhou, is covered by three big newspaper groups.

For more than three decades, both the circulation and advertising revenue of Chinese press titles were increasing year on year; however, in recent years, both readership and advertisers of the Chinese newspapers and magazines have been migrating from print to new forms of media outlets, including search engines, online news portals and mobile news. As a result of the decline in overall circulation and the drop of advertising revenues, some newspapers in China have had to cease printing. For example, Shanghai's local daily newspaper the *Evening News* was closed down on 31 December 2013.

It is argued that the Chinese newspapers' commercial success in the 1990s and 2000s permitted news and more critical forms of journalism to emerge in China (Shirk, 2011) and the investigative journalism conducted by some of the elite titles helped them to win brand authority and credibility. Yet, with the challenges posed by the internet and the new political climate in President Xi Jinping's government, there has been a trend for some newspapers to shift their flagship reporting away from the production of confrontational stories that expose elite wrongdoing (Li and Sparks, 2016). Print titles, vulnerable to the effects of recent technological, economic and political changes, have been challenged by Chinese online news portals and social media for credibility, authority, speed and cost and as a result, there has been a decline in their brand credibility, a decrease in journalistic integrity and an erosion of self-satisfaction among Party journalists.

Although also suffering from the shift of advertising and readership from print to online, Chinese magazines and periodicals are still growing both in terms of the number of publishers and their advertising revenue, but the rate of growth is slowing down. The total number of magazines and periodical publishers has grown from 2,793 in 2011 to 2,938 in 2016 and industry revenue has been increasing at an annualized rate of 5.3 per cent to $3.7 billion (IBIS World, 2016). According to China's Periodicals Association, by the end of 2013 there were 9,884 magazine titles registered with the General Administration of Press and Publication, with a total annual print run of 3.54 billion copies. However, among magazine titles, less than 1,000 titles are active in the retail market with approximately 800 titles available on subscription (FIPP, 2014).

It is essential to understand the domestic status of Chinese newspapers and magazines before examining their initiative of going global. The relationship between the press and the state, journalists' self-perception and the financial state of the print industry are the factors which impact on the response of Chinese newspapers and magazines to the Chinese government's going-out policy.

Global expansion

Over the past ten years, Chinese media's going-out project has been highly visible. From rapid expansion of multi-language services to significant bureau expansion and efforts in forming local partnerships, China's national broadcaster CCTV, national news agency Xinhua news agency, the English-language daily *China Daily*, the market-oriented subsidiary of the *People's Daily*, *Global Times* and the CCP's journal *Seeking Truth* have been leading elements in the Chinese media's march to the world.

The international expansion of Chinese newspapers is led by national titles using two key approaches: firstly the international distribution of their Chinese version with little or no localized content; secondly, publishing English editions abroad which report more on China's domestic issues, acting as a showcase for China. In 1981, China's first English-language daily newspaper, *China Daily*, was established and was distributed mainly in foreign embassies, multinational companies, five-star hotels, etc., to reach foreign readers who live, study or work in China. In 1985, national newspaper the *People's Daily* started publishing and distributing an international edition in Chinese to reach Chinese communities aboard as a showcase of China's development, policy and culture. Its distribution has now expanded to more than 80 countries globally.

With the introduction of government funding, from 2009 the two leading newspaper pioneers, the *People's Daily* and *China Daily* began to launch localized international editions to reach overseas audiences. *China Daily* launched its US edition in February 2009, its European and Asian editions in 2010 and an Africa edition in 2012 to expand its international outreach. The newspaper has set up branch offices in several major cities, including New York, Washington and London. In 2011, *China Daily's* America bureau moved to a much larger, 6,000 square foot office in Broadway, which is also home to ABC Television Times Square Studios.

The market-oriented subsidiary of the *People's Daily*, the *Global Times*, first launched an English edition in 2009 targeted at foreign readers in China to become the second English-language national daily and on 20 February 2013, launched its bilingual US edition, with 16 Chinese pages and 24 English pages printed in Los Angeles to 'cover world events from a Chinese perspective, introduce a real, complex and dynamic China and voice the Chinese public to the world in vivid, accurate reporting and in-depth analysis' (*Global Times*, 25 February 2013) and became the first newspaper from mainland China that launches both Chinese and English daily at the same time in the US. Sharing reporters aboard with its parent newspaper the *People's Daily*, the US edition of the *Global Times* has a better access to America's local stories. It is reported that *Global Times* has established an overseas team of reporters and writers with more than 500 people (*Global Times*, 2016). The *Global Times* also owns an English-language website, globaltimes.cn, which contains nearly all of the content of the newspaper's English and America editions; the weekend supplement *Global Times Weekend* is also available online in an e-paper format.

For regional newspapers, two commercially driven metropolis titles, Shanghai's popular local newspaper *Xinmin Evening News* and Tianjin's *Tonight Newspaper*, lead the march to reach the international market. *Xinmin Evening News* established its spin-off company in the US in 1994, specializing in publishing, distribution, advertisement and cultural exchange. In 1996, the newspaper extended its journalistic practice to the US by setting up its first international bureau and in the same year launched *Xinmin Evening News*'s American edition in Chinese, becoming the first evening post from China to be distributed daily overseas. In the same year that Hong Kong returned to mainland China, *Xinmin Evening News* registered its company in Hong Kong to manage the title's distribution there and expanded to Macao in 1998. In 2002, *Xinmin Evening News* formed an editorial partnership with Australia's Chinese newspaper *Sing Tao Daily* to have one page of the title edited by *Xinmin Evening News* daily. The same editorial partnership was introduced with Canada's local newspaper *Canada China Times* in 2004. With rapid expansion aboard, in 2004 the newspaper set up an international newsroom in its Shanghai headquarters specializing in providing content for its overseas editions. *Xinmin Evening News* has now expanded its international publishing to 28 overseas versions, reaching readers in 25 countries (Wei, 2010).

Following China's formal entry into the World Trade Organization in March 2002, the leading publication of Jinwan Media Group, *Tonight Newspaper* launched its first international edition in New York in partnership with America's Chinese newspaper, the *China Press*, and has rapidly expanded its distribution to 20 cities in 16 countries and territories with 23 local editions (Ma, 2012). As a market-oriented daily newspaper published in one of China's five national cities located in Tianjin, the newspaper claims to have a daily circulation of 700,000, with 12 to 16 pages in more than 30 provinces in mainland China. It is reported that the total weekly international circulation of its international editions reached 850,000 copies, serving more than two million readers a week (ibid.). According to the Director-Editor of *Tonight Newspaper*'s international edition, the purpose of investing in publishing international supplements is to showcase Tianjin's economic development, feature new government initiatives, inform the overseas reader of Tianjin's new investment opportunities and introduce human interest stories to create more mutual understanding (Guo, 2012).

Tonight Newspaper has formed partnerships with local newspapers in foreign countries and contributes original content gathered and produced by its newsroom in Tianjin to local newspapers branded with *Tonight Newspaper*'s title, as a supplement. In terms of selecting local partners, *Tonight Newspaper* favours influential local community newspapers that are targeted at people who study, work or live overseas, and newspaper titles funded by overseas Chinese as well as commercially successful

Chinese newspapers, such as *Sing Tao Daily*, which is originally published in Hong Kong but distributed globally.

Different from the *Global Times* and *China Daily*, which have editorial staff aboard for news-gathering and have the capability to produce English versions, the global strategy for regional newspapers is limited to publishing in Chinese and forming editorial or distribution partnerships with overseas Chinese newspapers to reach Chinese communities abroad. There is little to no localized content in its overseas editions and therefore they are even less effective than the free overseas Chinese community titles in reaching a local readership.

While Chinese newspapers are having difficulties with localizing content abroad and attracting foreign readers, transnational magazine companies have achieved significant success in their global expansion in China. Although the Chinese government has relaxed its control to allow foreign newspapers to be printed in China, foreign titles are still restricted in publishing and distributing in mainland China and only encouraged to print in China and then transport to other countries for distribution (*People's Daily*, 2004). But it is a different case for magazines. From the 1990s, the Chinese government began to allow foreign firms to form joint ventures with Chinese companies and publish magazines in China. Although the government has tightened its control, with the announcement that only magazine features on technology would be allowed to enter the Chinese market from 2004, leading international magazines in fashion and technology, as well as *National Geographic*, were already in China and soon established their brand and readership. By the end of 2015, 64 international magazine brands in total had been approved by the Chinese government to be published on a licensing basis. For example, the French publisher Hachette Filipacchi Media and Shanghai Translation Publishing House set up a joint venture to launch *Elle China* and *Marie Claire*; a Sino-Japan joint venture has been set up for the publishing of the Chinese *Rayli* and *Vogue* is a joint venture of China's People's Pictorial and Conde Nast Publications (Chen, 2010).

However, Chinese magazines' global expansion has been much harder and less successful than the entry into the Chinese market by international magazine brands. *Seeking Truth* launched an English edition in July 2009, with a selection of important theoretical articles adapted from the Chinese version to better serve international communication between the Communist Party of China and the world, and make this ideologically driven journal an important platform for international decision makers, academics and the public to understand the CCP's political thoughts and national strategies (Qiushi, 2009). Different from the Chinese edition, which publishes two issues a month, the English edition is now published as a seasonal periodical with four issues per year.

Within the commercially driven magazine groups, the leading examples are the women's magazine *NvYou* and text-based *The Reader*. Launched in 1988 with a special focus on fashion, beauty, health and family relationships, *NvYou* (*Women's Friend*) is China's leading women's magazine targeting female readers in their 20s and 30s. In 2001, *NvYou* released its Australia edition *Friends* (name changed to *Woman Friend* in 2011), claimed as the first Chinese magazine to have regular monthly distribution aboard. In 2004, the magazine partnered with a Vancouver-based local Chinese news-paper *Global Chinese Newspaper* (*Huan Qiu Huabao*) and expanded its publishing to Canada as *New You*. The Australian and North American editions are edited and printed in China and shipped to the two countries with its local partner responsible for advertising sales and distribution. In order to appeal to readers, *Nv You* has set up local bureaus in Australia and Canada and has 20 pages in both editions publishing stories and advertisements generated locally. In addition, the magazine endeavours to expand its influence on the local Chinese community through organizing events, sponsoring local celebrations of Chinese festivals and forming partnerships with writ-ers in Canada to encourage them to contribute to its content.

The Reader was established in 1981 with its title changed in 1993 from *The Reader's Digest* to avoid confusing it with the American *Reader's Digest*. It is one of China's most popular monthly magazines with a monthly circulation of more than eight million copies. In 2003, *The Reader* authorized an America company to distribute its North American edition priced at $2.50 per copy with a print run of 5,000 copies for the first year (Luo, 2006). Later in 2005, *The Reader* formed a partnership with a German company and Fujian Xinhua Bookstore's Australian branch to distribute the title in Europe and Australia. Different from its North American edition, the magazine only distributes 1,000 copies per month in the two countries and the copies are printed in China and shipped to its international market (ibid.).

However, compared with China's national broadcasters and news agency which have rapidly expanded their reach to international audiences through setting up regional news centres around the world or expanding offices and recruiting staff, the march of China's newspapers and magazines abroad is still comparatively slow and less influential. The most common approach for newspapers and magazines to expand globally is through what is called 'borrowing a boat to go to sea' which means 'identify vehicles that can effectively carry China's messages on behalf of China' (Sun, 2015: 408). To be more specific, the vehicles identified through the expansion practices con-ducted by national and regional newspapers, as well as magazine publishers include firstly, setting up, buying out, controlling the majority of share of or teaming up with foreign entities, such as *Xinmin Evening News*, *Nv You* magazine and *The Reader* and secondly, forming partnerships through content sharing, such as *Tonight Newspaper*.

There is still no indication of a clear business model to support these 'vehicles'. Newspapers and magazines are the biggest casualties of rapidly rising online news consumption in China. After more than 30 years' dramatic growth, China's econ-omy is still growing rapidly, but advertising expenditure on newspapers has begun to decline since 2012. Also, it is predicted that China's magazine industry will no longer maintain a similar rate of growth in their share of advertising spend; factors causing the erosion of revenue include the migration of readers and advertising to online publishing and the serious reduction in purchases of luxury products following the Xi government's crackdown on corruption (FIPP, 2015). Although the Chinese government has announced a 45 billion RMB funding scheme, it is hard for most newspapers and magazine groups to find the money to support investments in resources, facilities and staff to implement their global strategies.

On the other hand, there is a lack of commercial incentive for the media organizations to do so. The state-owned media organizations in China to some extent 'share the same expansionist logic that underpins the outward market expansionist imperative of Western media conglomerates' (Zhao, 2013). The competition to attract Chinese readers in major international cities, such as New York and London, is fierce between local Chinese community newspapers and the demand is still comparatively small. Therefore, there is little to no commercial interest for newspapers, in particular regional newspapers, which have less chance of receiving subsidies from the government's going-out funding scheme to invest in facilities and journalistic practices for global expansion. Meanwhile, in order to influence international readers, the English versions of China's print titles have to compete with the well-established, commercially driven transnational media companies, such as the BBC and News Corporation, which are either well respected and trusted or have extensive experience in running popular media.

Second, for press titles which have launched English editions aiming to provide China's voice on international issues and cover domestic stories in a way that is favourable to the Chinese government. It has been suggested that the international bureaus of Chinese media could follow the model of Al-Jazeera in staffing its news-gathering and production team with Western journalists who share the same news values and journalistic practices as the transnational media companies (Sun, 2015). When reporting news, China's media is heavily reliant on stories about sports, cultural and business activities to give an image of China as rich in culture and prosperity (Zhang, 2010). Although the Chinese newspapers and magazines claim to offer an alternative voice on international issues, China's media mainly cover stories on developing countries (ibid.).

Third, suffering from scepticism about China's rise, China's newspaper and magazine groups often only team up with overseas Chinese newspapers, which are mostly free publications targeting a niche market, and they find it difficult to form partnerships with established newspaper brands. For example, it is widely reported that the Southern Daily Group tried and failed to buy the international magazine *Newsweek*. The newspaper group teamed up instead with B-raymedia, a Shanghai-listed company based in Chengdu in Sichuan province that owns several metropolis papers, as well as a group of investors. The bid was described by Xiang Xi, managing editor of *Southern Weekly*, as 'a volunteer action of Chinese media professionals and investors' without any government involvement (*China Daily*). However, eventually the money-losing *Newsweek* was bought by an Australian audio equipment tycoon for a nominal amount reported to be just a single dollar. To some extent, it indicates the Western decision makers' unwillingness to hand over such a historical media outlet to Chinese control.

Government's role in newspapers and magazines' global expansion

Liu Yunshan, a leading member of the CCP's national committee, pointed out at the 2012 National Conference of Cultural Structural Reform that the going-out of

China's cultural and media sector should be 'oriented by the government, implemented by enterprises, participated [in] by the public and create a win–win partnership' (quoted in Xinhua, 2012). Michael Porter argues in his study on the competitive advantage of nations that government does not enhance the competitiveness of its companies, but acts as a catalyst and challenger. Its role is to encourage companies to improve their performances, stimulate early demand for advanced products and stimulate local rivalry by limiting direct cooperation and encouraging anti-trust regulations (Porter, 1990). However, Chinese newspapers and magazines' march abroad is primarily led by the party-state's political imperatives, rather than driven by commercial interest. Since the flow of information and the consumption of media content are demand-driven rather than supply-driven, a government-led global strategy for Chinese media becomes problematic (Zhang, 2010).

By 1994 more than 2,000 newspaper titles existed in China and the competition between these newspapers was fierce. In order to achieve economies of scale, the central government launched a top-down policy to promote press conglomeration. In June 1994, China's State Administration of Press and Publication began to foster a merger. Unlike in their counterparts in the West, where media conglomeration is driven by market forces, it was considered an imperative that popular commercially driven metropolitan and evening titles merge with CCP official titles. In addition, it was ordered that a proposal to set up a newspaper group must be initiated by a Party newspaper, and not the affiliated metropolitan titles. In 2002, the 'Making Media Big and Strong' strategy was launched, with the aim of creating powerful and profitable domestic media conglomerates with commercial strength and vitality that were prepared for global competition.

In a more marketized economy, mass circulation and the growth of advertising revenue enable the press to become comparatively more independent from the state and the Party and to be self-funded. The private ownership of newspapers also means that they can be more responsive to any change in the market to remain commercially competitive. In contrast, when the press is controlled as the instrument of the party-state, this results in what has been described as 'commercialization without independence' (Chan, 1993: 25) or 'liberalization without political democratization' (Zhao, 1998: 3). In the past ten years, with changes in news consumption behaviour and advertising spend, the press sector in China has responded much more slowly than the privately owned online news portals.

Although many newspapers have attempted to distribute in other countries and territories, funded by government subsidies, Chinese press titles have still not found a commercial motivation for their global presence. The march abroad is valued as a political achievement of government officials and as the responsibility of newspaper organizations to contribute to improving China's image aboard and promoting China's soft power. When political interests rather than commercial interests are the driving force for the march, political correctness rather than profitability and popularity is the priority for its global expansion. Thus, Chinese newspapers and magazine groups have responded much more slowly than other transnational competitors in terms of exploring new technology, finding alternative ways to improve newsroom efficiency, discovering ways of storytelling that are appealing to local audiences and eventually to build up their brand value and credibility abroad.

In addition, when driven by political rather than commercial interests, the allocation of resources, such as facilities and staff, is not determined through the interaction of free and self-directed market forces but by government interventions. When there is a mismatch between the need for an alternative Chinese voice and the effort put into promoting the newspapers and magazine titles abroad, it is a waste of time, facilities and money. Some argue that the leading state media organizations have turned the going-out march into a resource competition game to secure more political prestige and financial resources (Guo and Liang, 2011; Zhao, 2013).

Furthermore, with the Chinese government supporting Chinese media's going-out initiatives, it is harder for China's media to win over the sceptical global audience (Li and Sligo, 2012). With the party-state behind its march aboard, the credibility of the Chinese media in the global marketplace has been continuously undermined. Due to the political straitjacket and ideological complicity of the Chinese media, the content they produce is hardly appealing to Western decision-making elites and China's media is portrayed as an extension of the Chinese state or even intelligence system (Zhao, 2013).

An alternative approach?

Since electronic distribution of news first appeared in the early 1980s, pessimists have forecast the demise of print newspapers. Although it is premature to argue that the print newspaper is dying, since similar arguments have been repeated with every new communication technology, it is hard to deny that newspaper organizations have been challenged worldwide by these technologies in terms of credibility, authority, speed and cost (Chyi and Sylvie, 2001; Boczkowski, 2002; Allan, 2006). Due to the world-wide transformation of newspapers from print only to digital publishing, the demand for a print version has declined dramatically in countries where the readership has moved to online news consumption. Therefore, it is essential for China's newspapers and magazines to explore alternative approaches to reach the global audience.

Chinese media, like their Western counterparts, have been taking advantage of the internet and digital publishing to reach wider and younger audiences. China's newspapers and magazines began their migration to the internet from the late 1990s and this movement was led by the national and regional CCP newspapers. The *People's Daily* launched its website www.people.com.cn in 1997 and in 1999 opened China's first political bulletin board service. Besides the Mandarin version, the website has expanded its service into 14 other languages, including English, Arabic, French, Russian, Spanish, Japanese, German, Korean, Portuguese and Dutch. The content of the website is created by more than 70 bureaus at home and abroad. In 2011, the website's American bureau moved its office to the Empire State Building, a visible demonstration of its desire for global expansion.

The website of China's largest English-language newspaper, *China Daily* – chinadaily.com.cn – was launched in December 1995 and has editions in three languages, Chinese, English and French. The English edition has four versions of home pages, for China, the US, Africa and Asia. The English-language edition is also home to China's largest online English-language forums. In 2007, *China Daily* began its RSS service targeted at social elites and has more than 250,000 subscribers to its daily service. *China Daily*'s app for mobile and tablet was launched in 2009 and 2010 respectively and was the most popular app on Kindle in Asia. By 2016, the total number of users had reached more than five million from over 180 countries and territories (*China Daily*, 2016).

The editorial aim of the website is 'to bridge the world with multi-language news service' (ibid.). To be more specific, the website's English edition covers more stories about China with the purpose of introducing China to the world while its Chinese edition contains a large amount of international news aimed at creating one of China's most authoritative platforms for coverage and analysis on international issues (ibid.). *China Daily*'s website contains nearly all the content published in the newspaper group's print titles, as well covering a significant amount of online exclusive stories and providing a 24-hour rolling news service.

To some extent, the website has become one of the most important platforms for the Chinese government to make its voice heard globally, especially during a crisis. After a US navy spy plane collided with a Chinese fighter jet on 1 April 2001, the American media reported on the story immediately but without covering any response from the Chinese government, creating great tension in the relationship between China and the US. During the crisis, given the limitation of the print title's once-a-day editorial deadline, the website of the *China Daily* applied a digital first strategy during its coverage of the stories. It was the first to publish the Foreign Ministry spokesperson's response to the crisis and covered China's ambassador to the United States, Yang Jiechi's interview with CNN, so that the readers were well informed of the actions the Chinese government had taken at home and abroad, as well as its attitude towards the crisis. In addition, from 2003 the website has had an editorial partnership with the *PLA Daily*, publishing nearly 10,000 words of news and analysis about China's military, edited and translated by the *PLA Daily* (Cai and Yuan, 2003).

Wenzhou Newspaper Group is one of the few regional newspaper companies that has also explored global expansion via the internet. Wenzhou is one of China's most prosperous cities and is located in southeastern Zhejiang province. The city also has a large and historical tradition of overseas immigration, particularly to Europe and it is reported that there are no less than 500,000 immigrants from Wenzhou currently living in Europe. With the immigrants' demand for news and information from home, Wenzhou Newspaper Group launched a mobile newsletter service in 2011 in partnership with an Italian and a French company: in 2011 alone, more than 140,000 users subscribed to the free mobile news service (Wang, 2012).

Besides launching website and RSS services to reach international readers online, it has been suggested that using platforms outside the purview of the state media's external propaganda agenda, such as internet and social media, is another approach that could be used. The *People's Daily* has more than 22 million likes and 1.81 million followers on Twitter. Both of the social media accounts are constantly updated and carry a significant amount of multimedia content about China's culture, sports, natural beauty and social news. The *People's Daily* has published more than 37,000 tweets and more than 46,000 photos on Facebook. Foreign correspondents and readers can actively interact with posts through commenting or retweeting.

However, when it comes to coverage of news and current affairs online, in which social media are competing with traditional media in terms of speed, accuracy and depth, professional journalists are expected to uphold the credibility and integrity of their profession in informing the public and newspaper organizations are under pressure to enhance and extend their authority as trusted news brands online. Yet, the nature of Chinese newsrooms' workflow makes it difficult for them to enhance their competitiveness while the Western media companies have already applied strategies such as digital first, mobile first or live blogging. The control of the CCP over press titles means that when reporting sensitive international issues or domestic affairs, all newspapers need to wait for one of the three leading news providers, CCTV, Xinhua news agency, or the *People's Daily* to set up the agenda, which normally indicates the government and CCP's attitude towards the given issue. Therefore, it is impossible for China's media to compete with transnational media companies and social media for breaking news to eventually establish its credibility and brand value online.

In addition, for newspapers and magazines, revenues from advertising and circulation have plummeted and the business model of publishing online cannot support the newspaper at the same level as revenues from print. However, some of the Chinese press has found alternative means by which to fund its journalism and its global expansion online by investing in other ventures, such as real estate, and by

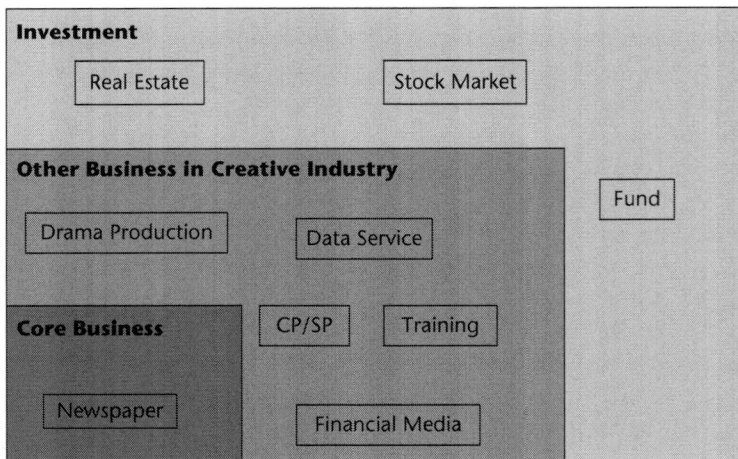

FIGURE 10.1   The transformation of Chinese newspapers' business model

Source: Adapted from Deloitte (2014) China Newspaper Breakthrough 2014.

raising capital from the stock market. For example, People.cn Co. is the holding company of the online business of *People's Daily* and was listed on the stock market in 2012, raising 1.4 billion yuan ($222 million) in a Shanghai initial public offering. It enables the *People's Daily* to set up separate online and print operations to allow the online website to develop without limiting its content diversity, originality, multimediality and interactivity (see Figure 10.1).

However, it is hard for other newspapers to copy the approach that *People's Daily* and *China Daily* have used to fund their global expansion and online journalistic practice.

Conclusion

With the Chinese government's significant funding scheme to support its media's global expansion and the pressure exercised on government officials by using the implementation of the going-out policy in their criteria for promotion, Chinese newspapers and magazines' march to the world is still mainly driven by political rather than commercial interests. Due to this, only a few of the national titles, such as the *People's Daily* and *China Daily*, have the capability to invest in facilities, staff and training to enable the titles to better reach their audiences abroad. Also, with the perception of Chinese media, in particular newspapers, as propaganda instruments tightly controlled by the government, it is hard for Chinese newspapers to compete with transnational media companies in terms of credibility and brand value and therefore convincingly convey China's voice to the world. Although many newspapers and magazines have made the attempt to establish editorial partnerships or to set up companies abroad to publish international editions, they have only made limited impact among overseas' Chinese communities or as a showcase for China's economic prosperity.

Nevertheless, Chinese newspapers and magazines have been enjoying the benefit of the country's growing economy, as both the advertisers and news readerships in China migrate rapidly to other forms of mass media. Chinese newspapers and magazines have to consider their business models for global expansion and will in the near future be driven much more significantly by their commercial success online. With the rapid development of communication technologies and the change of news consumption behaviour, Chinese newspapers and magazines have also explored alternative approaches to reach global audiences through online expansion. The impact of this on China's public diplomacy would be a fruitful area for further research.

References

Allan, S. (2006) *Online News: Journalism and the Internet*. Milton Keynes: Open University Press.

Boczkowski, P. J. (2002) The Development and Use of Online Newspapers: What Research Tells Us and What We Might Want to Know, in Lievrouw, L. and Livingstone, S. (eds.) *The Handbook of New Media*. London: Sage: 270–286.

Cai, J. F. and Yuan, D. (2003) *International Communication in a Global Perspective*. Beijing: China International Press.

Chan, J. M. (1993) Commercialization without independence: Trends and tensions of media development in China. *China Review*, 25–31.

Chen, P. Q. (2010) Magazines: An Industry in Transition, in Scotton, J. F. and Hachten, W. A. (eds.) *New Media for a New China*. Oxford: John Wiley.

China Daily (2016) Zhongguo ribao jianji [About China Daily]. Available at: www.chinadaily.com.cn/static_c/gyzgrbwz.html.

Chyi, H. I. and Sylvie, G. (2001) The medium is global, the content is not: The role of geography in online newspaper markets, *The Journal of Media Economics*, 14(4): 231–248.

Deloitte (2014) China Newspaper Breakthrough 2014. Available at: www2.deloitte.com/content/dam/Deloitte/cn/Documents/technology-media-telecommunications/deloitte-cn-tmt-china-newspaper-breakthrough-zh-140214.pdf.

d'Hooghe, I. (2007) *The Rise of China's Public Diplomacy*. Netherlands Institute of International Relations. Den Haag: Clingendael.

FIPP (2014) FIPP World Magazine Trends 2013/2014. Available at: www.fipp.com/insight/publications/fipp-world-magazine-trends-2013-14.

FIPP (2015) The Chinese Magazine Media Industry Continues to Expand Albeit at a Slower Rate. Available at: www.fipp.com/news/fippnews/the-chinese-magazine-media-industry-continues.

Global Times (2016) Huanqiu shibao jianjie [About Global Times]. Available at: http://hd.globaltimes.cn/html/abouthq/.

Guo, J. (2012) Analysis of *Tonight Newspaper's* international edition, *External Communication*, 10: 19–20.

Guo, Zh. and Liang, F. L. (2011) *China's Television Going Out and the Dynamics of Media Competition Within China. EAI Background Brief No. 598*, 10 February. Singapore: Singapore National University.

Hu, Z. R. and Guan, J. J. (2011) *Shijie zhuyao meitide guoji chuanbo zhanlue [International Communication Strategy of the World's Major Media]*. Beijing: Communication University of China Press.

IBIS World (2016) Magazine and Periodical Publishing Market Research Report | March by IBIS World in: *ibisworld.co.uk* [online]. Available at: www.ibisworld.co.uk/market-research/magazine-publishers.html.

Li, K. and Sparks, C. (2016) Chinese newspapers and investigative reporting in the new media age, *Journalism Studies*: 1–17.

Li, M. and Sligo, F. (2012) Chinese media going global: Issues of perception and credibility, *China Media Research*, 8(3): 116–128.

Liu, Y. (2009) Hui gu yu zhan wang [Looking Back and Forward]. Available at: http://politics.people.com.cn/GB/1026/8613794.html.

Luo, X. H. (2006) A Discussion on Chinese Magazine's International Market Strategies. Available at: www.ydbook.com/qikan/bkview.asp?bkid=104190&cid=296962.

Ma, L. (2012) Tonight newspaper: Travels to five continents in ten years, *Media*, 4: 24–26.

People's Daily (2004) Guowai baozhi jijiang jialin zhongguo, yinsha yu faxing shi liang hui shi [Foreign Newspaper is Coming to China, yet Printing is Different from Distribution]. Available at: www.people.com.cn/GB/14677/40710/40711/3043591.html.

People's Daily (2012) Xinwen chuban zongshu chutai 2012nian 'yi hao wen jian' licu zou chu qu [SARFT Released its First 2012 National Policy Pushing Chinese Media Going Out]. Available at: http://media.people.com.cn/GB/16835186.html.

Porter, M. E. (1990) The competitive advantage of notions, *Harvard Business Review*, 68(2): 73–93.

Qiushi (2009) Qiushi Sets up English edition. Available at: www.qstheory.cn/llzx/200909/t20090930_12642.htm.

Shirk, S. L. (Ed.) (2011). *Changing Media, Changing China*. Oxford: Oxford University Press.

Sun, C. (2013). *New Media in New China: An Analysis of the Democratizing Effect of the Internet* (Doctoral dissertation).

Sun, W. (2015) Slow boat from China: Public discourses behind the 'going global' media policy, *International Journal of Cultural Policy*, 21(4): 400–418.

Wang, Y. J. (2012) Wenzhou Ribao: Wenhua zou chu qu, shouyi zou jin lai [Wenzhou Daily, Brings Out Culture and Brings in Revenue]. Available at: http://data.chinaxwcb.com/epaper2012/epaper/d5257/d2b/201203/20005.html.

Wei, W. (2010) Traversing of international news in new media times – analyzing of 'crowd-sourcing' model for local newspaper, *Journalism Review*, 5: 81–84.

Wu, V. and Chen, A. (2009) Beijing in 45b Yuan Global Media Drive. Available at: www.scmp.com/article/666847/beijing-45b-yuan-global-media-drive.

Xinhua (2012) Quanguo wenhua tizhi gaige gongzuo huiyi juxing [National Culture Structure Reform Conference are Held]. Available at: http://news.xinhuanet.com/politics/2012-02/18/c_111540646.htm.

Xinhua (2015) 2014 nian quanguo xinwen chuban jiben qingkuang [Basic Figures of 2014 Chinese Press Sector]. Available at: http://news.xinhuanet.com/newmedia/2015-09/06/c_134593258_2.htm.

Zhang, X. (2010) Chinese state media going global, *East Asia Policy*, 2(1): 42–50.

Zhao, Y. (1998) *Media, Market, and Democracy in China: Between the Party Line and the Bottom Line*. Chicago: University of Illinois Press.

Zhao, Y. (2013) China's quest for 'soft power': Imperatives, impediments and irreconcilable tensions?, *Javnost – The Public*, 20(4): 17–29.

PART III

Discourses of Sino-globalization

11

THE EFFECTIVENESS OF CHINESE CULTURAL CENTRES IN CHINA'S PUBLIC DIPLOMACY

Xiaoling Zhang and Zhenzhi Guo

The importance of influence through cultural exchanges has long been recognised by governments around the world, and the Chinese government is no exception. Scholars (Zhang, 2013, 2016; Rawnsley, 2012) have observed that China has embraced the idea of soft power with overwhelming enthusiasm and has adopted soft power as a national policy. In its efforts to increase its state-centric and culture-focused soft power to secure an international environment conducive to its development and to generate goodwill abroad for its economic rise, Confucius Institutes (CIs) were established as part of China's 'going out' strategy.

According to the website of the Confucius Institute Headquarters, the Office of Chinese Language Council International, known as Hanban, 500 CIs and 1,000 Confucius Classrooms (CCs) have sprung up on campuses around the world since 2004.[1] Owned and overseen by Hanban, CIs, together with CCs, claim to be non-governmental, non-profit educational initiatives affiliated to the Chinese Ministry of Education. They partner with universities (for CIs) and colleges/schools (for CCs) or other educational institutions across the globe to provide Chinese language instruction, and scholarships for students to study in China and to promote greater understanding and appreciation of Chinese culture. Hanban provides partner universities and colleges/schools with grants of about $100,000 to $150,000 to cover the cost of set-up. Once established, Hanban funds the institutes' operations jointly with the host institutions. Hanban also provides teachers from China and supplies its own books, videos and other teaching materials to the institutes (Lumsden, 2015).

Between 2004 and 2011, Hanban spent an estimated $500 million establishing and funding CIs around the world (ibid.). CIs have thus become a global phenomenon across the world and have established partnerships with prestigious universities. However, since the first CI was established in 2004, CIs around the world have caused much controversy. Both the academic world and the media have joined the debate, questioning CI's intent, objectives and practices. Some worry about 'the real-political influence of the People's Republic' (Sahlins, 2014). It is believed to 'function as an arm of the Chinese state' and 'advance a state agenda in the recruitment and control of academic staff, the choice of curriculum and in the restriction of debate' (Sudworth, 2014). Many thus believe that because of all the controversy which leads to a lack of credibility, the CI has failed to play a successful role in China's public diplomacy (e.g. see Hubert, 2014; Wang and Adamson, 2015).

What has attracted far less attention but plays a similar role is the China Cultural Centre (CCC) under the Chinese Ministry of Culture. In contrast to the rapid speed and the accompanying debates around CIs and CCs, CCCs have demonstrated a different trajectory in their speed, operation, mode of collaboration and choice of host countries in spreading the knowledge of Chinese language and culture. Their importance may be said to have been overshadowed by the CI projects, operating in far more limited numbers and playing a quieter role in public diplomacy. However, they have drawn much less criticism from Western elites and have the potential to promote Chinese culture in the long run.

The main question this chapter asks is: since it attracts less criticism, does that mean the CCC is more effective than the CI in promoting Chinese language and culture and if so, why?

Through combined methods of analysis of relevant official websites (i.e. the website of the CCC Headquarters in Beijing and those of the individual CCCs around the world), a review of the limited academic and journalistic reports on CCCs in both Chinese and English, participant observation at the second China–Africa Cultural Industry Roundtable Conference in Beijing in May 2014, and in-depth interviews (i.e. interviews with the Director of the CCC Headquarters under the Ministry of Culture, the Director of the CCC in Benin, a local worker for the Benin CCC and a Benin cultural journalist), this chapter traces the development history of the CCCs, examines CCCs' development modes, activities, choice of host countries and channels for the promotion of Chinese language and culture, and assesses their impact. Drawing from literature, the chapter refers to CIs for comparison. The chapter concludes with discussions in the context of Joseph Nye's concept of soft power resources and soft power behaviour, and concludes that CCCs have so far been more successful, thanks to their gradualist and much less intrusive approach, collaboration with both governmental and non-governmental organisations both at home and overseas, ways of organising activities and, above all, the more invisible role the government plays. The chapter also points out the pitfalls CCCs should avoid in order to further their influence.

A brief history of CCCs' development

Since the establishment of the first CCCs in Mauritius and Benin in 1988, CCCs have gone through three periods – the exploratory period (1988–2002), the taking-off period (2002–2012), and the current rapid development period (Wang, 2014). As Table 11.1 shows below, the Mauritius and Benin CCCs remained the only two

TABLE 11.1 Establishment of China cultural centres around the world

Continents	Year established	Host countries/cities	Numbers
Africa			5
	1988	Mauritius	
	1988	Benin	
	2002	Cairo	
	2013	Nigeria	
	2015	Tanzania	
Europe			7
	2002	Paris	
	2003	Malta	
	2008	Berlin	
	2012	Moscow	
	2012	Madrid	
	2014	Copenhagen	
	2015	Brussels	
Asia			9
	2004	Seoul	
	2008	Tokyo	
	2011	Ulaanbaatar	
	2012	Bangkok	
	2014	Laos	
	2014	Sri Lanka	
	2014	Pakistan	
	2014	Nepal	
	2012	Singapore	
Americas			1
	2012	Mexico	
Oceania			3
	2014	Sydney	
	2015	New Zealand	
	2015	Fiji	

Source: Compiled from information on the website of the CCC at http://cn.cccweb. org/portal/site/Master/index.jsp, accessed 20 October 2016.

centres for a decade until 2002. Even today, with 25 having been established around the world, there is still less than one CCC established each year on average.

The year 2014 witnessed an increased speed in setting up the centres around the world, with six being established, followed by another four in 2015. By the end of 2014, the government had invested over 1.3 billion RMB in the development of CCCs. It was estimated by *Guangming Daily* (2015) that the investment amount would reach 360 million RMB in 2015, an increase of 181 per cent over 2014. Further development was announced in 2014 by Cai Wu, Minister of Culture. According to him the number of CCCs would reach 50 by 2020 (Lu, 2014). That means in the five years from 2015 to 2020, double the number of CCCs will be established as those set up in the previous 26 years. It is obviously a response to Hu Jintao's call to developing a 'Strong Socialist Culture in China' at the 18th Party Congress in November 2012, and its competition with the CI (*China Daily*, 2012).

But despite growing at a faster rate, the CCC, in sharp contrast with the CI and the CC, has adopted a more gradual approach in setting up CCCs around the world.

Activities, beneficiaries and setting ups

Do the CCCs around the world undertake activities different from those of CIs and CCs, and have they therefore avoided the kind of controversy the latter have faced? According to the website of the CCC Headquarters in Beijing,[2] its objectives include providing professional services and quality Chinese cultural activities for the general public in the host countries in order to improve mutual understanding and friendship. The CCC's website in Berlin captures well the essence of what CCCs want to achieve – 'quality, accessibility, friendship and partnership'.[3] An examination of the activities of different centres listed on their web pages shows that the main cultural products the centres try to promote in other countries are performances, exhibitions, art festivals, sports competitions and other cultural activities. These activities providing opportunities for participants to get involved prove the most successful in reaching out to the general public. Practical training programmes and cultural performances are the most popular. Training programmes include specialised sessions such as language training, cooking, martial arts, calligraphy, Chinese herbal medicine, tea-making, Dragon and Lion Dance, and acrobatics. Between 2007 and 2011, the CCCs held 2,500 activities altogether, with participants totalling 560,000 (Li and Su, 2012). For example, in 2014 centres ran training programmes ranging from Chinese painting and calligraphy, martial arts, to Chinese handicrafts. The CCC in Seoul on its own attracted over 2,000 participants that year (Jin, 2015).

Seminars are also regularly held on Chinese history, culture and life. However, the target audience of these talks is generally the local population and so they are designed to attract the general public rather than specific groups such as academics. In addition, the centres put on short-term training programmes of various kinds. For instance, the joint programme by the Ministry of Culture and the Cultural Bureau of Hunan Province successfully trained participants within a month to perform basic Dragon and Lion Dance movements. Another case in point is the practical cooking programme by the CCC in Berlin. It was well received, especially after it was on a local TV programme. 'Happy Chinese New Year' celebration activities have become CCCs' signature activities. For instance, in 2014, 'Happy Chinese New Year' celebration activities were held in 112 countries and 321 cities around the world, making it an important part of Chinese cultural soft power (Wang, 2015). In April 2014, the CCC in Paris organised a special cultural trip for over 20 French participants visiting Guangdong, Fujian, Jiangxi and Anhui, allowing them to fully experience the art and architecture in these regions (Li and Su, 2012).

In Benin, for example, an interview with the Director of the CCC there, conducted by Dr Gilbert as part of a UK research project 'Building Images: exploring 21st century Sino-African dynamics through cultural exchange and translation',[4] stated that activities designed to promote Chinese culture had four main focuses:

- Cultural – including shows, exhibitions, workshops, films, etc.
- Formation – year-long language classes and martial arts classes; short courses in Chinese painting, traditional medicine, ping pong, etc.
- Information/consultation – the library provides information for people who want to go to China.
- Dialogue between China and Benin – with Beninese experts who are interested in China. For example, the CCC regularly sends artistic groups to China (music, dance, etc.).

The activities of CCCs in Benin and in other countries around the world are not very different from those of CIs or CCs. Why should one be greeted with suspicion, receive a great deal of criticism and face significant resistance (Foster, 2014), while the other receives little criticism? We turn to the operations of the CCCs for an answer.

The operation of China Cultural Centres

Due to its close ties with the government, China's investment in higher education around the world has raised considerable concerns. Some describe the CI as a government entity, and see it as a vehicle for exporting China's soft power. However, the CCC gets no less support from the Chinese government. High-level officials, including the very top leaders have attended the opening ceremonies or related events for various centres. For instance, during his visit to Singapore in 2009, the then Chinese President Hu Jintao confirmed the setting up of the CCC in Singapore and in 2010, Xi Jinping, then Vice President, laid the foundation stone for the CCC in Singapore. In November 2005, both Hu Jintao and former German Chancellor Gerhard Schroeder attended the foundation stone-laying ceremony of the CCC. In 2013, it was announced by President Xi on his first trip to Africa that China would build a CCC in Tanzania. During his visit to Brussels in 2014, Xi mentioned many times the setting up of a CCC there. Also in 2014, during his visit to New Zealand, he announced that China would set up a CCC there. This high-profile attention also indicates that the CCCs are state-engineered, but there are differences.

What differentiates the CCCs from the CIs are the objectives, target beneficiaries, the way the activities are organised and the choice of host countries. While the CCC sets out to 'improve mutual understanding and friendship' between people, the CI is more ambitious. It aims to not only 'contribute to the development of multiculturalism and the building of a harmonious world', but also 'support educational institutions at different levels with the partner in the host countries'. Because it works with partners in the education sector, it has given rise to concerns of politically motivated academic interference. Such articles as 'Big Dragon on Campus: China's Soft Power-play in Academia' (Sudworth, 2014) or 'Confucius Institutes: the hard side of China's soft power', appear frequently (BBC, 2016). Some are concerned that the organisation's intentions may be less about promoting Chinese language and culture and more about expanding China's political influence over their host schools, and by extension, globally.

Some academics have expressed their fear of ceding control of their curriculum, academic freedom and intellectual integrity (e.g. Stanbach, 2014; Sahlins, 2014; Zaharna *et al.*, 2014). Hartig argues that, while he did not agree that the institutes are 'sinister' propaganda, 'the fact is that CIs are not apolitical organizations'(ibid.). In 2013, the Canadian Association of University Teachers (CAUT) called on colleges and universities in Canada who host Confucius Institutes to shut them down.[5] CAUT also urged schools in negotiations with Hanban to establish institutes to 'pursue them no further'. CAUT's Director, James Turk, said that the CIs are owned and operated by the Chinese Communist Party and 'beholden' to the politics of an 'authoritarian government'. In June 2014, the American Association of University Professors (AAUP) made the same call to US universities.[6] CIs, the AAUP statement said, 'function as an arm of the Chinese state' and 'advance a state agenda in the recruitment and control of academic staff, the choice of curriculum, and in the restriction of debate'.

Unlike CIs, CCCs are more flexible in their choice of partners, or in some cases, have no fixed partners in the host countries. The Ministry of Culture holds annual conferences to review CCCs' practices and experiences, explores new strategies and sets up new guidelines for the next year (Chen, 2015). In its practice, each CCC adopts what it sees as effective methods. An important element that differentiates the CCC from the CI are the CCCs' efforts in collaboration with local civil societies and organisations which allow them to have a better understanding of the local market and to have access to local resources on the one hand and to be seen as less intrusive and interfering than the CIs. For instance, the 'China Circus', established in 1989 by a German, went on a performing tour in over 160 cities in Europe, reaching out to millions of European audiences with such performances as 'Genghis Khan', 'the Last Emperor', 'Marco Polo', 'Buddha', 'Laozi', and 'Confucius'. Maurice Gountin is an example of a local employee making a great contribution to the running of the Centre in Benin because he has been the bridge of communication between the Chinese and local staff, acting as a translator, interpreter, teacher, programmer and public relations manager. Before Gountin worked for the CCC in Benin, he had studied for more than ten years in China and holds a PhD in the Diplomacy of Contemporary China. When he returned to Benin in 2009 he made the acquaintance of the previous Director of the CCC. The latter asked him to work for him while he was looking for a job. He is still there five years later.[7]

At home, the CCC takes advantage of the joint efforts between the Ministry of Culture and provincial level cultural bureaus so that while sharing the benefit, they also share responsibilities (see Table 11.2). In 2011, seven provinces and municipal cities sent 64 exchange groups of over 600 people to go and visit other countries. They also received 27 groups of visitors with 106 participants coming to China. That year, the CCCs held 89 activities, attracting more than 60,000 people.[8] 2014 saw 18 provinces and cities such as Hunan, Shandong, Tianjin and Beijing collaborating with the Ministry of Culture and held more than 200 cultural activities such as 'Henan Cultural Year' in Bangkok, 'Cultural Anhui' in Ulaanbaatar, 'Cultural Xinjiang Week' in Moscow and Berlin. Overseas audiences thus enjoyed different aspects of Chinese culture from different Chinese regions (Chen, 2015).

TABLE 11.2 Partnerships between CCCs and Chinese Provinces

Continent	Chinese Province	China Cultural Centre
Africa		
	Liaoning	Mauritius
	Hunan	Benin
	Shangdon	Cairo
	Jiangsu	Nigeria
Europe		
	Beijing	Malta
	Xinjiang Autonomous Region	Berlin
	Hubei	Moscow
	Guizhou	Madrid
	Shanghai	Brussels
Asia		
	Gansu	Seoul
	Hainan	Tokyo
	Anhui	Ulaanbaatar
	Henan	Bangkok
	Tianjin	Sri Lanka
America		
	Yunnan	Mexico
Oceania		
	Guangdong	Sydney

Source: Compiled by the authors based from information collected from the CCC headquarters website at http://cn.cccweb.org/portal/site/Master/index.jsp.

Another key element that differentiates the CCCs from CIs is the use of both official and informal domestic resources. Although CCCs are affiliated to China's Ministry of Culture just as CIs are to the Ministry of Education, they work closely with both state-owned organisations and private enterprises such as the China International Cultural Association, established in 1986, and the Chinese Culture Friendship Association, a non-profit national society for cultural exchange activities, established in 1987. In organising cultural exchange activities, they tap into the non-governmental organisations in China, such as performing groups and martial arts practitioners. Because of the nature of CCCs they have a wide range of social contacts, including links with the overseas Chinese diaspora. By using these resources, the CCCs maximise the quality and quantity of cultural products that can be delivered to people in host countries. By marketing cultural products such as Chinese New Year celebrations involving performers and artists from all over China, the CCCs have increased the social impact of Chinese culture around the world.

Our participation at the second China–Africa Cultural Industry Roundtable Conference held in May 2014 in Beijing allowed us to observe how the Ministry of Culture, together with the Ministry of Commerce, built a platform for Chinese enterprises in the Chinese cultural industry, both state-owned and private, to meet, exchange ideas, explore collaboration opportunities, and negotiate for businesses

TABLE 11.3 Favoured destinations for Chinese cultural institutions

Continents	Number of CIs	Number of CCs	Number of CCCs
America	157	544	1
Europe	169	257	7
Asia	110	90	9
Oceania	18	86	3
Africa	46	23	5

Source: Authors.

with officials and experts from the cultural sectors of 21 Francophone countries in Africa. Of the 150 people who attended the opening ceremony, many were cultural bureaus at the provincial level, state-owned enterprises, and non-government organisations including publishers, as well as monks from the Shaolin Temple, known for their martial arts performances. We witnessed representatives from both sides discussing and exchanging opinions on the related policies pertaining to Sino-African culture, industry, and their development, successful experience, bilateral demands and cooperative wishes.

An examination of the host countries on 20 November 2016 reveals a big difference: as Table 11.3 shows, the US is the most favoured destination for CIs and CCs and Europe is the second favoured destination. CCCs' favoured destinations are Asia and Europe, with Africa ranking third.

In sum, rather than working on its own, the CCC serves as a platform for such organised activities, encouraging and facilitating collaborations between official and non-official organisations in China and the host countries. It also chooses Asia as its most favoured destination while carefully working its way into other continents. In this way, the CCC succeeds in building a big network for promoting Chinese language and culture in a way that is acceptable to the host countries.

Challenges

Promoting positive images of one's country through language and culture is not new. Rodéric Abdon Dedegnonhou, one of the few cultural journalists in Benin, talked about the cultural relations between Benin and China positively.[9] Although he admitted that many local people remained sceptical towards the Chinese, he saw a lot of potential in this cultural relationship. He was covering the Chinese New Year for the local newspaper and thought the event brought people of different cultural backgrounds together. Like Rodéric, all our interviewees, be they Chinese or Beninese, were positive about the cultural exchanges between the two countries. Indeed, CCCs have so far experienced little criticism from the international community. However, there are challenges for furthering its role for China's public diplomacy.

Firstly, the dependence of CCCs on the Chinese government for financial support means the level of activities is not constant. Analysis of the activities and interviews reveals that the frequency of cultural activities in different host countries varies greatly. Activities increased greatly in response to Hu Jintao's government report in November 2012, when he called for the building of a strong cultural nation (*China Daily*, 2012). Activities also tend to be most frequent when a centre is first established. For instance, in 2015 shortly after it was established, the Sydney CCC held various kinds of activities, attracting media attention as well as large numbers of participants. But these activities tend to decrease after the first intensive period. Other centres arrange activities around the availability of visitors and opportunities. Both the Chinese and German versions of the website of the CCC in Berlin show intensive activities in 2015. But after the activities held in July 2015, nothing had been posted on the bulletin board when it was checked in November 2016, suggesting that there had not been much going on since then.[10] A check on the website of the CCC in Benin, Africa, also yielded little activity from July 2015 to November 2016.[11]

The interview with Guangming Bai, Director of the Benin CCC, is revealing.[12] Bai had served almost ten years at the CCC in Mauritius and one term in the cultural service of the Chinese Embassy in Tunisia before he took up the director-ship of the CCC in Benin in 2010. He spoke little French and his posting was for four years, but so far there had been no one to replace him and so he would remain there for the foreseeable future. When interviewed in 2015 he expressed his wishes that the two governments would invest more in cultural relations rather than just infrastructure/construction – he would like a larger budget to develop the CCC's cultural activities. Bai also claimed that it was difficult to continue making the cul-tural activities attractive to the public, for example, Happy Chinese New Year cel-ebration activities, because they were no longer a novelty, although there was still a high demand for the language classes.

The second challenge comes from a lack of reciprocity. Further research needs to be done in other continents, but interviews with people working for the CCC in Benin throw light on the cultural relationship between China and the host country. For instance, Mongadji,[13] a Benin journalist who had been to China at the invitation of the Chinese government, believed that the exchange of cultural activ-ities was often unbalanced. He also thought that Benin could learn a lot from China as a model. He illustrated his point by giving the example of the way China man-aged its unemployment problem. He was of the view that China had found its way by combining socialism and capitalism, and now Benin also needed to find its own path to development. However, Mongadji also thought that that Beninese people had certain prejudices towards Chinese people, and equally an initiative to show Beninese television programmes in China proved to be a non-starter.

Gountin also thought that although there were a lot of clichés circulating on both sides, there was a lack of understanding of each other's culture.[14] He pointed out that, while Beninese people were becoming more familiar with Chinese culture, it would take a long time for China to know 'African' (not 'Beninese') culture because he believed China was not investing enough in this direction. To him, even the Chinese people who were living in Benin only learned the local culture in a superficial manner. He believed that 'Un chinois qui le fait serait un chinois anormal' because 'Le Chinois est trop fier de sa proper culture' (A Chinese who knew Beninese culture is abnormal' because 'the Chinese are too proud of their own culture'). Bai perceived the geographical distance between China and Benin as another barrier, as it also made things difficult in terms of sending artistic groups to each other's countries.

Related to this, the third barrier lies in the language. For example, Bai, the Director of CCC in Benin, though he has a PhD in literature, could not share his enthusiasm with the students because he did not speak French. Gountin also saw language as the major barrier as it was almost always necessary to communicate between the Chinese and the local Beninese via an intermediary. In this case study of Benin, the major barriers concerning the cultural relations between China and the host country, which reflect the relations in other CCCs with their host countries, are the unequal exchanges between the two parties and the Chinese unwillingness to learn the host country's language.

Discussions and conclusion

Adjovi from the Ministry of Foreign Affairs in Benin has been to China twice, in 2009 and 2013 respectively.[15] He speaks highly of the cultural dimension of Sino-Beninese cooperation, rightly claiming that 'the culture allows the things that the diplomatic cannot achieve'. Cultural diplomacy is an important instrument in the toolbox for soft power.

Joseph Nye argues that successful states need both hard and soft power – the ability to coerce others as well as the ability to shape their long-term attitudes and preferences (Nye, 2004). Alongside its economic engagement with the international community, China has been promoting positive images around the world to win hearts and minds, tapping into its rich culture, a soft power resource, in order to produce attraction. Nye argues that cultural diplomacy is one of the public diplomacy instruments that governments use to mobilise the resources to produce attraction by communicating with the public rather than merely the governments of other countries (Nye, 2010). At the same time, post-modern publics outside China are generally sceptical of authority, and governments are often mistrusted. Although similar cultural organisations exist such as the Alliance Française, British Council, Goethe-Institut, Instituto Cervantes, Instituto Camões and the Japan Foundation, the Confucius Institute and the Confucius Classroom have been greeted with suspicion and criticism. At the same time, the CCCs, with the same kind of Chinese government support, have worked to provide opportunities for people on both sides to interact and to communicate with each other with much less negative attention. CCCs' experience tells us that it works a lot better if the government stays in the background and they work with private actors. Some non-governmental organisations enjoy more trust than governments do and, though they are difficult to control, they can be useful channels of communication. Companies can also take the lead in sponsoring specific public diplomacy projects.

CCCs have played an important role in helping create an attractive image of a country that can improve its prospects for obtaining its desired outcomes. In other words, CCCs have created an enabling environment for China's foreign policy. The study proves Nye's argument: the soft sell may prove more effective than a hard sell in the contemporary environment (Nye, 2010). Indeed, the US has excelled in projecting soft power with the help of its companies, foundations, universities, churches and other institutions of civil society. The CI's approach in terms of the way they are set up on campuses and the speed they proliferate has caused much debate and concern. Although it organises similar activities, the role of state actors in the dissemination of a nation's soft power is controversial.

In contrast, CCCs have sought to shape the foreign public's long-term attitudes and preferences in a more acceptable way to the host countries by working with both government and non-government organisations in both China and the host countries. Although it is affiliated with China's Ministry of Culture, the role of the government is less obvious in the activities CCCs organise in playing a more facilitating role. CCCs, or any other instruments of public diplomacy, cannot translate cultural resources into the soft power of attraction if they suffer from public distrust. After all, the effectiveness of public diplomacy is measured by minds changed rather than cash spent. The success of CCCs shows that the reputation and credibility of actors are important factors in cultural projects overseas. Successful promotion of soft power requires an understanding of the role of credibility and the role of civil society in generating soft power. Similarly, soft power depends upon an understanding of the minds of others. The best public and cultural diplomacy is a two-way street. Public diplomacy or propaganda that 'broadcasts' in one direction cannot produce attraction. It may produce consumption of soft power. China is learning to not only broadcast its messages to the world but also listen to what the others have to say. But from the interviews reported in this chapter, it is apparent that this is not yet happening in the developing world.

Our examinations and interviews show that developing long-term relationships is not always profitable in the short term, and thus leaving it simply to the market may lead to under-investment. While short training programmes (some are free in some countries) may pay for themselves, and non-profit organisations can help, many exchange programmes would shrink without support from the government.

Two organisations under two different ministries in China, with the same purpose of promoting Chinese language and culture, have achieved different impacts in the host countries. While succeeding in expansion at exponential speed, CIs have attracted attention and criticism for perceived interference in the educational systems in the host countries and for spreading communist ideology. CCCs have maintained a much lower profile in both numbers and the way they operate. They serve as organisers, facilitators and managers of cultural exchange activities between people on the ground in China and in host countries. They are either located in the Chinese Embassy or on their own, rather than in a partner educational institution like CIs. They work together with both official and non-governmental institutions at home and in the host countries in facilitating the exchange of cultural activities.

In addition to cultural exchange activities, the CCC also helps enterprises to explore business opportunities. They have helped spread Chinese culture, given China an international image and enhanced China's influence in a way more acceptable to the host countries.

The debate over the purpose of the Confucius Institute is ongoing. The different, but more successful approach adopted by the CCCs indicates that 'aggressive' promotion of Chinese culture overseas should be avoided, as Western and other societies may perceive these activities and behaviour as intrusive and interfering, especially if they take place on overseas campuses. Nye says the best public diplomacy issues spring from civil society. In this regard, the CCCs have an advantage over the CIs because they have strong links with civil society in both China and the host countries.

However, in the past few years, the reputation the CI has gained at home has stimulated the CCC to compete and develop at a faster pace. But now that the CCCs are expanding and putting on many cultural activities, they will have to develop sustainable strategies so that they can continue to operate without total dependence on the government. More importantly, CCCs need to develop reciprocity in cultural exchange activities, especially with developing countries, as is revealed by interviews with people in Benin: the lack of interest in learning French by local members of staff means communications are mostly done by interpreters, or by local people having to learn to speak Chinese. The complaint that the cultural exchange activities are not balanced, with many more Chinese activities happening in some countries rather than the other way around is of course not just an issue with CCCs but with other sectors in China as well.

The future of China's relations will increasingly be determined by the interactions of people on the ground. Cultural presence plays a vital role in sensitising peoples around the world to the diversity of Chinese culture and dispelling many of the myths that are currently in circulation. In some parts of the world such as Africa, it also helps to heal some of the wounds that have already been inflicted by intense Chinese economic engagement with many African countries.

Notes

1 http://english.hanban.org/, accessed 27 October 2016.
2 http://cn.cccweb.org/portal/site/Master/index.jsp, accessed 20 November 2016.
3 http://berlin.cccweb.org/cn/index.shtml, accessed 8 November 2016.
4 https://uscpublicdiplomacy.org/sites/uscpublicdiplomacy.org/files/useruploads/u25044/Confucius%20Institutes%20v2%20(1).pdf.
5 www.caut.ca/news/2013/12/17/universities-and-colleges-urged-to-end-ties-with-confucius-institutes, accessed 8 November 2016.
6 www.universityherald.com/articles/10105/20140625/aaup-universities-confucius-institutes-academic-freedom-american.htm#!, accessed 8 November 2016.
7 Interviewed in February 2015.
8 'The Building of Overseas China Cultural Centres Helps Chinese Culture to Reach the International Community'. 30 May 2012, from http://culture.people.com.cn/GB/22226/244082/244102/18028606.html, accessed on 8 November 2016.
9 Interviewed in Benin, January 2015.

10 http://berlin.cccweb.org/cn/whzxjs/zxjj/index.shtml, accessed 9 November 2016.
11 http://benin.cccweb.org/bj/whzxjs/zxjj/index.shtml, accessed 8 January 2015.
12 Interviewed in Benin, January 2015.
13 Interviewed in Benin, January 2015.
14 Interviewed in Benin, January 2015.
15 Interviewed in Benin, January 2015.

References

BBC (2016) Confucius Institutes: The Hard Side of China's Soft Power. Available at: www.bbc.co.uk/news/world-asia-china-30567743 [Accessed 8 November 2016].

Chen, L. (2015) Overseas China Cultural Centres: Painting Chinese Pictures on the Map of the World, *China Culture Press*, 1 August 2015. Available at: http://china.huanqiu.com/News/scio/2015–01/5362646.html [Accessed 8 November 2016].

China Daily (2012) Hu Jintao's call to developing a 'Strong Socialist Culture in China' at the 18th Party Congress. 19 November.

Foster, P. (2014) China Soft Power set back as US Universities Shut Second Confucius Institute in a Week. Available at: www.telegraph.co.uk/news/worldnews/northamerica/usa/11133921/China-soft-power-set-back-as-US-universities-shut-second-Confucius-Institute-in-a-week.html [Accessed 6 November 2016].

Guangming Daily (2015) China will Invest 360 Million RMB on CCCs this Year. Available at: http://cn.cccweb.org/portal/pubinfo/001002003005/20150227/1ac539eefd3f44bda228cc672175bffd.html [Accessed 18 October 2016].

Hubert, J. (2014) Ambiguous states: Confucius Institutes and Chinese soft power in the US classroom, *Polar, Political and Legal Anthropology Review*, 2014: 329–349.

Jin, S. (2015) Overseas Training Programs: Short Cut for Chinese Culture to 'go out', *China Culture Press*. Available at: http://cn.cccweb.org/portal/pubinfo/001002003005/20150323/5415c5a79a964c8ea8d8bc1046680906.html.

Li, X. and Su, X. (2012) Promote Chinese Culture Better and More Widely. Available at: http://roll.sohu.com/20120628/n346735394.shtml. [Accessed 10 November 2016].

Lu, P. (2014) China will Build 50 Overseas China Cultural Centres. Available at: www.wenming.cn/wmzh_pd/jj_wmzh/201402/t20140225_1762992.shtml [Accessed 30 October 2016].

Lumsden, A. (2015) Big Dragon on Campus: China's Soft Power-play in Academia, *Council on Hemispheric Affairs*. Available at: www.coha.org/big-dragon-on-campus-chinas-soft-power-play-in-academia/ [Accessed 9 November 2016].

Nye, J. (2004) *Soft Power: The Means to Success in World Politics.* New York: Public Affairs.

Nye, J. (2010) Soft Power and Cultural Diplomacy, *Public Diplomacy Magazine*, University of Southern California. Available at: http://publicdiplomacymagazine.com/soft-power-and-cultural-diplomacy/ [Accessed on 9 November 2016].

Rawnsley, G. (2012) Approaches to soft power and public diplomacy in China and Taiwan, *Journal of International Communication*, 18(2): 121–135.

Sahlins, M. (2014) *Confucius Institutes: Academic Malware.* Available at http://apjjf.org/-Marshall-Sahlins/4220/article.pdf.

Stanbach, A. (2014) *Confucius and Crisis in American Universities: Culture, Capital, and Diplomacy in US Public Higher Education.* New York and London: Routledge.

Sudworth, J. (2014) Big Dragon on Campus: China's Soft Power-play in Academia. Available at: www.thenassauguardian.com/opinion/op-ed/58010-big-dragon-on-campus-chinas-soft-power-play-in-academia/ [Accessed 12 November 2016].

Wang, D. and Adamson, B. (2015) War and peace: Perceptions of Confucius Institutes in China and USA, *The Asia-Pacific Education Researcher*, 24(1): 225–234.

Wang, J. (2014) Deputy Minister of Culture Ding Wei: Let CCCs Tell a Good Story of China. Available at: http://cn.cccweb.org/portal/pubinfo/001002003005/20150202/5b 1a57a6160c4ffc989f56c98759ddf7.html [Accessed 9 November 2016].

Wang, J. (2015) China Culture Centres have reached 20 in numbers, *People's Daily*, 9 January 2015. Available at:http://paper.people.com.cn/rmrb/html/2015–01/09/nw.D110000renmrb_ 20150109_2–12.htm [Accessed 10 November 2016].

Zaharna, R. S.; Hubbert, J. and Hartig, F. (2014) Confucius Institutes and the globalization of China's soft power, *CPD Perspectives on Public Diplomacy*, paper 3.

Zhang, X. (2013) How ready is China for a China-style world order?: China's state media discourse under construction, *African Media Studies*, 34(3): 79–101.

Zhang, X. (2016) A World of Shared Influence, in Zhang, X.; Wasserman, H. and Mano, W. (eds.) *China's Media and Soft Power in Africa: Promotion and Perceptions*. New York: Palgrave Macmillan.

12

FOREIGN CORRESPONDENTS IN CHINA: PARTNER OR LIABILITY IN CHINA'S PUBLIC DIPLOMACY?

Wanning Sun

Existing works, as well as many chapters in this volume, point to a number of new pathways the Chinese party-state has adopted in pushing its media out into the global mediasphere. We also know that Chinese state media has increased its investment in international broadcasting (Zhang, 2011; Sun, 2010, 2014, 2015). However, how foreign media shape the success or failure of China's effort to improve its international image is not at all clear. Yet knowing the answer to this question is crucial if we are to understand the depth and breadth of the challenges facing China's soft power goals. Writing about the lessons to be learned from the history of public diplomacy in various national contexts, Cull stresses the importance of letting others speak on behalf of the self. It is his firm belief that sometimes the most credible voice in public diplomacy is not one's own, and for this reason, the government would often be better off not blowing its own trumpet (Cull, 2010). Furthermore, if public diplomacy is about 'working with others to achieve our goals' (Leonard, 2002: 54), China's Other – foreign media – is pivotal to China's public diplomacy efforts. After all, foreign publics are the ultimate targets of China's 'media going global' initiatives. And news stories and coverage of China by foreign correspondents are instrumental in shaping foreign publics' opinion of China. For this reason, it is safe to say that the foreign correspondent is still a missing figure in our examination of China's public diplomacy strategies and practices. It is also safe to say that the role of foreign correspondents in China – whether partner or liability – in China's impression-management initiatives constitutes a major blind spot in our study of China's soft power and media 'going global' exercises.

This chapter aims to make a start in addressing this blind spot. Centring upon the figure of the foreign correspondent in China, it raises the empirical and conceptual question of the role of the foreign correspondent in China's public diplomacy agenda. The main objective of this chapter is to chart a new direction in the examination of China's soft power, public diplomacy and communication strategies.

Combining institutional and historical analyses, the chapter aims to do a number of things. First, it provides a discussion of the salient aspects of China's public diplomacy efforts, paying particular attention to how they are played out in the context of the Chinese government's management of foreign correspondents in China. Second, it considers the historical and geopolitical contexts which continue to shape today's foreign correspondents' work practices. Third, drawing on interviews with foreign correspondents, the chapter outlines the institutional, professional, and individual factors which contribute to an entrenched antagonism between the Chinese government and foreign correspondents.

Policies, goals, and actors in China's public diplomacy

Public diplomacy is widely understood to have three integral realms, i.e. news management, strategic communication, and relationship building. Each of these three realms is seen to yield public diplomacy impact in three different time scales. News management, conducted on a routine basis, is expected to generate immediate influence and shape perceptions and opinions on day-to-day issues about the nation for foreign media and public. Strategic communication, which involves communicating a set of strategic messages to promote the nation through a series of planned activities, is seen to operate on an intermediate time frame. Finally, public diplomacy also aims to conduct cross-cultural exchanges of individuals, such as exchange students, business people, and tourists. Although this long-term process may often produce a more close-up, 'warts and all' understanding of the initiating nation, it is believed that such contacts will ultimately foster goodwill and good relations (Leonard, 2002).

Relationship building between nations and cultures is the earliest form of public diplomacy undertaken by the Chinese government. For more than a decade, promoting Chinese culture through language teaching and hosting of many and various event-based activities and exchange programmes are all examples of intermediate and long-term public diplomacy goals. Well-documented initiatives include the operations of the Confucius Institute in many developed countries, as well as the corporate sector's engagements in aid projects, low interest loans, economic collaborations, and direct investment, especially in the developing, mostly African countries (Tang and Li, 2011). In contrast, it is only in recent years, particularly since the 2008 Beijing Olympics, that policy-makers, evidenced in a series of statements made by the then Propaganda Chief Li Changchun, turned to the agenda of shaping the international community's public opinion of China through news media. Research on how to expand China's influence in the global community of public opinion and improve China's national image has gained momentum among state-supported academics and intellectuals in China. Similarly, in professional and industry publications targeting media practitioners, analyses and discussions aiming to canvass and develop creative ideas and effective strategies have also proliferated. Although there is a lack of consensus on how to achieve these aims and objectives, it seems that nobody questions the rationale behind the perceived need to improve China's international image (Wang and Nye, 2009). There is a consensus that China's global influence in the domains of politics, economics, and international relations has grown exponentially, yet the international community's understanding and knowledge of China is disproportionate to China's economic power. China's public diplomacy policies, practices, and initiatives, which moved into a 'higher gear' (d'Hooghe, 2008) around the time leading up to the Beijing Olympics, have also started to generate responses and assessment in English-language scholarship (e.g. Kurlantzick, 2007; d'Hooghe, 2008; Cho and Jeong, 2008; Wang, 2011; Nye, 2009; Sautman and Li, 2011; Edney, 2012).

Two domains are instrumental in determining the effectiveness of China's efforts to influence foreign publics' opinion of China through media. The first is Chinese media's coverage of China, and the second is foreign media's coverage of China. In terms of the former, China has in recent years invested an enormous amount of money, to the tune of $6 billion, to achieve an increased global media presence in order to claim China's 'discursive right' to compete with the West's monopoly over its China coverage (Hu and Ji, 2012). In terms of the latter, the Chinese government has indeed made some efforts at becoming more open and transparent. Between 1981 and the present, the State Council of the People's Republic of China has issued three regulatory policies regarding foreign correspondents in China. The 'Temporary Rules Regarding the Management of Foreign News Organizations and Journalists in China', issued in 1981, consisted of fourteen rules. This document required that foreign journalists and their organizations go through a mandatory and strict process of application, documentation, and registration, and foreign correspondents' activities, including entering and exiting the country, visa extension, accommodation, interview itinerary, and communication set-up, were to be closely monitored. This document was replaced by 'Rules of Managing Foreign News Organizations and Journalists in China' issued in 1990. Consisting of eight additional rules, the 1990 document was more detailed, and included rulings regarding foreign reporters' coverage of issues pertaining to China's national security.

The last policy document was released in 2007, in anticipation of the Beijing Olympics. In the 2007 document, the government relaxed its regulation and control of foreign journalists, allowing them to travel extensively except to a few restricted regions and areas, and permitting them to interview people as long as the interviewee agreed. A number of breakthroughs are identified in this set of new rules. For instance, foreign reporters are no longer required to be accompanied by Chinese organizations and individuals when conducting investigations and interviews and foreign journalists can hire Chinese assistants through agencies (Guo, 2009). Some believe that this represents a marked improvement to the 1990 regulation, which put more stringent restrictions on foreign journalists in China (Zhang, 2008). Others think that while these policies represent an incremental level of openness in terms of the Chinese government's control of foreign correspondents, they also feature a fundamental paradox between a desire for control and a willingness for openness (Tang, 2013).

China's public diplomacy is intended to build 'an objective and friendly publicity environment' (*People's Daily*, 2004), and 'actively cooperate with Chinese national development strategy and gradually change China's image in the international society from negative to neutral to positive' (Wang, 2008: 269). It has four stated nation-branding objectives: First, China seeks understanding for its politics and policies, which are based on the principles of 'harmonious society' and 'scientific development'; second, China wants to be seen as a stable, reliable, and responsible economic partner which does not pose a threat; third, China wants to be seen as a trustworthy and reliable member of the international community, and actively contribute to world peace; finally, China wants acknowledgement and respect for its contributions in culture and civilization (d'Hooghe, 2008). In juxtaposition to these stated nation-branding objectives is a prevalent sense of dissatisfaction with foreign media's reporting on China. In general, foreign reporting on China is perceived by China to be straitjacketed by some recurring themes, including 'China as a threat', 'the collapse of China', 'China as a demon', 'China as an opportunity', and 'China's development' (Guo, 2009: 4). A sense of urgency for the public diplomacy push is to a large extent fuelled by this acute sense of dissatisfaction with foreign media's reporting on China.

It has been observed that, in recent years, state actors in China have had less control over what they want to achieve, and they also have to rely more and more on the actions of non-state actors in their public diplomacy tactics and exercises. As China extends its public diplomacy abroad on many fronts, it inevitably involves the state and non-state actors on the part of both the Chinese side and the foreign countries. On China's side, there are government bodies at national and provincial levels, as well as corporations, civic organizations, and individuals who come into contact with foreign countries and their representatives, either based in China or in the target country. On the side of the 'target', there are the government organizations of the target countries at various levels, as well as civic and business communities, institutions and individuals which do business with, and study and work in China (d'Hooghe, 2008).

In the domain of communication and media practices, there has been a shift from an emphasis on the concept of propaganda to that of public relations (Brady, 2008; Chen, 2004). This shift has implicitly done away with the notion of the 'enemy', a concept and terminology which was much utilized in international relations and in China's foreign policy during the socialist period to describe and account for China's foreign affairs decisions. Instead, the West has been re-imagined as the key and most difficult target of China's 'external propaganda' (*wai xuan*), whose unfavourable, negative, and unfriendly view of China needs to be corrected and changed.

Despite this, scholarship on China's public diplomacy, both in English and Chinese, has continued to focus on the policies, practices, and challenges facing the state players and actors. This is, to a large extent, understandable, given the dominant role played by the Chinese government. In this context, the role of key actors, such as the State Council Information Office, the Office of External Publicity, and the Ministry of Foreign Affairs is considered to be crucial in the formulation and implementation of public diplomacy policies and initiatives. It is believed that these state actors still play a predominant role. A recent development involving these government bodies is the Government Spokesperson System, and the stipulation of Regulations for the Work of News Spokespersons in 2008, which defined the spokesperson's role in shaping foreign reporting on China so as to enhance international understanding and support of the country (Chen, 2011). Important as these insights are, the question remains as to how these government initiatives are received by their target groups.

Foreign correspondents and the Chinese government: mutual distrust

Foreign correspondents in China clearly fit into this target group. According to the registration issued by the Department of Foreign Affairs, approximately forty countries currently have their media organizations stationed in China, with most of them being based in Beijing and some others in Shanghai, Guangzhou, and Shenzhen. With the exception of a few friendly countries such as North Korea and Pakistan, it is a long list of potentially useful but currently hostile actors. The number of media outlets from these countries varies considerably, ranging from as many as more than thirty media organizations from the US, to one or two from other smaller countries. Western European countries such as Germany and France have relatively large contingencies, having usually around a dozen media organizations each. The importance of China to its two wealthy neighbours, Japan and South Korea, is evidenced in the numerous news organizations they send, each country boasting of having more than a dozen media outlets in China. Another figure provided by a Chinese source suggests around 600 long-term correspondents in China and another 3,000 to 5,000 reporters in China on short visits each year (Guo, 2009: 2). Besides these officially registered foreign correspondents, there are a large number of freelance journalists and special correspondents, many of whom are writing about China and operating under the radar of official scrutiny. The size of this category is hard to ascertain, especially given that many of them may travel to China on tourist visas or reside in China assuming identities – business people, students, or researchers – other than that of a journalist. But it is safe to speculate that the number is considerable. Another category of foreign correspondents is that of 'parachute correspondent' sent to China to cover important events such as the Olympics. During the Beijing Olympic Games, as many as 24,000 foreign journalists went to cover China (Guo, 2009: 2). This category also includes foreign journalists who go to China at the invitation of the Chinese government. Increasingly, this has become a standard public diplomacy exercise engaged in by the Chinese government to extend hospitality to selected foreign journalists in the hope of securing favourable reporting of China.

On the whole, it is safe to say that many, if not most, foreign correspondents have a view of a suspicious and controlling Chinese government. This is evidenced in the information published on the official website of Foreign Correspondents Club of China (FCCC), an organization to which most foreign correspondents in China belong but which has no officially recognized status. Members are advised which topics are politically taboo in China, as well as how to protect their safety and rights as journalists in cases of harassment by the Chinese authorities. The 'Sensitive Areas and Topics' page lists a number of sensitive places including Tibet, Xinjiang, and a range of other hotspots, including places with a high concentration of HIV-Aids patients, as well as areas experiencing land disputes, particularly over big projects such as the Three Gorges Dam. Its list of sensitive issues is long and extended, including social problems (pollution, HIV/AIDS, forced land acquisition), corruption, political dissidents, religion, Falungong, or North Korea refugees.

As a preamble to this long list, the Club advises its members:

> Let's face it: China is a great story. The booming economy, intriguing politics and fast-changing society make this a great time to be working as a journalist here. Yet reporting in China also presents special challenges. Some authorities still hope to control the information flow; they regard foreign media with suspicion. While the new reporting regulations have helped open-up the provinces, many local authorities have yet to implement them properly, and foreign correspondents still encounter harassment, interference and detentions.
>
> *(FCCC, n.d.)*

This suspicion is also evidenced in a survey conducted by the FCCC in 2007 among 163 foreign journalists in China. While 47 per cent of the respondents felt that there was an improvement in their reporting environment, as many as 67 per cent of them believed that the Chinese government failed to fulfil its own promises to relax policies towards foreign journalists. For those reporters who participated in the survey, their biggest problem was not being able to access the government officials of their choice (Guo, 2009).

Despite the rhetoric of the new public diplomacy, a geopolitical view of the world marked by the binary relations between friend and enemy has not disappeared in the imagination of either side. In the minds of the Chinese government, foreign correspondents spend more time perpetuating and reinforcing misperceptions than correcting them. Instead of being China's advocates, they are more often than not its critics and detractors. And this sense of grievance and injustice against the Western media, buttressed by an enduring anti-imperialistic memory, has become a strong emotional resource sustaining nationalism, particularly among young people. The Chinese government and its think tank firmly believe that global media narratives consistently present a stereotypical, biased, and largely negative picture of China, and wilfully ignore many favourable and positive aspects of China (e.g. Wu, 2007). Furthermore, it is felt that the Chinese government has so far not been able to effectively deal with foreign media (Li, 2011b). According to Hu and Ji, China implements the costly 'going out' strategy because of the widely held belief that China is not fully represented in the global media due to a 'Western-dominated structure of information flow' (Hu and Ji, 2012: 33). Much influenced by Professor Li Xiguang and his colleagues' influential and controversial book *Behind a Demonised China* (1996), there is a widespread belief among both the policy-makers and ordinary people that foreign media, particularly Western media, engage in mostly 'negative' (*fu mian*) reporting of China, and seldom write about China in a 'positive' (*zheng mian*) way.

Despite the Chinese government's relaxation of its restrictions on foreign journalists in China, the relationship between the Chinese government and foreign media is often described as one of 'continuous conflict' between the 'cooperative antagonists', whereby neither side trusts the other, yet each has to live with the other (Zhang, 2008). Among various other factors, history plays an important role in shaping such an antagonistic relationship. Mike Chinoy was CNN's senior Asia Correspondent and its first Beijing Bureau Chief from 1987 to 1995. Reflecting on the history of foreign correspondents in China, he points out that, during the few decades of socialism when China was closed off from the West, reporting on China was virtually impossible. A few foreign correspondents did find their way to China in the 1960s but they were either under house arrest or trapped in their residential compounds. Most of the journalistic coverage of China was produced not by China corrrespondents, but 'China watchers', most of whom were stationed in Hong Kong. For this reason, Hong Kong was a very important place from which to observe and report China (Chinoy, 2011).

Economic reforms which started towards the end of the 1970s and the subsequent open-door policy changed all that. Much as it is clear that it is never wise to 'invite the wolf into your house' (*yinlang rushi*), the foreign correspondent is the 'wolf' which the Chinese government has to let in and learn to live with. For this reason, in the eyes of the Chinese authorities, foreign correspondents in China are, more often than not, a necessary evil. The overriding impression the Chinese authorities have of foreign correspondents is that they are uncooperative and unfriendly at best, and hostile, distrusting, and ruthless at worst. This is an enduring perception, evidenced in the writings of foreign correspondents such as George Morrison's reporting on China for *The Times* as early as the turn of the nineteenth century. A seven-part documentary film, *Assignment China*, featuring many US foreign correspondents' reminiscences of their time in China over six decades or so, also testifies to this.

It is true that China's economic reforms and open-door policy have been welcomed on the world stage and China's economic development has become a crucial and integral part of the global economy. However, a view of China as a communist, authoritarian regime has persisted, and has assumed a multitude of contemporary forms. These range from a concern with China's rising military power, its environmental crisis, to its failure to conform to international law, especially in the area of intellectual rights. They also include the perennial issues of Tibet and other ethnic regions, its treatment of political dissidents, and its close relations with corrupt regimes.

From the point of view of foreign, in particular Western, journalists stationed in China, the general environment in which they work has changed little over the last few decades. While most acknowledge the benefit of the Internet and social media in accessing and researching for news stories, the dominant perspective of reporting

China – its lack of transparency, credibility, and freedom of speech and expression – has more or less remained unchanged. It may well be for this reason that Wang Jian sees China's challenge in the form of number of divergences, the most important one being the divergence between how China sees itself and how the world sees China (Wang, 2011: 6).

Interestingly, although many of the current public diplomacy initiatives aim to transcend the old geopolitical mapping of the world on the basis of whether a country is China's friend or enemy, the historical context of China's diplomatic relations with particular countries is still relevant in particular for 'the West' – usually referring to the liberal democracies of North America, Western Europe, and New Zealand and Australia. These nations – endowed as they are with dual public and commercial sectors and long-established policies controlling foreign media ownership, content, and practices – are the most difficult symbolic spaces for the Chinese media to penetrate. In addition, they tend to be among the wealthy nations, whose news media and organizations send their own correspondents to China. And given that China has been playing a crucial role in these countries' economies, foreign policies and domestic politics, it is not surprising that they invest considerable resources and staffing in generating first-hand reporting of China. Furthermore, seeing themselves as the harbingers of free speech, freedom of information, individual rights and liberty, their reporting of China may have played a significant role in perpetuating and sustaining images of China that even now linger on from the Cold War. A number of Western media personalities were responsible for putting these images centre stage early in the Mao era, including, for instance, Henry Luce. Luce was born in China to missionary parents, and became imbued with the mission to bring the 'blessing of liberty' to the communist regime. He and the magazines he founded – including, most notably, *Time* – were instrumental in shaping the West's imagination of China after World War II (Herzstein, 2006). Also influential were reports on China by Theodore White, the *Time* journalist considered to be 'America's best-known war time correspondent in China' (French, 2009: 229). The number of countries represented by these foreign correspondents is admittedly small. However, their influence in shaping the image of China has been global, given that the content generated by this handful of correspondents is accessed not only by the publics of their own countries, but also by the social and cultural elites of many other nations in the world. In short, those Western nations with an established tradition of locating foreign correspondents in China pose the biggest challenge to the country's efforts to improve its international image. It may be for this very reason that those Western journalists who are sympathetic to China, such as Edgar Snow and Rewi Alley, hold such a cherished place in the official memory of China.

Pursuing the China story: same story, different scripts

Besides historical and geopolitical factors, the aspirations and ambitions of foreign journalists also shape their work in China. Interviews with several foreign correspondents who are now working in or have returned from China[1] make it clear that China is often perceived as a place promising adventure, exciting challenges, or even danger. Michael Bristow, a former BBC correspondent who reported on China for five years from 2008 to 2012, says that

> there has never been a better time to be a foreign journalist in China. The country is undergoing a radical transformation that is changing the lives of everyone who lives there – and reporters have a ringside seat. What makes this an even better assignment is that there are relatively few foreign journalists reporting from a country that is still little understood by the outside world. But there are difficulties, not least from a sometimes hostile government that thinks foreign reporters are at best misguided, at worst anti-China.
>
> *(author's communication with Bristow, 2012)*

To many of these correspondents, assignments in China are exciting and adventurous, precisely because of the potential difficulty involved. After a few years' stint as the *Australian* newspaper's correspondent, Michael Sainsbury decided to stay on in Beijing and switched to the UK's *Daily Telegraph*. When asked why he preferred to stay on in China, despite its bad pollution, difficulty of getting a good story, and the likelihood of being 'hassled' by the Chinese government, Sainsbury's reply was straightforward yet revealing. 'Australian politics is too boring. In China, it is difficult to get scandals, particularly involving top national leaders, but you can keep trying. And it is exciting' (author's interview with Sainsbury, 2013). In other words, China is the Promised Land to journalists in pursuit of a 'good story'.

From time to time, this determination to breach the sensitive or taboo topics in order to pursue a good story lands the correspondent in trouble with the Chinese authorities. For that reason, there is a sense that expulsion and danger are only a few steps away from doing a proper job. China offers the possibility of frisson which foreign correspondents are known to seek. To a considerable extent, this sense of allure and adventure derives from the fact that China is a communist country under an authoritarian regime. Usually taking great pride in their commitment to cut through the noise of the lies and propaganda of the Chinese Communist Party, most foreign correspondents in China see it as their professional duty to discover the 'real China' behind the smokescreen of harmony and unity and bring it to the audiences back at home. Conversations with foreign correspondents reveal a strong sense of solidarity and collective identity, forged in the feeling of a lone but intrepid truth-seeking individual stationed in a hostile foreign land, fighting against the odds of a repressive regime and an uncooperative bureaucracy. Most foreign correspondents also emphasize the challenge of working in a country where they do not speak the language.

Often, an unwritten assumption among foreign correspondents is that the more unpopular a foreign correspondent is with the Chinese authorities, the better and more professional he or she is as a journalist. For this reason, the experience of being expelled from China by the authorities or having visas denied can be worn as a badge of honour and bestows on the individual an aura of heroism and objectivity. As a result, incidents of foreign correspondents' expulsion from China can become newsworthy. This 'foreign correspondent versus an oppressive regime' narrative has various manifestations, including the expulsion of the Australian journalist writing for Reuters and the *New York Times*, Chris Buckley, for his story on the family wealth of Chinese Premier Wen Jiabao (Gaunaut, 2013). Such narrative also includes, for instance, the story of the alleged Chinese computer espionage campaign against the *New York Times* for tarnishing the images of China through the reporting of its China correspondents on corruption stories (Perlroth, 2013). They also include the refusal of a visa to Melissa Chan and the shutdown of the *Al Jazeera* bureau in Beijing (Reuters, 2012).

More than personal and historical reasons, a significant obstacle in China's public diplomacy is the foreign journalists' innate distrust of governments. Talking to two Chinese scholars about his work as *New York Times'* Asia correspondent, Edward Gargan has this to say:

> I believe in this principle: all governments are liars. Whether it is the government in China, the US, UK or France . . . As far as I am concerned, as long as you write news stories about the government, you should listen to the views which are critical of the government.
>
> *(Gargan in Zhang and Ye, 2009: 110)*

While foreign journalists may be indiscriminate in their distrust of governments, including their own, this 'healthy' scepticism of governments often comes across to the Chinese government as evidence of a hard-wired determination to avoid all 'good stories' about China and instead only to produce 'bad' ones. This is compounded by the fact that most foreign correspondents are frustrated with their inability to talk to government officials directly. Peter Ford from the *Christian Science Monitor* finds China to be the most 'difficult' country he has worked in, mainly because of the way the Chinese government handles information:

> It would be good if the government was willing to publicize information. In China, it is very hard to find an official who is willing to speak their minds. All you can get is their views published in the official Chinese media . . . The press spokesperson system in China works differently from its counterparts in the West. The Chinese spokesperson often gives you ambiguous answers, or simply dodges the question . . . Western journalists often finds it hard to know how to find information about the government.
>
> *(Ford in Zhang and Ye, 2009: 123)*

Foreign journalists' distrust of the Chinese government's spokesperson system is indeed ironic. Designed to counteract the foreign media's distrust of the government and to project an image of openness and cooperation, the spokesperson system sometimes has the effect of reinforcing the view of a suspicious and controlling Chinese government. Steven McDonell, formerly Australian Broadcasting Corporation's foreign correspondent in Beijing, now covering China for the BBC, says:

> The Chinese government has become much more friendly to us now. They hold press conferences regularly; in fact, more often than we care to go. And they are very patient when we ask them questions. Even though you know they are only feeding you the Party line, you have got to admit they are very patient. But when you try to get a real story by going off the officially allowed track, you will find that the public security people are not far behind you wherever you go.
>
> *(author's communication with McDonell, 2012)*

Perhaps the most fundamental impasse facing China's public diplomacy efforts in relation to foreign correspondents is China's failure to understand a number of things, including what foreign correspondents' journalistic standards are, how their institutional affiliations shape their news selection, gathering, and writing, and how their professional training informs their understanding of objectivity. The Chinese government's inability to understand how foreign correspondents work may be understandable, given that it expects its own media to toe the 'Party line' and maintain – rather than challenge – its political legitimacy. However, if it can be convinced that Western journalists almost by definition tend not to trust their governments, and that they are always on the lookout for problems rather than good news – even when they are reporting on their own countries – then they may at least learn not to take foreign journalists' critical reporting 'personally'. Of course, the Chinese government – like any other potential target of Western reporters – has no obligation to make an effort to understand the different values and practices of foreign correspondents. However, it would certainly serve their interests well to make such an effort. The Party's demonstrated inability to do this to date lies at the heart of China's problems with foreign correspondents, and goes a long way towards explaining China's seemingly contradictory posture of control and openness.

At the same time, Western journalists are at pains to stress that their critical reporting is not an indication of their dislike of China; instead it is motivated by their conviction of what news should be like. Henrik Bork, from the German paper *Süddeusche Zeitung*, says:

> For me, a society which has no problems and where the government handles everything well is of no interest to me. News is by definition problems and 'bad news'. In selecting my stories, I focus on things which are interesting or problematic. But this does not mean that everything in China is like this.
>
> *(Bork in Zhang and Ye, 2009: 81)*

Foreign journalists believe that the benchmark for journalistic professionalism should be to produce credible and balanced coverage. They make it clear that whether their news stories end up being read as having a negative or positive impact on China is of little concern to them. 'To me, I don't care if my news story is negative or positive, as long as it is fair and interesting and credible', says Lindsey Hilsum, Britain's Channel 4's correspondent in Beijing (Hilsum in Zhang and Ye, 2009: 147). This is echoed by Richard McGregor from the Australian *Financial Review*, who sees it as his duty to go beyond what is fed by the press release:

> Our paper wants to dig deep into the background and the significance of the event. We want to understand the process leading to this. We want to avoid our stories looking like a press release. In our stories, we try to identify important people, who they are, and what they say. In doing so, our stories may end up being either negative or positive.
>
> *(McGregor in Zhang and Ye, 2009: 45)*

These foreign journalists make it clear that they operate within an institutional and professional framework which may run up against the primary objective of China's public diplomacy, even though individual journalists may not intend to 'demonize' China. Nevertheless, not surprisingly, in most cases, foreign correspondents' reporting of China is far too critical for the Chinese authorities' liking. To make matters worse for China, foreign correspondents' reporting of China is the main source of news about China for the international reading public. Equally problematically, compared with the Western media's coverage of China, China's self-representation is more positive and upbeat, but it is widely perceived by the international community to lack credibility and persuasive power (Sun, 2010).

Conclusion

If nothing else, this discussion makes it abundantly clear that, so far, foreign media have proved to be the biggest detractor of China's attempts to spruce up its international image. How to manage and live with this liability is the ultimate challenge facing China's public diplomacy ambition in the realm of news media. The foreign correspondent has been a missing figure in our examination of China's public diplomacy strategies and practices. However, as this discussion also makes clear, the foreign correspondent assumes an increasingly important but fraught role in China's public diplomacy initiatives for a number of reasons. Successfully managed, they are potential assets for China's public diplomacy objectives of listening and advocacy. Clumsily managed, they can do more damage to China's international image than any amount of clever power can repair and restore. Speaking initially in the context of the American cultural influence in the world, Nye defines 'soft power' as the ability to get what you want through attraction (Nye, 2004); by implication, soft power is the opposite of coercive power. Adapting the concept to the Chinese situation, Li Mingjiang believes that soft power lies in the 'soft use of power to increase a state's attraction, persuasiveness and appeal' (Li, 2011a: 7). Li argues that an examination of the soft-power approach in China should shift the focus from resources of power to how a state uses its capability. Following this logic, and considering the behaviour of the Chinese government in its management of foreign correspondents, we can say that 'clumsy power' is the state's attempt to repair the damage done to its own soft power efforts by falling back on coercive measures, and in doing so, incurring further damage. As this discussion suggests, China's public diplomacy in the realm of news media faces an impossible double bind, and foreign correspondents in China constitute one of the most problematic aspects of China's soft power ambition.

Note

1 Interview material cited in this chapter comes from two sources. The first is communication with some foreign correspondents in the period of 2012 to 2013 conducted by the author. The second is a collection of interviews conducted by Zhang and Ye (2009). Zhang and Ye's collection is in Chinese, and the interview material from this collection is translated by the author.

References

Brady, Anne-Marie (2008) *Marketing Dictatorship: Propaganda and Thought Work in Contemporary China*. Lanham: Rowman and Littlefield.

Chen, Ni (2004) From propaganda to public relations: Evolutionary change in the Chinese government, *Asian Journal of Communication*, 13(12): 96–121.

Chen, Ni (2011) The Evolving Chinese Government Spokesperson System, in Wang, J. (ed.) *Soft Power in China: Public Diplomacy Through Communication*. New York: Palgrave Macmillan: 73–94.

Chinoy, Mike (2011) Assignment China, Keynote Presentation at Sydney University, 15 June.

Cho, Young Nam and Jeong, Jong Ho (2008) China's soft power: Discussions, resources, and prospects, *Asian Survey*, 48(3): 453–472.

Cull, Nicholas (2010) Public diplomacy: Seven lessons for its future from its past, *Place Branding and Public Diplomacy*, 6(1): 11–17.

d'Hooghe, Ingrid (2008) Into high gear: China's public diplomacy, *The Hague Journal of Diplomacy*, 3: 37–61.

Edney, Kingsley (2012) Soft power and the Chinese propaganda system, *Journal of Contemporary China*, 21(78): 899–914.

FCCC (n.d.) Foreign Correspondents' Club of China. Available at: www.fccchina.org/.

French, Paul (2009) *Through the Looking Glass: Foreign Journalists in China, from the Opium Wars to Mao*. Hong Kong: Hong Kong University Press.

Gaunaut, John (2013) China Expels Journalist After Wen Revelations. *Sydney Morning Herald*, 1 January.

Guo, Ke, Preface to Zhang, Zhi'an and Ye, Liu (2009) *Zhongguo Zengme Yang (What is China Like: How Foreign Correspondents Tell Their China Stories)*. Guangzhou: Nanfang Daily Press.

Herzstein, Robert (2006) *Henry R. Luce, Time, and the American Crusade in Asia*. Cambridge: Cambridge University Press.

Hu, Zhengrong and Ji, Deqiang (2012) Ambiguities in communicating with the world: The 'going-out' policy of China's media and its multilayered contexts, *Chinese Journal of Communication*, 5(1): 32–37.

Kurlantzick, Joshua (2007) *Charm Offensive: How China's Soft Power is Transforming the World*. New Haven: Yale University Press.

Leonard, Mark (2002) *Public Diplomacy*. London: The Foreign Policy Centre.

Li, Mingjiang (2011a) Soft Power: Nurture Not Nature, in Li, M. (ed.) *Soft Power: China's Emerging Strategy in International Politics*. Lanham: Rowman and Littlefield: 1–18.

Li, Mingjiang (2011b) Soft Power in Chinese Discourse: Popularity and Prospect, in Li, M. (ed.) *Soft Power: China's Emerging Strategy in International Politics*. Lanham: Rowman and Littlefield: 2–44.

Nye, Joseph (2004) *Soft Power: The Means to Success in World Politics*. Cambridge, MA: Perseus Books.

Nye, Joseph (2009) Hard decisions on soft power: Opportunities and difficulties for Chinese soft power, *Harvard International Review*, 31(2): 18–22.

People's Daily (2004) The 10th Conference of Chinese Diplomatic Envoys Stationed Abroad Held in Beijing, 30 August.

Perlroth, Nicole (2013) Hackers in China Attacked *The Times* for Last 4 Months. *The New York Times*, 30 January.

Reuters (2012) Al Jazeera English Shutters China Bureau After Beijing Expels Reporter. *Reuters*, 8 May.

Sautman, Barry and Li, Ying (2011) Public Diplomacy from Below: The 2008 'Pro-China' Demonstrations in Europe and North America. *CPD Perspectives on Public Diplomacy*, Paper 11. Los Angeles: Figueroa Press.

Sun, Wanning (2010) Mission impossible: Soft power, communication capacity, and the globalization of Chinese media, *International Journal of Communication*, 4(1): 19–26.

Sun, Wanning (2014) Foreign or Chinese: Reconfiguring the symbolic space of Chinese media, *International Journal of Communication*, 8: 1894–1911.

Sun, Wanning (2015) Slow boat from China: Public discourses behind the 'going global' media policy, *International Journal of Cultural Policy*, 21(4): 400–418.

Tang, Lu and Li, Hongmei (2011) Chinese Corporate Diplomacy: Huawei's CSR Discourse in Africa, in Wang, J. (ed.) *Soft Power in China: Public Diplomacy Through Communication*. New York: Palgrave Macmillan: 95–116.

Tang, Min (2013) State, Control, Openness: Reading the National Regulations on Global Media and Foreign Correspondents in China, International Communication Association Annual Conference, London, June.

Wang, Jian (ed.) (2011) *Soft Power in China: Public Diplomacy Through Communication*. New York: Palgrave Macmillan.

Wang, Jisi and Nye, Joseph (2009) Hard decisions on soft power: Opportunities and difficulties for Chinese soft power, *Harvard International Review*, 31(2). Available at: http://hir.harvard.edu/agriculture/hard-decisions-on-soft-power.

Wang, Yiwei (2008) Public diplomacy and the rise of Chinese soft power, *The ANNALS of the American Academy of Political and Social Science*, 616: 257–273.

Wu, Xu (2007) Zhongguo ruan shili buneng chi laoben (China's soft power cannot rest on its laurel), *Shiji Xing (Century)*, 6: 47–48.

Zhang, Juyan (2008) Making sense of the changes in China's public diplomacy: Direction of information flow and messages, *Place Branding and Public Diplomacy*, 4(4): 303–316.

Zhang, Xiaoling (2011) China's International Broadcasting: A Case Study of CCTV International, in Wang, J. (ed.) *Soft Power in China: Public Diplomacy Through Communication*. New York: Palgrave Macmillan: 57–72.

Zhang, Zhi'an and Ye, Liu (2009) *Zhongguo Zengme Yang (What Is China Like: How Foreign Correspondents Tell Their China Stories)*. Guangzhou: Nanfang Daily Press.

13

CHINA IN AFRICA: REFIGURING CENTRE–PERIPHERY MEDIA DYNAMICS

Yu Xiang

The beginning of the twenty-first century witnessed the emergence of a new order of global power. With the vigorous growth of developing countries in the Global South, the world has now entered a new era where the dualistic structure of centre and periphery is changing. The rise of countries like BRICS (Brazil, Russia, India, China and South Africa) represents the increasing ascendency of semi-peripheral countries in the world system. Although the semi-peripheral countries in the current capitalist world economy are more likely to 'contribute to global neoliberal regime maintenance' rather than to create an alternative economic mechanism to change the hierarchical world system (Bond, 2015: 15), the political, economic and cultural challenges from these countries still contribute enormously to the exploration for a new analytical frame to explain the complicated dynamics between countries. The complexity of bilateral interactions in South–South cooperation is increasing as there are more layers within the Global South than was the case two decades ago. One new and striking example of enhanced South–South cooperation is that of China with the continent of Africa.

After the global financial crisis triggered by the recession in the United States in 2008, China, with its rapidly growing economy, is regarded by some as the new dominant power in the global sphere (Jacques, 2009), though many doubt the feasibility of China's economic power leading the world (Kawanami, 2016). Accordingly, China's exponentially growing investment in and trade with Africa since the early 2000s was seen as the driving force accelerating 'a new round of scramble' in Africa (Moyo *et al.*, 2012). Along with increasing economic influence, the growth of China's state media in Africa has also aroused fierce discussion. Because of the subordinate position of China's state media to the Chinese government, most Sino-African media studies concentrate on the diplomatic function of China's media in Africa to promote the soft power of China (Wu, 2014; Zhang *et al.*, 2016). A few critically focus on the internal and external political-economic structure of China as a semi-peripheral country in the world system which is unlikely to be adequately explained by the international relations theory of realism. Furthermore, while scholars are fascinated by the intriguing content and policies of China's media in Africa, few are paying enough attention to the importance of its reception among audiences in African nations.

The ideological values delivered by the media are significantly conditioned by the economic structures of ownership, as the media system 'is not only closely linked to the ideological dictates of the business-run society, it is also an integral element of the economy' (McChesney, 1999: 281). On one hand, in order to acquire a comprehensive understanding of the ideological core of China's media in Africa, it is important to analyse the structural basis of Sino-African relations. On the other hand, reception analysis of the African audiences of China's media in Africa helps us to understand the dynamic process of Sino-African media flow. Therefore, this chapter aims to provide a structural analysis of the media dynamic between China and Africa from a critical, political-economic perspective, using the case study of CCTV in Africa and empirical data from interviews with African consumers of Chinese media.

In the first section, there is a general discussion of the semi-peripheral characteristics of China in terms of interacting with the continent of Africa mainly in economic terms, and how the discourse of China's media in Africa resonates with the Sino-African economic agenda. The second section provides a theoretical illustration of the structural alliance of the semi-peripheral and peripheral elite groups, underpinned by joint economic interests and reinforced by the ideological consent promoted – directly or indirectly – by international news. The third section examines the specific case of CCTV-Africa on how international media target elite audiences in local societies in order to manufacture ideological consent to serve the structural agenda. The fourth section looks at the media dynamic between semi-periphery and periphery by bringing in reception analysis of African audiences of CCTV-Africa. This chapter aims to set out in embryonic form a new analytic frame within which to view Sino-African media flows, and thus contribute to the development of Sino-African and South–South media studies.

China in Africa: harmony of interests between semi-periphery and periphery

In Immanuel Wallerstein's theory of world systems, there are three main types of countries: core/centre countries, semi-peripheral countries and peripheral countries, which can be identified in history from the time the concept of modern nation states was established (Wallerstein, 1976, 2006). In the capitalist world economy, 'semi-peripheral states play a particular role' which is 'based on the double antinomy of class (bourgeois-proletarian) and function in the division of labour (core-periphery)' (Wallerstein, 1976: 462). On one hand, semi-peripheral countries 'act as a peripheral zone for core countries', and on the other hand 'they act as a core country for some peripheral areas' (ibid.: 463). This definition of 'semi-peripheral states in the capitalist world economy' resonates with the notion of 'semi-imperialist' countries as the latter also refers to the ones which 'do not just transfer surplus value to imperialist centres but also succeed in appropriating weaker countries' surplus value by displacing some of the contradictions specific to dependent capitalism' (Luce, 2015: 34).

According to Mathias Luce's summary in his 2015 article 'Sub-Imperialism, the Highest Stage of Dependent Capitalism', this in-between position is also one of the 'five determining elements that make sub-imperialism's relatively autonomous expansionist policy possible through state action' (Luce, 2015: 33–34). For example, although the income of the working-age population has been rising (Roach, 2016), China still remains one of the main international users of sweatshop working, as the case of Foxconn shows (Chan and Pun, 2010). But at the same time China has become the biggest trader with Africa and the fourth largest country for foreign direct investment in the continent after Britain, the United States and Italy (*The Economist*, 2015). An increasing number of Chinese factories have moved to Africa for cheaper labour (Wonacott, 2014) and natural resources. The in-between economic character of China as semi-peripheral country is, therefore, an important analytical category.

However, according to the structural theory of imperialism formulated by Johan Galtung, which has a quite different perspective from that of realist international relations which focus more on the conflicts rather than the harmonies of interest, the dominant global structure underpinned by the capitalist world economy is maintained by the harmony of interests between central classes from countries in different stages of development (Galtung, 1971). In speaking of harmony of interests, Galtung refers to the compatible goals pursued by different parties (Galtung, 1971: 81), which are easily observed in the case of Sino-African bilateral cooperation.

The economic interests of China in Africa can be summarized in four points, according to the analyst Sun Yun from the Henry Stimson Center: firstly the rich natural resources of Africa as the raw materials for production; secondly the stable support from local African governments as a result of historical effort; thirdly the potential market of Africa to consume Chinese goods, and fourthly the 'untapped' labour resources in Africa which replace China's labour-intensive industries and assist China to 'move up in the global supply chain' (Sun, 2014: 6). More importantly, as a transitional country, from semi-periphery to centre, China is now facing many economic dilemmas. Among them, the most frequently mentioned one in recent years is overcapacity, mainly in the steel industries (Mitchell and Shepherd, 2016).

The ambitious 'One Belt One Road (OBOR) Initiative' launched by the Chinese government in 2013 'covering about 65 per cent of the world's population, about one-third of the world's GDP, and about a quarter of all the goods and services the world moves' (Ngai *et al.*, 2016) is expected to absorb, if not the whole, then a significant part of the overcapacity of the domestic heavy industries in China (Fulco, 2016). As a part of OBOR's territories, Africa is also expected to consume the surplus Chinese products such as steel and cement and turn them into magnificent buildings like stadiums and convention centres, something which is already happening in Africa (Hao and Lei, 2015). China invests capital and technology in infrastructure and in return Africa offers China natural resources and access to local markets, which has been described as a 'give-and-take' of the Sino-African relationship (Ighobor, 2013).

China needs Africa to complete its transition from semi-periphery to centre as much as Africa needs China to complete its transition from periphery to semi-periphery. As the former Vice-President of the World Bank, Yifu Lin said, the key for a poor economy to 'transform itself into a middle – or even higher – income urban economy' is 'to capture the window of opportunity for industrialization arising from the relocation of light manufacturing from a higher income economy', so Africa should welcome the idea of building industrial parks for Chinese companies and see it as the powerhouse for the world (Lin, 2015). As the South African President Jacob Zuma once claimed in a Sino-African summit, Africa and China will be a 'win–win' cooperation as both sides want to 'prosper together' (BBC, 2015).

The function of international media in maintaining and reinforcing the global structural dominance is to foster and promote ideological consent among its target audience through producing the deliberately encoded linguistic and visual media content. Therefore, the economic agenda of promoting bilateral cooperation is inevitably reflected in the media discourse of China's state-controlled media in Africa, such as CCTV, because the priority of state media in China is to serve the purpose of central government, despite the fact that communicative techniques have become much more sophisticated than crude propaganda. As Zhu Ying wrote in her study of CCTV news: '[t]he state continues to manage CCTV as an agent of ideological control, but the game has changed' (Zhu, 2012: 5). In order to understand how China's international state media function in Africa in terms of who its target audience is and why, it is useful to look at how structural theory can provide a framework for analysing the dynamics of Sino-African relations.

Structural theory and manufacturing ideological consent among elites

The structural theory of imperialism devised by the Norwegian scholar Johan Galtung in the 1970s provides us with a systematic and thorough explanation of the mechanism underlying the global structure of relations between centre and periphery countries: 'periphery-centre relationships', according to Galtung, 'are maintained and reinforced by information flows and through the reproduction of economic activities' (Thussu, 2006: 51). As indicated in Figure 13.1, nations are not unified entities but rather are formed from two main classes of people who are also designated by Galtung in terms of centre and periphery, with the centres constituting the elite groups. This centre–periphery model is 'highly protective of the centre as a whole' (Galtung, 1971: 82). While the centres of centre and periphery are tied through 'harmony of interests', the peripheries of centre and periphery are separated by 'disharmony of interests' (Galtung, 1971: 84). The existence of disharmony of interests between

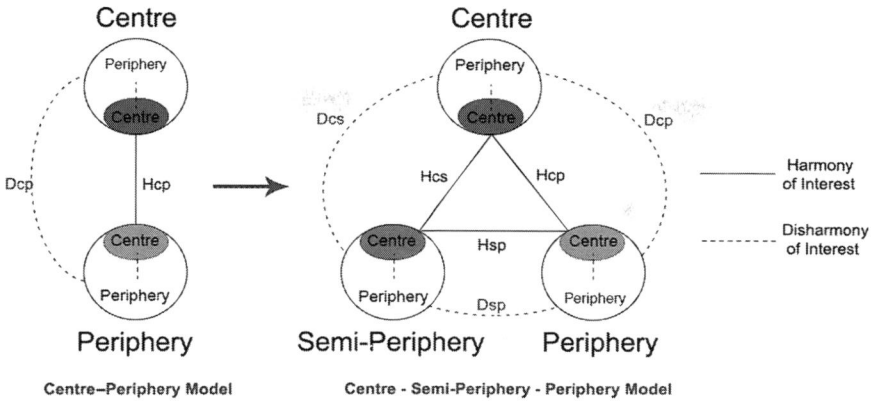

FIGURE 13.1 Revision of centre–periphery model

Source: Author.

peripheral groups, arising from the ideology of nationalism, means it is difficult for the vertical peripheral groups to unite to resist the elites in the global central groups.

The insightfulness of Galtung's structural theory remains relevant 40 years later, although the map of global powers has become more complicated with the decline of traditionally dominant countries and the emergence of new economies such as BRICS. In the case of Sino-African relations, China's involvement as a semi-peripheral country with countries in Africa has been very different from that of centre countries in terms of political and economic goals, as well as ideological approach. Therefore adding the variable of semi-peripheral actors to Galtung's centre–periphery model produces a revised three-body model with the participation of three types of nations interacting with each other, as shown in Figure 13.1.

In this revised model, the centres of the centre, semi-periphery and periphery are tied to each other by harmony of interests. However, what needs to be further spelled out here is that the 'harmony of interests' between centre and semi-periphery, centre and periphery and semi-periphery and periphery is not the same in all cases, which is the essential point of the revision. Although it has been argued that the global expansion of transnational corporations will lead to a stateless globe, which was predicted by Karl Marx as the result of the 'exploitation of the world market given a cosmopolitan character to production and consumption in every country' (Marx and Engels, 2015: 7), the concept of a unified global ruling/elite class is still unrealistic given geopolitical contradictions between nation states.

What makes the harmony of interests between semi-periphery and periphery different from any other 'harmony of interests' relies on the in-between position of semi-peripheral countries which makes their goals in the interactions with peripheral countries different from that of the centre. In the 1960s, dependency theory argued that the central/developed countries managed to keep the underdeveloped countries underdeveloped to secure their central positions in the world system 'to make conditions suitable for "dependent development"' (Thussu, 2006: 47). This dependent development model led to an increasing gap in living conditions between people in centre and periphery countries (Galtung, 1971: 87–88). However, in the case of semi-periphery and periphery, such dependent development becomes less significant as it has been replaced by a dynamic process involving a long-term objective. In the previous model of centre–periphery, the dualistic structure is relatively static, and centre countries have dominant political, economic and military power over peripheral countries. In the new model, while the hegemonic power of the centre is declining, the semi-periphery is still not as influential as the centre to peripheral countries. This situation enables peripheral countries to seek a certain degree of autonomy from the centre.

This complex of semi-peripheral and peripheral interaction can be seen in many examples in the case of Sino-African relations, including that of the media flows from China to Africa. Galtung wrote that 'major agencies are in the hands of the centre countries, relying on centre-dominated, feudal networks of communication' (Galtung, 1971: 93). However, in the case of China's media in Africa, although China has been trying to penetrate the local news industries in African countries for many years, the mainstream of the African journalistic profession remains largely Westernized. In many African countries, studies have shown, the mainstream Western media such as CNN and BBC are much more influential than Chinese media (Gorfinkel et al., 2014: 86). This is one of many concrete cases indicating that Sino-African relations cannot be maintained as a centre–periphery relation. As Chinese media are not as popular or international as Western media, which gained influence during the colonial age, the strategy used by Chinese media for entering the African news market is much more focused on manufacturing ideological consent among its target audience – the elite class – rather than setting a global agenda through international news. Therefore, it is important to understand the underlying economic base of 'harmony of interests' among Sino-African elite classes as the basis for the ideological consent promoted by CCTV-Africa.

The elite target audience of CCTV-Africa

Political, economic and cultural domination in the peripheral countries can be made interchangeable 'by regulating the flow of information' by the centre countries (Galtung, 1971: 99). International media play a crucial role in the process of regulating the information flow from centre to periphery as well as semi-periphery to periphery. In the case of China's media flow to Africa, China's international media in Africa are mostly state-owned and state-controlled. State-owned media in China, despite their financial autonomy from the newly commercialized domestic media industries, remain largely 'the agent of ideological control . . . at the behest of the state' (Zhu, 2012: 3–5): 'China Central Television (CCTV) is still the mouthpiece of the [China Communist Party] CCP' (ibid.: 8) and therefore has the mission of promoting the image of China in the global sphere (Yu, 2008). Driven by the national project of 'going out', 'CCTV stepped onto the global step [sic] with the establishment of CCTV-International' (Zhu, 2012: 169).

CCTV, together with other Chinese media in Africa, has shown a different reporting style to traditional Western critical journalists' modus operandi. There appears to be a new style of 'positive reporting' which is defined by Gagliardone as 'a style of journalism that focuses on collective achievements, rather than divisive issues (e.g., political crisis) or sensational, negative news (e.g., famine)' (Gagliardone, 2013: 32). This innovative reporting style of Chinese media has been extended into a new journalistic paradigm called 'constructive journalism' (Zhang and Simon, 2016). However, a discourse analysis of the *Africa News* programme of CCTV-Africa conducted by Zhang Xiaoling has shown that this positive reporting style is more often seen in the China-related content than in general reports about Africa (Zhang, 2013: 13). Limited by the need to report objective facts rather than rosy reality, it seems that CCTV-Africa's comprehensive news programme has a rather balanced reporting style not necessarily driven by an official agenda to promote 'economic development' and 'political stability'. However, the case of the business programme *Global Business* is rather different, as the media content is more directly connected with the political-economic goals of the Chinese government. A frame analysis of *Global Business* has indicated that the programme has a focus on emphasizing the importance of political stability and advocating economic innovation in local markets (Xiang and Zhang, forthcoming).

Additionally, CCTV-International has also focused on the target audience of elite classes to promote its ideological values. In the development paradigm of international communication studies in the 1950s, mass media was seen to be capable of educating the people in developing countries with current knowledge and information much more efficiently because 'the scale of the audience that mass media produce meant that they could reach into the minds of vast numbers of people at the same time and for vastly less cost' (Sparks, 2007: 23). And 'the early adopters' of the new knowledge and ideology 'would tend to come from elite groups' (Rogers, 1992, cited in Sparks, 2007: 26). As Marx and Engels once wrote, 'the ruling ideas of each age have ever been the ideas of its ruling class' (Marx and Engels, 2015: 31). Because of the harmony of interests between elite groups in semi-periphery and periphery, ideological consent is most easily forged through the cooperation between elite classes in their 'centres' and then reinforced by the international media.

According to statistics from research in 2009, the CCTV News channel could reach 98 per cent of the earth's surface through six satellites, and had 40 million audiences across Asia, Europe and America (Yan and Ke, 2009: 70). Although the audience profile has long remained unclear, one consultant of CCTV News, when interviewed, confirmed the specific target, saying that 'the channel should be directed at the foreign audience, particularly overseas, and in particular at "opinion makers"' (Jirik, 2008: 241). Research conducted by Guo and his colleagues in 2005 indicated that about 77 per cent of CCTV News' foreign audience are from the middle or upper class and their occupations included 'entrepreneurs, educators, politicians and technology-developers' (Guo *et al.*, 2005: 4). Similarly, in the case of the African audience of CCTV, research on the CCTV-Africa business programme

Global Business indicates that, judging from the appearance of the speakers in the reports, the media content of *Global Business* has an obvious focus on the interests of the elite class (Xiang and Zhang, forthcoming). CCTV News seems to have a clear strategy, based on the 'two-step flow' theory, of targeting opinion leaders, who are often the elite classes in those countries (Li, 2013: 30).

However, what remains under-researched is the African audiences' perception of China's media. Although there have been some surveys conducted by both Chinese and foreign researchers to find out how African people perceive the image of China (Chen, 2015; Nassanga and Makara, 2015; Tang, 2015), few are analysing how exposure to China's media in Africa has influenced (or not) local people's perceptions. The main reason why audience studies which focus specifically on the elite classes in African countries are rare is possibly a lack of data due to the infancy of Sino-African media studies. In addition, because of this the limited influence of China's media in Africa makes it difficult for researchers to conduct systematic audience research. Under such circumstances, the community of African students in China become the chosen research subjects for audience studies since they are more likely to watch Chinese media and 'are going to be in positions of power and influence . . . within the next couple of years' (Allison, 2013).

Yan surveyed African students who were journalism professionals on a training programme from June 2013 to June 2014, organized by China's State Administration of Press, Publication, Radio, Film and Television. Results showed that 92 per cent of the 358 participants watched CCTV though not CCTV-Africa particularly, and 23.5 per cent voted CCTV as one of their top three favourite international television channels next to BBC (40.2 per cent), France 24 (36.9 per cent) and CNN (24 per cent) (Yan, 2015). According to Yan's research, CCTV and Chinese media are regarded as important information sources for the elite African audience. Therefore, how these audience groups perceived the media content indicates whether the national ideology

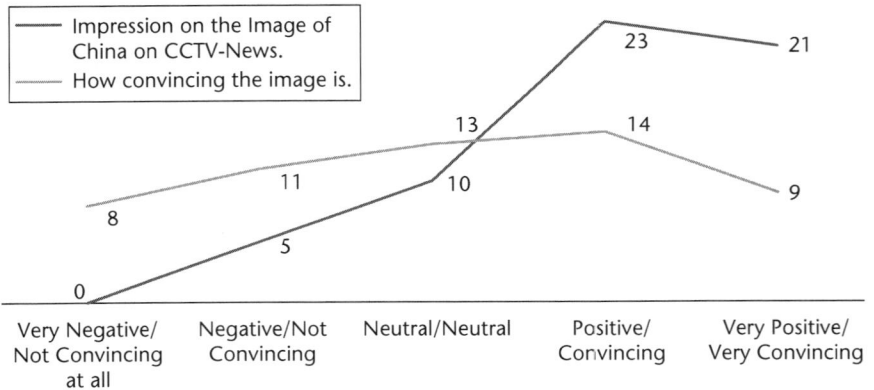

FIGURE 13.2 African students' perception of the image of China on CCTV News (2014)

Source: Author.

promoted by China is being absorbed by the target audience or not. As indicated in Figure 13.2, in an online questionnaire conducted by the author in 2014 with the participation of 60 African students from 13 African countries, the results have shown that although about 75 per cent of African students do have the impression that CCTV News is delivering a positive image of China, only 37 per cent of them are convinced by that image. Despite the fact that African students in China are not fully representative of the local elite class, these divergent opinions among the educated population are an interesting phenomenon which needs to be further studied.

African audiences' reception of CCTV-Africa

The mixed-method field research deploying both quantitative questionnaires with 89 participants and qualitative individual interviews with 36 interviewees from 18 African countries was conducted by the author in the summer of 2016 from the end of May to the beginning of July. All participants either for the questionnaire or the interviews were African students studying Bachelor, Master or PhD degrees in China, assumed to be potential members of the elite class in their local societies. One clear result of the questionnaire survey is a general trend in African students' perceptions of CCTV-Africa. The ideological agenda of CCTV-Africa is to promote bilateral economic cooperation between China and Africa by highlighting the importance of neoliberal economic development and China's critical involvement in enhancing such development.

As shown in Figure 13.3, among the 89 participants, 63 per cent had a positive impression of CCTV-Africa, and only 13 per cent thought of it negatively. In order to further understand how the African students perceive the media content produced by CCTV-Africa positively and negatively, in-depth individual interviews were conducted with interviewees selected from the questionnaire results: 36 interviews were conducted in four cities (Changchun, Harbin, Jinhua and Ningbo)

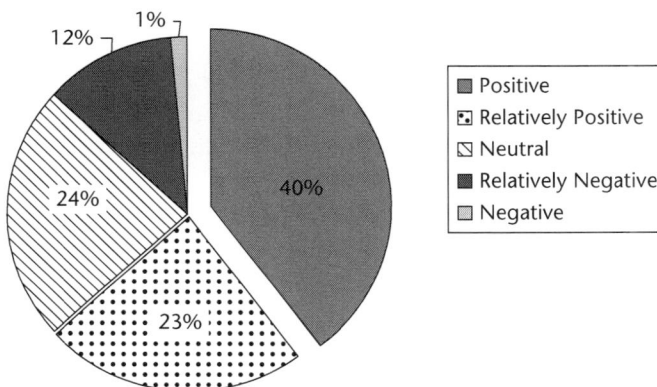

FIGURE 13.3   African students' impressions of CCTV-Africa (2016)

Source: Author.

TABLE 13.1 Typology of audience's reception of media content (revised from Fuchs, 2015: 87)

	Agree with the ideological agenda	Agree/disagree with parts of the ideological agenda	Disagree with the ideological agenda
Unconscious of the ideological agenda of CCTV-Africa	1) Do not recognize it in CCTV-Africa, but agree with it in reality	2) Do not recognize it in CCTV-Africa, but partly agree as well partly disagree with it in reality	Do not recognize it in CCTV-Africa, but disagree with it in reality
Conscious of the ideological agenda of CCTV-Africa	3) Recognize it in CCTV-Africa, and agree with it in reality **(Hegemonic Code)**	4) Recognize it in CCTV-Africa, and partly agree as well partly disagree with it in reality **(Negotiated Code)**	5) Recognize it in CCTV-Africa, but disagree with it in reality **(Oppositional Code)**
Partly conscious of the ideological agenda of CCTV-Africa	6) Partly recognize it in CCTV-Africa, and agree with it in reality **(Hegemonic code)**	Partly recognize it in CCTV-Africa, but partly agree as well partly disagree with it in reality	Partly recognize it in CCTV-Africa, and disagree with it in reality

in three provinces (Zhejiang, Jilin and Heilongjiang) and three municipalities (Beijing, Shanghai and Tianjin).

The typology deployed in this research to categorize interviewees' perceptions of the agenda of CCTV-Africa is based on the typology of ideologies summarized by Fuchs (2015). In the typology shown in Table 13.1, there are nine categories of an audience's perception of the ideological agenda of media content. The empirical results collected from the interviews in this research fall mainly into six categories:

- Unconscious of the ideological agenda of CCTV-Africa but agree with it;
- Unconscious of the ideological agenda of CCTV-Africa and agree with only parts of it;
- Conscious of the ideological agenda of CCTV-Africa and agree with it;
- Conscious of the ideological agenda of CCTV-Africa but only agree with parts of it;
- Conscious of the ideological agenda of CCTV-Africa but disagree with it;
- Partly conscious of the ideological agenda of CCTV-Africa but agree with it.

According to Stuart Hall in his 'Encoding/Decoding', there are mainly three types of codes deployed by audiences to decode the message encoded in media content which are: hegemonic codes, negotiated codes and oppositional codes (2006: 171–173). Hegemonic codes refer to the reception that audiences decode 'the message in terms of the reference code in which it has been encoded' (2006: 171). Negotiated codes refer to the mixed reception of adaptive and oppositional understanding of the encoded media message (2006: 172). Oppositional codes refer to the reception that the audience understands very well the connotative meaning of the media content, but decodes the message in a 'globally contrary way' (2006: 172).

Matching the three types of codes with the typology of the audience's reception of CCTV-Africa, it is clear that the categories of 'conscious of the ideological agenda and agree with it' and 'partly conscious of the ideological agenda but agree with it' fit the hegemonic codes well; the category of 'conscious of the ideological agenda but only agree with parts of it' resonates with the negotiated codes, and the category of 'conscious of the ideological agenda but disagree with it' conforms to the oppositional codes.

The premise of the three reception codes is that the significant moments of encoding and decoding do happen. But for the audience that is unconscious of the ideological agenda of the 'connotative levels of signifiers' in media content (Hall, 2006: 169), the moment of decoding fails to happen thoroughly, if at all. Hall aimed to provide an analytic frame to understand audience's reception only from the perspective of media discourse which is simultaneously a detonative reflection and a crucial part of the grander societal structure. For the audience unconscious of the media agenda, and hardly influenced by the ideology expressed by the media discourse, their agreement and disagreement with the ideological agenda encoded in the media content arise from the context of the reality of their lives within the wider societal structure. Therefore, the formation of the ideology of audience, as indicated in the typology in Table 13.1, is not only influenced by the media but more likely conditioned by the wider political-economic structure.

The students' reception of the news produced by CCTV-Africa is not consistent, as Hall predicted that there is no guarantee that people from the same class would have a similar ideology (Hall, 1986). Nevertheless, the field results of this research show a certain degree of favourable interpretation by the interviewees of the ideological agenda of CCTV-Africa. The African audiences in the first, third and sixth categories, whether they are conscious of the agenda of the news of CCTV-Africa or not, appear to agree with that agenda. As one interviewee from Burundi said,

> CCTV is Chinese. It depends on the political agenda they have between Burundi and China. So they don't really go to the negative side as well as the positive side of the political crisis . . . But I still think CCTV is good because it is not trying to take any part or any kind of position . . . CCTV is just trying to show the hot news . . . They are just showing what the news in that country . . . So they just show what is happening, and they just want to sell what is happening . . . Personally, I think it is good (to sell the good image of Africa) . . . Because the bad news will shock people . . . most of what CCTV Africa shows is about business . . . [Chinese government] encourage[s] the Chinese investors to invest in Africa.
>
> *(Male, 21, 14 July 2016)*

Interviewees with this understanding usually have a positive attitude towards China–Africa economic cooperation and welcome investment from China: as one student from Tanzania said:

> my government's attitude towards China is very positive and good, considering the fact that Tanzania and China have had good relations for a long time. The relationship with Beijing is a cooperative one and I support my government's opinion of cooperating with the Chinese government.
>
> *(Female, 22, 24 July 2016)*

These kind of positive attitudes are demonstrated in views of the differences in behaviour between China and Western countries in Africa:

> we like Chinese. China has been signing contracts [with African countries]. Because for America, even you don't have a bill, you still have a gun. Africa would totally be afraid of something [like that], but Chinese won't [do that]. And we still make a lot of contracts with China.
>
> *(Male, 26, Djibouti, 14 July 2016)*

This kind of positive influence is also reflected in the audience's trust in the credit of CCTV-Africa: 'I believe in CCTV . . . CCTV will tell the truth' (Male, 28, South Sudan, 29 May 2016).

For the African audience who partly agree/disagree with the ideological agenda of CCTV-Africa, as indicated in the second and fourth categories, they have a more complex understanding of the message the news of CCTV-Africa is trying to convey. They are not unconditionally accepting the messages encoded in the news content of CCTV-Africa, whether they are fully conscious of the agenda or not. Most of the interviewees of this type have a rather dialectical understanding of the objectivity of news. Although they probably do not recognize clearly what agenda CCTV-Africa has, some believe that 'every media has an agenda . . . they are selling ideas' (Male, 34, Ghana, 25 May 2016). The ones conscious of the agenda seem rather neutral about it. As one student from Ghana said: '(there is) an agenda that China is pushing to strengthen the ties between China and Ghana . . . I don't think it's a very bad idea . . . but depending on the strings that might be attached to it' (Female, 35, Ghana, 26 May 2016). However, despite all their concerns, they are still supportive of Sino-African economic interaction, as the 'cooperation between the two governments is approved by all because the changes are visible in the country' (Male, 22, Cameroon, 8 July 2016).

The group of interviewees who decode the news of CCTV-Africa in an oppositional way are more critical of the content, although they comprehend very well the connotative meaning of the news. The reasons for this lack of credibility of CCTV-Africa are various. Some interviewees believe the ideological agenda serves China more than Africa, as an interviewee from Tanzania told the author that 'CCTV is yours, use (it for) whatever you want' (Male, 24, 15 July 2016). Other interviewees, like one female student from Democratic Republic of Congo are concerned about the elite orientation of the economic agenda expressed by the news because 'even if it (Sino-African cooperation) does bring in money, the population would never get to see . . . only the people in the elite (class) . . . they (the general population) would never be able to get access to it' (Female, 21, 30 May 2016). And one interviewee expressed his concern that China was becoming another colonist country:

> when the French came into my country, they said that they will help you guys, they do everything, like teaching us language . . . But at the end of the day, till today, we want to get free from these people . . . They exploited us in all types of ways . . . I just hope China won't do the same thing.
>
> *(Male, 26, Guinea, 27 May 2016)*

As indicated in Figure 13.4, the interviewees who agree with the agenda (categories 1, 3, 6) occupy the biggest proportion (53 per cent). Audiences who partly agree with the agenda are at 30 per cent, and only 17 per cent of them critically interpret the news of CCTV-Africa following the oppositional codes. The diverse opinions on CCTV-Africa, which are indicated here, among the African students in China, provide us with a multi-dimensional panorama of the ideological dynamic of the

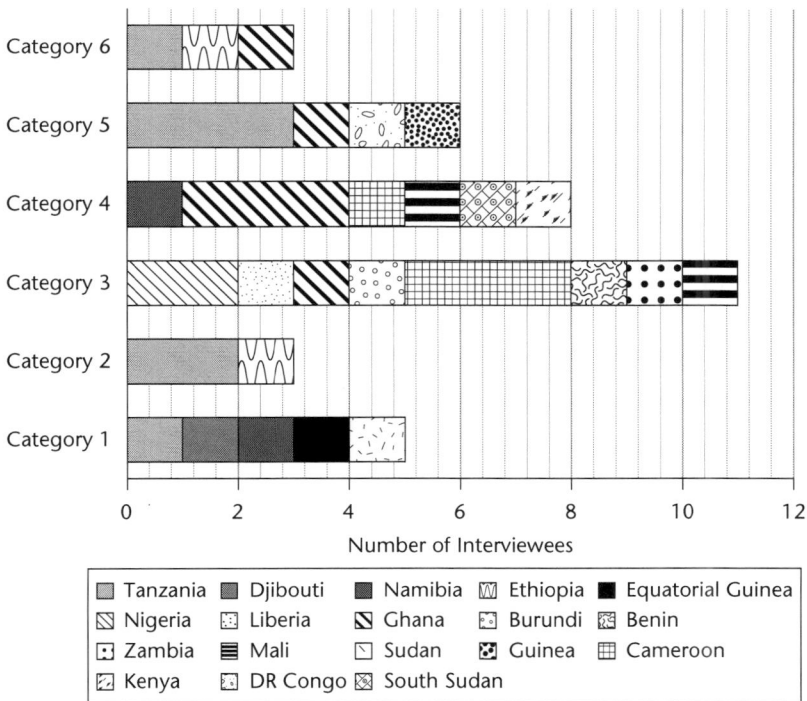

FIGURE 13.4 African students' reception of CCTV-Africa

Source: Author.

would-be elite African class. As illustrated in the section about the structural theory on the harmony of interests among transnational elites, international news usually has a positive influence in terms of fostering and reinforcing ideological consent for the transnational elites. As we can see from this case study of African student audiences of CCTV-Africa in China, most of the interviewees who have an interest in Sino-African economic cooperation, as they are living and studying in mainland China, have a rather positive understanding of the news content and interpret the message following the dominant code.

This finding resonates with the argument made by Hall that 'polysemy must not, however, be confused with pluralism' (2006: 169). People from different cultures and societies would probably have a different understanding of foreign media because of the different dominant orders of their local 'social life, of economic and political power and of ideology' (2006: 169). However, in the cases such as Sino-African media flow where the different societies are gradually aligned with each other within the political and economic structure dominated by the global economy of neoliberal capitalism, the African interviewees watching CCTV-Africa, conditioned by their elite position, are more likely to follow hegemonic codes to decode the message encrypted in the international news.

Conclusion

The unprecedented scale of globalization underpinned by the expanding capitalist world economy contributes to the ever-growing divergence between elites and masses as indicated in the recent international political events such as Brexit and the election of President Donald Trump in the United States. Revisiting Galtung's structural theory of 'harmony of interests' between elites and 'disharmony of interests' with the majority population is a timely contribution to explaining the ever-growing nationalism and rightist extremism in the globe. However, while Western democracies are experiencing a relative decline in their global influence, many non-Western developing countries with steadily growing economies are increasing cooperation. The practice of South–South collaborations in these circumstances is of importance not only in revitalizing the global economy but also in reshaping the global order.

As discussed above, the Sino-African economic interactions and the ideological content of China's media demonstrate a different pattern of semi-periphery–periphery model compared to that of centre–periphery. China's multi-dimensional engagements in Africa, while resonating with the global expansion of neoliberal capitalism, have shown many African countries an alternative development path paved by a different political and economic regime which is characterized as political meritocracy with limits of democracy (Bell, 2015). Nevertheless, although the United States world hegemony has been eroded, the hierarchical world system has been maintained and managed to secure the interest of the centre core countries such as the United States. Whether the South–South cooperation will provide the world an alternative model for political, economic and communication transnational interactions is a critical question that remains to be answered.

References

Allison, Simon (2013) Fixing China's image in Africa, one student at a time. *The Guardian*. Available at: www.theguardian.com/world/2013/jul/31/china-africa-students-scholarship-programme [Accessed 15 November 2016].

BBC (2015) Zuma says China-Africa co-operation 'win-win'. Available at: www.bbc.co.uk/news/world-africa-35018241 [Accessed 1 January 2017].

Bell, Daniel (2015) *The China Model: Political Meritocracy and the Limits of Democracy*. Princeton: Princeton University Press.

Bond, Patrick (2015) BRICS and the Sub-imperial Location, in Partrick, B. and Ana, G. (eds.) *BRICS: An Anti-Capitalist Critique*. London: Pluto Press: 15–26.

Chan, Jenny and Pun, Ngai (2010) Suicide as protest for the new generation of Chinese migrant workers: Foxconn, global capital, and the state, *Asia-Pacific Journal*, 37: 2–10. Available at: http://japanfocus.org/-Jenny-Chan/3408 [Accessed 14 September 2016].

Chen, Xuefei (2015) The image of China in the eyes of Africans: A research based on the local African media content (非洲人眼中的中国形象：基于非洲本地媒体视角的考察). *Utopia*. Available at: www.wyzxwk.com/Article/guofang/2015/04/341461.html (In Chinese). [Accessed 15 November 2016].

The Economist (2015) One Among Many. Available at: www.economist.com/news/middle-east-and-africa/21639554-china-has-become-big-africa-now-backlash-one-among-many [Accessed 25 September 2017].

Fuchs, Christian (2015) *Culture and Economy in the Age of Social Media*. New York: Routledge.

Fulco, Matthew (2016) Solving the prickly issue of overcapacity in China. *CKGSB Knowledge*. Available at: http://knowledge.ckgsb.edu.cn/2016/06/14/chinese-economy/solving-the-prickly-issue-of-overcapacity-in-china/ [Accessed 29 December 2016].

Gagliardone, Iginio (2013) China as a persuader: CCTV Africa's first steps in the African mediasphere, *Ecquid Novi: African Journalism Studies*, 34(3): 25–40.

Galtung, Johan (1971) A structural theory of imperialism, *Journal of Peace Research*, 8(2): 81–117.

Gorfinkel, Lauren; Joffe, Staden; Van Staden, Cobus and Wu, Yu-Shan (2014) CCTV's global outreach: Examining the audiences of China's 'new voice' on Africa, *Media International Australia*, 151: 81–88.

Guo, Ke; Wang, Wei and Sang, Cuilin (2005) On the international influence of English TV media in China: Case study of CCTV-9. Available at: www.xizuo.com/yingyujiaoshi-bokejingxuan/yingyulunwen/31999.html [Accessed 10 March 2016].

Hall, Stuart (1986) The problem of ideology – Marxism without guarantees, *Journal of Communication Inquiry*, 10(2): 28–44.

Hall, Stuart (2006) Encoding/decoding, in: Durham, M. G. and Kellner, D. M. (eds.) *Media and Cultural Studies: Key Works* (Revised Edition), Cornwall: Blackwell Publishing, 163–173.

Hao, Wangle and Lei, Ming (2015) 中国援非项目已成非洲当地亮丽风景 (Aid projects from China become beautiful view in Africa). Available at: www.fmprc.gov.cn/zflt/chn/zxxx/t1315256.htm (In Chinese) [Accessed 1 August 2017].

Ighobor, Kingsley (2013) China in the heart of Africa. *Africa Renewal*. Available at: www.un.org/africarenewal/magazine/january-2013/china-heart-africa [Accessed 1 January 2017].

Jacques, Martin (2009) *When China Rules the World: The Rise of the Middle Kingdom and the End of the Western World*. London: Penguin Books.

Jirik, John (2008) *Making News in People's Republic of China: The Case of CCTV-9*. Doctoral dissertation. University of Texas at Austin.

Kawanami, Takeshi (2016) US opposes granting China market economy status. *Nikkei*. Available at: https://asia.nikkei.com/Politics-Economy/International-Relations/US-opposes-granting-China-market-economy-status [Accessed 1 August 2017].

Li, Zhi (2013) The two step flow strategy of outward communication – a case study on China Centre Television (对外传播中的'二级传播'策略 – 以中央电视台为例), *International Communication*, 2: 30–33. Available at: http://m.xzbu.com/1/view-4007772.htm (In Chinese). [Accessed 13 November 2016].

Lin. Yifu Justin (2015) Africa's path from poverty. *Project-Syndicate*. Available at: www.project-syndicate.org/commentary/africa-development-route-by-justin-yifu-lin-2015-02?barrier=true [Accessed 1 January 2017].

Luce, Mathias (2015) Sub-Imperialism, the Highest Stage of Dependent Capitalism, in Partrick, B. and Ana G. (eds.) *BRICS: An Anti-Capitalist Critique*. London: Pluto Press: 27–44.

Marx, Karl and Engels, Friederich (2015) *The Communist Manifesto* (translated by Moore, S.). London: Penguin Books.

McChesney, Robert (1999) *Rich Media, Poor Democracy: Communication Politics in Dubious Times*. New York: New Press.

Mitchell, Tom and Shepherd, Christian (2016) China says its steel capacity will remain. *Financial Times*, 28 December.

Moyo, Sam; Yeros, Paris and Jha, Pravee (2012) Imperialism and primitive accumulation: Notes on the new scramble for Africa, *Agrarian South: Journal of Political Economy*, 1(2): 181–203.

Nassanga, Goretti and Makara, Sabiti (2015) Perceptions of Chinese presence in Africa as reflected in the African media: Case study of Uganda, *Chinese Journal of Communication*, 9(1): 1–17.

Ngai, Joe; Sneader, Kevin and Zecha, Cecilia Ma (2016) China's One Belt, One Road: Will it reshape global trade? *McKinsey Podcast*. Available at: www.mckinsey.com/global-themes/china/chinas-one-belt-one-road-will-it-reshape-global-trade [Accessed 11 November 2016].

Roach, Stephen (2016) Why China is central to growth. World Economic Forum. Available at: www.weforum.org/agenda/2016/09/why-china-is-central-to-global-growth [Accessed 11 November 2016].

Rogers, Everett (1992) *The Diffusion of Innovation*, fourth edition. New York: The Free Press.

Sparks, Colin (2007) *Globalization, Development and the Mass Media*. London: SAGE.

Sun, Yun (2014) *Africa in China's Foreign Policy*. John L. Thornton China Centre and the Africa Growth Initiative, Brookings. Available at: www.wlv.ac.uk//media/departments/faculty-of-social-sciences/documents/Africa_in_China_Brookings_report.pdf [Accessed 1 August 2017]

Tang, Ying (2015) The status quo of China's image in Africa (中国国家形象在非洲的现状). *Foreign Affairs Observer*. Available at: www.faobserver.com/NewsInfo.aspx?id=11002 (In Chinese). [Accessed 15 November 2016].

Thussu, Daya (2006) *International Communication: Continuity and Change*. London: Hodder Arnold.

Wallerstein, Immanuel (1976) Semi-peripheral countries and the contemporary world crisis, *Theory and Society*, 3(4): 461–483.

Wallerstein, Immanuel (2006) *World-Systems Analysis: An Introduction*, fourth edition. Durham: Duke University Press.

Wonacott Peter (2014) China Inc. Moves Factory Floor To Africa. *The Wall Street Journal*. Available at: www.wsj.com/articles/china-inc-moves-factory-floor-to-africa-1400099895 [Accessed 25 September 2017].

Wu, Yu-Shan (2014) *China's Media and Public Diplomacy: Illustrations from South Africa.* Beijing: China and Africa Media, Communications and Public Diplomacy.

Xiang, Yu and Zhang, Xiaoling (forthcoming) Revisiting cultural imperialism at the intersection of class and nation: A case study of Sino-African media flows. *Chinese Journal of Communication.*

Yan, ChengSheng (2015) The status quo, characteristics and reviews on China's Television in Africa (中国电视对非洲传播的现状、特点与思考). Available at: http://media.people.com.cn/n/2015/0605/c396798-27110574-2.html (In Chinese). [Accessed 3 April 2016].

Yan, Lifeng and Ke, JinHuang (2009) Analysis on the international communicative strategies of CCTV-9: A case study of CCTV-News (以CCTV News为例评析CCTV－9国际传播策略), *Exploration & Contention*, 12(241): 70–72. (In Chinese).

Yu, Miao (2008) Interview with the vice president of CCTV–Let CCTV be seen in every corner of this world (让世界每一个角落看到央视的节目 – 专访中央电视台副台长张长明), *International Communications* (2008/02), 8–13. (In Chinese).

Zhang, Xiaoling (2013) *How Ready is China for a China-style World Order? China's State Media Discourse under Construction.* China Policy Institute, The University of Nottingham. Available at: www.nottingham.ac.uk/cpi/documents/working-papers/working-paper-8.pdf. [Accessed 1 August 2017]

Zhang, Xiaoling; Wasserman, Herman and Mano, Winston (eds.) (2016) *China's Media and Soft Power in Africa.* London: Palgrave Macmillan.

Zhang, Yanqiu and Simon, Matingwina (2016) Constructive Journalism: A New Journalistic Paradigm of Chinese Media in Africa, in Zhang, X., Wasserman, H. and Mano, W. (eds.) *China's Media and Soft Power in Africa.* London: Palgrave Macmillan: 93–106.

Zhu, Ying (2012) *Two Billion Eyes: The Story of China Central Television.* New York: The New Press.

14

THE RISE OF CHINA'S FINANCIAL MEDIA: GLOBALIZING ECONOMY VS. GLOBALIZING ECONOMIC DISCOURSE

Jingwei Piao

Financial media, as a news subgenre, play an important role in the functioning of economic activities. On the one hand, financial media play a watchdog role in monitoring the market and shaping the economic agenda. On the other hand, the market economy needs the media to disseminate information, boost business, and form a favourable economic culture. Thus, the power relations between the media and the market are key in shaping the economic discourse (Parsons, 1990; Parker, 1997). Since China began to embrace market principles in 1978, China's financial media have prospered in association with the fast-growing economy. However, little has been written about their role in the shift from socialist economic values to those of the free market and free trade; and in propagating an economic discourse from 'capitalist-socialist' paradox to global norms (Sigley, 2006). To remedy the situation, this chapter attempts to explore the interrelationship of the Chinese economy, and role of the financial media in establishing a new economic discourse.

The rise of Chinese financial media can be divided into four phases that reflect a slower pace of media development, compared with the economic reform. Such mismatched developmental processes resulted in the media facing fiercer competition with other financial institutions and PR companies, and the move to separate editorial and management teams within media outlets. In the early stage of market reform, China's financial media played a successful educational role in formulating a new economic language and business culture. However, as the economic agenda has evolved, the economic discourse used by the media does not seem to have developed fast enough to stay in sync with the global norms of the neoliberal business mentality. However, a small circle of elite financial media with a globally oriented perspective have in common the advocacy of the free market and free trade with their Western counterparts.

From market reform to economic globalization

In the West, financial media have historically played a key role as mediator between markets and governments, as well as being an important prerequisite for the liberalization of economics and politics (Gussow, 1984; Schuster, 2006; Davis, 2006; Greenfield and Williams, 2007). In China, the financial media sit at the very core of the country's market reforms. By linking the Chinese economy with the development of financial media, China's financial media have developed in two dimensions (Table 14.1). Being predominant in the first two phases of development, the horizontal dimension implies that media aim to educate the public in the new economic culture, and enlarging the audience that consumes economic news. In the latter two phases, the vertical dimension illustrates that the media landscape has been increasingly stratified and diversified to cater for specific readerships, as the market is more liberal and globally integrated.

Phase One: enlightenment

The first phase of development began in 1978, when Deng Xiaoping promulgated market reform, including the de-collectivization of agriculture on a massive scale, dismantling the Soviet-style central planning industries, and opening up to the international marketplace (Huenemann, 2013). The *Frontline of Finance and Trade* and *Economic Daily* were founded as vital party organs to disseminate economic

TABLE 14.1 Four-phase dual development of China's financial media and economics

	Economics	*Financial media*
Phase One (1978–1991)	**Market decentralization at local levels** • Market reform since 1978 • Growth slow down	**Enlightenment** • Advocate free market ideas • Educate public in market principles • Influence economic agenda-setting
Phase Two (1992–2001)	**Centrally initiated reform** • Economic framework building • Domestic capital market re-established in 1990s	**Stratification** • Business management type • Capital markets type • Policy making, and social consequence type
Phase Three (2002–2008)	**Global Integration** • Accession into WTO • 'Go Global' policy • Foreign IPOs	**Convergence** • '21st Century' group • 'CBN' group • 'SEE' group
Phase Four (2009–2015)	**Influential role in global economy** • Second largest economy • 'One Belt, One Road' policy • Founding a multilateral development bank: AIIB	**Digitalization and capitalization** • From mainstream to private startups • From traditional platforms to Internet plus and mobile apps

policies. In the early 1980s, as a subdivision of the *People's Daily*, the *Market Paper* deviated from the propaganda discourse and socialist ideologies, covering market issues from daily consumption to stocks that China did not have (Yuan, 2013; Qin, 2015). These state-owned newspapers shared the common goal of advocating free market ideas, educating the ignorant public with market principles hitherto lacking. Meanwhile, privately funded newspapers also emerged. The *World Economic Herald*[1] was founded by the Shanghai Academy of Social Science, with close ties to China's 'elitist movement', popularizing the notions of 'science' and 'democracy' (Cheng and White, 1991). In the early 1980s, it had the reputation for being the most forthright, liberal newspaper. *China Business Times* was set up in the late 1980s and pushed the rhetoric of reform firmly throughout its reporting. As China's first commercial newspaper, it cultivated many prominent professionals building the current prosperity of the financial media, such as Hu Shuli (*Caijing*), Liu Jian (*Economic Observer*), and Lv Pingbo (*China Times*) (Qin, 2015).

In the late 1980s, China's economy slowed down mainly because of corruption and inflation. In 1984, the *Economic Daily*, *World Economic Herald*, and some other financial media, together with the young economists convened a meeting to discuss the urgent problems of reform (Liu, 2014). The so-called Moganshan Conference had a profound influence on the history of China's economic liberalization and for academic economists. With the leadership paying close attention and providing support, the conference made a significant contribution to price reform, which had used the 'dual-track' approach for deregulation and adjustment of the country's price mechanism (Fewsmith, 1994: 137).

Phase Two: stratification

Deng Xiaoping's southern tour in 1992 marked the second phase of reform, from decentralization at local level to centrally planned institutional rebuilding. Financial media emerged from a wave of commercialization and stratification. In the aftermath of the 1989 Tiananmen events, the top leadership was divided into 'reformers' and 'conservatives' as a side effect of the economic liberalization that challenged political and social stability. Deng was a 'private citizen' with no official title outside the Beijing government. To restart the reform momentum, the southern trip was his personal intervention to bring reform back on course. Thus the tour was intentionally ignored by Beijing and national media, which were under the control of Deng's political rivals. While the mainstream media ignored him, *Liberation Daily*[2] and *Shenzhen Special Zone Daily* were the first to publish articles to support Deng's trip and his speeches advocating reform. *China Business Times*, as a private newspaper without party background, reprinted those reports. After several months, the national media finally reported the tour. The 14th Party Congress in the same year formally endorsed Deng's economic policy, leading to a series of centrally initiated reforms, including the implementation of stock exchanges, the large-scale state-owned enterprise (SOE) reform, and the Constitution's granting of full legal status for private business (Wong and Zheng, 2001).

As Chinese society became more stratified and diversified, financial media also needed to further commercialize in order to accommodate the demands of an increasingly heterogeneous audience (Qian and Bandurski, 2011). There emerged some party-run media with the authority to discuss economic policies, targeted at an elite readership, such as *China Economic Times* and *China Economic Herald*, which were founded by the Development Research Center of the State Council and National Development and Reform Commission respectively. Channel 2 of China Central Television (CCTV) was also adapted to specialize in broadcasting economic programmes. Since the mid-1990s, the rise of Chinese entrepreneurs ushered in new business periodicals. *China Entrepreneur* (*zhongguo qiyejia*) and *China Business* (*zhongguo jingyingbao*) were restructured to educate China's emerging entrepreneurial class. *Business* (*shang jie*) and *China Marketing* (*xiaoshou yu shichang*) were also influential business journals with the editorial stance of proclaiming that 'entrepreneurship is the key driver to economic prosperity' (Qin, 2015). In the global explosion of the dotcom bubble, Internet companies pioneered China's business world. The IT specialist media articulated strong messages about conducting commerce in the digital age. *China Info World* (*zhongguo jisuanji shijie*), *Global Entrepreneur*[3] (*huanqiu qiyejia*) and *CEOCIO China* (*IT jingli shijie*) were set up to educate a new Chief Information Officer class in China's corporate world.

The establishment of two national stock exchanges inspired the emergence of a variety of financial media in reporting capital markets. *China Securities Daily*, *Shanghai Securities News*, and *Securities Times*,[4] known as the 'Three Big Papers' (*sandabao*), were founded with party-backed authority to provide information on the stock markets (Ma, 2003). Additionally, *Capital Week* was a privately owned magazine but with direct personal connections with Beijing. Its parent company, Stock Exchange Executive Council (known as SEEC or *lianban*) was founded by Wang Boming and Gao Xiqing, who were early overseas returnees from Chinese elite families[5] (Zhang *et al.*, 2011). These four media organizations together created a new discourse focusing on discussing China's capital markets. In 1998, originally as the monthly supplementary of *Capital Week*, the founding of *Caijing* magazine signalled a new era for 'muckraking' coverage of listed companies.

Phase Three: convergence

The market, government policies and financial media have all evolved dramatically in the third phase. In 2000, the government implemented the 'Go Global' (*zouchuqu*) policies, providing national endorsement for Chinese companies' being globally competitive and recognized. In 2001, China officially became a member of the World Trade Organization. Since then, the volume of output and trade experienced substantial increase; the number of firms being listed on foreign exchanges (IPO) tripled and dominated the overall foreign IPOs (Initial Public Offerings) in global securities markets, and SOEs took leading role in cross-border mergers and acquisitions and bidding for global brands.

Some of the earlier forms of financial media faded away. Many remaining business media evolved to be one of the most elite and professional forms of journalism in

TABLE 14.2 China's financial media groups and media convergence (2002–2008)

	CBN Shanghai Media Group	21st Century Nanfang Daily Media Group	SEEC SEEC Media Group
Newspapers	China Business News	21st Century Economic Herald, 21st Century Global Report (shut down)	
Periodicals	CBN Weekly	21st Century Business Review, Global Entrepreneur, Money Week, Fast Company	Caijing, Capital Week, Properties, Time Out (Beijing, Shanghai editions), La Revue du Vin de France, Sports Illustrated, Better Homes, Harvard Business Review Chinese …
Websites	China-cbn.com	21st Century website (shut down), 21st Century Finance Search online service	Finance Net (caijing wang), Harvard Business Review Chinese online
TV/video	CBN Finance (including three cable channels)		
Market index	Dow Jones China Total Market Index		
Others	Think tank: CBN Research		Series of high profile annual conferences on subjects of economics and finance

China. They had shifted from centrally funded to privately owned, and research institutes dominated, from Beijing to the economically developed south, from information dissemination to in-depth investigation, and from sensational reformist rhetoric to rational discussion of the economic agenda and infotainment for the less financially literate lay audience (Developmental strategies of China's financial media, 2007). In line with global trends, media convergence is the most influential changing characteristic. Through the processes of collaborating between diverse media forms (Erdal, 2011), and the early forms of digitalization (Chon *et al.*, 2003), the convergence categorizes the landscape of China's financial media into three major groups: CBN (China Business Network) group (*yicai xi*) based in Shanghai, 21st Century group (*21 shiji xi*) based in Guangdong, and SEEC group (*lianban xi*) based in Beijing (see Table 14.2).

Born from CBN,[6] *China Business News* soon became the most circulated daily business newspaper for timely and engaging reporting, embedded in the global context. CBN also had a professional-quality broadcast service covering major cities through the cable TV *CBN Finance*, the first Chinese media publishing the

Dow Jones China Total Market Index which includes the performance of China's capital markets. The *21ˢᵗ Century Economic* (or *Business*) *Herald*[7] was founded in 2001, by the same media company, Nanfang Daily Press, as *Southern Weekend*, which was one of the earliest outspoken liberal media in China. *Southern Weekend*'s section of 'New Economy' in the 1990s laid a foundation for the newspaper, as they share the same editorial values of being opinion-shaping in economic policies and concerns about the social impact of economic developments among Chinese elites. 21st Century Media owns a variety of newspapers and magazines providing business analysis. *Global Entrepreneur* is a representative case of Chinese financial media in promoting the internationalization of Chinese companies. In 2000, under the management of SEEC Media Group Limited (*caixun chuanmei*), *Caijing* was separated from *Capital Week*. Through a series of taboo-breaking coverage of corporate wrongdoings and capital market scandals, *Caijing* has been pioneering critical and investigative reporting on capital markets. In a broader sense, it sets a unique example of journalistic professionalism with global perspective in a Chinese context (Piao, 2015). SEEC not only owns the most influential and profitable financial media including *Caijing*, *Capital Week* and *Properties*, it also has copyright cooperation with global media brands, such as *Time Out* (UK).

Phase Four: digitalization and capitalization

In the fourth phase, financial media are deepening the digitalization in media convergence and catching up with the new trend of digital media startups that global venture capital is flowing into. Since the Split Share Reform in 2005, China's stock markets have exploded, with the Shanghai Composite Index reaching the high point of 6,124. The bull market created new dynamics, further expanding traditional financial media like the 'Three Big Papers'; and more importantly, enabled the emergence of online financial websites for individual investors on a massive scale (Qin, 2015). These websites include not only the finance segments from well-established portal sites (e.g. Sina, Sohu, Tencent, etc.), but also the specialized platforms offering professional services for investment and personal finance (e.g. Hexun, Stockstar and JRJ), and financial data vendors based on the concept of Internet Plus financial service (e.g. Wind.com, Easymoney and Great Wisdom). The digital media platforms rapidly grew to be the main channel for obtaining financial information and consuming data analysis, playing an active role in the development of domestic capital markets. The Internet also provides an alternative route for foreign financial media to enter the Chinese market. A significant example is *Financial Times Chinese*, with 2.3 million subscribers by 2015 (ibid.). The Chinese versions of *Forbes*, *Wall Street Journal*, *Nikkei* and *Reuters* have all attracted different readership groups online.

Besides the explosive emergence of digital media, veteran journalists and editors have started their own private media ventures (Table 14.3). The landmark is the resignation of Hu Shuli with the majority of her editorial team from *Caijing* in 2009. Consequently, Hu started Caixin Media,[8] including the relaunched magazine *New Century Weekly*. The chief editor of *China Entrepreneur*, Niu Wenwen, also resigned

TABLE 14.3 Veteran financial media professionals turning into private media ventures

Veteran practitioners	Time	Original position in traditional media forms	New startup project
Hu Shuli	2009	Chief editor in *Caijing*	Caixin Media
Niu Wenwen	2008	Chief editor in *China Entrepreneur*	*Entreprendre magazine*
Wang Lifen	2011	Anchor and producer in CCTV	Youmi.com
Liu Donghua	2011	Proprietor in *China Entrepreneur*	Zhisland.com
Wu Xiaobo	2014	Financial writer, and founder of Blue Lion Publishing	'Wu Xiaobo Channel' in WeChat, Youtube, iQiyi
Qin Suo	2015	Chief editor in *China Business News*	'Chin@Moments' in WeChat

and founded *Entreprendre* – the name refers to entrepreneurs and venture capitalists. *Entreprendre* attempted to build up a shared identity among Chinese business leaders who are innovative and have a forward-thinking business mentality. The skyrocketing growth of the microblog (Weibo) and the launch of WeChat[9] have transformed the careers of veteran financial editors from traditional to digital media platforms. In the surge of 'Internet Plus' startups, financial media practitioners can be at the cutting edge with their professional knowledge and resources in both domains of business and news production. As a producer of many influential economic programmes on CCTV, Wang Lifen left the preeminent state broadcaster in 2011 to found Youmi. com – a video website providing subscribed online courses to emerging startups. Most recently, Qin Suo also quit *China Business News*, and kick-started his own official account 'Chin@Moments' in WeChat (Fang and Xu, 2015).

Professionalism of financial media: Chinese and Anglo-American contexts

This section explores how journalistic professionalism is redefined for financial media, particularly in relation to the circumstances in which the production of economic discourse takes place. Hallin and Mancini's (2004) three interrelated dimensions are relevant in analysing the degree of professionalism: *autonomy*, based on 'esoteric' knowledge; *professional norms*, including ethical principles and standards of 'newsworthiness'; and *public service orientation*. The measurement will take account of the deviation of China's socio-political settings from Anglo-America's capitalist democracy, and the core nature of financial media as a special subgenre.

(i) The blurry 'red line'

Because of media censorship, China's liberal media run great political risks in reporting controversial stories. However, the financial media have mostly survived control from the CCP's (Chinese Communist Party) propaganda department (Hu, 2011) partly because of the general lack of professional knowledge of economics and finance among government officials in media regulatory bodies. Before 1989, economic deregulation and privatization were at the top of the political agenda, so that the initial forms of a financial press were closely supported by government to communicate its economic policies and advocate reform. For example, the State Council founded the *Economic Daily*; Ding Wang, who used to work at the *Economic Daily*, then established *China Business Times*; and the Three Big Papers were officially sponsored securities dailies. Though their journalistic practices were constrained by the political regime (some were shut down after 1989), it was a time when the media agenda on free market advocacy coincided with the political agenda of market reform. Even after the Tiananmen Square crackdown in 1989, financial media managed to stay relatively propaganda-free, because of public ignorance of market principles.

There are also other factors that help to create a broad grey area in which financial media can keep pushing the 'red line'. Compared with financial media's thousands of copies circulation, the propaganda department is keen to maintain closer watch over television and mass-market newspapers that reach millions, even though financial media cater for a readership that includes the most influential decision makers in government, companies, and academia (Osnos, 2009). On the other hand, support from reform-minded party officials has been a minimal factor in financial media's effective functioning in investigative reporting. For example, the founder of SEEC Wang Boming is a scion of the former deputy foreign minister. The magazine is also said to be backed by Wang Qishan, who was the son-in-law of a vice-premier, and Zhou Xiaochuan, who was then the governor of China's central bank. Since capital markets emerged, the China Securities Regulatory Commission (CSRC) allows financial media to publish negative stories of securities market failures, in pursuit of transparency of the market (Hu, 2011: 79). Though CSRC does not have the same regulating authority as the propaganda department, it sees a close connection between financial media and market stability.[10] Another notable factor is that sometimes, in order to protect editorial integrity, the news content could deliberately stay away from political discussion, such as the 'talking only business' policy that entirely lacked political content in *China Business Times*, and the 'only stocks' policy that limits the reporting to nonpolitical news on capital markets in the Three Big Papers (ibid.: 82).

(ii) Market parallelism

'Market parallelism' is coined and modified from the concept of political parallelism, which means the media is tied to certain organizational or political groups (Piao, 2015). A higher degree of political parallelism implies lower journalistic professionalism in the Anglo-American context (Hallin and Mancini, 2004). Market parallelism says that journalistic practices should be considered as an integral part of market activities. If the media agenda were more closely related with the economic agenda, the financial media could be more professional. Market parallelism obliges media practitioners not only to grasp sound professional knowledge in economics and finance, but also to arguably play a 'watchdog' role, because of their closer relationship with the commercial world than other media genres. Therefore, the media–market relationship is at the core of accessing market parallelism, encompassing a range of issues in defining professional norms of financial media. The Chinese market manifests mixed characteristics of neoliberalism and contesting ideologies inside the Communist Party. China's financial media have played a much more complex role under an authoritarian regime for over three decades of marketization. Tentatively, China's market economy is not able to sustain the full capacity to integrate media as one driving market force in its overall development.

As financial media inhabit a highly unregulated business world, editorial integrity could be inherently influenced by business and politics. Sometimes, China's financial journalists collude with securities analysts or corporate officials. Along with stock markets expansion, analysts and economists become media celebrities to internally manipulate market movements. 'Blackmail celebrity' (*hei zui*, literally meaning black mouth) constantly shows up on local televisions to feed a speculative public with investment advice and to hype shares, in order to share illegal earnings with security companies (Shi, 2014: 40). The credibility of business reporting is also undermined by rent-seeking activities, through the journalistic practice of asking companies to purchase paid news for favourable coverage or paid salience for avoiding negative publicity (Hassid, 2015). In 2011, CCTV-2 uncovered the fact that an Italian company, DaVinci Furniture, had deceived Chinese consumers with the origins of its high-end products. Hu Shuli's *New Century Weekly* has been the first media outlet to challenge the monopolistic broadcasting programme, revealing the fact that the media fabricated false reports and extorted money from the company. In 2014, the 21st Century Media website was shut down and the prominent *21st Century Business Herald* was suspended, because they were blackmailing listed companies and companies planning to go for IPO, marking a new era of tighter scrutiny of financial media.

Such corrupt phenomena reflect that Chinese financial media demonstrate a slower pace of development, compared with the market reform. These mismatched developmental processes result in financial media's involvement in fierce competition not just with the journalistic peers, but also and more importantly, with financial institutions and PR sectors in companies, as they offer much higher earnings (Hassid, 2015). The income discrepancy is considered as a key reason for media extortion. A more fundamental reason is the separation of the management and editorial teams. *Newsweek, Fortune* and *Wall Street Journal* all adopt such a code of conduct. However, in China, *Caijing* magazine under SEEC and Hu Shuli's Caixin media are perhaps the only financial media that set editorial staff free from trading news content for profit. As financial media are a decisive parameter for the functioning of economic activities, the core issue of the media–market relationship is the power play over the economic discourse. On the one hand, the financial media play the watchdog role in monitoring the market and shaping the economic agenda.

On the other hand, the market economy needs the media platform for disseminating information, boosting businesses, and forming a favourable economic culture. China still lacks proper law enforcement to deal with the few people on each side who collude and share the economic 'rent' from corrupt activities. Additionally, media censorship and the authoritarian regime add more complexity to the context of culture, economics and politics.

(iii) In sync with economic policy making

The elite communication position of financial media is a 'crucial intersection between the world of finance and world of government' (Palmer, 1970: 98). As China's financial media rise with the wave of market reform, economists and politicians have made the foray into media to publicize their ideas and debates. However, the phenomenon is not primarily because of the changing relationship between financial media and government but because of the changing context of financial news itself. According to Yu Guoming, rich political resources ensure financial media's profound impact on large-scale social transformations. Deng Xiaoping's southern trip in 1992 left a permanent mark on China's financial media. In the subsequent years, they have pioneered the industry as the most forthright media, with a news agenda that integrates the internal agenda of economists and external agenda of political debates. In this golden era, China's financial media play the same role as Western counterparts that serve as a focus for political debate and commercial discussion. In this transition, the economic discourse gives business a language and legitimacy which China had hitherto lacked.

Notwithstanding China's non-democratic political structure, economic prosperity has been the top priority for political legitimacy. Thus, China's financial media imbue the values of free market and free trade with the same sort of coherency and intellectual respectability that are embedded in the Chinese context and provided for the legitimacy of the CCP. One unprecedented case is the sharply worded joint editorial by the *Economic Observer* and twelve regional newspapers, calling on China's legislature to abolish the system of household residential permits (*hukou*). Despite its dissemination being banned, it generated wide discussion and soon the government proposed partial reform of the *hukou* system, though not its abolition as demanded by the editorial (Shirk, 2011).

A more recent example is how the media generated the discussion that led to the complete abolition of the over three-decade long one-child policy. Since 2012, as an Internet entrepreneur and economist specializing in demographic economics, Liang Jianzhang (also known as James Liang) started a debate by highlighting the potential danger of China's one-child policy in the *Wall Street Journal* (English and Chinese editions) and Caixin Media, where he co-authors a column with Huang Wenzheng, a statistician and economics graduate from Johns Hopkins University. Based on economic rationale and statistical accuracy, they argued that the sharply decreasing workforce would unseat China's competitive advantage as a global manufacturer, along with other potential social and political dangers. The heated debates have gradually transformed the public's perception and influenced the government in making the decision to end the outdated policy.

However, also because of the non-transparent political regime and market system, sometimes the media become a negative factor in economic agenda making. Chen Zhiwu, a renowned liberal-minded economist and professor of finance at Yale University, warns that in China the policy cycle has been subject to the news cycle (Chen, 2012). Because of the pressure from 'economists' in the media, the government released a four trillion RMB fiscal stimulus package hoping to stabilize growth and calm investors in 2008. Two years later, a bubble in the real estate industry emerged and forced the policy to change drastically. Chen claimed that the so-called experts as media celebrities were to be blamed, because of their prominent position in manipulating public discussion of economic policies (ibid.: 38). The sentimental economic language that lacks solid knowledge in economics is an inseparable part of state intervention and should be eliminated.

Representing China's economy to a global audience

Economic globalization is a complex and multi-faceted 'big' phenomenon, with economic, political and cultural aspects (Fairclough, 2006). Before discussing how financial media represent Chinese economic globalization, it is necessary to separate the actual economic situation from the media's representation of economic reality and how media draw upon certain discourses rather than others (ibid.). Based on the previous discussion, it is evident that China's financial media play an educational role in formulating a new economic language and business culture. However, the economic agenda that evolved in the new century was very different to that which had emerged in the 1980s in one crucial respect: economic liberalization has shifted from focusing on domestic prosperity to global expansion. In a neoliberal framework, the intellectual context of the policy agenda and of economics as news has also been in the process of transformation. However, this section will argue that the economic discourse, which was shaped for the early stage of capitalist development, has not evolved fast enough to match the new agenda of the economy going global.

According to the founder of *Entreprendre*, Niu Wenwen, how the Chinese media portray China's business community and economic culture differs from the way it is portrayed by leading international financial media such as the *Financial Times* and the *Wall Street Journal* (Niu, 2007). The discourse being too inward-looking is suggested as the main reason for the difference between Chinese and global economic discourses of China's economic globalization. In the Chinese context, big state-owned enterprises (*yang qi*) that spend billions of dollars on overseas investments are represented as monopolistic and unethical. On the contrary, in Western media they are called 'emerging market multinational companies', with positive connotations for global business communities. Private enterprises (*min qi*) are usually seen as being rich but less educated in the Chinese media, whereas most of the Western financial media regard private enterprise as the private sector as opposed to state institutions. Another example is the unique expression of *gu min* (literally it means 'ordinary people in stock market') in China's financial media. *Gu min* are often presented in the context of being powerless grassroots and easily deceived. Outside the Chinese narrative, *gu min* are referred to as individual investors, as distinguished from institutional investors. This 'introverted' discourse indicates that the Chinese media agenda is not yet in tune with the global norms of the neoliberal business discourse.

The differences of economic discourses in Chinese and global contexts may be of greater significance for financial media specializing in reporting corporates, securities and industries. However, it is less evident in the narrower circle of elite communication. Primarily, elite financial media are themselves part of the political and economic intellectual circle in agenda-setting. Their political resources allow greater government tolerance of taboo-breaking coverage that could include radical new economic ideas and political rhetoric, further blurring the 'red line'.

Piao (2015) interviewed some foreign correspondents from *Forbes* and *The Economist* specializing in reporting China. Most of them claim that besides reaching for original sources the only Chinese media they may refer to are *Caijing* and the new *Caixin* by Hu Shuli, so as to better understand the background and context of the news and its implications. Nevertheless, while China's financial media have yet to collectively formulate a new influential economic discourse for a global audience, it is undeniable that the leading financial media such as *Caijing* share similar narrative structures with the most globally oriented media such as *The Economist* (ibid.). The economic discourse with a slant on the neoliberal editorial stance features a crucial characteristic that the value and belief in the free market and minimal state intervention are 'morally superior' (Peters, 2001: 19), even compared to the advocacy of political liberalization. To construct such neoliberal discourse, there are two important prerequisites: (i) a high degree of market parallelism that reveals the nature of financial media being an integral part of market; (ii) privileged access to political resources that could shield the media from the wrath of the censors.

In the trajectory of two intertwined sets of development of media and market, the achievements of China's financial media can be divided into two distinct phases. When market liberalization was the top priority in the economic and political agenda, the media played a successful role in *educating* the ignorant public with market principles, and *winning converts* by propagating ideas of the free market and free trade. However, when the Chinese economy was beginning to internationalize and impact across the globe, China's financial media were in the process of *synthesizing* economic and political agendas with media agenda, and *disseminating* the commercial information and neoliberal economic reasoning to cater for heterogeneous audiences. Even though financial media have undergone the convergence, digitalization and capitalization which are all part of the globalization of the media industry, they have yet to commit to construct a new economic discourse that could demonstrate global appeal to audiences outside Chinese communities. One crucial reason for shifting from the pioneering to the fallback position of economic globalization is that the media agenda has been transforming the focus from the formation of business language to organizational restructuring.

What is worth noting is an underlying trend behind the media's changing focus – it is the same group of professional elite journalists moving from well-established traditional media to digital platforms (see Table 14.3), from shaping public opinions to searching for a more stratified audience. There are some key figures in this intellectual circle: for instance, Hu Shuli, who originally worked at *China Business Times* and had been the chief editor at *Caijing,* started her own media venture Caixin Media in 2009. Wu Xiaobo is a celebrity columnist and writer of many books promoting stories of Chinese markets and companies, and the founder of a publishing company specializing in business and financial stories. He launched his personal brand 'Wu Xiaobo Channel' on WeChat, YouTube and iQiyi, a Chinese video website. As founder and chief editor of *China Business News* for a decade, Qin Suo also set up a personal account 'Chin@Moments' on WeChat to publicize tailor-made content on current market events. In a recent and heatedly discussed article with over 100,000 views on WeChat, Wu Xiaobo pointed out that mainstream financial media have lost the dominance of the economic discourse in investigating, representing and making sense of ongoing events (Wu, 2015). He concludes that there is a 'collective disappearance' of investigative journalists with experience and expertise from mainstream media, resulting in the 'hollowness' of professionalism in financial media.

Conclusion

This exploratory study has centred around two key questions: (1) what role the financial media play in China's economic transformation and globalization; (2) how and to what extent the economic discourse reflects and/or affects the economic reality within and outside the national boundaries. At an early stage of market decentralization and privatization (1978–2001), the media played a key role in conveying and rationalizing economic policy making, educating an ignorant public with market fundamentals, and articulating free market ideas as a new economic culture in a language that secured a sound understanding by Chinese audiences. As economic globalization deepened (2002–2015), the developmental path of financial media shifted to a vertical dimension that they shed more light on converging different media platforms, and digitalizing the content so as to reach more stratified audiences.

Through recontextualizing the concept of journalistic professionalism in Chinese institutional settings, there are three interrelated dimensions in which to evaluate the professionalization of financial media. The blurry 'red line' indicates a considerable grey area that survives censorship, because of the lack of specialist knowledge in economics and finance in propaganda departments, and muted support from reform-minded government officials. 'Market parallelism' of financial media is argued as being relatively low, because on the one hand, the incomplete market economy cannot sustain the full capacity to integrate media as a driving force in economic development. On the other hand, some journalistic practices are attuned to media extortion through either colluding with 'expert' sources or bullying corporates. As a decisive parameter in economic activities, China's financial media also play a similar role as their Western counterparts in formulating a political economy discourse, serving as a focus for political debates, but for the primary purpose of political legitimation.

It is evident, based on these dimensions, that there was a discrepancy of trends between economic and media development, when the economic agenda shifted from domestic prosperity to global expansion. Before 2000 was the golden era for China's financial media being not only the pioneering force in challenging conservative ideology, but also the key driver in forming and promoting a business mentality for China's emerging financial class. With the Chinese economy being more globally integrated, financial media have yet to construct a new economic discourse that could match the internationalizing commercial dynamic, and demonstrate a global appeal to audiences outside Chinese communities.

According to Bagehot (Parsons, 1990), the production incentive of financial media features a causality of business cycle and 'idea cycle'. When the economic situation plummets, media's incentive for advocating more abstract economic ideas increases; when the economy prospers, media tend to cover more commercial stories in a factual, statistical approach. The theory pertains to the trend discrepancy of China's financial media. When China's economy was prospering within the domestic landscape, free market advocacy and liberal political rhetoric dominated the media discourse. When the domestic market was gradually exposed in the neoliberal framework, the opinion-shaping function was replaced with the organizational restructuring towards more stratified ways of information dissemination, to tailor to the diverse needs of audiences.

However, it is too early to conclude that the media fail to perform the role of being an influential factor in China's capitalist expansion, because in comparison to Anglo-American history, China has experienced much concentrated capitalist development over merely three decades. There are exceptional cases, such as *New Century Weekly* or its former version *Caijing*, that have the prerequisites for both maintaining a high degree of market parallelism and privileged access to economic and political resources. In the political-economic context of China, such a high level of professionalism cannot be easily achieved. Or, to put it another way, China's financial media are still in the learning process of establishing a proper 'model' or 'consensus', in order to gain the hegemonic power of economic discourse in reflecting, representing and propagating Chinese economic culture. Such power of economic discourse is a crucial intersection between hard power (referring to the economic and political powers), and soft power (referring to how the outside world understands China's internationalizing business and global economic policies). Will China's economic discourse become more globally oriented? Will China's financial media have a greater impact on the economy's global integration? And what do the journalistic professionals need to do in order to facilitate the reconstructing of a more globalized, or neoliberal discourse? These questions remain for further research.

Notes

1 The founder Ding Wang used to be the deputy editor-in-chief of the *Economic Daily*, when the Moganshan Conference was organized. The paper was shut down because of it showing sympathy to Hu Yaobang and anti-corruption rhetoric, amidst the political turmoil of the Tiananmen Square incident in 1989. It is said that the closure closely related to Jiang Zemin.
2 At the time the editorial board of *Liberation Daily* in charge of covering Deng's southern trip was led by Zhu Rongji, who then became the prime minister sparking off the national level SOE reform.
3 The chief editors, Li Rong and Yang Fu, came from the 'New Economy' section the *Southern Weekend* founded in 1999.
4 The Chinese titles of *China Securities Daily, Shanghai Securities News*, and *Securities Times* are correspondingly *Zhongguo zhengquan shibao [*中国证券报*]*, *Shanghai Zhengquan shibao [*上海证券报*]*, and *Zhengquan shibao [*证券时报*]*.
5 Wang Boming was born and grew up in a elite family. His father had served PRC as deputy minister of foreign affairs until 1975. Together with Gao Xiqing, whom he met in Wall Street during his study abroad, they first drafted the proposal to establish capital markets in China. Since coming back to China in the late 1980s, they helped to develop the Shanghai and then Shenzhen Stock Exchanges (Zhang *et al.*, 2011). SEEC has gained direct support from Wang Qishan who is now the member of the seven-man Politburo Standing Committee at central government in charge of the massive anti-corruption campaign, and Zhu Rongji who was the sharp reform-oriented premier during 1998 to 2003 (Yuan, 2013). Such personal connection with Beijing gives SEEC's publications considerable leeway for uncovering sensitive news that should be controlled by media censorship.
6 The name CBN was initially unified with the merger of *Shanghai TV Finance Channel* and *Oriental Broadcasting* in *Finance*. In Chinese it literally means 'the number one finance and economic daily'.
7 The Chinese name literally meaning '21st century economic report' (*21 shiji jingji baodao*), rather than 'herald'. And the title of another paper is translated as economic herald but originally is *21st Century Economic Insights*. There are ambiguities in English-Chinese translation in the titles.
8 Caixin Media includes not only the *New Century Weekly*, but also *China Reform, Comparative Studies*, online website, TV/video programs in partnership with SMG, and a think tank *China Institute for Reform and Development*.
9 WeChat (*weixin*) is a mobile text and voice messaging communication serive by Tencent. After releasing in 2011, it soon became the largest messaging app in China. It provides services such as instant messaging, public accounts for citizen journalists or other types of media practitioners to deliver contents, moments as social networks for text, image and music, and payment/money transfer.
10 According to Hu (2011: 80), CSRC uses a system called designated information disclosure (*zhiding xinxi pilu*), to control media coverage of the securities sector.

References

Chen, Z. (2012) Hold the Hand of Government [把握住政府之手]. In: S. Hu (ed.) *China and the World: Strategizing Sustainable Growth [*寻找真实的成长：中国*2012]*, Nanjing: Jiangsu wen yi chu ban she.
Cheng, L. and White, L. (1991) China's technocratic movement and the World Economic Herald. *Modern China*, 17(3):342–388.
Chon, B.; Choi, J.; Barnett, G.; Danowski, J. and Joo, S. (2003) A structural analysis of media convergence: cross-industry mergers and acquisitions in the information industries. *Journal of Media Economics*, 16(3):141–157.

Davis, A. (2006) Media effects and the question of the rational audience: lessons from the financial markets. *Media, Culture & Society*, 28(4): 603–625.

Developmental strategies of China's financial media [中国财媒发展大战略论坛实录 (2007). In: *China Financial Media Summit*. [online] Beijing: Sina Finance. Available at: http://finance.sina.com.cn/hy/20070425/17023540787.shtml [Accessed 4 May 2014].

Erdal, I. (2011) Coming to terms with convergence journalism: cross-media as a theoretical and analytical concept. *Convergence: The International Journal of Research into New Media Technologies*, 17(2): 213–223.

Fairclough, N. (2006) *Language and Globalization*. London: Routledge.

Fang, Z. and Xu, W. (2015) *The last 'watchdog' turns to startup: Qin Suo's new 'Moments'*. [online] Tencent Finance. Available at: http://finance.qq.com/original/zibenlun/qscy.html [Accessed 19 November 2015].

Fewsmith, J. (1994) *Dilemmas of Reform in China*. Armonk, NY: M.E. Sharpe.

Greenfield, C. and Williams, P. (2007) Financialization, finance rationality and the role of media in Australia. *Media, Culture & Society*, 29(3): 415–433.

Gussow, D. (1984) *The New Business Journalism: An Insider's Look at the Workings of American's Business Press*. New York: Harcourt Brace Jovanovich.

Hallin, D. and Mancini, P. (2004) *Comparing Media Systems*. Cambridge: Cambridge University Press.

Hassid, J. (2015) *China's Unruly Journalists: How Committed Professionals are Changing the People's Republic*. New York: Routledge.

Hu, S. (2011) The Rise of the Business Media in China. In: S. Shirk (ed.) *Changing Media, Changing China*. New York: Oxford University Press.

Huenemann, R. (2013) Economic Reforms, 1978–Present. In: W. Timothy (ed.) *Oxford Bibliographies: Chinese Studies*, New York: Oxford University Press.

Liu, H. (2014) Thirty anniversaries of Moganshan Conference: a phenomenal event in economic academia. *The Economic Observer*. [online] Available at: http://finance.sina.com.cn/china/20140904/112220211868.shtml [Accessed 2 December 2015].

Ma, Q. (2003) *History of Chinese Securities Market: 1978–1998*. Beijing: China Citic Press.

Niu, W. (2007) In making Chinese media's global power of discourse [打造中国媒体的国际话语权]. In: *China Financial Media Summit*. [online] Beijing: Sina Finance. Available at: http://finance.sina.com.cn/hy/20070425/14463540192.shtml [Accessed 4 July 2015].

Osnos, E. (2009). The forbidden zone: how far can a provocative editor go? *The New Yorker*. [online] Available at: www.newyorker.com/magazine/2009/07/20/the-forbidden-zone [Accessed 12 November 2014].

Palmer, J. (1970) The Harlot's Prerogative. In: R. Boston (ed.) *The Press We Deserve*, London: Routledge and Kegan Paul.

Parker, R. (1997) The public, the press, and economic news. *Harvard International Journal of Press/Politics*, 2(2): 127–131.

Parsons, D. (1990) *The Power of the Financial Press*. New Brunswick, NJ: Rutgers University Press.

Peters, M. (2001) *Poststructuralism, Marxism, and Neoliberalism*. Lanham, MD: Rowman & Littlefield.

Piao, J. (2015) *Financial Media, Globalisation, and China's Economic Integration–Comparing Narrative Construction of* The Economist *and* Caijing. PhD. University of Westminster, London.

Qian, G. and Bandurski, D. (2011) China's Emerging Public Sphere. In: S. Shirk (ed.) *Changing Media, Changing China*, New York: Oxford University Press.

Qin, S. (2015) Review and revelation of China's financial media in the new era. *China Business News*.

Schuster, T. (2006) *The Markets and the Media*. Lanham, MD: Lexington Books.

Shi, Y. (2014) *Zhongguo cai jing mei ti chuan bo shi ling xian xiang yan jiu* =. Beijing: Zhongguo she hui ke xue chu ban she.

Shirk, S. (ed.) (2011) *Changing Media, Changing China*. New York: Oxford University Press.

Sigley, G. (2006) Chinese governmentalities: government, governance and the socialist market economy. *Economy and Society*, 35(4): 487–508.

Wong, J. and Zheng, Y. (2001) *The Nanxun Legacy and China's Development in the Post-Deng Era*. Singapore: Singapore University Press.

Wu, X. (2015). The expendables still exist, special forces vanish [敢死队犹在，特种兵已死]. [Blog] Channel Wu. Available at: https://mp.weixin.qq.com/s?__biz=MzA3OTM5 NTkxNA==&mid=401890239&idx=1&sn=0c74fd3d2096ae8de8da2f2afc9623cd#rd [Accessed 30 Dec. 2014]

Yuan, Z. (2013) Evolving history of China's financial media. [Blog] Available at: www. guancha.cn/YuanZuoGong/2013_12_27_194642.shtml [Accessed 12 October 2015].

Zhang, W.; Wang, H. and Alon, I. (2011) *Entrepreneurial and Business Elites of China*. Bingley: Emerald Group.

15

THE THREE PATTERNS OF CHINESE INTERNATIONAL COMMUNICATION

Qing'an Zhou and Yanni Wu

After the 2008 Beijing Olympic Games, Chinese mainstream media started a new round of capacity building for international communication. From the perspective of public diplomacy, recent years have witnessed a growing interest by Chinese media in nation branding and international communication activities with increasingly diversified approaches and significant achievements. For Chinese mainstream media, the strengthening of international communication capacity also reflects an increasing professionalism. It is worth noting, however, that the approach adopted by Chinese media in this area is different from those of their counterparts in other countries.

This chapter aims to study the international communication patterns of Chinese media. Six media organizations were selected, including Xinhua news agency, *People's Daily*, CCTV, China Radio International (CRI), *China Daily* and Chinese News Service. They represent the major force of Chinese international communication capacity building, and have launched massive projects to achieve that goal since 2009. This is also one of the national strategies set out after the 2008 Olympic Games. China's growth to become the second largest economy in the world has profoundly affected the process, with growing investment in this area. However, research on Chinese mainstream media has shown that the way in which they participate in international communication differs from those of other countries. The roles that traditional media and new media respectively play in international communication are also different. This chapter aims to analyse China's international communication strategy and approaches through reviewing these patterns.

The development of China's communication capability

The concept of international communication in the Chinese political context has three patterns, including 'to explain the world to China', 'to explain China to the world' and 'to explain the world to the world'. For Chinese media, the difficulty of the three patterns increases progressively, representing different perceptions and phases of China's modernization. The nature of China's international communication is closely related to its modernization process and is significantly affected by it. The process began with the establishment of the consciousness of being a nation, followed by the consciousness of being a sovereign state and finally being a participant in the system of global governance. Chinese society also went through a parallel process in relation to international communication. On one hand, international communication is regarded as a way in which China can learn from the developed world's experiences, while the media is regarded as a communication channel to maintain social norms. On the other hand, international communication is also an important way to express China's own identity, in how it presents China's mode of development to gain the respect of the world. This is equally important to the Chinese public, even the officials, who are influenced by the emotion of nationalism. Within the three phases of the Chinese international communication and modernization process, several patterns can be detected.

The first phase is 'international news reporting' in which, for quite a long time, the main task for Chinese mainstream media was to explain the world to China. This phase can be described as containing the 'national pattern' of international communication, given that the priority for international news reporting in traditional media is actually to explain the world. Through purchasing news or dispatching correspondents, significant international news and politics of other countries are reported as an indication of China's modernization. The Chinese public, meanwhile, has also developed an international outlook, with a growing demand for international news. Even in the era of new digital media, Weibo and WeChat are filled with energetic independent freelancers, whose job is to translate news articles written in various foreign languages. This situation is not unique to traditional mainstream media. Commercial media that emerged in the 1990s and social media that took off in the twenty-first century also shared it. The integration of commercial media into the international communication system is based on satisfying the needs of the audience for international news. For instance, after successfully founding the '21st Century Business Herald', the 21st Century media group marched into entertainment and international news, publishing the '21st Century Global Herald', at a time when the two active newspapers with large circulation are *Reference News* and *Global Times*, whose speciality is international news reporting.

The second phase is to present China's development to the world through establishing its own voice in multiple foreign languages. In the Chinese political context, this phase is to 'explain China to the world', which can be described as containing the 'sovereign state pattern' of international communication. This pattern emerged with the state's foundation in 1949 when it had begun to engage in international communication activities and needed a narrative that countered the misunderstandings and prejudices of Western media, which was effected by establishing two forms of media channel. On the one hand, multi-language platforms for international news were established, such as the home news for the overseas service department of the Xinhua news agency, the overseas page of the *People's Daily*, and *China Daily*, founded in the 1980s. On the other, several specialized media for international news were established whose major business was to explain changes in China to the world, such as the *Beijing Review*, which is affiliated with the China International Publishing Group, along with *China Today*, *ChinAfrica*, etc. China also established a nine-language website, China.org.cn, as an important platform for international communication.

However, this pattern is rarely seen in Chinese domestic media, whose audience is more localized, thus giving them no incentive to invest in overseas news in a competitive free market. Therefore, so far there have been only two commercial local media engaged in international news reporting, *Shanghai Weekly* and *Shenzhen Weekly*. Despite this, the willingness to have cross-national cooperation in commercial media is increasing. More and more reporters with these media are applying for overseas study or obtaining degrees from European and American schools of journalism and communication before they enter the industry.

The emergence of the 'sovereign state pattern' marks the starting point of China's willingness to build international communication capacity as a sovereign state. This phase has gradually transformed Chinese international communication from passive delivery of world news into an active news reporting process, with more self-confidence. With the combination of sovereign-state consciousness and the government's powerful lead, this phase has long been called 'external publicity' in China's historical narrative. The creation and development of the sovereign-state pattern is also closely related to the nation's ambition of being accepted by international society. The most evident case happened in 2008, after the 14 March turmoil in Tibet, when China was facing harsh criticism from the West and challenges during the Olympic torch relay. At the same time, the 12 May Wenchuan earthquake was considered an opportunity for China to project its voice and broadcast its efforts to international society. The Beijing Olympic Games that followed shortly afterwards gave China a wealth of opportunities to brand its national image.

The third phase is a status that Chinese media is hoping to achieve, which is 'to explain the world to the world'. This phase can be described as containing the 'global pattern' of international communication. With the massive capacity-building projects of international communication launched in 2009, Chinese media have gradually realized that introducing China to the external world needs to be more than a one-way communication with limited effects. In contrast, the development of other international mainstream media has not been through participation in the global dialogue only as state media, but as independent media whose focus is mainly on their own independence and domain. Therefore, most Chinese scholars argue that real international mainstream media should be capable of delivering a variety of international news to different countries, instead of delivering only its own news.

This phase features the development of better conditions for its own news reporting, based on massive overseas investment and hardware construction. Chinese media are also paying more attention to agenda-setting and have realized that 'explaining the world to the world' would actually enhance the media's accountability and agenda-setting capacity. Meanwhile, the development of this phase is also linked to the rise of professionalism. The role of Chinese media has been transformed from an instrument simply for public relations to increasingly globalized professional institutions. In international communication, particularly, the freedom to select topics and professionalism has increased. Admittedly, although Chinese commercial media and social media have yet to achieve full capacity, the emergence and popularity of this global strategy demonstrates the aspirations for the media's role in China's modernization.

These patterns – national, sovereign-state and global – coexist in Chinese international communication. However, the emphasis of each pattern is different and each has a different historical background. The national pattern is the most established; the sovereign-state pattern is more politically oriented, which is determined by the nature of the Chinese media system; the global pattern is actually just beginning. Since 2013, with the changing communication strategy of the new government, Chinese media are making every effort to strengthen the sovereign-state pattern and expand the global pattern.

International communication strategies of mainstream media

The media have played a paramount role in China's international communication and public diplomacy strategy, including mainstream media, commercial media and social media. Whether or not they take part in international communication activities depends on both the political apparatus and market economy. Although some of the media are still funded by the state's financial allocation, most of them are becoming more and more commercialized.

The first strategy is that of 'global distribution'. Represented by Xinhua news agency and CCTV, this strategy features an active deployment all over the world of a large number of correspondents to establish bureaus and desks in major countries and regions or to upgrade the bureaus into stations and news centres. For instance, the Xinhua news agency has established over 160 bureaus that have exceeded the number of overseas bureaus of AP, Reuters and AFP respectively, with over 3,000 local correspondents and staff recruited.[1] After 2009, both Xinhua news agency and CCTV have expanded their overseas branches. CCTV America, CCTV Africa and CCTV Europe are respectively established as well as dozens of correspondent stations. CCTV America and CCTV Africa have also recruited a large number of local staff, including the former producer of CNN and the production team of Kenya Broadcasting Station, whose local news is produced and broadcast on CCTV News.

The feature of this strategy is to gain first-hand news materials at the scene by investing substantial resources, thus challenging the timeliness and exclusiveness of Western media. The major appeal of capacity building in international communication is to obtain first-hand material quickly so that China's voice can be heard. During the outbreak of the 2003 Iraq War, the correspondent with the Xinhua news agency in Baghdad was among the first to report on the Iraqi airstrike by the American air force. Xinhua is a news agency while CCTV is a TV station, but the commonality is that their core competitiveness lies in obtaining first-hand material and the strategy of global deployment manifests the fight over that.

As a substantial investment in Chinese international communication, the aim of this strategy is to create the infrastructure needed to transform a quantitative change into a qualitative change. The evidence shows that the increasing number of overseas correspondents and localized news has improved the capacity of mainstream media in breaking news reports, thus endowing them with more power of discourse in international news reporting.

The second strategy is 'cross-national cooperation'. Unlike the Xinhua news agency and CCTV, the lack of substantial funds and investment has constrained other media to follow the strategy of global deployment, even though their multi-language news platform is relatively mature. The epitome of this type is *China Daily*. Founded in 1981, *China Daily* is one of the most important platforms for international communication after the 'Opening Policy'. Leaders from different countries often publish articles highlighting their political priorities in *People's Daily* and *China Daily* as a communication method shortly before their official visits to China. *China Daily* is essentially an English-language international publication owned by China.

The strategy of *China Daily* is principally cross-national cooperation. In international communication activities, publishing newspapers in foreign countries invariably involves registration, application, authorization and other legal processes, which is the weak point of Chinese media. However, *China Daily* established itself by cooperating with local newspapers, such as adding inserts and co-publishing to achieve its international communication aims. For instance, in Washington, *China Daily* cooperated with the *Washington Post* to publish its inserts 'China Watch' inside the weekend edition. The same methods have been adopted in the *Wall Street Journal* and London's *Daily Telegraph*.[2] Meanwhile, different editions of *China Daily* are also a type of cross-national cooperation, which usually rely on partnerships with local media, and there are now seven international editions of *China Daily* of this kind.

The cross-national strategy is one of localization, emphasizing the audience's needs. This audience-oriented communication pays more attention to the different preferences for information in different countries and regions. This requires sensitivity to local customs and cultures as well as meeting the demand for Chinese information. For *China Daily* and other media alike, the lack of funds has prevented them from using overseas correspondents, which makes them short of information. However, the cross-national strategy has created a new path for Chinese media to present China's information to local audiences through selecting ideologically neutral partners and even purchasing advertising.

The third strategy is technology acquisition, which is represented by CRI. The method is to acquire local media or make strategic investments. This involves, on the one hand, the acquisition of technology facilities, such as the acquisition and successful operation of short-wave radio stations in Bangkok and Helsinki.[3] On the other hand, China has been investing in larger acquisitions to develop media capacity.

Since China realized it is lagging behind the world's mainstream media and the huge cost for catch-up, it has been using acquisitions to narrow the gap. As a method of capital operation, technology acquisition has long been discussed in relation to trade barriers in international communication studies. However, most researchers concentrate on the cross-national sales of media products. With more developed culture industries, Western countries have gained the upper hand in the trade of media products, thus resulting in the imbalance of sales. However, globalization has contributed to the increasing dynamics of cross-national capital and China is no longer satisfied with local investment, focusing more on cross-national capital cooperation. Chinese capital owners are quite active in Hollywood as well as centres of global media such as London. Although acquisition at present is influenced by various factors, including markets and politics, the trend is irreversible and has been regarded as a more efficient strategy for international communication. The large capital owned by China is adequate to support its acquisitions in the international communication market. This behaviour is not only led by the state; first-class international media with high-quality production are also promising investment targets for Chinese capital owners.

Since 2009, these three strategies have coexisted in the capacity-building process. Because of the different characteristics and investment across different media, the communication effect of each strategy also varies. In general, Chinese international communication patterns have changed greatly, compared with party-state propaganda dating back to 1949. For the last few decades, China has been sticking to the concept of being 'self-centred', especially emphasizing traditional Chinese culture, tourist resorts and arts. At the local level, so far, international communication is still mainly about tourist resorts and culture. However, since 2009, particularly with the new leadership coming in in 2013, the focus has explicitly shifted. On 19 August 2013, President Xi Jinping announced at the Publicity Seminar the guidance rules of 'telling good Chinese stories and spreading Chinese voice' and further refined the concept of the Chinese dream to strengthen people's identity internally and present Chinese developments and achievements externally.

China's investment in international communication is comprehensive, including not only infrastructure construction, but also human resources as soft power. Although it is said that over 40 billion yuan were invested into international communication, these investments were actually pre-existing rather than being added to the budget. With this increasing investment came more focus on using soft power, including producing content exclusively for new media platforms and training programmes designed for young international news reporters.

China's international communication has also started paying attention to localization in target countries. The aim is to blend Chinese stories and global issues to create new communication habits for local populations. Chinese media believe that localization, for content creation, means selecting topics of most concern to locals according to their own political, economic and cultural conditions, thus engaging them with the communication by answering those concerns. For technology applications, localization means using the communication technology most accepted and used in the target country, according to their stage of development. For instance, most cooperation in the Middle East and Latin America is carried out through radio stations, while print media, in contrast, play the main part in Asian countries, and in European countries, TV channels are the most common medium for cooperation.

It is important to note that the three strategies do not include the use of new media, as they reflect investments in international communication between 2009 and 2015. With the fast development of new media, the three strategies are facing new challenges and changes, especially the changes in the international communication narrative, which is bound to reconstruct the communication patterns and enhance the international communication capacity.

Narrative patterns of Chinese international communication

At the same time as the development of these strategies, two trends at the macro level of international communication studies can be identified. First of all, the narrative is increasingly becoming more Chinese. This is not a Chinese monologue; rather, it is a closer interplay between news topics and China's development, as well as between the news and Chinese people's own worldviews.

The Chinese narrative does not intrinsically contradict the global one. Since China is becoming one of the most important parts of the global system, topics related to China are also rising up the international media agenda. Especially since 2008, the media from various countries have shifted attention to Chinese affairs, as well as participating in the discussion of the Chinese model and its development path. They are curious about China and how this reflects upon Western institutions, as China's economic development and social condition has defied traditional Western explanations.

Apart from the Chinese narrative, a 'modern' narrative is also emerging. Traditional international communication studies since the 1980s concentrated mainly on China's positive features, namely history, culture and Chinese customs, avoiding controversial contemporary social topics. The concern is that Chinese culture and history already have a solid foundation among certain audiences, while contemporary topics were always controversial, and this may have had counter effects. However, for news reporting, the 'modern' narrative features not only modernity, but also the common issues of concern to both China and the international society. China's development has long been interpreted in a historical context to make comparisons with its own past, but news reporting is all about the present instead of the past, which makes the audience eager to know about the nation's present condition. Therefore, international communication studies are required to interpret contemporary China through the lens of present reality, even problems and issues in which a Chinese solution can be seen.

Firstly, there is the emergence of a story-telling pattern among media workers reflecting a shift from 'impressions of China' to 'China's story'. To date, most communication has concentrated on a grand narrative, such as the historical comparison of China's development. However, telling stories has become an imperative for

China's international communication as dialogue with international audiences has become routine. This is not only a basic characteristic of news reporting, but also a method to engage in international dialogue. Even though Chinese stories are not perfect, a vivid and realistic representation of China that shows the ordinary life of Chinese people is effective.

From impression to story, details and plots are required. Detail means truly reporting the news at the scene and telling the stories and plot means a logic that can connect the details. Chinese stories can only stand out when the plots and details meet the requirements and embody the qualities of the 'Chinese' and 'modern' narratives. Meanwhile, in-depth reporting has become a major standard in international media. Traditionally, in-depth reporting means coinciding with the narrative of Chinese ideology which is the narrative of mainstream discourse and the Communist Party. In contrast, contemporary in-depth reporting is more aligned with universal values or cultural pluralism.

Secondly, a sensitive mode of international communication has emerged. Reports on sensitive and controversial topics should become the next wave. Western media have always had a monopoly in the international communication environment, which in recent years, however, has been challenged by rising media from developing countries. They have delivered different angles and perspectives on news topics and content. Good examples are Al Jazeera during the Iraq war in 2003, and RT (formerly Russia Today) during the Ukraine and Syrian civil conflicts. The reason why these two media organizations have risen quickly is the different perspectives they have provided on international issues, which complement public opinion on international and regional affairs in major countries. Admittedly, both organizations are isolated by Western mainstream media for their perspectives and their countries of origin, but their efforts have opened up new potential in the international communication system.

The sensitivity of sensitive news derives from huge gaps of understanding between the East and the West which further construct the value systems and judgements of the development choices of particular countries. That is why many countries remain cautious while reporting sensitive news. However, it is the proposition of the modern Chinese international communication mission that goes far beyond historical and cultural narratives to define its deeper requirement of modern dialogue. For instance, even a news report on the commemoration of Chinese history and peace is required to be embedded in contemporary topics such as Chinese modern development and military build-up. If Al Jazeera is considered as offering an alternative voice from the Middle East that was different from the West during the Iraq war in terms of cultural and social recognition, RT is playing its own communication role by implementing a different ideology and reconstructing a new value system. Topics in international communication since 2009 have been increasingly focusing on sensitive issues. Taking the promotional video of China's national image as an example, Chinese astronauts are boldly included for the first time ever. Even though the video has received different comments, it is unquestionably a breakthrough in traditional silence on sensitive issues. Several animations such as

'How to Become a Leader' produced by FUXINGZHILU studio, SHISANWU published by Xinhua news agency and XIDADA (Uncle Xi Jinping) produced in 2006, are all international works designed for new media that have received a positive response.

Thirdly, a dialogue mode has been constructed, which is also a trend in international communication. For a long time, the mission of international communication was nation branding and development, some of which was essentially national public relations, thus mainly one-way communication. The reality, however, has required producers to put themselves into the audience's shoes, urging them to participate and observe dialogues between China and the rest of the world, even to understand China's development through foreigners' eyes. Dialogue means constructing effective communication and interactions, engaging more people in the topics instead of one-way transmission.

In international communication, remoteness and strangeness can lead to curiosity-seeking rather than fact-finding, thus reducing the news to conflict and difference, which could be seen as a form of orientalism. To change this situation, a dialogue mode should be promoted in active international communication methods and provide different perspectives instead of simply describing the phenomenon or so-called value judgements. In fact, with the development of new media, the dialogue mode is now deeply rooted: audiences have become used to interactivity as they consume as well as produce the new media. If dialogue and interaction between different classes and perspectives can be constructed, a closer bond can be made with audiences and a more convincing interpretation of a diverse world will be reflected in international communication.

New patterns of international communication in new media

The Report on China's National Image issued by China International Publishing Group in 2016 surveyed 19 countries of the G20, among which the young (18–35), the middle-aged (36–50) and the older group (51–65) scored 6.6, 6.1 and 5.6 respectively on China's national image.[4] Apart from not being traditionally biased, the reason why the evaluation among the younger generation scored the highest is because they obtain information primarily from new media platforms. Twitter, Facebook and YouTube are more pluralistic and adapted to independent and innovative ideas. On these platforms, more and more Chinese young netizens venture beyond the firewall and even voluntarily participate in international communication activities in an organized manner. China's stance on many issues of nationalism, especially the sovereignty issue, is expressed by them.

From the perspective of communication methods, even though Twitter and Facebook are still not allowed to operate in China, Chinese international communication scholars have pointed out that social media is indispensable in China's capacity building for international communication. Furthermore, social media has created a chance for China to 'overtake on the bend'. Therefore, the Xinhua news agency, the *People's Daily* and CCTV have all created their own social media accounts overseas. Among them, Xinhua has the most frequent and diversified news feed; the number of *People's Daily* followers has reached 9.6 million to take second place worldwide, following the *New York Times*; and CCTV America on Twitter sent 19,000 tweets between 2012 and 2016. All of these increasing numbers demonstrate the dynamics of Chinese media on new media platforms.

A more important change stems from the content. Since the first one-minute promotional video of China's national image was played at Times Square in New York, more and more visualized content has been created. Chinese international communicators realized that presenting more Chinese content on new media by visualization will have a positive effect on communication. The change in content also coincided with the three narrative patterns mentioned above, which are storytelling, sensitive issues and dialogue. The music video 'How to Become a Leader' released on YouTube and the 'Shisansu' released by Xinhua news agency's Twitter account are more condensed, aiming to explain the hard issues recognized by international society: China's political institutions. This visualized content was used to explain the institutional issues and help new media users get China's points firsthand instead of reading second-hand materials edited by the Western mainstream media as the 'gatekeepers'.

The international communication strategies presented by new media will become a major investment target for China. Particularly with the financial problems and stagnancy of traditional media, more and more international media are cutting back their expenses, calling back overseas bureaus and correspondents and depending more on new media to transform and develop. Although China has been investing in international communication, with the challenges of the new media landscape, Chinese media have begun to realize that they are positioned in the same development phase as international mainstream media. Therefore, future investment will be targeted more on new media, thus creating new communication methods as narrative patterns evolve.

Notes

1 http://news.xinhuanet.com/newmedia/2011-10/29/c_122212821_2.htm.
2 www.chinadaily.com.cn/static_c/gyzgrbwz.html.
3 www.thepaper.cn/newsDetail_forward_1392992.
4 http://mt.sohu.com/20160829/n466595196.shtml.

PART IV

Media with Chinese characteristics

16

ADVERTISING IN CHINA: GLOBAL IMPLICATIONS AND IMPACTS

Shanshan Lou and Hong Cheng

Since the 1970s, the world has not only witnessed a booming Chinese market and an emerging global economic powerhouse but also seen a fast-growing advertising industry in the country. Chinese society has been in a process of transformation over recent decades, from 'a traditional society with an economy based on agriculture to one based on industry' (Nicholson, 2016), from 'the receiving side of the innovation in the past' to an active contributor to shaping that innovation and from having 'low demand for data and technology' to 'a high demand for data and technology' (Chow, 2016). With the world's largest population, the more than 1.4 billion people living in China continue to offer a huge consumer base to the world (Nicholson, 2016). China's advertising market ranks firmly as second in the world in terms of advertising spending (about $51 billion in 2015) (World Advertising Research Center [WARC], 2016).

With China's rapid rise, it is generally realized that 'the Chinese market has become more complicated for Western players' (Dodd and Zhou, 2015). More specifically, what does this huge advertising market mean for the global advertising and global media industries? With an increasing number of Chinese companies going global, what role is Chinese advertising playing in the international arena? What implications does Chinese advertising's presence overseas have for the global market? In particular, what influence does Chinese mobile advertising have on the global mobile advertising market when leading advertisers tend to allocate their digital expenditure to the mobile phone market? More broadly, what impact is Chinese advertising beginning to have on global media and culture? This chapter aims to address these questions.

An overview of advertising in China

Since advertising came back to life in China in 1979, shortly after the country began an economic reform and reopened to the outside world in 1978, it has grown phenomenally (Xu, 1990; Cheng, 1996, 2000; Yu and Deng, 2000). From a humble beginning nearly 40 years ago, advertising spending in China has been second only to that of the United States (WARC, 2016). In 1979, advertising spending in China was approximately 10 million yuan ($1.43 million) (Zhang, 2008 cited in Cheng, 2010). Even in 2000 when the London-based World Advertising Research Center, the authoritative annual worldwide advertising expenditure data provider, first included China's advertising data in its annual listings of worldwide, country-by-country advertising expenditure, China's total media spending was $3.96 billion (WARC, 2016). According to WARC, China's advertising spending in 2015 jumped to $51.02 billion (WARC, 2016), way above that of Japan ($38.86 billion), although still far behind that of the US ($166.83 billion) in the same year. In fact, according to WARC (2016), China surpassed Japan in terms of annual total advertising spending in 2013, claiming the second-largest advertising industry in the world.

In 2014, Internet advertising spending ($20.05 billion) overtook that of television ($15.67 billion), the largest advertising medium in China for years, becoming the most-invested medium for advertising in the market (WARC, 2016). In 2015, China's Internet advertising spending reached $25.63 billion, a 27.8 per cent increase on the previous year. Compared with their counterparts in the US and Japan, 'Chinese companies spend relatively more on the Internet, and relatively less on print' (Yeh and Zhang, 2013). In 2016, Internet advertising revenue was forecast to reach 275.6 billion yuan ($41.4 billion), while estimated TV advertising revenue continued to decrease (CIW Team, 2016a). Some researchers believe that the online advertising market in China may reach 410.5 billion yuan ($63.49 billion) in 2018 (CIW Team, 2016a).

As far as mobile advertising is concerned, although it does not take a substantial portion of overall ad spending in China, given that mobile advertising still struggles to generate profits, it is on a fast track of growth (Yeh and Zhang, 2013). The annual spend of mobile advertising jumped from $400.6 million in 2011 to $4.83 billion in 2014, according to WARC's (2016) latest report. A major momentum for the rapid increase in advertising spending on digital media is Chinese users' average daily time spent on digital media (50.4 per cent), which in 2015 for the first time surpassed that spent on television (43.6 per cent), the most popular medium in China for decades (CIW Team, 2016a). The market volume of mobile Internet in China was merely 12.01 billion yuan ($1.79 billion) in 2008 and 391.8 billion yuan ($58.65 billion) in 2015, but it was forecast to be up to 618.8 billion yuan ($92.63 billion) in 2016 and 1,186.8 billion yuan ($177.66 billion) by 2018 (Statista, 2016) (see also Table 16.1).

With the rapid development and popularity of mobile Internet and smartphones, Chinese consumers have become more adapted to ads that promote products and brands on their mobile devices. For instance, a great number of companies utilize Tencent's WeChat, the most popular all-purpose social app in China, to create official promoted accounts in order to engage consumers. It has been shown to effectively reach potential consumers (CIW Team, 2016c). Some global marketers have also realized the potential of online and mobile advertising in China. In order

TABLE 16.1 China media spend by category 2011, 2014, and 2015, $billion

China	Total media spend	Internet ad spend	TV ad spend	Mobile ad spend
2011	31.78	7.15	13.24	0.40
2014	46.98	20.05	15.67	4.83
2015	51.02	25.63	15.48	——

Source: WARC (2016).

to prevail against the competition, they need to better understand the changing habits of Chinese media users and adapt to the highly developed e-commerce market in China. In the past four years, Chinese users' average daily time spent on digital media increased from 35.8 per cent (1.78 hours per user) to 50.4 per cent (3.08 hours per user) (CIW Team, 2016a). Studies have documented that the secret to convincing China's 'infamous' savers to spend their money is 'all about being online' (Burkitt, 2013). According to McKinsey, 'China's e-commerce market, the largest in the world behind the US, is booming, with sales expected to reach $420 billion to $650 billion by 2020' (Burkitt, 2013). The same data report also analysed consumers' online spending behaviour in 266 cities in China and the result showed that around 40 per cent of China's consumers would not have made the purchase had it not been for the option of e-commerce (Burkitt, 2013). This new purchasing pattern has major business implications for global marketers when analysing Chinese markets and consumers today. Global marketers need to rethink their strategies and the answer to the question below becomes increasingly important: should companies expand their brick-and-mortar stores first before rolling out online in China, or does the order of operations not matter anymore?

Successful advertising campaigns have confirmed that marketing on online platforms, Sina Weibo and Tencent's WeChat, is one of the most effective methods to promote brands and companies in China (Incitez China, 2016a). While WeChat is an all-purpose social app, Weibo is the most popular and influential Twitter-like social media in China. Users of these two social media platforms mainly access them through smartphones, as confirmed in a recent digital consumer study, that messaging and social media are among the primary functions for mobile use among the Chinese. While Weibo currently has 222 million monthly active users, WeChat has 650 million (CIW Team, 2016c).

Mobile online advertising opportunities in China for global marketers

Mobile advertising can be defined as 'using a wireless medium to provide consumers with time-and-location-sensitive and personalized information that promotes goods, services and ideas, thereby benefiting all stakeholders' (Scharl *et al.*, 2005: 165). China is well ahead of the global average on this front. WPP's GroupM has forecast that 31 per cent of worldwide ad budgets this year will go online. Advertisers in

China are taking cues from how quickly consumers have embraced the online world, especially mobile phones, for streaming videos and movies online, shopping from Alibaba's e-commerce empire and using WeChat to communicate, book services and pay household bills. Mobile online advertising in China 'is growing at about twice the rate of general online spending' (Doland, 2016). GroupM identified the rapidly increasing consumer use of digital media, the 'much more strictly regulated' television advertising market, and 'the high cost of ad buys on television' in China as the major reasons for the rapid growth of mobile and Internet advertising and the significant decline in television advertising spending in the country (Doland, 2016).

As the demographic using smartphones and other mobile devices continues to increase, advertisers and marketers have begun taking advantage of various mobile channels to deliver commercial information to users (Khan and Allil, 2010). The popularity and fast adoption of mobile devices drives the growth of the mobile advertising market. In 2009, the revenue size of China's mobile TV advertising market was approximately $115 million (ChinaRealNews, 2009). According to a separate report, the mobile advertising market in China was ranked number five in the world by volume in 2012, and grew between 2011 and 2012 by up to 120 per cent (ChinaRealNews, 2012). China's mobile ad spend nearly doubled, from $7.5 billion in 2014 to $14 billion in 2015 (Greiff, 2015). Reporters from *Fierce Mobile Market* estimated that, in 2016, advertisers in China would spend $22.14 billion to reach customers via tablets and mobile phones (Burt, 2015).

Researchers predicted that the increase in China's mobile online ad spend would correlate with its number of mobile users, with an estimate of two billion smartphone users in China by the end of 2016 (Greiff, 2015). Such rapid growth of mobile marketing has caught the attention of both Western and Chinese players, whose advertising business needs to be boosted to compete with Chinese companies like Baidu, the Chinese Internet search giant often called 'the Google of China' (ChinaRealNews, 2012). Baidu was predicted to reach second place in search-ad revenue worldwide in 2015 (Flynn, 2015). Chinese research company analysis listed Baidu, Tencent, Sogou, Youku, Alibaba, Liebao, 360, Sohu, Google China, Weibo, Autohome, Letv, Netease, Sina and Soufun as 'the most innovative companies in China's online advertising market' (Incitez China, 2016b).

Innovation capacity is mainly determined by the manufacturers' media operations. Baidu, Alibaba and Tencent, in particular, have a great impact on China's Internet market due to their capacity for innovation. Baidu launched Duer in 2015, which offers full-time secretarial services by 'learning and alternating people's behavior' (Incitez China, 2016b). Alibaba's Deharma Sword is one of the few big data platforms in China that can help develop targeted marketing services. Alibaba further expanded its user data after the acquisition of Tudou, a video-sharing website. Tencent offers Wide Click-through service through its social marketing service: By providing analysis of user data, it allows advertisers to reach their potential consumers. Advertisers now have the tools to generate precise profiles of their targeted consumers, which makes their marketing strategies more individualized.

Mobile penetration correspondingly means the growth in popularity and use of social media. Today, China is a leading country for social marketing – 63 per cent of smartphone users between 16 and 64 in China are using social networking sites. Chinese millennials, in particular, love to browse, chat, and make friends online (Dodd and Zhou, 2015). Since Twitter and Facebook together with YouTube are all inaccessible in China, colleges and universities outside China turn to China's homegrown social media, Sina Weibo, the most popular and influential Twitter-like social media in China, to attract prospective students and engage with their Chinese students and alumni (Glogou, 2012). For example, on 6 June 2012, the University of Illinois in the US established a Sina Weibo account to connect with its Chinese alumni and students (Glogou, 2012). Some international celebrities have also established Weibo accounts to build more interactive relationships with their fans in China. In 2015, Sina Weibo set up a department specifically for the purpose of helping international celebrities to overcome cultural and language barriers to facilitate better communication between them and their Chinese fans (Zhang, 2015). In order to seek new revenue sources to maintain robust growth, Sina Weibo announced the launch of video advertising (Incitez China, 2015).

Like Sina Weibo, Tencent's WeChat is another highly effective tool to promote brands and businesses in China. One good example of the use of this social media e-commerce platform is China Southern Airlines, which launched its WeChat account in 2013 and now has two WeChat service official accounts with over eight million followers. The number of app downloads has reached nearly five million, visits to the e-commerce platform increased by 85 million, and most importantly, its ticket sales via WeChat almost tripled in 2015 (CIW Team, 2016b).

Research has suggested that mobile marketers should pay attention to China, especially the large amount of 'smartphone-geared ads' (Johnson, 2014a). According to Johnson (2014a), 'while US broadcasters and companies try to play catch-up with more mobile content, new research from the Interactive Advertising Bureau shows how smartphones and tablets have become the primary way to watch videos in China'. Adam Kmiec, Campbell's global digital marketing and social media director, has commented that 'Asia has been ahead of the curve when it comes to mobile for nearly a decade' (Heine, 2013). 'Mobile commerce is much more advanced (in China),' said CEO of Spil Games Asia. 'Companies like Taobao, which is the Chinese version of eBay, have very advanced mobile apps that are easy to use' (Heine, 2013).

As early adopters of mobile devices and mobile apps, Chinese users are becoming more familiar with different formats of mobile advertising. Short Messaging Services or SMS have been shown to be very successful in China for a long period of time (Xu, 2006). Xu's study indicated that personalization is a strong predictor of consumer attitudes towards mobile advertising (ibid.). Tencent's WeChat is an interesting case for analysis from a mobile advertising perspective. WeChat is the one of the most popular messaging platforms around the globe (Brown, 2015). The app is available in various operation systems and in 16 different languages. In 2015, registered users increased to 1.12 billion. WeChat distinguishes itself from other pure mobile messaging apps through different features. For instance, WeChat allows users to share their 'Moments', which is similar to Facebook's 'Newsfeed'. Users' WeChat friends can 'Like' and comment on posts. WeChat also makes it easier for users to group their contacts and set up the visibility of each 'Moment' for different friends. With such features, WeChat has successfully increased its efforts to monetize users' personal 'Moments' feed by rolling out advertisements.

In 2015, WeChat utilized a new advertising system that was different from the self-serve advertising system for public accounts to monetize the traffic of their accounts. The system has a CPM (cost-per-impression) sales model, which means the number of views of an ad determines the cost structure. For instance, 1,000 views of an ad in smaller cities cost around 40 yuan (app. $6), 1,000 views of an ad in key cities (e.g. Guangzhou) cost 90 yuan (app. $14), and 1,000 views cost 140 yuan (app. $21) in major cities (Beijing and Shanghai). Tencent picked 50 brands to launch their ad campaigns on WeChat 'Moments', among which Vivo, BMW and Coca-Cola were the first three brands to debut their ads on 'Moments'.

Many users perceived the kinds of ads they got as indications of what Tencent's big data machine thought about them. If you saw a BMW ad, you were probably considered a wealthy user by Tencent. And if you saw the Coca-Cola ad, it means that you were not among the elite or middle-class followers. WeChat 'Moments' was later made open to all advertisers. Tencent gave any brand access to its target consumers according to their location, gender, age and interests (Loras, 2015). 'Moments' ads work well for well-known brands with visually appealing campaigns. Less well-known brands or smaller companies can consider other channels that WeChat provides, such as WeChat banner ads. In 2015, Tencent announced that it would open up its data to Dentsu Aegis Nework and WPP's GroupM (Doland, 2015c). This provides an opportunity for smaller companies to better target users and evaluate the effectiveness of Tencent's products.

Another service that places WeChat further into mobile commerce territory is allowing customers to purchase items or services within the app. The new in-app purchase in WeChat is called Weixin Payments, referring to the app's Chinese name. The portal takes the form of a WeChat Wallet. At least one in five WeChat users signed up for Weixin Payments by linking a banking or credit card to the users' account in the Wallet (Chan, 2015). The importance of the Wallet is that it facilitates instant transactions between users and all official accounts that sell products and services. To use Weixin Payments, the customer just needs to find the products' official account in WeChat, and check the Weixin Payments option. Users can also pay for taxi rides, utility bills, phone bills, and make donations through Weixin Payments. In this sense, WeChat has become a success story of the evolutionary use of social networks.

Another popular method for Chinese consumers to make payments and get promotion information from the companies' official accounts that they follow is the QR code feature. QR codes are very common in China; they appear on almost every ad you see and business you contact. WeChat tends to serve as an agent between the vendor and the consumer. For instance, WeChat provides more services than making payments. It can help users make reservations at restaurants. Once the user picks a restaurant, they can use WeChat to join the virtual queues to wait for tables. They can view menus, place orders once they are seated and pay their bills, all within the WeChat platform. When it is time to pay for meals, restaurants will give customers QR codes to scan. Once a customer scans a QR code within WeChat, a meal will be paid for using WeChat Wallet. In some restaurants, users can even get discounts if they use WeChat as their payment method. The majority of Chinese consumers are paying for products and services using WeChat Wallet. Not only because it is convenient, but also because it is deemed reliable and trustworthy by WeChat users. For brands, Chinese and foreign alike, presence on WeChat has marketing benefits; it allows consumers to have easy access to their products and services, which makes any promotion strategies more direct and efficient.

For Western users, although online shopping is popular, payments on social media platforms are still not that common. WeChat has been experimenting with processing payments offline via the QR codes the app generates at stores, vending machines and restaurants. The level of integration and frictionless mobile-first experiences that WeChat provides is unprecedented. In China, many people do not bring their wallets nowadays; they can use WeChat to pay for almost everything they need to, from transportation to entertainment and dining. Chinese users quickly adapt to this style of living. In the US, although much research has been done to explore the mobile app's capacity to generate more interactive and personalized user experiences, designs of most apps are limited, not maximizing all advanced functions of smartphones (Chan, 2015). Despite having a great number of users, US-based social media apps (such as Facebook, Twitter, Instagram and SnapChat) provide limited services other than social networking functions and content sharing. Unlike WeChat, most social media apps do not connect consumers and business or vendors directly, which limits the commercial potential of these social media apps. In addition, Western users have not developed a strong trust towards mobile apps and online payments. Mobile payments require users to link their mobile wallet to a bank account. For the majority of Western users, the risks of purchasing products and services through an app may still outweigh the benefits. Consumers tend to be concerned about the safety of mobile transactions. Network safety issues and uncertainty about technology may be obstacles in the development of mobile marketing and advertising.

Chinese companies and consumers going global

As one of the biggest emerging markets in the world, China has become the most dynamic one in the new media era. According to Haines (2015), 'the Asian market is particularly dynamic and vastly different from anything you'll experience in the West'. China accounts for 20 per cent of the world's population, 13 per cent of global GDP, and five per cent of total worldwide advertising (Johnson, 2014b). Since China overtook Japan to become the world's second-largest advertising market in 2013 based on its ad spend, the country has been eager to enter the international market and burnish its brand images. This gigantic market is incredibly challenging, while providing amazing opportunities for global investors (Doland, 2015a).

Going out of the China market seems to have become the new trend of Chinese companies (Compass, 2016). The government is increasing financial support to encourage Chinese companies to both invest and operate aboard (Tiezzi, 2014): for example, according to China's Ministry of Commerce, 'Chinese overseas investment totaled $61.6 billion by the end of September 2013 – a 17.4 per cent year-on-year increase,' (Backaler, 2014). As a result, 'going out' became a buzzword throughout 2015 (Compass, 2016). With examples including Lenovo's acquisition of IBM and Geely's purchase of Volvo, Chinese private enterprises have triumphed in many industries (The State Council, 2016). Chinese firms now operate in at least 35 of the 50 states in the US (Rosen and Hanemann, 2012). Renren, a Beijing company that began in 2005 as a Facebook-like social media platform, has led a $10 million investment in a Washington-based startup that uses big data to forecast legislation (Purnell, 2015). Dalian Wanda, a Chinese multinational conglomerate corporate, made a name for itself with its $2.6 billion acquisition of AMC Entertainment in the US in 2012. Huawei, a global telecommunications equipment manufacturer headquartered in Shenzhen, also expanded its business to the US by having many of its new products featured at the 2015 Consumer Electronic Show in Las Vegas (Backaler, 2015).

The 'going out' effort comes with challenges as well as opportunities for Chinese businesses. Like the international companies that first entered the Chinese market decades ago, Chinese companies face a similar learning curve of understanding market rules and adapting their strategies to survive and win. Choosing the right advertising platforms in overseas markets is important to those companies to maximize exposure to their potential customers. One of the biggest challenges China encounters today is that people around the world rarely know many Chinese brands even though they may hold the perception that many products are 'made in China'. Recent research showed that only 22 per cent of consumers outside China can actually name a Chinese brand. 'Though some Chinese brands sell well internationally – appliance-makers Haier and Hisense, for example – they lack name recognition' (Doland, 2015a). Therefore, for Chinese companies, it is now critical to brand their products to expand international markets and build trust among their global users, in order to attract investors outside China.

Promoting brand recognition of Chinese companies to the outside world is one of the most critical tasks that need to be well done to help China 'going out'. Without strong and effective promotion, it would be difficult to fulfil the mission of 'going out'. Doreen Wang, Global Head of BrandZ at Millward Brown, says she does not see many ads for Chinese brands in the US. One reason is that many Chinese companies are not accustomed to spending the time and money necessary to sell themselves in foreign markets (Doland, 2015a). Nevertheless, several successful Chinese companies have realized the importance of branding. For instance, Li-Ning, a top Chinese sports brand, is making a second pass at the US market with branded e-commerce as its strategy (AdAge, 2011). Li-Ning made a strong presence at the 2012 London Olympic Games by sponsoring top-tier athletes. 'With more name recognition and grassroots pride and popularity than ever, the brand launched a massive expansion programme that included international markets and a global branding campaign' (Sauer, 2012).

In view of the current situation, Chinese enterprises tend to choose professional overseas marketing service providers to open foreign markets. For example, despite being blocked in China, Chinese companies are using Twitter to buy advertising space on its service, which is used by more than 300 million people elsewhere in the world. Specifically, Twitter already works with Chinese smartphone maker Xiaomi, online shopping giant Alibaba Group, white goods producer Qingdao Haier, and flagship carrier Air China to target customers abroad (Wong, 2015). Facebook is another popular social media platform that is blocked in China, but is chosen by Chinese companies to promote their products to consumers in other countries (Tong, 2014). They believe Facebook offers a higher return on investment than search engine advertising, and also helps retailers to connect with potential consumers in the rest of the world.

When doing business in a foreign environment, advertisers have to face greater challenges and higher risks. Due to differences in markets and consumers, as well as cultural differences and other multiple factors, it is hard for advertisers to enter foreign markets (Compass, 2016) but there are a few successful examples to learn from. A few years ago, Alibaba, China's e-commerce giant, started to seek 'going out' opportunities after its huge success in China. In 2012, Alibaba produced a commercial that ran in New York City's Times Square to promote the power of small business. It was not as successful as the company had expected, as many Americans were still confused about the difference between Alibaba and Amazon. The company then posted more videos and examples on its corporate website to explain business models in order to communicate with and acquire overseas investors and partners (Doland, 2015b).

Nowadays, Alibaba 'makes most of its money through merchant advertising, which secures page views', allowing 'merchants to sell directly to consumers' (Mann, 2014). In fact, its business model set an example for global merchants to follow in using this vast platform for advertising opportunities. Darren Burns, President of Weber Shandwick China, believes that 'in many ways China is creating a parallel or pioneering universe for the internet and e-commerce – one that's different from the Anglo world' (Doland, 2015b).

The growing Chinese market and changing consumer patterns have caught the attention of international brands. Many have adapted marketing strategies to appeal to Chinese customers. According to Griffiths (2015), Chinese consumers are early adopters of new technologies and they are familiar and comfortable buying goods online and using their mobile phones to make purchases. Alipay, an online payment platform, launched within Alibaba's digital ecosystem in 2014, has become a major mobile-payment player. Some international brands have started accepting Alipay on their sites to keep up with the needs of Chinese consumers purchasing from overseas (Griffiths, 2015).

Collaboration between agencies and companies in China with those of other countries is becoming increasingly common. In view of the rapid development of the Chinese e-commerce marketplace, including Alibaba and other online companies, international marketers and agencies have developed partnerships with their Chinese counterparts to work together on data and research (Doland, 2015c). This represents international companies' growing interest in the Chinese market. It also indicates Chinese agencies' ambitions to expand their influence. According to WEMCB research, most countries hope to reach potential consumers through WeChat OA, standing for WeChat Official Account (CIW Team, 2016c). Since WeChat was officially introduced into the overseas market in 2013, it has taken an industry-leading role (Appcoach, 2015). In the same year, Tencent hired Argentine soccer star Lionel Messi as a pitchman and spent $200 million plugging WeChat abroad (Doland, 2015a).

In 2011, the Chinese government launched a commercial shown on screens in New York's Times Square. The commercial was designed to promote China's image to the world. It featured different groups of Chinese people, from ordinary citizens to celebrities, including basketball player Yao Ming and film director John Woo. The commercial also introduced a great number of successful Chinese entrepreneurs and their companies, artists and politicians. It presented many prominent landmarks in China, including the Birds Nest national stadium in Beijing and the Monument to the People's Heroes on Tiananmen Square (Chao, 2011). In the summer of 2014, Xinhua, China's state-run news agency, took over a prime advertising spot on Times Square. Many perceive Xinhua's presence to this landmark US public sphere as an effort to burnish the country's global image and promote its local brands and products. A Beijing-based marketing firm partnered with Clear Channel Outdoor in this promotion to help Chinese brands attract US consumers (Pasquarelli, 2014). Digital media in Times Square such as video billboards were used to advertise Chinese electronics, entertainment and tourism brands.

However, many Americans see these campaigns as failures. In his book, *The End of Cheap China: Economic and Cultural Trends That Will Disrupt the World*, Rein (2012) argued that China's efforts to reach global audiences did not establish a connection with the US public and tourists from around the world. The reason is that people appearing in these campaigns – Chinese scientists, athletes, artists and businessmen – were not recognizable in the US. To the US public, none of them represented how China was viewed. Interestingly, Alibaba Group founder Jack Ma, one of the celebrities in the 2011 Times Square campaign, was also little known to most Americans then. However, his e-commerce empire, Alibaba, listed on the New York Stock Exchange in 2014, with its stock up for 38 per cent to land a market valuation of $231 billion on its first day of trading on the New York Stock Exchange (McCarthy, 2014). Alibaba's business model was reported and studied extensively in many countries.

Another prime example of collaboration is the public-service advertising (PSA) during the 2014 CCTV Lunar New Year Gala. This annual entertainment gala could be regarded as China's equivalent of the US Super Bowl, except that no commercials are permitted during the gala while PSAs are acceptable (Doland, 2014). The 2014 gala attracted around 700 million viewers worldwide – in the Chinese mainland as well as overseas – during its four-hour presentation, featuring musicals, comedies, dances and drama performances. Few audience members perhaps knew that the PSAs shown during this gala were produced by McCann Erickson Shanghai and Saatchi & Saatchi Beijing, two global advertising companies' operations in China. Both ads focused on the 'Chinese Dream', a phrase Chinese President Xi Jinping first used in public in 2012, which soon became a widely adopted national slogan and theme in China (*The Economist*, 2013). Several agencies, both foreign and local, pitched for public-service spots at the gala. McCann's PSA used chopsticks as a cultural heritage symbol of family values. The PSA was comprised of several short stories, in which chopsticks represented various meanings and connotations such as sharing, caring and love. With English subtitles, the PSA could be easily understood by non-Chinese speaking audiences.

Saatchi's PSA depicted how Chinese New Year was celebrated worldwide. 'Our idea is that at Christmas, a lot of people celebrate it whether they are Christian or not, and when it comes to the Chinese New Year, with so much of the world's population being Chinese, I think it's worthy of celebration as well,' said Tian Ng It, executive creative director of Saatchi & Saatchi Beijing. 'The ad shows people around the world celebrating the holiday in quirky ways' (Doland, 2014). Both PSAs subtly delivered the pride of being Chinese. The story-telling techniques in both PSAs were creative. Unlike traditional PSAs aired in China, the McCann and Saatchi spots not only took a close look at China's heritage but also showed how China and Chinese culture could be presented to the rest of the world. The success of the PSAs produced by McCann and Saatchi provides a valuable lesson for Chinese local advertising agencies. Although local agencies may have a better insight in cultural values and customs, they need to understand how to market these values on a global platform. Chinese brands and products need to be known by the global audiences and entrepreneurs. Local agencies can take advantage of this growing demand and build bridges between local and global markets.

Conclusion

Accumulated cross-cultural advertising studies suggest that advertisements that reflect cultural values appeal to target audiences (Han and Shavitt, 1994; Kim and Markus, 1999; Liang *et al.*, 2011). As a cultural artefact, advertising is also a major source for people to learn about and understand how to interpret other cultures. From the billboards at Times Square to the FIFA soccer fields, Chinese ads have not only made more local brands and products known to global consumers, but have also stimulated interest in Chinese culture.

From examples in this chapter, we can see that the majority of campaigns for those 'going out' Chinese companies are handled by global advertising agencies in their global endeavours. Collaboration between local agencies and global agencies has its advantages. The innovation and operational capacity of advertising agencies such as McCann Erickson can guarantee the quality of advertising campaigns. However, Chinese advertising agencies should take advantage of the growing need for targeted and value-generated campaigns. Compared with global advertising companies, Chinese advertising agencies may have a more accurate and deeper understanding of Chinese culture and its target consumers. They should strive to advance their creativity and innovation in order to prevail in the competition. An increasing number of global brands have realized the fast-expanding market opportunities for e-commerce in China. At the same time, Chinese advertisers are gaining understanding of the global market and collaborating with international agencies as their first step of their 'going out' efforts. Many Chinese brands have become prominent because of continuous innovation. However, success in the global market calls for much more than innovation. Advertising that effectively represents its clients and targets their markets is pivotal. Whether exploring with global advertising partners, or adventuring on their own, Chinese advertising agencies should spearhead Chinese companies' endeavours in the global market.

References

AdAge (2011) China's Li-Ning takes on Nike, Adidas with U.S. e-commerce site. Available at http://adage.com/article/cmo-interviews/china-s-li-ning-takes-nike-u-s-e-commerce-site/231642/ [Accessed 31 July 2016].

Appcoach (2015) China's apps go overseas. Available at: www.appcoachs.com/chinas-apps-go-overseas/ [Accessed 31 July 2016].

Backaler, J. (2014) 14 Chinese companies going global in 2014. *Forbes*. 10 January.

Backaler, J. (2015) 10 Chinese companies going global in 2015. *Forbes*. 14 January.

Brown, N. (2015) How to advertise on Wechat Social Media Week. (Blog) Social Media Week. Available at http://socialmediaweek.org/blog/2015/03/how-to-advertise-on-wechat/ [Accessed 31 July 2016].

Burkitt, L. (2013) Where Chinese consumers are spending their cash. *The Wall Street Journal*. 21 March.

Burt, T. (2015) Global mobile ad market to top $100B in 2016; US, China biggest spenders. FierceCMO. Available at www.fiercecmo.com/story/global-mobile-ad-market-top-100b-2016-us-china-biggest-spenders/2015-04-07 [Accessed 31 July 2016].

Chan, C. (2015) When one app rules them all: The case of WeChat and mobile in China. Andreessen Horowitz. Available at http://a16z.com/2015/08/06/wechat-china-mobile-first/ [Accessed 31 July 2016].

Chao, L. (2011) Pro-China ad debuts in Time Square. *The Wall Street Journal*. 18 January.

Cheng, H. (1996) Advertising in China: A Socialist Experiment, in Frith, K. (ed.) *Advertising in Asia: Communication, Culture, and Consumption*. Ames: Iowa State University Press: 73–102.

Cheng, H. (2000) China: Advertising Yesterday and Today, in Jones, J. (ed.) *International Advertising Realities and Myths*. Thousand Oaks: SAGE: 255–284.

ChinaRealNews (2009) Revenue size of China mobile TV advertising market mounts to RMB 788 million. Newstex Global Business Blogs. Available at: http://chinarealnews.typepad.com/chinarealnews/ [Accessed 31 July 2016].

ChinaRealNews (2012) Google eyeing China mobile advertising market. Newstex Global Business Blogs. Available at: http://chinarealnews.typepad.com/chinarealnews/ [Accessed 31 July 2016].

Chow, L. (2016) How Unilever, UnionPay and Coca-Cola use big data in China. WARC. Available at: www.warc.com/Security/Login/Paywall.aspx?OriginalUrl=/Content/Content Viewer.aspx?ID=c9980782-3395-4839-8062-fbb556545de8&CID=A107979&PUB=EV ENT-REPORTS&MasterContentRef=c9980782-3395-4839-8062-fbb556545de8 [Accessed 31 July 2016].

CIW Team (2016a) China advertising revenues forecast 2016–2018. *China Internet Watch*. Available at: www.chinainternetwatch.com/17819/ad-revenues-2016-2018/ [Accessed 31 July 2016].

CIW Team. (2016b). China southern airlines ticket sales via WeChat almost tripled in 2015. [online] China Internet Watch. Available at: www.chinainternetwatch.com/17124/china-southern-airlines-wechat-2015/ [Accessed 31 July 2016].

CIW Team. (2016c). WeChat marketing insights in 2015. [online] China Internet Watch. Available at: www.chinainternetwatch.com/16559/wechat-marketing-insights-2015/ [Accessed 31 July 2016].

Compass (2016) Overseas mobile advertising marketing of Chinese companies. Available at: www.doingbusinessinchina.org/marketing_in_china/mobile_marketing_in_china/Overseas_Mobile_Advertising_Marketing_of_Chinese_Companies_I321.html [Accessed 31 July 2016].

Dodd, P. and Zhou, R. (2015) Uncommon sense: China-rise of the local giants. Nielsen. Available at: www.nielsen.com/us/en/insights/news/2015/china-rise-of-the-local-giants.html [Accessed 31 July 2016].

Doland, A. (2014) China's super bowl equivalent: 4 hours, 700 M viewers, 0 ads. *Ad Age*, Available at http://adage.com/article/global-news/china-s-super-bowl-equivalent-4-hours-700m-viewers-0-ads/291632/ [Accessed 31 July 2016].

Doland, A. (2015a) Chinese brands want to go global; here's why it's still so tough. *Ad Age*. Available at: http://adage.com/article/cmo-strategy/tough-chinese-brands-global/300101/ [Accessed 31 July 2016].

Doland, A. (2015b) Chinese Internet giant Tencent opens its trove of data to agencies. *Ad Age*. Available at: http://adage.com/article/digital/chinese-internet-giant-tencent-opens-trove-data-agencies/301867/ [Accessed 31 July 2016].

Doland, A. (2015c). Chinese Internet giant Tencent opens its trove of data to agencies. Ad Age, [online]. Available at: http://adage.com/article/digital/chinese-internet-giant-tencent-opens-trove-data-agencies/301867/ [Accessed 31 July 2016].

Doland, A. (2016) Half of China's ad spending will go toward the Internet this year. *Ad Age*. Available at: http://adage.com/article/digital/half-c/303175/ [Accessed 31 July 2016].

The Economist, (2013). Xi Jinping's vision: Chasing the Chinese dream. [online] Available at: www.economist.com/node/21577063/print[Accessed 31 July 2016].

Flynn, K. (2015) China ban hits Google's search ad share; Baidu gains. *International Business Times*. Available at: www.ibtimes.com/china-ban-hits-googles-search-ad-share-baidu-gains-1864852 [Accessed 31 July 2016].

Glogou (2012) China's most popular social media Weibo helps overseas universities engage with their Chinese audience. Available at http://glogou.com/china/chinas-most-popular-soical-media-weibo-helps-overseas-universities-engage-with-their-chinese-audience/ [Accessed 31 July 2016].

Greiff, F. (2015) Global mobile ad spending will climb to $100 billion in 2016. *Ad Age*. Available at: http://adage.com/article/digital/global-mobile-ad-spending-climb-100-billion-2016/297889/ [Accessed 31 July 2016].

Griffiths, T. (2015). China's mobile payments war is going global. *Ad Age*, [online]. Available at: http://adage.com/article/opinion/china-s-mobile-payments-war-global/301488/ [Accessed 31 July 2016].

Haines, J. (2015) 5 Reasons a job in Asia will propel your creative career forward: Gaining hugely marketable insights. *Adweek*. Available at: www.adweek.com/news/advertising-branding/5-reasons-job-asia-will-propel-your-creative-career-forward-167446 [Accessed 31 July 2016].

Han, S. and Shavitt, S. (1994) Persuasion and culture: Advertising appeals in individualistic and collectivistic societies, *Journal of Experimental Social Psychology*, 30(4): 326–50.

Heine, C. (2013) For mobile marketing that really works, just look to Asia. *Adweek*. Available at: www.adweek.com/news/technology/mobile-marketing-really-works-just-look-asia-147135 [Accessed 31 July 2016].

Incitez China (2015) Weibo to offer video advertising in H1 2016. *Weibo News Watch*. Available at: http://weibowatch.com/weibo-to-offer-video-advertising-in-h1-2016-3028/#. V4ru0-l5j58 [Accessed 31 July 2016].

Incitez China (2016a) China Internet quick overview for 2015. *China Internet Watch*. Available at: www.chinainternetwatch.com/16758/internet-companies-marketing-capacity-2015/ [Accessed 31 July 2016].

Incitez China (2016b) 6 successful social media campaigns in China in 2015. *China Internet Watch*. Available at: www.chinainternetwatch.com/16796/successful-social-media-marketing-cases-2015/ [Accessed 31 July 2016].

Johnson, B. (2014a) What you need to know about the global ad market. *Ad Age*. Available at: http://adage.com/article/global-news/global-ad-market/296104/ [Accessed 31 July 2016].

Johnson, L. (2014b) Study: Mobile marketers should pay attention to China where 71% of consumers watch videos on the go. *Adweek*. Available at: www.adweek.com/news/technology/study-mobile-marketers-should-pay-attention-china-161367 [Accessed 31 July 2016].

Khan, M. and Allil, K. (2010) Determinants of mobile advertising adoption: A cross-country comparison of India and Syria, *International Journal of Mobile Marketing*, 5(1): 41–59.

Kim, H. and Markus, H. (1999) Deviance or uniqueness, harmony or conformity? A cultural analysis, *Journal of Personality and Social Psychology*, 77(4): 785–800.

Liang, B.; Runyan, R. C. and Fu, W. (2011) The effect of culture on the context of ad pictures and ad persuasion: The role of context-dependent and context-independent thinking, *International Marketing Review*, 28(4): 412–434.

Loras, S. (2015) Tencent opens WeChat Moments to all advertisers. Clickz. Available at: www.clickz.com/clickz/news/2423654/tencent-opens-wechat-moments-to-all-advertisers [Accessed 31 July 2016].

Mann, R. (2014) Alibaba preps e-commerce site for worldwide shoppers and advertisers: English version is in the works. *Adweek*. Available at: www.adweek.com/news/advertising-branding/alibaba-unleashing-its-e-commerce-giant-taobao-world-161605 [Accessed 31 July 2016].

McCarthy, T. (2014) Alibab IPO: Market values e-commerce giant at $231bn in enthusiastic opening day-live. *The Guardian*, 19 September.

Nicholson, C. (2016) Global marketing tips: Connecting with Chinese culture. *Lingualinx*. Available at: http://lingualinx.com/blog/global-marketing-tips-connecting-with-chinese-culture/ [Accessed 31 July 2016].

Pasquarelli, A. (2014) Times Square makes way for 'Made in China'. *Crain's*. Available at: www.crainsnewyork.com/article/20140702/RETAIL_APPAREL/140709971/times-square-makes-way-for-made-in-china [Accessed 31 July 2016].

Purnell, N. (2015) China's Renren invests in U.S. startup FiscalNote. *The Wall Street Journal*. 2 February.

Rein, S. (2012) *The End of Cheap China: Economic and Cultural Trends That Will Disrupt the World*. New Jersey: John Wiley.

Rosen, D. and Hanemann, T. (2012) China's growing presence abroad brings new competition but also commercial opportunities. *China Business Review*. Available at: www.chinabusinessreview.com/the-rise-in-chinese-overseas-investment-and-what-it-means-for-american-businesses/ [Accessed 31 July 2016].

Sauer, A. (2012) London 2012: Success as Li-Ning 'makes a change' in Olympics strategy. Brandchannel. Available at: http://brandchannel.com/2012/08/13/london-2012-success-as-li-ning-makes-a-change-in-olympics-strategy/ [Accessed 31 July 2016].

Scharl, A.; Dickinger, A. and Murphy, J. (2005) Diffusion and success factors of mobile marketing, *Electronic Commerce Research Applications*, 4(2): 159–173.

Statista (2016) Market volume of mobile internet in China from 2008 to 2018 (in billion yuan). Available at: www.statista.com/statistics/278530/market-volume-of-mobile-internet-in-china/ [Accessed 31 July 2016].

The State Council, the People's Republic of China (2016) Chinese enterprises enter 'Go Global' era 4.0. Available at: http://english.gov.cn/news/top_news/2016/04/11/content_281475325205328.htm [Accessed 31 July 2016].

Tiezzi, S. (2014) China urges companies to 'go global': Increasing China's outbound investment is part of Beijing's long-term economic and political strategy. *The Diplomat.* Available at: http://thediplomat.com/2014/12/china-urges-companies-to-go-global/ [Accessed 31 July 2016].

Tong, F. (2014) Chinese e-retailers advertise to overseas shoppers on Facebook. *Internet Retailer.* Available at: www.internetretailer.com/2014/06/04/chinese-e-retailers-advertise-overseas-shoppers-facebook [Accessed 31 July 2016].

WARC (2016) World AdSpend: 1980–2016. World Advertising Research Center. Available at: www.warc.com/NotesOnAdspendData [Accessed 31 July 2016].

Wong, S. L. (2015). Blocked in China, Twitter still courts Chinese firms for ads. [online] Reuters. Available at: www.reuters.com/article/twitter-china-idUSL3N0YH2J720150527 [Accessed 31 July 2016].

Xu, B. (1990) *Marketing to China: One Billion New Customers.* Lincolnwood: NTC Business Books.

Xu, D. (2006) The influence of personalization in affecting consumer attitudes toward mobile advertising in China, *Journal of Computer Information Systems*, 47(2): 9–19.

Yeh, J. and Zhang, M. (2013) Taking the pulse of China's ad spending: A big shift in Chinese advertising spending is underway. *McKinsey Quarterly* . Available at: www.mckinsey.com/industries/media-and-entertainment/our-insights/taking-the-pulse-of-chinas-ad-spending [Accessed 31 July 2016].

Yu, H. and Deng, Z. (2000) *A History of Contemporary Advertising in China.* Changsha: Hunan Science and Technology Press.

Zhang, J. (2008) An Examination of Chinese Advertising Growth in 30 Years. Cited in Cheng, H. (2010) Advertising: Wings of the Media, in Scotton, J. and Hachten, W. (eds.) *New Media for New China.* Malden: Wiley-Blackwell: 128–140.

Zhang, X. (2015) Hollywood meets Sina Weibo. *Global Times.* Available at: www.globaltimes.cn/content/921049.shtml [Accessed 31 July 2016].

17

SOCIAL MEDIA AND GLOBAL CONVERSATION

David Feng

During the Mao era, China's communication with the outside world was less that of active dialogue and more one of propagating political messages, disseminating the Communist Party line (Zhao, 2001). This was mostly aimed at a domestic audience but with some expectation that it could find an audience in the outside world. In the wider world, though, there was only limited support amongst traditional communist allies, such as North Korea, the Soviet Union, and Albania, who could, to varying degrees and at different times, identify with Beijing propaganda.

A new reform-oriented – and opening-up – policy was espoused by Deng Xiaoping, who succeeded Mao as China's 'paramount leader'. This was as much about permitting more foreign media into the country as spreading Beijing's messages to the outside world. Both infrastructure-wise as well as in terms of actual media business connections, the years from 1978 (when the reforms were first established) through to 2001 (when the nation joined the World Trade Organisation) were dynamic, with policies which were generally seen as more open than restrictive, although there were limitations at different times for different technologies.

With China becoming a full member of the World Trade Organisation in 2001, it cemented its presence and status as a very visible member of the world community, of almost constant relevance. China's economic strength is of particular note: by nominal GDP, it is the second largest worldwide; by purchasing power parity, it is the largest economy in the world (World Bank, 2015). Debate regarding China in the mass media has also increased, with it receiving almost uninterrupted coverage. The years through to 2022 and beyond will see China rise to even greater prominence on the world stage, although it is also important to note that in spite of the unprecedented importance of the country, and the growth of media and communications industries in China, and other emerging markets, much of the global media, in particular their discourses, are still dominated by the United States (Thussu and Nordenstreng, 2015).

Topics concerning China are, if not an everyday part of worldwide news, an increasing part thereof, and coverage is afforded to China not only on its shortcomings, but also on its successes. The rapid development of the country is a paradox to many Western observers, however, as it combines an economic powerhouse with only limited avenues of democracy, particularly if seen from a purely Western point of view. Whilst a privately held economy appears to have been legalised (Chen, 2013), the expected Western society-oriented democracy that many Anglophone observers see as 'naturally' a part of this has yet to make its presence felt. Yet no matter what fabric the country is made up of, its rise can no longer be ignored. As a result, the country is more visible on the world stage, with noticeable influence – although this is the result of much effort, as it seems to be painting only rosy pictures of itself, when international reports appear more critical (Hu, 2015).

Social media play an integral part in how Chinese messages are being communicated. In this chapter, general policy towards Chinese social media by its official media bodies is examined, as well as two specific examples, one highlighting a current issue in China, and the other an achievement: respectively, smog and pollution in China, and the nation's exceptionally successful high-speed railway network. In doing so, the research will mostly utilise quantitative analysis of recent (April 2016) content on Twitter, by means of its Twitter search for 'top' posts (influential content), and take into account both visibility of the content in official Chinese media, and how it is being reflected upon.

China's electronic presence: diversity in conversation but also scepticism of official channels?

China's population, be it offline or online, is the largest around the globe. In recent years, expansion in the population of China in cyberspace has evolved from merely 'growing numbers' to an equal focus in 'growing quality' (Luo and Mi, 2014).

Perplexingly, China is both seen as officially unitary in viewpoints, and very much diverse in its arts. Great poets, artists, and thinkers, such as Li Bai, Confucius, and Xu Beihong, are well-known to audiences both inside and outside the nation, yet official media outlets, be it the Di Bao from imperial times, or the current-day *People's Daily*, are known for what outsiders might initially consider visibly lopsided reporting. The Chinese expression, *bao xi bu bao you* ('report the good, never the bad'), is seen to apply with few exceptions to official reports.

Although critics, from at home and abroad, might further contend that Chinese media systems, in particular their regulators (or as seen by some censors) also desire to keep the audience in the dark regarding scandals involving government, the Chinese situation is not a unique case. There is coverage of current affairs as desired by a national government, or even political spin, even in other nations such as the United States (Qiu and Shi, 2013). It is only with the increasing visibility of social media that new forms of public opinion are possible. The government is not blind to this development: it understands that information can be received and disseminated from any computer connected to the World Wide Web. This being such a paradigm shift in communicating messages, the government needed to take an active part, in particular during events which might focus on negative coverage of the authorities (Cao, 2010). A particular point to note is the speed at which such messages are conveyed, communicated, and disseminated online.

China is attempting to make its voice better heard in the contemporary stream of world communications, although its effort is met internationally with scepticism and criticism, especially in this neo-liberalist economy of communications (Hu and Li, 2014). Hence, China might appear to struggle to find its position in the contemporary global media scene, where Anglophone media remain more or less dominant, as they often present outsiders with an outdated or otherwise unrealistic view of situations in the country. Upon a closer examination of the present-day situation in China, one can conclude reality is quite different and that there are limits to the ways in which Western media theories can be applied in China.

Traditional views on international communication

Chinese media have always aimed to broaden the audience receiving its messages. It feels entitled to: the country argues it needs its own voice, in particular in the context of its rise in power and importance. This has, to many observers and lay people, always been the case. However, this has been particularly amplified since the current President, Xi Jinping, became more proactive, both domestically and with his many state visits around the world (Xu, 2015). With this activity, however, comes also a great variety of views and, amongst these, misunderstanding is ultimately inevitable. The country is at times misunderstood and such misunderstanding is as detrimental to its own interests as it is to the interests of the wider international community. As neighbouring countries feel uncomfortable about the rise of China, Beijing itself feels an equal degree of unease, or threat, even, when it finds it has to contend with the major force in Asia, the United States (de Burgh, 2006).

In communicating a China-based voice, it has to utilise international channels of communication. China-based media intended for international audiences include the country's international broadcasters: amongst them are the Xinhua news agency, China Central Television, and China Radio International. (If one elects to ignore the developments brought about by the internet and online presence of other China-based media, these three would in essence be the 'sole' presence of the country outside its borders.) By this definition, international broadcasting is the use of media, electronic and otherwise, by one society (China) to shape the opinions of the people and leaders of another (Price, 2002). Chinese media tend to propagate news of the country's positive achievements and, whilst this is worthy of being communicated, it fails to capture the attention of worldwide audiences, in particular in the rather sensationalised world outside Chinese borders and particularly in Western societies. Western audiences would expect also to find coverage on negative issues, a matter the Chinese media has struggled to do well.

At the time when Severe Acute Respiratory Syndrome (SARS) hit China in 2003, there was plenty of publicity on the changeover of power from Jiang Zemin to Hu Jintao, but visible coverage of SARS only happened after the parliamentary session concluded. Access to foreign media was restricted until the sackings of former Beijing Mayor Meng Xuenong and former Health Minister Zhang Wenkang were announced, and only then were the media given significant access. In 2008, Beijing appeared to have learnt its 2003 lessons by granting access to both national and international media organisations just hours after the Wenchuan earthquake struck southwestern China. Access permitted this time was much wider than before, giving a more positive image to foreign media (Pan, 2011).

However, coverage of China by its own media organisations, whether using traditional or 'new' media, remains controversial. It is made even more complicated if Beijing's use of media, especially for an international audience, is considered. If propaganda is defined as an attempt to affect the personalities and to control the behaviour of individuals towards ends considered unscientific or of doubtful value in a society at a particular time (Doob, 1966), this is far less the case in contemporary communications than at an earlier period in the history of communist China, especially regarding Mao-era elements such as personality cults and what can be termed the politicisation of the masses. Coverage, dissemination and propaganda itself, as seen in China, has changed, certainly on the surface, since 1976, but Beijing is still unwilling to make fundamental changes in its communications policy, with some even claiming that there is good reason for China to continue not just propaganda, but also its theoretical research and analysis. Beijing is also very conscious of anti-Beijing rhetoric by what it terms 'Westernisers' or 'splitters' (Wu, 2015) and their messages to the detriment of China. There is also pressure, however, from academics and professionals, arguing that there is a need to change methods of communication from 'propaganda to an international audience' (*duiwai xuanchuan*) to 'communicating to an international audience' (*duiwai chuanbo*), and this is needed if China is to be better 'explained' to a more global audience (Zhang, 2014).

From a more holistic perspective, though, there is no doubt that the Beijing authorities have a message – or many messages – to convey. The form they are communicating this in appears rather mixed: at times such outward journalism or communication is too official or with too much of a 'missionary' purpose (Schneider and Raue, 2003); at other times, though, the reporting is more balanced. In recent years, Chinese authorities have attempted to expand their international reach, making their messages travel further. In doing so, upgrades and new editions of government-funded or government-controlled media have been rolled out, and more focus has been given to what Beijing deems its 'external publicity work' (Jacques, 2012). Clear examples include the 24-hour Xinhua TV, as well as the CCTV-News channel, now in a multitude of languages, reaching a claimed audience of 125 million. Other key players in this include the Xinhua news agency, China Central Television, China Radio International, *China Daily*, *People's Daily*, the China International Publishing Group, and the China News Service (Yao, 2014). But as important as it is to communicate the messages from a traditional, authoritative source, China must also leverage the channels that are social media, both domestically on WeChat, Weibo, Youku, and Tudou (Wolf, 2015), and internationally.

Sea changes of social media: how is China adapting?

The Information Age does not, according to Castells (2010: xix), 'present a formal, systematic theory of society'; rather, new concepts, as well as new theoretical perspectives in understanding trends characterising the structure and dynamics of the societies all belonging to the contemporary, twenty-first-century world, are proposed. The arrival of the internet has also meant the arrival of major changes. On the one hand, some causes for concern include conflicts regarding legal issues, forms and paradigms of communications, as well as the incomes and lifestyles of some members of society. However, the impact of the internet upon society will also see an increasing influx of information, as well as further globalisation in society. In addition, there will be major changes in economic structures, the importance of the information industry will be further emphasised and there will be changes in the labour market (Hu, 2008).

China has been connected to the internet since 1994 and, through the evolution of the Web, it has changed its tactics, even if these may not be very visible to the outside world. During the pre-Web 2.0 era, otherwise known as the Web 1.0 era, there was greater focus on simply moving content online, if only to foil any containment policies the West may have had for China. One of the earliest such cases was the 1995 launch of *China Daily*'s official website (Liu *et al.*, 2014). The Web 2.0 era was much more centred on multimedia and variety in broadcasting China's messages online to the outside world, with a main focus on communicating, not merely propagating its messages to cyberspace. However, even this underwent significant changes, especially with the arrival of new media, particularly social media. The arrival of new technology is coupled with an increasing focus, desire even, to communicate the country's messages beyond its borders, given its importance in the contemporary world.

New media has resulted in deep-seated changes in how messages are being disseminated. What was previously a means of communicating messages, made possible only by resorting to expensive, one-to-many means of communication, is now being replaced by a more diversified means, which can even involve user-generated content (Qiu and Chan, 2009). Indeed, social media is visibly participatory and this model is often opposed to the mass media and broadcasting model typical of (and previously generally seen in society) the era of newspapers, radio, and television (Fuchs, 2014).

The arrival of the World Wide Web has also meant, for the Chinese government, that it must regard the Web as a force to be reckoned with. Whereas, previously, reports unfavourable to the government could be censored or controlled, sometimes with force, this is clearly no longer the case (Li, 2012). Indeed, the tendency is for quite the opposite of blocking – it also calls for increased transparency. On a domestic level, 'official' participants, starting with individuals in government, have been on social media since late 2009 (Guo, 2010). However variable their early success might have been, Chinese 'officialdom' decided it did not want to miss out on the rise of social media. More recently, official Chinese media – seen by some as government mouthpieces and others as authoritative sources – have expanded beyond their existing operations, providing content to local users in Chinese and are now expanding their footprint to the wider world by using non-Chinese social media platforms, including Twitter and Facebook.

Branding and communicating with a relatively unified voice to the rest of the world are necessary for any organisation, and Xinhua news agency has not been blind to this. On 1 March 2015, Xinhua relaunched its social media platforms under a new brand, New China (Xiang, 2015). In doing so, it also stressed the importance of building an 'online news agency' to enhance its influence via new media, as stated by the news agency's executives. This move comes as part of China's series of actions on ensuring its state-operated media have a voice overseas. In spite of China's solidly being part of Weibo and WeChat, and possessing its own smartphone apps, it is the overseas market outside the Chinese mainland that is the new target for building influence.

Given the rapid emergence and prevalence of social media – blogs and otherwise – external communications must be adaptable to new challenges. In particular, when there are issues of concern, a conversation must be maintained as much between non-state entities as between governments and the wider public (Scoble and Israel, 2006). When Beijing's policies – especially if they are of concern to the world community – are discussed at length the world over, China must not appear weak or remain blind to such developments. As an example, the Chinese economy has, since entering the 12th Five-Year Plan period in 2011, not registered the double-digit growth it was well-known for during the earlier period of its reform policies. Both at home and abroad, economic analysts have shown concern, even pessimism, and theories of China's economy poised to 'hit a brick wall', or that, in China, the 'bubble is about to burst', continue unabated (Cai, 2015). Beijing is fully aware of the situation and of the views, both locally and internationally.

Views are, at times, restricted in Chinese cyberspace, which the outsider may see as 'censorship'. Whilst certainly arising from a different state and state of affairs than in a typical liberal democracy that many in the Anglosphere might be familiar with, Chinese internet regulations are not entirely random and laws at national level are being drafted and implemented. Early hopes that the internet would bring about a fundamental change in the political system have hit 'hard reality'; instead, the Chinese nation-state has seemingly 'harnessed' the internet, although in a very different way than Westerners might assume. In more recent years, the rhetoric that the internet is supposed to, in Western terms, 'free' China, is less and less realistic. Since the financial crisis of 2008, China, which the West traditionally sees as a 'closed' society, has done visibly better than 'open' ones (Cohen, 2013). Some in Chinese officialdom questioned, as a matter of fact, why Americans were so adamant that China should allow free speech, on terms such as those in the United States, when the latter was going through a crisis and China was booming. In spite of a basic ban on Twitter and Facebook for mainland users, which has existed since mid-2009, exceptions appear to have been made for its government-run media to the outside world, in particular in the wake of key visits by Chinese leaders – such as

President Xi Jinping's visit to the US in autumn 2015 (CNN, 2015). Such 'exceptional' coverage has attracted attention – and critical attention at that – by mainstream Western media.

This apparently perplexing and exceptional situation has been made even more complex with official media in China apparently increasingly interested in how they are seen from outside. A new Xinhua column, launched in 2015, takes a look at 'What's being said on Twitter about China', this coincidentally also being the name of the column itself (Florcruz, 2015). While China intends to permit more views on the country, it also desires to retain control as to what is actually being covered. Hand-picked Twitter feeds from international news organisations, including CNN, or even the Milan Expo feeds, portray non-controversial topics about the country.

What must be noted, however, is that social media, in terms of audience reception versus communication, function in a different paradigm than traditional media. Whereas in traditional media it was comparatively difficult for the audience to 'talk back', or to communicate further, this is not true with social media. Social media incorporate a public sphere, although, at best, a limited version of that and, at worst, one that is visibly flawed in function. On social media, not just the views of the broadcaster are visible, but also those of the audience. There is apparently greater equality here; audiences, too, join in the discourse. Not only is access granted to all (who choose to take part), but all may confer, or engage in discourse, so possess also the rights of the auditor and of the speaker (Sparks, 1998). As will be made clearer later in this chapter, China-based government-funded media are far from being the sole participants in any discourse related to China.

Chinese issues: the examples of smog and pollution

Before the economic development resulting from the reform and opening-up policies espoused by a 'second generation' of leaders centred on Deng Xiaoping, the skies around China were visibly less polluted, thanks to comparatively limited production activity and fewer cars. Since the 1980s, and in particular since the late 1990s, however, car ownership has mushroomed, new buildings have appeared almost everywhere and polluting activity has continued to increase.

In Beijing, for example, the city was the victim of sandstorms in the early to mid-2000s before smog became a matter of concern. In fact, smog was hardly an issue in the official eyes of city mandarins – the government tended to regard this more as 'fog' as opposed to real smog. Initially, Beijing residents, whilst concerned about poor air, saw it as part of the modernisation of the Chinese capital. Chinese state-owned media did remarkably little in introducing the wording itself – 'smog' – tending to favour 'fog' instead. In the late 2000s, however, this saw a visible change, and in the early 2010s, concerns from citizens reached fever pitch.

Awareness of Beijing's polluted air came from a source that must have appeared rather innocuous: in 2008, the US Embassy in Beijing installed a rooftop air-quality monitor which would tweet air-quality data hourly (Wired, 2015). Instead of reporting based on evaluations of PM 10, the much finer and critically important PM 2.5 particles – which can enter people's bloodstream and penetrate lungs, and are thus a much more felt health hazard – were the basis of reports tweeted by the embassy's Twitter account, @BeijingAir. Beijing residents could now (at first directly, then indirectly) obtain more detailed information about air pollution – which became an issue when the city authorities, using the outdated PM 10 standard, reported a 'blue-sky' day when the US Embassy's Twitter account reported much more severe circumstances.

In recent years, the Chinese government has become more open and willing to 'face the music' when it comes to the sensitive issue of air pollution. Official media now also provide a fair number of good insights; the authorities also are more open regarding the effects of global warming and climate change (van Kerckhove, 2012). The enactment of a revised Environment Protection Law, which, in the newest version that took effect on 1 January 2015, saw no upper limit for fines that could be imposed on polluters, was just one of the many actions the Chinese authorities took to tackle smog.

The matter was brought before a huge nationwide audience both inside and outside China by Chai Jing's 2015 documentary, 'Under the Dome'. Amidst this backdrop of developments, former CCTV anchorwoman Chai Jing's 2015 documentary, 'Under the Dome', took a personal (from Chai's view) but also relatively comprehensive look at the situation of China and smog. Using statistics and one-on-one interviews, from both the US and China, the documentary was publicised merely days before the start of the 2015 *lianghui* – when the National People's Congress and the Chinese People's Political Consultative Conference met in Beijing.

The documentary was already highly popular immediately following its release. Communications-wise, it made use of very simple-to-understand, very approachable language. The addition of context-relevant statistics also made it appear more credible. Finally, Chai, in spite of coming in close contact with Chinese officialdom, did not elect to use such views or language as are typically used by the Beijing authorities (LSE China Development Society, 2015). Released on the eve of the 2015 *lianghui*, or annual session of the Chinese parliamentary bodies – both the national legislature, the National People's Congress, and the 'advisory body', the Chinese People's Political Consultative Conference – the documentary was banned before the official start of the legislature's session, but its arguments had already 'slipped through the doors' of China's huge governing complex.

In December 2015, under new guidelines published by the Beijing municipal government, the revised regulations, including the first-ever actual enforcement of 'red alert days' for poor air quality, was new and newsworthy not only for Beijing, but also for the rest of the world. In relation to its reputation for poor air quality, the Chinese capital had hit an all-time nadir, certainly in recent memory. Twice the city hit the red alert threshold, 7 December 2015 being the first. A great many measures had to be enforced: 50 per cent of cars were forced off the road in the odd–even numberplate system, construction sites and factories were shut, and schools were closed for over three days (Connor, 2015).

Smog on social media

This case study on smog is based on quantitative analysis of recent (April 2016) content on Twitter, by means of its Twitter search for 'top' posts (influential content), taking into account visibility by official Chinese media and how it is being reflected upon. In this research, a fixed timeframe of between 19:37 and 19:43 British Summer Time on 15 April 2016 was set. Twitter Search for 'top' (influential) posts were limited to the search strings set out below (representative in terms of the general search string used, content with an official Chinese media organisation being @mentioned, and mentions during the two sessions with the #lianghui hashtag). As a major body of official Chinese media, the Xinhua news agency @XHNews was used as the sole representative and account-in-question.

The search terms employed were as follows:

- Beijing smog (Twitter, 2016a)
- China smog (Twitter, 2016d)
- @XHNews pollution (Twitter, 2016g)
- @XHNews smog (Twitter, 2016h)
- #lianghui pollution (Twitter, 2016k)
- #lianghui smog (Twitter, 2016l)

The 'Off.' (Official Interactions) column notes the following interactions:

- L = link present leading to article on Chinese media site (here: Xinhua)
- R = content retweeted or @mention-retweeted (older-style retweet)
- @ = Xinhua was @mentioned or @replied to in relation to this tweet

Table 17.1 sets out the first 15 results (in the order as provided by the Twitter listing itself); in some circumstances, a lesser number of results were provided.

From the above, it appears that official Chinese media, with Xinhua as the example, appears only to have limited reach and influence in the search terms as described above. There was an almost full absence of official Chinese media, represented by Xinhua (@XHNews), when generic terms, including 'China smog' and 'Beijing smog[1]', were being searched on Twitter Top Tweets. The official account only emerged in a slightly more visible fashion when it was specifically mentioned as part of the search string.

Interaction was most visible where @XHNews was mentioned or part of the conversation. There appeared to be slightly more cases of @mentions (11 out of 30 tweets) than retweets (7 out of 30), although it is important to note that there were three such tweets where there was both a @mention and a retweet, most likely to cite the source of such coverage as from @XHNews.

It is of interest, however, to note that another authoritative Chinese news source, the Beijing Review (@BeijingReview), was made more visible when the search string included #lianghui. Although this particular research did not consider the

TABLE 17.1 Results based on case study on smog

	China smog	Date	Off.		Beijing smog	Date	Off.
1	@nytimesworld	12 Apr 2016		1	@DaneeBound	13 Apr 2016	
2	@from_UGND	15 Apr 2016		2	@RobotUnderscore	12 Apr 2016	
3	@HeidiKarlsson	13 Apr 2016		3	@NewsFB	12 Apr 2016	
4	@SaveTheWater	13 Apr 2016		4	@oceanwave11	14 Apr 2016	
5	@StanfordEnergy	12 Apr 2016		5	@UrbanPlanner34	14 Apr 2016	
6	@calestous	14 Apr 2016		6	@RFA_Ed	14 Apr 2016	
7	@EcoMarketplace	14 Apr 2016		7	@RFA_Ed	14 Apr 2016	
8	@Julian_Doczi	14 Apr 2016		8	@KendellRizkall	14 Apr 2016	
9	@TaigaCompany	13 Apr 2016		9	@Socraplastotle	14 Apr 2016	
10	@insideclimate	13 Apr 2016		10	@choe_sarah	13 Apr 2016	
11	@johnupton	12 Apr 2016		11	@NonsenseFinder	13 Apr 2016	
12	@Brent_Huffman	12 Apr 2016		12	@Himalayacool	12 Apr 2016	
13	@wrobertsfood	12 Apr 2016		13	@Koreatown213	12 Apr 2016	
14	@kunktation	12 Apr 2016		14	@Natasha_Parry28	12 Apr 2016	
15	@EconomicTimes	12 Apr 2016		15	@Janiceontv	12 Apr 2016	

	@XHNews smog	Date	Off.		@XHNews pollution	Date	Off.
1	@NRDCChina	13 Apr 2016	L	1	@XHNews	12 Apr 2016	T L
2	@atrueblueaussie	12 Apr 2016	@	2	@xiejiafu520	10 Apr 2016	@
3	@JuettC	13 Apr 2016	@	3	@DibakarGhosh111	10 Apr 2016	@
4	@Jenmus88	01 Apr 2016	@	4	@bodhibrian	10 Apr 2016	@
5	@davidfreelander	01 Apr 2016	R	5	@ICD_climate	08 Apr 2016	@
6	@XHNews	31 Mar 2016	T L	6	@KariKarijoh	06 Apr 2016	@
7	@XHNews	29 Mar 2016	T L	7	@Teddywade32	05 Apr 2016	@
8	@smog_wawelski	20 Mar 2016	R	8	@davidfreelander	01 Apr 2016	@
9	@bikejourno	17 Mar 2016	R	9	@manana_phoenix	01 Apr 2016	@
10	@BrujoUfoAlien	11 Mar 2016	@	10	@sarimasari	26 Mar 2016	@ R
11	@ThusSpeaksYHWH	08 Mar 2016	@	11	@RosenthalEllery	26 Mar 2016	@
12	@Shehu_III	05 Mar 2016	R L	12	@XHNews	23 Mar 2016	T L
13	@ChinaAirQuality	04 Mar 2016	@	13	@XHNews	22 Mar 2016	T L
14	@anilbhattarai	04 Mar 2016	@ R	14	@XHNews	18 Mar 2016	T L
15	@luxferorr	03 Mar 2016	@	15	@acasislumi	17 Mar 2016	@

	#lianghui smog	Date	Off.		#lianghui pollution	Date	Off.
1	@DavidFeng	05 Mar 2016		1	@clemtan	08 Mar 2016	
2	@BeijingReview	07 Mar 2014		2	@DavidFeng	05 Mar 2016	
3	@BeijingReview	07 Mar 2014		3	@DavidFeng	05 Mar 2016	
4	@BeijingReview	06 Mar 2014		4	@BeijingReview	13 Mar 2014	
5	@DavidFeng	05 Mar 2014		5	@BeijingReview	07 Mar 2014	
6				6	@CAMG_Media	06 Mar 2014	
7				7	@NatdiMontgo	05 Mar 2014	
8				8	@chinafrica1	04 Mar 2014	
9				9	@BeijingReview	03 Mar 2014	

Beijing Review as a key player or a representative official Chinese news voice, its actual placing in the Chinese news system means it should also be seen as an official Chinese voice.

The quantitative investigation as undertaken here presents an initial overview of the presence of Chinese official media on social media (using Xinhua @XHNews as a representative), as well as interactions and reactions. Objectively speaking, it can be considered an adequate method of analysing how visible Chinese media are on Twitter on certain topics, how they are being viewed and which ways the interactions take place, as well as how influential they are. It also focuses on the usage of @mentions and #hashtags on Twitter on pertinent topics, two elements of Twitter which are of increasing importance.

Xinhua is viewed as a key representative of Chinese official media, but it cannot, for all its 'officialness', be viewed as the sole authoritative voice of even state media for the country. Furthermore, the selection of solely Twitter as an area of analysis limits how discourse on other networks is seen. The varied presence or lack of results – with some results yielding far less than the minimum 15 sought after – may have indicated a lack of results; alternatively, network failure could have been blamed as well, although a relatively reliable public wireless network was used when the Twitter search system was used. In the interests of uniformity and accuracy, subsequent searches of results were not conducted. In spite of the importance of China in the contemporary world, the fact that Twitter has a largely Anglophone audience, and this audience's tendency to focus more on matters 'at home', mean that the results as presented are conceivably disproportionate with what would be expected. It could be conjectured that such shortcomings would be absent or less of an issue should this be repeated in future, when the service would have been populated with more relevant content.

Whilst content regarding pollution, often a rather difficult and uncomfortable topic, was predictably negative about the current situation in China, different results were found when research was conducted on a topic often seen as a success for China: its high-speed railway system.

Chinese successes: the example of the national high-speed rail project

To many Chinese citizens, the train is probably the most familiar mode of transport in getting around such a vast nation. In the 1970s, the aeroplane remained very much off-limits to many; a letter of introduction, or for the very small number of Chinese expatriates abroad, a passport was required to secure a train ticket. The development of commercial aviation, combined with the loosening of travel restrictions, have put the plane closer to the reach of millions, if not billions, but contemporary air travel is beset with, at times, massive delays.

The evolution of Chinese high-speed rail (HSR) offers a cleaner and lower-cost alternative. China's first 350 km/h (217 mph) HSR line opened on 1 August 2008, with the 120 km (75 mi) Beijing–Tianjin Intercity Railway linking the two northern

Chinese metropolises in just around half an hour. Newer links have opened in subsequent years, with the opening of the Beijing–Shanghai High-Speed Railway on 30 June 2011, a major event with VIP patronage (NetEase, 2011).

On 23 July 2011, however, Trains D301 and D3115 crashed just north of Wenzhou, southeastern China: 40 lives were lost, and the nationwide HSR project took a major hit. Amongst other causes, the crash was blamed on corruption and mismanagement (Wolf, 2012); others have also hinted at errors or failures related to signalling. While some criticism had existed before the crash due to the roll-out of the national HSR network, in the immediate months following the Wenzhou disaster public opinion towards HSR was highly critical. Calls for Sheng Guangzu, then the leader of the Chinese mainland authorities in charge of national railway operations, to resign, were only one example of the largely negative messages being conveyed; some newspapers went further, resorting to expletives and other foul language to criticise the Chinese mainland rail authorities.

In the wake of such a crisis, much of the rhetoric concerning Chinese HSR remained negative, with opposition and doubts about the system being particularly noticeable. Noelle-Neumann (1993) defined the theory of the 'spiral of silence' as when views differing from the main, or dominating viewpoint, are silenced, or are giving such limited airing that the majority viewpoint is easily favoured. As only a few would intend to be seen as dissenting, or not conforming with the 'mainstream' view, the views of the 'mainstream' continued to grow in volume.

In this environment of mostly negative coverage of the national HSR project, new lines were delayed, downgraded, or in isolated cases, cancelled or paused. Passenger numbers shrank; the once high-flying Beijing–Shanghai HSR was reported to be carrying less than 30 per cent the number of people than there were seats, with business class completely empty (Zhu, 2011).

The worst effects for Chinese HSR did not last long, however; funding eventually resumed, thus saving the project and getting it back on track, as it was realised that the project had potential (Feng, 2013). In early 2012 and throughout 2013, HSR 'bounced back' and more high-speed lines were opened. Two major lines opened up to traffic by 2014: the 2,298 km Beijing–Guangzhou HSR, and the 1,777 km Lanzhou–Ürümqi HSR. Passenger numbers increased as did the number of trains, and the introduction of internet and smartphone ticketing made ticketing much easier for the population.

Amidst this background, it would be only natural that construction of new trunk lines would continue, but particularly noteworthy was the resumption of a whole range of new lines built for 217 mph (350 km/h). As is the case with many of these new lines under construction, the main reasons for their construction, apart from completing and expanding the national HSR network, also included linking more provinces more comprehensively, accelerating the process of urbanisation, stimulating economic growth in the cities situated along the new lines, better developing the role of the railways in the national integrated transport system, and serving a greener society (*Shanghai Railway Daily*, 2015). By late 2015, the national network spanned 19,000 km, with 60 per cent of the world's HSR rails in Chinese territories, with 2020 figures envisioning a 30,000 km national high-speed railway network (National People's Congress of the People's Republic of China via Xinhua, 2016). To improve efficiency, 350 km/h railway services resumed operations at this speed in September 2017.

This research analysed how, through social media, the world perceived the Chinese national HSR project on social media, which in general has been seen as a major success. Whilst not analysing China Railways's own social media strategies, it is also of note that they have used a period of two years to become a major social media communicator – very remarkable for a body which was, before the 2013 reforms, mainly seen as a 'political propaganda organ' for the railways.

Chinese high-speed rail on social media

As with the previous research, a fixed timeframe of between 19:37 and 19:43 British Summer Time on 15 April 2016 was set. Twitter Search for 'top' (influential) posts were limited to the search strings listed below (representative in terms of the general search string used, content with an official Chinese media organisation being @ mentioned, and mentions during the two sessions with the #lianghui hashtag).

As was previously the case, the Xinhua news agency @XHNews was used as the sole representative of Chinese state media, and remained the account-in-question. The search terms employed were as follows:

- China high speed rail (Twitter, 2016b)
- China HSR (Twitter, 2016c)
- #lianghui high speed rail (Twitter, 2016i)
- @XHNews high speed rail (Twitter, 2016e)
- @XHNews HSR (Twitter, 2016f)
- #lianghui HSR (Twitter, 2016j)

To the benefit of this research, frequently used derivations of a term, such as both the fully written-out term 'high speed rail', were employed, as well as the frequently used abbreviation HSR, which caused the research to encompass a wider focus.[2]

As was previously the case, but also in addition, the 'Off.' (Official Interactions) column notes the following interactions:

- F = tweet mentioned general railway developments overseas
- H = tweet mentioned railway developments in Hong Kong / Macao / Taiwan
- I = tweet mentioned Chinese railway involvement overseas
- L = link present leading to article on Chinese media site (here: Xinhua)
- R = content retweeted or @mention-retweeted (older-style retweet)
- @ = Xinhua was @mentioned or @replied to in relation to this tweet

Table 17.2 sets out the first 15 results (in the order as provided by the Twitter listing itself); for some there were fewer results.

As was the case with smog and pollution, @XHNews only made appearances in results where the Twitter account was specifically mentioned in the search string.

TABLE 17.2 Results based on case study on Chinese high-speed rail

	China high speed rail	Date	Off.		China HSR	Date	Off.
1	@Whtapl	13 Apr 2016		1	@jarrodmyrick	15 Apr 2016	
2	@ColbyBermel	12 Apr 2016		2	@aditnamasaya	13 Apr 2016	
3	@andreaventura01	12 Apr 2016		3	@JOHARIWINDOWS	12 Apr 2016	
4	@Whtapl	12 Apr 2016		4	@oneinbillion	11 Apr 2016	
5	@eububble	14 Apr 2016		5	@Sublevelcaver	10 Apr 2016	
6	@guideme_japan	14 Apr 2016		6	@maglevboard	09 Apr 2016	
7	@KSDA	14 Apr 2016		7	@highspeedrai_dp	07 Apr 2016	
8	@RailAnalysis	13 Apr 2016		8	@JuruteraAwam	06 Apr 2016	
9	@China__agent	13 Apr 2016		9	@JuruteraAwam	06 Apr 2016	
10	@oscarco81074367	13 Apr 2016		10	@DavidFeng	05 Apr 2016	
11	@MGliksmanMDPhD	12 Apr 2016		11	@klscoop	04 Apr 2016	
12	@KhanAsid_Speaks	12 Apr 2016		12	@carnewsm	04 Apr 2016	
13	@jmwdvin	11 Apr 2016		13	@klspeed	04 Apr 2016	
14	@NicholasJThomas	11 Apr 2016		14	@cheechoong	04 Apr 2016	
15	@shellzzz	11 Apr 2016		15	@ShazGhaF	04 Apr 2016	

	@XHNews high speed rail	Date	Off.		@XHNews HSR	Date	Off.
1	@XHNews	05 Mar 2016	T	1	@tekhelet	24 Jan 2016	@
2	@VOAStevenson	03 Mar 2016	—	2	@knol2go	12 Dec 2015	@
3	@XHNews	26 Feb 2016	T L I	3	@XHNews	12 Dec 2015	T
4	@XHNews	13 Feb 2016	T L	4	@SRA525	05 Dec 2015	@
5	@XHNews	06 Feb 2016	T	5	@jaipurvinayrs	24 Sep 2015	@
6	@XHNews	06 Feb 2016	T H	6	@XHNews	05 Feb 2015	T L F
7	@PabloFootball	24 Jan 2016	@	7	@XHNews	30 Jan 2015	T
8	@Geopolitica	19 Jan 2016	@	8			
9	@XHNews	27 Dec 2015	T	9			
10	@knol2go	12 Dec 2015	@	10			
11	@shenolm	24 Dec 2015	R @ F	11			
12	@XHNews	24 Dec 2015	T	12			
13	@XHNews	17 Oct 2015	T I	13			
14	@XHNews	17 Oct 2015	T L I	14			
15				15			

	#lianghui high speed rail	Date	Off.		#lianghui HSR	Date	Off.
1	@clemtan	07 Mar 2016		1	@DavidFeng	05 Mar 2016	
2	@DavidFeng	15 Mar 2014		2	@DavidFeng	05 Mar 2015	

However, @XHNews does appear to be far more visible as part of the search string when HSR was being searched, rather than when pollution was the main search term.

Coverage made by Xinhua in such situations tended to focus on China-centric rail developments, although with China's increased activity overseas, focus on overseas rail involvements was mentioned as well; three out of 21 tweets mentioned China's involvement abroad.

The topic of Chinese HSR could be slightly less relevant with regard to global discourse, as it is not given the same amount of attention as was the case with smog and pollution. It is possible this is due to the fact that smog and pollution cause acute and visible harm to people, whereas HSR was of slightly lesser concern due to it being less of a health hazard. It should also be remarked that most of the content of the tweets analysed were largely in favour, or envious of China's HSR system.

Social media 'stage time' for China: increasing visibility and managing issues regarding misconceptions

As can be inferred from the results, of most concern is a relative lack of presence of official Chinese media on matters which are of general discussion: the Chinese media do not appear to be addressing these two issues using context-relevant hashtags or other content. A lack of presence on the part of the Chinese media, however, can be seen also in an alternative way, in that the Chinese media outlet does not appear to be too 'visible' and thus, in the eyes of more critical observers, too 'interfering' in this discourse. This, however, could also be to the detriment of Beijing, as it risks 'losing' the discourse. Key here, however, is the recognition that Twitter is what can be referred to as 'international cyberspace'; thus the population of content tweeted by other sources, particularly private and non-Chinese sources, is expected to be more visible.

On a number of topics, which are outside the issues discussed in this chapter, this may well not be the case, and Chinese media may have a more visible role. For example, coverage of the full government sessions (*Lianghui*), as well as President Xi's official visits overseas, may make use of other hashtags or otherwise contain content which may elevate the visibility of Chinese media. On the two topics discussed here, however, visibility of the Chinese official media sources is limited by their approach to social media.

Certainly, if viewed from Beijing's position, if it wished to be a guiding, influential force on a China-centric topic, increased presence and dissemination of its content would be desirable. In particular, should there be coverage with views or events detrimental to the positive image Beijing wants to project, the government would need to act appropriately for the digital age, i.e. with speed, content, and attitude – as scandals and negative coverage have a tendency to be disseminated very rapidly and often at great detriment to the parties concerned (Pöksen and Detel, 2012). However, in the interests of more diversified discourse, the presence of other Twitter users would also be of use. Objectively speaking, it is vital for

Beijing to have a voice if it wishes to communicate messages of importance – such as elaborating its stance on a controversial topic. It is best served, however, if its visibility is restricted so that it is more retweeted, rather than merely being visible, for a retweet broadens its dissemination and visibility amongst other private individual users.

Governing bodies in charge of China's official presence on social media would benefit from a greater understanding of the meaning and effects of social media on contemporary society and vice versa. The internet is faster than merely 'electronic' media; it stores and disseminates what is almost limitless content. Its form as a convenient, free, and open community will also mean a new type of online community that is worthy of analysis (Chen and Yu, 2012). As is the case in current media policy in the country, the media are to be controlled by the ruling party (Zhao, 2008). In doing so, the political apparatus expects to convey messages to its benefit, also to the world by means of a wide variety of channels. It is here that particular attention needs to be paid – neither the overuse of 'official' content where not needed, nor a 'hands-off' approach is conducive to managing its voice to the outside world. At the same time, it cannot be blind to assumptions the outside world has regarding government-run media apparatus. This is further complicated by the novelty of social media and particularly to China's official presence. In using its official channels to 'talk down the microphone', it would also be wise to 'listen to the conversation' and turn to a 'one-to-the-masses' form of communication, transforming official stances, as was the case with traditional media (Bi, 2002), into a more conversational form.

Notes

1 The research was confined to Beijing but broader research could include other sources of pollution and other heavily polluted cities (including Lanzhou, Western China, or Xingtai, Northern China), which would have provided for a more in-depth analysis of the matter. Similarly, less polluted cities, such as Sanya, Hainan, could also be analysed.
2 In terms of the high-speed rail research, it is important to note that contents which are somewhat related to 'China' and 'HSR' but were actually of a different topic, such as the export of China HSR technologies or overseas HSR projects with Chinese involvement, were included though not intentionally.

References

Bi, Zheng (2002) Xinwen Boyin (News Announcing), in Zhang, S. (ed.) *Zhongguo Boyinxue (Broadcasting Announcing in China)*. Beijing: Communication University of China Press: 388–403.

Cai, Fang (2015) Dispelling pessimism over China's economic outlook, *Qiushi* (English edition), 7(22): 48–52.

Cao, Jinsong (2010) *Zhengfu Wangluo Chuanbo (Government Internet Communications)*. Nanjing: Jiangsu People's Press.

Castells, Manuel (2010) *The Rise of the Network Society. The Information Age: Economy, Society, and Culture*, second edition, Vol. 1. Malden, MA: Wiley-Blackwell.

Chen, Changfeng and Yu, Xin (2012) *Wangluo Shidai de Shengshi Weiyan – Hulianwang yu Shehui Bianqian (The Cyber Age: The Internet and Social Change).* Beijing: Beijing Publishing House.

Chen, Jie (2013) *A Middle Class Without Democracy: Economic Growth and the Prospects for Democratization in China.* Oxford: Oxford University Press.

CNN (2015) Beijing Uses Banned Social Media to Promote Xi's U.S. Visit. Available at: http://money.cnn.com/2015/09/27/technology/china-facebook-xi-jinping-ban/ [Accessed 22 December 2015].

Cohen, Nick (2013) *You Can't Read This Book.* London: Fourth Estate.

Connor, Neil (2015) Beijing Issues First-Ever Smog 'Red Alert' to Shut Down City. *The Guardian,* 7 December.

de Burgh, Hugo (2006) *China: Friend or Foe?* Cambridge: Icon Books.

Doob, Leonward (1966) *Public Opinion and Propaganda,* second edition. Hamden, CT: Archon Books.

Feng, David (2013) Zhongguo Xuyao Gengkuai Genghao de Gaotie (China Needs Faster and Better High Speed Rail). *People's Railway Daily.* Available at: www.peoplerail.com/rail/show-467-134145-1.html [Accessed 19 October 2016].

Florcruz, Michelle (2015) Is China Opening Up To Twitter? New Xinhua News Agency Column Using Twitter Despite Censorship. *International Business Times.* Available at: www.ibtimes.com/china-opening-twitter-new-xinhua-news-agency-column-using-twitter-despite-censorship-1959113 [Accessed 19 March 2016].

Fuchs, Christian (2014) *Social Media: A Critical Introduction.* London: Sage.

Guo, Liang (2010) *Weibo Jiang Dailai Shenme? (What Will Weibo Bring?).* Beijing: Chinese Industry and Commerce United Press.

Hu, Zhengrong (2008) *A General Theory of the Studies of Communications.* Beijing: Communication University of China Press.

Hu, Zhengrong (2015) Tell the China Story Well, Improve its Voice on the World Stage (Jianghao Zhongguo Gushi, Tigao Guoji Huayuaun). *National Governance Daily,* July.

Hu, Zhengrong and Li, Jidong (2014) How to Build China's Voice on the World Stage (Ruhe Goujian Zhongguo Huayuquan). *Guangming Daily,* 17 November, 11.

Jacques, Martin (2012) *When China Rules the World: The End of the Western World and the Birth of a New Global Order,* second edition. London: Penguin.

Li, Dongxiao (2012) *Intermediary Politics: Sociological Examinations of Chinese Media and Counter-Corruption (Jujian Zhengzhi: Zhongguo Meiti Fanfu De Shehuixue Kaocha).* Beijing: Communication University of China Press.

Liu, Yang; Shan, Chengbiao and Liu, Hui (2014) Zhongguo Wangluo Meiti Duiwai Chuanbo Fazhan Baogao (Report on the International Communication of Chinese Internet Media), in Hu, Z.; Li, J. and Ji, D. (eds.) *Blue Book of International Communication: Annual Report on the Development of China's International Communication (Guoji Chuanbo Lanpishu: Zhongguo Guoji Chuanbo Fazhan Baogao).* Beijing: Social Sciences Academic Press: 255–275.

LSE China Development Society (2015) Bridging Minds Symposium: Under the Dome: It Made People Think About the Environment – Beyond the Clip: Social Issues, Media Literacy, Education, and Tolerance of Viewpoint Diversity, 16 March. Available at: http://mp.weixin.qq.com/s?__biz=MjM5NDAzNzczOQ==andmid=207737942andidx=1andsn=902c82582b21be41b732310cc44eee9eandscene=5andsrcid=0321OryUED PMWFknknk1GtpG#rd [Accessed 20 March 2016].

Luo, Yan and Mi, Hui (2014) An Overview of Developments in New Media in China (Zhongguo Xinmeiti Fazhan Gaikuang), in Hu, Z.; Tang, X. and Li, J. (eds.) *New Media Industries Frontiers (Xinmeiti Qianyan Fazhan Baogao).* Beijing: Social Sciences Academic Press: 187–204.

National People's Congress of the People's Republic of China via Xinhua (2016) Outline of the Thirteenth Five-Year Plan of National Economy and Social Development of the People's Republic of China. (Zhonghua Renmin Gongheguo Guomin Jingji He Shehui Fazhan Di Shisange Wunian Guihua Gangyao). Available at: www.npc.gov.cn/npc/ dbdhhy/12_4/2016-03/18/content_1985670_8.htm [Accessed 18 March 2016].

NetEase (2011) Jinghu Gaotie Chepiao Kaishou Shoutang Chepiao 10 Fenzhong Shouqin (Tickets on Beijing–Shanghai High Speed Railway Sold Out Ten Minutes After Being on Sale). Available at: http://news.163.com/photoview/00AN0001/15299.html [Accessed 30 April 2012].

Noelle-Neumann, Elisabeth (1993) *The Spiral of Silence: Public Opinion – Our Social Skin,* second edition. Chicago: University of Chicago Press.

Pan, Xianghui (2011) The internet connection between crisis and the media system change in Chinese context – case study of the Wenchuan earthquake and the group events, *Communication and Society*, 15: 33–70.

Pöksen, Bernhard and Detel, Hanne (2012) *Der entfesselte Skandal: Das Ende der Kontrolle im digitalen Zeitalter (The Provoked Scandal: The End of Controls in the Digital Age).* Köln: Herbert von Halem Verlag.

Price, Monroe (2002) *Media and Sovereignty: The Global Information Revolution and Its Challenge to State Power.* Cambridge, MA: MIT Press.

Qiu, Jack Linchuan and Chan, Joseph (2009) Approaching new media events, *Communication and Society*, 9: 19–37.

Qiu, Jack Linchuan and Shi, Anbin (eds.) (2013) News, politics, social movements, and digital media, *Communication and Society*, 26: 1–31.

Schneider, Wolf and Raue, Paul-Josef (2003) *Das Neue Handbuch des Journalismus (The New Handbook of Journalism).* Reinbek bei Hamburg: Rowohlt Verlag GmbH.

Scoble, Robert and Israel, Shel (2006) *Naked Conversations: How Blogs Are Changing the Way Businesses Talk with Customers.* Hoboken, NJ: John Wiley.

Shanghai Railway Daily (2015) Hefei Zhi Anqing Gaotie Kaijian (Hefei–Anqing High Speed Railway Now Under Construction), 31 December, 2.

Sparks, Colin (1998) Is There a Global Public Sphere?, in Thussu, D. K. (ed.) *Electronic Empires: Global Media and Local Resistance.* London: Arnold: 108–124.

Thussu, Daya Kishan and Nordenstreng, Kaarle (2015) Introduction: Contextualizing the BRICS Media, in Nordenstreng, K. and Thussu, D. K. (eds.) *Mapping BRICS Media.* London: Routledge: 1–22.

Twitter (2016a) Beijing Smog – Twitter Search. Available at: https://twitter.com/search?src= typdandq=Beijingper cent20smog [Accessed 16 April 2016].

Twitter (2016b) China High Speed Rail – Twitter Search. Available at: https://twitter.com/ search?src=typdandq=Chinaper cent20highper cent20speedper cent20rail [Accessed 16 April 2016].

Twitter (2016c) China HSR – Twitter Search. Available at: https://twitter.com/search?src= typdandq=Chinaper cent20HSR [Accessed 16 April 2016].

Twitter (2016d) China Smog – Twitter Search. Available at: https://twitter.com/ search?src=typdandq=Chinaper cent20smog [Accessed 16 April 2016].

Twitter (2016e) @XHNews High Speed Rail – Twitter Search. Available at: https://twitter. com/search?src=typdandq=percent40XHNewspercent20highpercent20speedpercent20 rail [Accessed 16 April 2016].

Twitter (2016f) @XHNews HSR – Twitter Search. Available at: https://twitter.com/search ?src=typdandq=percent40XHNewspercent20HSR [Accessed 16 April 2016].

Twitter (2016g) @XHNews Pollution – Twitter Search. Available at: https://twitter.com/sea rch?src=typdandq=percent40XHNewspercent20pollution [Accessed 16 April 2016].

Twitter (2016h) @XHNews Smog – Twitter Search. Available at: https://twitter.com/searc h?src=typdandq=percent40XHNewspercent20smog [Accessed 16 April 2016].

Twitter (2016i) #lianghui High Speed Rail – Twitter Search. Available at: https://twitter. com/search?src=typdandq=percent23lianghuipercent20highpercent20speedpercent20 rail [Accessed 16 April 2016].

Twitter (2016j) #lianghui HSR – Twitter Search. Available at: https://twitter.com/search? src=typdandq=percent23lianghuipercent20HSR [Accessed 16 April 2016].

Twitter (2016k) #lianghui Pollution – Twitter Search. Available at: https://twitter.com/sear ch?src=typdandq=percent23lianghuipercent20pollution [Accessed 16 April 2016].

Twitter (2016l) #lianghui Smog – Twitter Search. Available at: https://twitter.com/search? src=typdandq=percent23lianghuipercent20smog [Accessed 16 April 2016].

van Kerckhove, Gilbert (2012) *Toxic Capitalism: The Orgy of Consumerism and Waste: Are We the Last Generation on Earth?*. Bloomington: AuthorHouse.

Wired (2015) Opinion: How the US Embassy Tweet to Clear Beijing's Air. Available at: www.wired.com/2015/03/opinion-us-embassy-beijing-tweeted-clear-air/ [Accessed 28 April 2016].

Wolf, David (2012) High Speed Rail in China: A Reassessment. *Wolf Group Asia*. Available at: www.academia.edu/8603019/High-Speed_Rail_in_China_A_Reassessment [Accessed 20 March 2016].

Wolf, David (2015) Economic Resilience Will be Determined by the Chinese People, presented at The Fletcher Forum of World Affairs 2014, Global Risk Forum. Available at: www.fletcherforum.org/2015/02/05/wolf-2/ [Accessed 20 March 2016].

World Bank (2015) Gross Domestic Product 2015. Available at: http://databank.worldbank. org/data/download/GDP_PPP.pdf [Accessed 19 October 2016].

Wu, Hao (2015) Lizhi Qizhuang Di Kaizhan Zhongguo Xuanchaunxue Yanjiu (Confidently and justifiably launch the research of China propaganda studies), *Hongqi Wengao*, 312(24): 9–12.

Xiang, B. (ed.) (2015) Xinhua Officially Launches Global Social Media Presence. *Xinhua news agency*, 1 March. Available at: http://news.xinhuanet.com/english/2015-03/01/c_ 134027886.htm [Accessed 20 December 2015].

Xu, Fangqing (2015) Foreign policy: Ringing endorsement, *China Report*, 20: 18–22.

Yao, Yao (2014) *Xin Zhongguo Duiwai Xuanchanshi: Jian'gou XIandai Zhongguo de Guoji Huayu Quan (The History of China's International Publicity: The Creation of Modern China's Say in the World)*. Beijing: Tsinghua University Press.

Zhang, Zhao (2014) Zhongguo Dianshi Jiemu Duiwai Chuanbo Celue Fenxi (On International Communication Strategy for TV Programmes in China), in Hu, Z.; Li, J. and Tang, X. (eds.) *Blue Book of Global Media: Annual Report on the Development of Global Media (2014) (Quanqiu Chuanmei Lanpishu: Quanqiu Chuanmei Fazhan Baogao 2014)*. Beijing: Social Sciences Academic Press: 255–275.

Zhao, Yuezhi (2001) Media and elusive democracy in China, *Javnost – The Public*, 8(4): 21–44.

Zhao, Yuezhi (2008) *Communication in China: Political Economy, Power, and Conflict*. Lanham: Rowman and Littlefield.

Zhu, Lingqing (2011) Beijing–Shanghai HSR: At Most 70 Percent Seat Vacancy. *Tianya*, 1 August. Available at: http://bbs.tianya.cn/post-worldlook-372254-1.shtml [Accessed 22 March 2016].

18

TRANSFORMING ENTERTAINMENT TELEVISION THROUGH TRANSNATIONAL FORMATS

Hong Li and Rong Zeng

With the introduction of advertising in China in the late 1970s, commercialization started to change television. Since the late 1980s, in response to the tidal wave of media commercialization, entertainment television has boomed: television drama, which has until recently been at the centre of entertainment media, broadcast 15,000 episodes in 2013.[1] However, increasingly prime-time television is being dominated by the growth of format shows. The deployment of transnational formats has been seen by broadcasters as a means of expanding audience share by transmitting programmes already well established as popular entertainment in other markets.

Contracting to buy the format and agreeing to abide by the rules requires the adoption of processes and operations unfamiliar to production staff in China. In order successfully to make and transmit formats originated abroad, knowledge, skills, competencies, management procedures, work styles and production practices have to change. Hence, the popularity of formats in China suggests not only Chinese entertainment television's increasing interconnectivity with global television networks but also the standardization of content and technology.

This chapter will first review the context of entertainment television and its development over the last few years in the context of globalization and internationalization. Then it will look at the television format business, the relationship between China and the outside world, and how changes in entertainment television are coming about through foreign involvement. Finally, it will examine how the entertainment industry is orienting itself towards export in the course of pursuing higher degrees of internationalization and will review the success of China's entertainment television abroad.

Entertainment television: Chinese TV's response to media commercialization

Following the implementation of the reform and opening-up policy in 1978, the television industry, like most of the other sectors of the economy, began to develop rapidly and gradually be liberalized. At the same time, advertising was introduced into Chinese television, which signalled the start of its commercialization. It was not until the late 1980s, however, that entertainment became an increasingly important means to attract audiences. In the Chinese context, Gray (2008: 3) defines television entertainment as:

> programmes, segments, or channels that enjoy, amuse, delight, and perhaps even enlighten. Given the vast differences in individual notions of what actually is entertaining and what is not, by television entertainment, I mean programming designed with entertainment as the primary goal.

During the period from 1984 to 1989, approximately 6,000 episodes of television dramas were produced domestically (Zeng, 2009: 2).

In some sense, this period can be regarded as inaugurating the age of Chinese entertainment television, when media professionals came upon the idea of experimenting with the soap opera approach to drama.

In 1990, China's first domestically produced soap opera *Yearnings* (渴望) seized the whole nation's imagination and caused a sensation across the country. It was not the first serial drama that was aired in China, but it was the first drama to focus on relationships between friends and families and on the dreams of ordinary Chinese people, making it what some people called China's first real 'soap opera' (Latham, 2007). In the next three years, many other soap operas such as *Stories in the Editor's Office* (编辑部的故事), *I Love You Absolutely* (爱你没商量), and *Beijinger in New York* (北京人在纽约) were broadcast, using *Yearnings* as the model for the new Chinese television drama. These dramas, in a thematic sense, dealt with various sensitive issues and concerns that ordinary Chinese people could relate to, rather than serious topics such as national politics or Chinese history. Since then, television dramas have flourished and now constitute a major part of the cultural landscape in contemporary China, as well as attracting much scholarly attention.

The commercialization process continued throughout the post-Mao era after advertisements were introduced in the late 1970s. In 1992, Deng Xiaoping made his speech about the move to take bolder steps in economic development and reform, which marked the point at which the market economy in China was formally established. Not only were the media regarded as the Chinese Communist Party (CCP)'s mouthpiece and ideological instrument, but also media workers saw it as a medium of aesthetic and intellectual engagement which had commodity value. The year 1992 has been widely recognized as transforming the face of Chinese television through an increased degree of media commercialization.

Advertising revenues soared for several consecutive years, which resulted in television replacing newspapers as the leading advertising medium. As market-oriented institutional organizations proliferated and provincial stations launched satellite channels to seek for wider audiences, the competition for advertising revenues intensified. It was recognized that television drama had become essentially a medium for advertisement and advertising became financially important to television stations. Even state-funded and 'propaganda-themed dramas aimed to emulate commercial entertainment' (Bai and Song, 2015: 3).

In contrast to television dramas that were, and still are, an unrivalled form of television entertainment in terms of output, the supply of entertainment programmes such as variety shows, game shows and dating shows grew steadily in the 1990s. Throughout the 1990s, entertainment programmes took up an increasing share of the total hours of television programming, from approximately 26 per cent in 1992 to 44 per cent in 2000 (Zhang, 2002).

CCTV took the lead by launching two entertainment programmes in 1990 – *Zhengda Variety Show* (正大综艺) and *Variety Panorama* (综艺大观). While it was sponsored and co-produced by a Thai-Chinese agricultural fertilizer company (Zhengda Consortium) based in Thailand, *Zhengda Variety* can be considered as China's first authentic variety show format and remains the most influential variety show in China. However, by 1997 it began to suffer the fate that most successful programmes would face in China. As *Zhengda Variety* became widely circulated and heavily imitated throughout China, its market value generally diminished. Like other economic sectors in China, the television industry is evidence of what the Chinese call 'duplicate construction', that is, 'everyone rushes in and produces the same kinds of products and targets the same markets within a particular locality' (Keane, 2001: 224).

However, Hunan Satellite Television (HSTV) made its way to become a leading force in Chinese television entertainment by liberally borrowing from successful television shows. For example, HSTV launched *The Citadel of Happiness* (快乐大本营) in 1997, a game show targeted at the youth audience, and *A Date with Roses* (玫瑰之约) in 1998, a dating show. Shortly after first being aired *The Citadel of Happiness* became the most popular entertainment show in China, which demonstrated that the shortcut for provincial television stations to compete in the domestic market was to concentrate on entertainment.

The first decade of the new century: the era of format television arrived

While Chinese television producers have borrowed from successful foreign content since the 1980s, it is only in the past decade that increasing use of international entertainment formats has been witnessed. With China's accession to the World Trade Organization in 2001 and its sponsorship of the Beijing 2008 Olympic Games, China has been facing a great number of unprecedented opportunities as well as challenges. As Lee stated, 'China and its media have been caught in the crosscurrents of nationalism and globalism' (2003: 1). An order by the State Administration of

Radio, Film and Television issued in October 2011, which came into effect on 1 January 2012, reduced entertainment broadcasts by two-thirds during prime time, which showed that the government was trying to retain its 'monopoly over tremendous coercive power and resources' (Lee, 2003: 2). However, because of the changing nature of audience consumption of online and mobile media, this curb on 'excessive entertainment' has not prevented, but rather driven some among the audience to turn to video-streaming sites with entertainment content (Chao and Tejada, 2012).

The launching of the 'Going Out' policy has offered Chinese broadcasters a promising prospect to step out of the Chinese market and export more of their own creative content. It had long been the dream of Chinese broadcasters to be global players in the worldwide market but this meant that Chinese media had to meet challenges from competitors abroad as well as those inland. According to Zhao, 'although the media are still owned by the state, their economic basis has been shifted from complete reliance on state subsidies to increasing dependence on commercial revenue from advertising, sponsorships, and business operations in other areas' (Zhao, 1998: 67). In addition, with the development of multi-channelling (increasing number of channels) we can see the appearance of audience fragmentation, namely, lower average audiences per channel (Economic Analysis, 2004), which means that audiences have more choices and that competition among media conglomerates has also intensified (Chen, 2008).

Therefore, Chinese television stations increasingly began to search for the formula for popular entertainment that had proved successful in other markets. As Chen argued, 'those who can generate more resources and create more popular programmes will be the winners in the market' (ibid.: 16). But as to why Chinese broadcasters tended to simply buy formats rather than create their own, according to Lei, the

> media business is a risky business as the taste of audiences is unpredictable. The most important part in content production is the idea, which is equivalent to the corporate R&D function. Buying some successful formats can surely reduce the risk comparatively and to some extent have cost efficiency.
> *(Chen, 2008: 24)*

In this context, the deployment of formats from foreign countries in the Chinese television industry has also been seen by Chinese broadcasters as a means of increasing audience share.

Ever since the format *Got Talent* （达人秀） achieved such great success in China, we have seen the growth of format franchising and Chinese industry's reliance on Western expertise. Television formats have provided Chinese TV professionals with not only new creative inputs into indigenous production practices but also a licence to experiment with ideas that may not fit in with the national culture or the brand of the channel or network. Producer Chen Qian said:

> Propaganda documentaries dominated the television industry in the 1980s and 1990s. But now, the viewers have been provided with abundant reality

shows featuring flashy set designs. And we, as producers, have subsequently learned the systematic production process through the adoption of formats and the collaboration with global networks.

(Interview 2, 2013)[2]

From the perspective of the Chinese television industry, the adoption of international TV formats is a new mode of production, which brings in advanced norms and the means to internationalize and professionalize provincial TV networks in particular and Chinese TV in general. In the following sections this chapter will illustrate how Chinese professionals perceive the development of their practices and that of the whole TV industry consequential upon the adoption and localization of formats. In doing so, it will describe how changes in entertainment television are coming about through foreign involvement, and also examine how Chinese professionals perceive the production knowledge they gain from international formats and what transnational television formats mean for Chinese TV.

Technology transfer is a crucial mechanism for the continuous growth of format adoption in China. The Chinese television industry seeks to absorb the dominant international advantages by gaining crucial know-how and practices from foreign independent production companies, and thus make it possible to obtain a prime position in the global TV market. The increasing use of foreign television formats has provided opportunities for China to connect with global TV production practices and professional culture. In this respect, technology comes in various forms. As the director Chen Qian mentions,

> Television formats are a good medium for these technologies, including specific knowledge about R&D, as well as those found in machinery and physical goods. They contain not only detailed information about how to make particular format shows, but also offer more general lessons and insights into the framework and structures from which they are derived.
>
> *(ibid., 2013)*

Transition from in-house production to independent production

In this emerging post-broadcasting environment, a proliferation of independent companies has emerged, all jockeying for position in the rapidly forming TV market. In many instances these production companies are operating with greater degrees of flexibility than was allowed over the past few decades, when production units were linked directly with television stations. In this regard, old relationships and structures are changing. One of the changes in the Chinese TV landscape brought about by the format adoption is the transition from in-house production to massive independent production, which will be illustrated through the following three points.

Firstly, television format production is sub-contracted out to independent production companies, which aim to follow 'a publishing model'. As Liu noted, 'independent companies have taken the lead in defining the international TV format market' (2009: 32).The shift to independent production began with American television networks in the 1950s, allowing production to be 'outsourced' to independent producers. The trend towards independent production occurred later in Europe, with Channel 4 in the UK established in 1982 as the catalyst for change. With the first independent company officially registered in 1994, independent production occurred much more recently in China, due to 'the nature of the market and a propensity on the part of governments to regulate control of content by opting to deal with broadcasters' (Liu, 2009: 32). And in recent decades, they have moved quickly into making format shows. Compared with state-owned TV stations, as the CEO of IPCN said,

> Independent companies have less resource but they are more flexible and efficient in producing programmes. Most of the founders of independent companies began their careers in the state-owned TV stations, so they maintain close relationships with the personnel of stations after leaving from there. This enables them to have local connections and at the same time keep themselves more space to be creative.
>
> *(Interview 3, 2013)*[3]

There are currently three modes of programme production in China. In the first, programmes are produced in the studio of the state-controlled TV station. For the state-owned media system, each TV station has its own production units. In particular, news programmes, including political discussion, are kept for in-house production. The second mode is that independent companies devise and produce programmes for broadcasters. In return for the content, broadcasters trade a certain amount of advertising time through which independent companies attract sponsors to gain financial profits. As producer Lin Mi mentioned, some channels have traded substantial channel time to independent companies for the content provided, such as Beijing TV's Life Channel and Hainan's Travel Channel. The third production mode is that TV stations, which used to produce everything in-house, cooperate with independent companies to make programmes. For instance, one of Dragon TV's brand shows, *So You Think You Can Dance* (舞林争霸), is produced by an independent production company, Canxing Productions.

Lu Wei detailed the usual way in which independent production companies and television stations work together:

> The way that production companies deal with the entire production process and television stations is they simply make a decision about whether to buy the show and broadcast it after viewing the demos. The broadcasters will set the price for buying the show mainly based on its potential viewer ratings and estimated advertising revenue. After receiving the fixed fee paid by the

network, the production companies will get no more profits related to the show, no matter how much is generated from commercials and sponsorships.

(Interview 4, 2013)[4]

This way of organizing the collaboration usually compels production companies to skimp on production costs at the expense of programme quality in order to maximize net profits. With the advent of the mainstream adoption of transnational formats in China, a new mode of cooperation between independent production companies and television stations has gradually emerged in the Chinese TV landscape.

Secondly, in co-producing *The Voice of China* (中国好声音), Canxing Productions and Zhejiang Satellite Television formed a joint venture, a partnership in which both parties share both the revenue and the risk. It is unprecedented in China's TV broadcasting history that an independent production company and a television station have started to collaborate with each other in the way of 'both parties' inputting, risk sharing and profit sharing' (共同投入、共担风险、共享利润).

Jin Lei, the chief director of Canxing Productions, echoes the point above on the cooperation mode:

> This new mode of cooperation puts both parties in the same boat, which means that the broadcasters have to take on a greater amount of financial risk than before. It is really a good thing for us; however, at the same time, it took us quite a lot of time to find a network that was willing to sign on at the very beginning.
>
> *(Interview 5, 2013)*[5]

Compared with the traditional way of cooperating, the new partnership motivates both Canxing Productions and Zhejiang Satellite Television to invest in the best possible resources. As Lu Wei revealed,

> Since there is no cap on profit sharing, both parties are willing to make their best efforts to offer the best possible show and related promotional campaigns. With this kind of motivation we've got, we invested large amounts of money to make sure that everything from stage setting, sound equipment to post production are top-class. At the same time, Zhejiang TV put forth its best efforts in the advertising bidding and successfully attracted a title sponsorship deal worth 60 million RMB with Wong Lo Kat, a beverage company. The fierce bidding also drove advertisement placements during the shows of the first season to reach 360,000 RMB per 15 second slot.
>
> *(Interview 4, 2013)*

Thirdly, in recent decades, the term 'commissioning' (separation of production and broadcasting) was frequently discussed by television producers and media scholars (Korp and Olig, 2007). However, this advanced business operation framework has not yet been properly introduced to the Chinese television industry. Television professionals tend to see the new mode of cooperation between independent production companies and broadcasters as a big move towards the 'real sense' commissioning. As the SAPPRFT (State Administration of Press, Publication, Radio, Film and Television) researcher Ming Chao noted,

> The Chinese television industry is going through a stage of development as the British industry did in early 1980s. Nowadays, the separation of manufacture and broadcast has been well established to direct the British TV industry toward innovation. In order to encourage the TV content to be diverse, the British government requires broadcasters to commission independent production companies to produce a certain proportion of their programmes. It has also been supporting the growth of the independent sector deliberately by granting independent production companies more rights, such as production rights and international franchising rights, after the sector took off in early 1980s.
>
> *(Interview 6, 2014)*[6]

This is echoed by Paul Jackson, former ITV and BBC Director of Entertainment Programming and now Creative Director of Beijing-based independent production company Houghton Street Media: 'Regulatory rules are made that guarantee independent production companies will get reasonable payments of commission from broadcasters, and this has made London the centre of the innovative television industry' (Interview 7, 2013).[7]

In China, independent companies were given the rights to produce TV programmes in 2004. A growing number of private companies have been gaining recognition from broadcasters and viewers in recent years, especially after Canxing Productions successfully produced *The Voice of China* for Zhejiang Satellite TV. However, independent production companies are constantly facing financial risks in a situation where there is no proper legislation, especially before the appearance of the new cooperation mode. Gao Ya from IPCN explained:

> Independent production companies are sometimes required by broadcasters to sign a contract promising to reach a certain viewer rating. The payment will be deducted if they fail to reach it. In another scenario, production companies are paid a certain amount of fee, which includes their profits, to make a show. They have to dip into the profit margin when broadcasters keep requesting changes once the production has started. This kind of contracts discourages the sustaining TV innovation.
>
> *(Interview 8, 2013)*[8]

Shift from genre production to format production

'The format is a stage of development in the evolution of television, anticipating and responding to the media post-broadcasting environment of increased market uncertainty' (Keane, 2005: 84). Keane (2005) argues in his study of television formats that their dramatically increasing use is a sign of unprecedented change in the television industries worldwide. The global television industry has been compelled to reconsider what it can do, how its viewers have drifted, and how it can generate revenues. In China, producers have used television formats as a strategy to break away from stereotypical, traditional genres. One of the major changes in Chinese television has been a shift from genre production to emergent practices of formatting. In academic critiques, genres and formats are usually considered together but formats function differently from genres. A format at its most basic is a core idea or a concept of a programme (Moran, 2006). Moran (1998) uses the 'pie and crust' metaphor to imply that formatting is basically a matter of providing the television format with local filling when it travels to local territories. In this research, formatting is a generic term for licensing television formats' copyright in different geographical markets. Genre deals with a bundle of narrative forms within standardized conventions that are widely agreed upon; that is, they are closely associated with narrative structure. However, it does not make much sense to talk of the trade in television genres. In today's global television we can see an unprecedented level of change in modes of production, workflows, product life-cycle planning and advertising and marketing strategies, as in Chinese television. These changes are occurring as global formats travel to local territories, viewers migrate away from television screens to interactive choices, and viewers have diminishing loyalty to channels and programmes. In the fierce competition for quality content and the struggle for ascendancy in the multi-platform era, the television industry has gradually used format adoption as the new engine for industry development. As Lu Wei pointed out,

> Television format plays a role as a catalyst for change in local content. We can see from the recent popularity of talent shows and reality shows in China that the adoption of global formats turns out to be a shortcut for TV institutions to make their content more diverse and competitive. Dragon TV, ZJTV, HSTV and JSTV have all benefited commercially from the format production. *China's Got Talent* (中国达人秀), *The Voice of China* (中国好声音), *Divas Hit the Road* (花儿与少年) and *If You Are the One* (非诚勿扰) made these top four provincial satellite channels nationally famous respectively. Television formats in the end help the Chinese TV institutions stand out from the fierce and homogeneous content competition under the strict content control of the state.
>
> *(Interview 4, 2013)*

What television format means for Chinese TV: a new engine for growth

In the distribution market of global television, China used to be categorized as a 'D level territory' which features the lowest value, 'simply because of the low return and high probability of cloning' (Keane and Moran, 2008: 166). However, the production of *China's Got Talent* signals 'an important change of heart of global format conglomerates concerning the value of the Chinese market' (Ouellette, 2014: 529). In recent years, Chinese television professionals have gradually realized the benefits of purchasing formats properly than copycatting, and turned their attention to format production as a whole new approach for the development of the Chinese TV industry.

As McCabe argues, 'emergent television territories like China have only recently entered the global TV marketplace, and so what is required from a TV format is not necessarily the same as what the Germans or Spaniards want' (2013: 12). As when they licensed the format *The Voice*, what Chinese producers wanted from the format deal was not only the content but also, more importantly, an industry development strategy. The knowledge about financial decisions about 'product placement, artist packaging services, programme promotion and derivative product arrangements' (McCabe, 2013: 13) is mostly wanted by Chinese producers. Based on the ethnographic observation of *The Voice of China*, product placement had a direct and important impact on the format's local production. As the programme's title sponsor, Wong Lo Kat appeared frequently in the programme and was built into the narratives of the competition. On 10 August 2013, the team was producing the battle rounds within Na Ying's team, during which the director ordered the photographer specifically to give the Wong Lo Kat trademark close-ups on several occasions.

The prevalence of format franchising in China has been the result of many developments in the Chinese media environment and the formats' own advantages. Firstly, in technological terms, buying in TV formats is seen as an effective means of increasing the competitiveness of the TV stations amid the fierce market competition of China's media industry. When a format is franchised to other territories, its production package may contain narrative elements, scripts and character dialogue. It may also provide suggestions for staging (camera angles, musical arrangements) and distribution (promotion, auxiliary markets) (McCabe, 2013: 12). In other words, format franchising is the transfer of expertise. Regarding the question of weakening Chinese media institutions' creativity and innovation by importing formats, there have been political and economic discussions among scholars. However, as De Burgh *et al.* (2011) stated, the 'TV format is among all sorts of modern media software that has to learn from the successful western experience of economizing the creative and culture industries' (quoted in Zhang and Fung, 2014: 515). To a certain degree media institutions have to rely on the advanced expertise of the West, especially in the 'adolescence' of their development.

According to Zhao (2008), China has integrated into global capitalism since the post-Mao economic reform. Based on Huang's (2007) observation, China's media industry is 'in a transformation from a pure propaganda machine to a market socialism model or a state-controlled capitalist corporation model' (Zhang and Fung, 2014: 515). However, the Chinese TV sector is still not fully developed despite decades of reform and has a huge number of television stations that compete with each other in a chaotic market environment that has few high-quality programmes (Keane, 2002). In addition, with the advent of multi-channelling and the convergence of delivery platforms, the demand for TV content has been increased dramatically. Since the TV format is known for its transfer of expertise, fashioning formats has become an industry development strategy for Chinese broadcasters.

Secondly, in financial terms, as Miller noted, 'executives optioning formats for development prefer the sense of security obtained through formats having been "proven" in a market with similar tastes' (Miller, 2010: 203). Formats, as a proven record of success, are usually adopted in China as a means of financial and cultural insurance, which somehow reduces a sense of risk. Thirdly, in cultural terms, the TV format is known, upon localization, for having the advantage of cultural proximity to local audiences. By combining both local preferences for cultural tastes and the basic components of a TV format, local versions of formats reduce cultural gap by modifying original format frames. In the process of format franchising and reproducing, cultural hybridity, as a result of the global trade in television formats, eliminates the problem of contradictory ideology at the level of audience reception in China.

Conclusion

Since the tidal wave of media commercialization, television dramas have attracted much scholarly attention and come to constitute a major part of the cultural landscape in contemporary China. However, in recent years, an increasing number of television format shows have dominated prime-time television in China. The deployment of transnational formats has been seen by Chinese broadcasters as a means of increasing audience share by transmitting programmes already well-established as popular entertainment in other markets.

After initially copycatting such formats, the broadcasters found that they might get a more marketable product by purchasing the formats legitimately. Contracting to buy the format and agreeing to abide by the rules requires the adoption of processes and operations unfamiliar to production staff in China. In order successfully to make and transmit formats originated abroad, knowledge, skills, competencies, management procedures, work styles and production practices have to change. From examples of format localization, this chapter argues that the adoption of television formats is not only increasing Chinese broadcasting's interconnectivity with global television networks but also changing the landscape of the Chinese television industry. Technology transfer is a crucial mechanism for the continuous growth of the format trade in China. Technology in this sense mainly comes in two forms: one is specific knowledge about particular television formats (ideas and know-how) as described above; the other is general insight into the structures and framework from which they are originated. One of the changes in the Chinese TV landscape brought about by format adoption is the transition from in-house production to massive independent production.

Notes

1 According to the *Annual Report on Development of China's Radio, Film and Television* (2014).
2 Interview with SMG producer, 14 August 2013.
3 Interview with CEO of IPCN, 10 November 2013.

4 Interview with publicity director of Canxing Productions, 13 August 2013.
5 Interview with chief production director of Canxing Productions, 12 August 2013.
6 Interview with researcher of SAPPRFT, 12 July 2014.
7 Interview with creative director of Houghton Street Media, 13 November 2013.
8 Interview with researcher of IPCN, 10 November 2013.

References

Bai, R. and Song, G. (2015) *Chinese Television in the Twenty-First Century*. New York: Routledge.
Chao, L. and Tejada, C. (2012) Web Takes Star Turn in China. *Wall Street Journal*.
Chen, S. (2008) *Format Trading at GBS*. Master's thesis.
De Burgh, H.; Zeng, R. and Chen, S. (2011) Chinese television 'internationalization' and the search for creativity, *Creative Industries Journal*, 4(2): 137–154.
Economic Analysis of the TV Advertising Market, PwC, December 2004. Available at: www.ofcom.org.uk/research/tv/reports/tvadvmarket.pdf [Accessed 20 May 2015].
Gray, J. (2008) *Television Entertainment*. London: Routledge.
Huang, C. (2007) Trace the stones in crossing the river: Media structural changes in post-WTO China, *International Communication Gazette*, 69(5), 413–430.
Keane, M. (2001) Cultural technology transfer: Redefining content in the Chinese television industry, *Emergences: Journal for the Study of Media and Composite Cultures*, 11(2): 223–236.
Keane, M. (2002) As a hundred television formats bloom, a thousand television stations contend, *Journal of Contemporary China*, 11(30): 5–16.
Keane, M. (2005) Television drama in China: Remaking the market. *Media International Australia*. 115, 82–93.
Keane, M. and Moran, A. (2008) Television's new engines, *Television and New Media*, 9(2): 155–169.
Korp, M. and Olig, S. (2007) *Internationalization of the Chinese TV Sector*. Munster: LIT Verlag.
Latham, K. (2007) *Pop Culture China!: Media, Arts and Lifestyle*. Santa Barbara, CA: ABC-CLIO.
Lee, C. C. (2003) The Global and the National of the Chinese Media: Discourses, Market, Technology and Ideology. In *Chinese Media, Global Context*. New York: RoutledgeCurzon: 1–32.
Liu, R. (2009) New strength: Independent television companies in China's television industry, *Ejournalist*, 9(1), 31–44.
McCabe, J. (2013) *TV's Betty Goes Global: From Telenovela to International Brand*. London: I.B. Tauris.
Miller, J. (2010) Ugly Betty goes global: Global networks of localized content in the telenovela industry, *Global Media and Communication*, 6(2): 198–217.
Moran, A. (1998) *Copycat Television: Globalization, Programme Formats, and Cultural Identity*. Luton: University of Luton Press.
Moran, A. (2006) *Understanding the Global TV Format*. Bristol: Intellect Books.
Ouellette, L. (2014) *A Companion to Reality Television*. Malden, MA: Wiley-Blackwell.
Zeng, Q. (2009) Recent 50 years of Chinese TV drama, *Culture Review*, 3:3.
Zhang, T. (2002) Spring and autumn of the media: Observations about the orbit of the party state, *Journal of Communication*, 50: 3–26.
Zhang, X. and Fung, A. (2014) TV formatting of the Chinese 'Ugly Betty': An ethnographic observation of the production community, *Television & New Media*, 15(6): 507–522.
Zhao, Y. (1998) *Media, Market, and Democracy in China: Between the Party Line and the Bottom Line*. Chicago: University of Illinois Press.
Zhao, Y. (2008) *Communication in China: Political Economy, Power, and Conflict*. Lanham: Rowman and Littlefield.

19

YUNNAN MEDIA RHETORIC ON THE 'GATEWAY' TO SOUTHEAST ASIA

Jiao Yang and Mei Wu

In the traditional definition of international communication, the national boundary is the dividing line. However, in an age of globalization, we are facing an environment of transnational 'global media flows and contra-flows' (Thussu, 2006: 11). Even though transnational communication has become a part of people's lives with the Internet, information exchange activities between people are still confined, to a large extent, to a geographic region and linked to regional culture. Globalization has promoted transnational flows on five dimensions: flows of capital, information, technology, organizational interaction, and images, sounds and symbols (Appadurai, 1996). In over 30 years of reform and opening up, China has set up ports and exchanged personnel, trade and media with neighbouring countries, which has accelerated regional flows of information (Congressional Research Service, 2008). Situated along national borders with neighbouring countries, several regional information hubs have gradually been forming in China. And the formation of these hubs is determined not only by the trend of globalization and location advantages, but also by China's foreign policy and the games of interest played between local governments and the central government.

Located in southwest China, which is adjacent to its border with Myanmar, Vietnam and Laos, Yunnan Province was dubbed 'the tail end of China's reform and opening up'. From 25 to 28 July 2009, when President Hu Jintao visited Yunnan, he said explicitly that Yunnan Province should be built into a 'gateway of China' to the Southeast and South Asia. On 6 May 2011, 'Opinions of the State Council on Supporting Yunnan Province to Accelerate the Construction of an Important Gateway Opening up to the Southwest' was issued. Thus 'gateway', a concept originally linked to the idea of the 'road-bridge' economy, became a new metaphor for the Yunnan government to define its position in the new era of opening up.

This chapter focuses on the process by which *Yunnan Daily*, the representative of Yunnan's official media, constructed the 'gateway strategy' rhetoric before and after the strategy was issued. The analysis in this chapter employs symbolic convergence theory (SCT) and fantasy theme analysis (FTA) to answer the following questions: firstly, what fantasy themes about the 'gateway strategy' did *Yunnan Daily* construct? Secondly, what rhetoric did these fantasy themes create? Finally, how can these rhetorical terms be evaluated?

Symbolic Convergence Theory and Fantasy Theme Analysis

American communication scholar Ernest Bormann and his research team developed SCT in the context of Cold War ideology, political propaganda and audience consciousness analysis. The theory provides a framework to analyse symbolic communication and ideological landscapes. It treats abstract human consciousness, exchanges and communication as symbolic realities that are composed of various symbols – such as language, words, images, orientations, visions, worldviews and ideologies. Symbolic reality converges in human consciousness and forms a layered and symbolized 'ideology landscape'. The surface layer is composed of basic elements such as words, vocabularies and images. These elements converge into opinions, consciousness, worldviews and value orientations, and then into an ideological and discourse system. At the end, the core value of a civilization emerges.

Through exchange and communication, people tend to seek a valid explanation for a new thing, derived from a symbolic reality that is deeply rooted in their mind, and the resulting resonance (a 'chain-out') reaching into communities creates the same or similar symbolic landscape. Ultimately, a 'fantasy theme' is generated. The fantasy theme will further converge in communication into a 'rhetorical vision', namely 'a fantasy phenomenon with a more precise structure, and a more complex drama' (Bormann *et al.*, 2004: 284). A shared rhetorical vision is a symbolic reality identified by communities. The mass media convey deliberately constructed fantasy themes and rhetorical visions to their audiences in order to provoke a 'chain-out' and form a symbolic reality agreed to by the public. Therefore, studying mass media texts is an important approach to discerning the media communicator's symbolic system, and measuring the rhetorical realities that media are propagating to the public.

This study employs SCT and FTA to focus on how the official media construct the rhetoric of a nation's development policy in the regional information flow. SCT is based on two assumptions: that communication creates reality, and that the meanings we hold for symbols can converge to create a shared reality (Foss, 1996). There are three basic concepts of SCT and FTA. They are fantasy theme, fantasy type and rhetorical vision (Bormann, 1972). People who have identical fantasy themes will gather together, mainly because they share a common experience. Similar fantasy themes can be extrapolated to a fantasy type. 'Fantasy types provide known reference points for help with understanding and making meaning out of future phenomena' (Lee and Hoon 1993: 529). Finally, rhetorical vision is described as a 'composite drama that catches up large groups of people into a common symbolic reality' (Bormann, 1996: 4). This theoretical construction, although derived mostly from the Western context – which emphasizes the power of fantasy – provides a useful conceptual frame within which to investigate a deeper layer of meanings and interpretations.

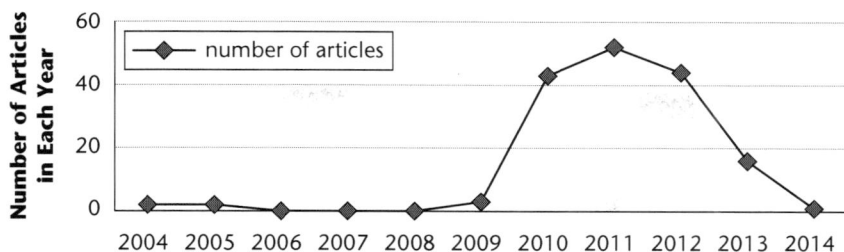

FIGURE 19.1 Articles with the word 'gateway' in the title

Source: CNKI Newspaper Database 2004–2014.

Methodology of the case study

Yunnan Daily is the official newspaper of the Communist Party Committee of Yunnan Province. Founded on 4 March 1950, it is a party newspaper and communication organ of the provincial government with the highest circulation in Yunnan Province. This research analysed 163 news reports from *Yunnan Daily* between 2004 and 2014 using the keyword 'gateway' in the titles. The data were collected through the CNKI newspaper database. The distribution diagram in Figure 19.1 presents the number of news reports with the word 'gateway', issued between 2004 and 2014.

In their essay published in 1996, Bormann *et al.* (1996: 2) explained that the Cold War rhetorical vision was characterized by the life cycle of 'consciousness creating, consciousness raising, consciousness sustaining and consciousness declining'. Taking reference from Bormann's 'four continua' in the life cycle of a rhetorical vision, we discover that the *Yunnan Daily's* rhetorical interpretation of 'gateway' exhibited a change that could be defined along the three phases of consciousness creating, consciousness raising and consciousness declining. The first phase (2004–2009) was consciousness creating; the second phase (2010–2012) was consciousness raising and the third phase (2013–2014) was consciousness declining. Our findings are organized around the three major actors, namely the Yunnan Provincial Government, Yunnan local government and local industries.

Consciousness-creating phase for the gateway rhetoric, 2004–2009

The use of 'gateway' here has special connotations in studies on the 'road-bridge' economy. The use of 'gateway' in *Yunnan Daily* focuses on the meaning of the first city in an economic belt. During this period, the fantasy was created around 'seizing opportunities'.

Through rhetorical analysis of fantasies in *Yunnan Daily*, we discovered several elements in this early stage. Firstly, the use of 'gateway' was sporadic and random. Articles with the word 'gateway' first appeared in *Yunnan Daily* in 2004. Baoshan City, which borders on Myanmar, was first mentioned in 'the construction of "gateway" in opening up to South Asia' (2004: 1). In 2005, after being established as a border trade zone, Dehong was also mentioned in the 'the construction of "gateway" in opening up to ASEAN and South China' (2005: 2). Starting from 2004, Baoshan City, Dehong Prefecture and other border cities and prefectures were among the first actors in the construction of the 'gateway' in terms of the 'road-bridge' economy.

Between 2006 and 2008, there were no articles in *Yunnan Daily* using 'gateway' in the title. In 2009, 'gateway' appeared again, which enlisted Yunnan University in the 'gateway' rhetoric, saying: 'It has become a "gateway" for traditional Chinese medicine to the world.' In July 2009, when then President Hu Jintao paid a visit to Yunnan, he said that Yunnan Province should be built into an important gateway in China's opening up to Southeast and South Asia. On 26 December 2009, the article whose title contains 'the construction of "gateway"' appeared on the front page of *Yunnan Daily* for the first time. Henceforth, the gateway rhetoric entered into a new period when its new connotations were produced, developed and shared.

Secondly, from the very beginning, the rhetorical terms of 'new opportunities' and 'seizing opportunities' were established. However, at this point they were aimed at the 'local governments' as actors. These terms were associated with a narrow concept of the road-bridge economy. It was only after the national leader's visit to Yunnan when the central government issued a new development policy for Yunnan that the rhetorical themes of 'gateway' started to carry a broader meaning.

Consciousness-raising phase for the gateway rhetoric, 2010–2012

From 2010 to 2012, the number of *Yunnan Daily* articles with the word 'gateway' in their titles grew exponentially. During this period, the study conducted FTA around the four fantasy objects, namely the gateway, Yunnan Provincial Government, Yunnan local governments and industries, to dissect the construct of the gateway symbolic reality by *Yunnan Daily* from the perspectives of consciousness creating, consciousness raising and consciousness sustaining.

During this period, *Yunnan Daily* created in the consciousness-raising phase of 'gateway,' a 'national strategy' fantasy type, and the 'historical opportunity' and 'new opportunity' fantasy types. Meanwhile, in order to achieve a 'chant-like' resonance, *Yunnan Daily* introduced two prominent symbolic cues like 'new' in 'new positioning', 'new pattern', 'new approach', 'new progress' and 'new breakthrough', as well as 'big' in 'big base', 'big platform', 'big window', 'big pathway', 'big portal' and 'big industry' in the construction of the above rhetorical fantasies.

According to Bormann, a symbolic cue is a shorthand indicant or code that stands for a fantasy theme such as a sign or symbol or an inside joke (Bormann *et al.*, 2004: 283) The words 'new' and 'big' were symbolic cues for the historical opportunity fantasy type. As argued in one article published in *Yunnan Daily*, 'the gateway construction is an enormous systematic project'. It reflects the interest game played between local governments at various levels, including different industries and enterprises and many governmental agencies. But *Yunnan Daily* resolved the incompatibilities and conflicts of different parties and constructed a symbolic reality of 'historical opportunity' warmly welcomed by all.

Consciousness-declining phase for the gateway rhetoric, 2013–2014

In this period, the 'gateway' rhetoric entered into the consciousness-declining phase, which was shown by the number of articles sharply dropping and the reemergence of a new competitive rhetoric. As seen in Figure 19.1, the number of articles in 2013 had sharply decreased compared with those published in 2012. In 2014, there was only one article whose title included 'gateway' published in *Yunnan Daily.* The 'gateway' rhetoric lost its initial appeal, and turned into a discourse framework for daily routines.

During this period, the large majority of articles contained the fantasies of 'Yunnan Provincial Government' and 'industries and enterprises', but they did not create new fantasy types. Instead they continued the 'new opportunities' type created in the previous phase. Because *Yunnan Daily* failed to supply the 'new opportunities' fantasy type with new symbolic impetus, the former 'historical opportunities' rhetoric gradually lost its initial rhetorical attractiveness, which had the ability to inspire its audience's imagination. And the 'gateway' rhetoric was reduced to a regular discursive framework for daily routines.

Bormann (1996) argues that three rhetorical principles (explanatory deficiency, exploding free speech, and resurfacing of competitive rhetoric) results in the declining of rhetorical fantasies. In 2014, the new strategies of 'One Belt and One Road' and 'Bangladesh-China-India-Myanmar Economic Corridors' were introduced, which gradually replaced the 'gateway' policy. Thus new and more competitive rhetorical fantasies appeared.

In 2014, the only article with 'gateway' in its title read:

> The nation's proposal of 'One Belt and One Road' strategy is a significant strategic decision made based on the consideration of the overall domestic and international picture, the conformity to the historical trend and the current situations, and the all-around plan for strategic prospects. The positioning of opening-up to South Asia and Southeast Asia in Yunnan's 'gateway' construction is compatible with the goal of opening up to Central Asia and Western Asia in the 'Silk Road Economic Belt' and to Southeast Asia in the 'Maritime Silk Road', which forms multi-directional patterns of opening up to surrounding countries. Yunnan's 'gateway' construction is a very important content of, foundation for, link to, and precursor in the implementation of the 'One Belt and One Road' strategy.
>
> *(Yong, 2014)*

Evidently, *Yunnan Daily* paved the way for the later resurfacing of the 'gateway' rhetoric by incorporating the 'gateway' policy into the rhetorical framework of the 'One Belt and One Road' strategy.

Conclusion and discussion

Through analysing the 'gateway' rhetoric of *Yunnan Daily* in the last decade, we can conclude the following series of points:

1. *National policy plays a significant role in determining the direction of regional information flow in China.*

   In the last decade, the 'gateway' rhetoric of *Yunnan Daily* experienced a consciousness-creating phase, consciousness-raising phase and consciousness-declining phase. From sporadic and random use at the beginning to Yunnan's new positioning in the general structure of China's policy of opening to the outside world, the 'gateway' rhetoric underwent two turning points. Firstly, President Hu Jintao said explicitly that Yunnan Province should be built into a gateway for China to open up to the Southwest when he visited Yunnan in July 2009 and the 'Opinions of the State Council on Supporting Yunnan Province to Accelerate the Construction of an Important Gateway Opening up to the Southwest' as issued in May 2011. However, after 2014, the strategy of 'One Belt and One Road' and 'Bangladesh-China-India-Myanmar Economic Corridors' (BCIM Economic Corridor) became the strategic landscape of China's policies for opening to the outside world in a new period. It is against the background of this national strategic planning and configuration that the 'gateway' rhetoric has been created and sustained – and during which it also eventually declined. Therefore, we can conclude that changes in national development policies determine the regional communication flow and rhetorical construction of local official media.

2. *Local official media opt for building a positive rhetorical fantasy in the framework of hard propaganda.*

   In the consciousness-raising phase of the 'gateway' rhetoric, *Yunnan Daily* constructed the fantasy type that 'gateway' policy brings very rare 'historical opportunities'. The newly constructed rhetorical fantasy resulted in an outbreak of a series of positive fantasy themes that were expressed through some symbolic cues such as 'new' in 'new positioning', 'new pattern' and 'new approach' as well as 'big' in 'big gateway', 'big platform', 'big route-way' and 'big industry'. These themes were presented within the hard propaganda framework of 'good start, remarkable achievements and significant effects'. Therefore, it is difficult for such rhetorical constructs to inspire more symbolic imagination from the local audience to visualize the pioneering role of Yunnan in the new national development strategy with South and Southeast Asian countries. During the course of its propagation, they gradually lost their initial rhetorical appeal and became reduced to a discursive framework for daily propaganda. Moreover, the implied connotation in the word 'gateway', a bridge gate that dominates its neighbouring areas, tends to be missed by overseas audiences.

3. *Local official media place the interests of local government first.*

   According to our research published in 2011, local official media gradually came to hold the dominant position in the regional flow of communication

(Wu and Yang, 2012). Although the national policy played a significant role in determining the construct of rhetorical themes and types of local official media, the interests and propaganda direction of local governments defined the rhetoric framework of official media in a more substantial and detailed way. In the construction of the 'gateway' rhetoric, the local government-centred rhetorical symbol 'building Yunnan into a promising ecological economy, an ethnic cultural diversity and a gateway in China's opening up to the Southwest' expanded and enriched the rhetorical connotations of 'gateway'.

4. *The process of constructing the rhetoric of 'gateway' actually reflects the interest game played among local governments at different levels in Yunnan Province.*

    The rhetorical symbol of 'new opportunities' used by *Yunnan Daily* ran through the 'gateway' rhetorical construction, but the fantasies built around the 'new opportunities' type varied in different phases. In the consciousness-creating phase, the rhetorical symbol of 'new opportunities' was set for the 'local governments of Yunnan Province'. In the consciousness-raising phase, the same fantasy type spread to other agents such as 'Yunnan Provincial Government', 'local governments' and 'industries and enterprises'. And in the consciousness-declining phase, the 'new opportunities' type was intensified for 'Yunnan Provincial Government' and 'industries'. However, the fantasy type got lost for 'local governments'. In essence, this reflects an interest game played between Yunnan Provincial Government and the local governments at different levels.

5. *The construct of the 'gateway' rhetoric reflects a pragmatic master analogue.*

    When analysing Cold War rhetoric, Ernest Bormann and his research team put forward three master analogues or deep structures, which are righteous, social and pragmatic (Bormann *et al.*, 1996: 4) According to their argument, a righteous master analogue emphasizes the right way of doing things; a social master analogue is linked to primary human relations; and a pragmatic master analogue emphasizes expediency, practicality and utility – whatever it takes to get the job done. Apparently, a pragmatic master analogue is the deep structure that substantiates the rhetorical construction of 'gateway' by *Yunnan Daily*. Pragmatic fantasies are evident in phrases such as 'The gateway policy has changed Yunnan from being at the tail end of opening-up to its forefront', 'The gateway construction should be put in the central place of the social and economic development of Yunnan', 'The gateway policy is a powerful engine for the economic rise of Yunnan Province' and 'The gateway policy elevates Yunnan's position in the general structure of China's policy of opening to the outside world', and so on.

Strategically, the 'new opportunities' fantasy type in *Yunnan Daily's* rhetoric of 'gateway' entails the deep social and economic contradictions in the development process of Yunnan Province. The official media coverage places all hopes of Yunnan's future development on the 'gateway' policy. And the reason why the policy is an enormous systematic project is because it aims not only at Yunnan Province but the whole area to the south and southeast of China. Nevertheless, it is not easy to 'explain what the gateway policy refers to regarding the Vietnamese and Thai businessmen' (Liu and Duan, 2010). Thus, if the official rhetoric maintains confused in their imagination of the 'gateway', and if it is hard for them to 'tell the Yunnan stories' well enough to audiences in South and Southeast Asia, the 'new opportunities' constructed by *Yunnan Daily* will probably turn out to be nothing more than a rhetorical and symbolic carnival.

References

Appadurai, A. (1996) *Modernity at Large: Cultural Dimensions of Globalization*. Minneapolis: University of Minnesota Press.

Bormann, E. G. (1972) Fantasy and rhetorical vision: The rhetorical criticism of social reality, *Quarterly Journal of Speech*, 58(4): 396–407.

Bormann, E. G. (1996) Symbolic convergence theory and communication in group decision making, *Communication and Group Decision Making*, 2: 81–113.

Bormann, E. G., Cragan, J. F. and Shield, D. C. (1996) An expansion of the rhetorical vision component of the symbolic convergence theory: The Cold War paradigm case, *Communication Monographs*, 63: 1–28.

Bormann, E. G., Cragan, J. F. and Shield, D. C. (2004) Three decades of developing, grounding, and using symbolic convergence theory (SCT), *Communication Yearbook*, 25: 271–313.

Congressional Research Service (2008) Comparing global influence: China's and US diplomacy, foreign aid, trade and investment in the developing world. Available at: www.fas. org/sgp/crs/row/RL34620.pdf. [Accessed 12 September 2011].

Foss, S. K. (1996) Fantasy Theme Criticism in *Rhetorical Criticism: Exploration and Practice*. Long Grove, IL: Waveland Press: 109–150.

Lee, S.K.J. & Hoon, T.H. (1993) Rhetorical vision of men and women managers in Singapore. *Human Relations*, (46), 527–542.

Liu, J. and Duan, J. (2010) New snail bay: To create a 'gateway' business strategy of the observatory. *Yunnan Daily*, 4 June 2010.

Thussu, D. K. (ed.) (2006) *Media on the Move: Global Flow and Contra-Flow*. London: Routledge.

Wang, B. and Padmore, L. (2005) Preface, in Zhan, Y. (ed.) *China Goes Global*. London: The Foreign Policy Centre: ix–xii.

Wu, M. and Yang, J. (2012) *Yunnan's New Strategy of Media and Communication with Southeast Asia*. CSCEXV Macau Conference, Macau.

Yong, M. (2014) It is suggested that the state should speed up the construction of gateway in the implementation of 'One Belt One Road'. *Yunnan Daily*, 7 March.

INDEX